# The Origin of Tongues

*by*
*Nick Thom*

Grosvenor House
Publishing Limited

All rights reserved
Copyright © Nick Thom, 2007

Nick Thom is hereby identified as author of this
work in accordance with Section 77 of the Copyright, Designs
and Patents Act 1988

The book cover picture is copyright to Nick Thom

This book is published by
Grosvenor House Publishing Ltd
28-30 High Street, Guildford, Surrey, GU1 3HY.
www.grosvenorhousepublishing.co.uk

This book is sold subject to the conditions that it shall not, by way of
trade or otherwise, be lent, resold, hired out or otherwise circulated
without the author's or publisher's prior consent in any form of binding or
cover other than that in which it is published and
without a similar condition including this condition being imposed
on the subsequent purchaser.

A CIP record for this book
is available from the British Library

ISBN 978-1-906210-32-8

# Preface To Second Edition

This book represents a personal journey of discovery. I have always been fascinated both by languages and by ancient human history but, until recently, had never really appreciated the full significance of the one to the other. That all changed after reading Luigi Cavalli-Sforza's book *Genes, Peoples and Languages*, where I was struck by the contrast between the brilliant and detailed work carried out by geneticists and the relatively crude analysis of linguists. Yet both were attacking the same problem. Geneticists were carrying out precise measurements of the difference in genetic make-up between different human populations, whereas linguists were still talking in vague terms about language families and possible inter-relations between them. That was the impetus which drove me to formulate what I believe to be a genuinely sound approach to measuring the difference between human languages and then to turning these measurements into language 'family trees' with real historical meaning.

For me, the exciting element is the light which is thrown on human history. Archaeology can tell us a certain amount but the picture which it gives is inevitably just a series of snapshots, dependent on the rather hit-and-miss nature of archaeological exploration. A proper appreciation of the way in which languages have spread across the face of the earth, on the other hand, gives a direct view of the spread of culture. Where archaeological evidence exists, the two stories should logically be one; where there is no archaeology, language history gives us a totally unique view of events. Where archaeological evidence is disputed, for example on the subject of human colonisation of America, language has the potential to settle matters – and I believe it does.

I hope you enjoy the ride. This is not a book aimed particularly at specialists. It is intended for anyone who has an interest in the human past and, of course, anyone who has an interest in language. The story it tells is, in many parts, absolutely new. I am taking you far beyond any region of academic consensus, out into hitherto uncharted territory. I am also taking you into areas which genetics, for all its brilliance, cannot touch, because the story told here is one of cultural history and, in many instances, this has little to do with genetic history. That is what gives this particular story its absolutely unique flavour.

I would particularly like to express my gratitude to George Starostin of the Russian State Academy for the Humanities for his helpful comments on the first edition of this book. This second edition includes some additional analysis, notably of Old English, Ancient Chinese and Sumerian, which has led to minor revision of dates and geographical deductions. However, the overall picture remains essentially unchanged from that of the first edition and, of course, any error remains my own.

On the subject of error, I continue to invite comment and criticism. This work is surely far from perfect still and, as someone who is on the search for truth rather than error, I genuinely value anything which brings us nearer to that truth.

Nick Thom
University of Nottingham
June 2007

# Contents

| | | |
|---|---|---|
| **CHAPTER 1:** | INTRODUCTION | 1 |
| **CHAPTER 2:** | THE LANGUAGES OF THE EARTH | 9 |
| **CHAPTER 3:** | LANGUAGE CHANGE | 21 |
| **CHAPTER 4:** | MEASURING THE CHANGE | 35 |
| **CHAPTER 5:** | DIVIDE AND CONQUER | 52 |
| **CHAPTER 6:** | THE GERMANIC TRIBES | 66 |
| **CHAPTER 7:** | THE INDO-EUROPEANS | 79 |
| **CHAPTER 8:** | INDO-EUROPEAN ORIGINS | 98 |
| **CHAPTER 9:** | OUT OF AFRICA | 116 |
| **CHAPTER 10:** | TO THE URALS AND BEYOND | 128 |
| **CHAPTER 11:** | HUNS, MONGOLS AND TATARS | 142 |
| **CHAPTER 12:** | BEHIND THE GREAT WALL | 159 |
| **CHAPTER 13:** | PEOPLES OF THE PACIFIC | 178 |
| **CHAPTER 14:** | A NEW BEGINNING IN A NEW WORLD | 196 |
| **CHAPTER 15:** | ROOTS | 221 |
| **WORLD LANGUAGE FAMILY TREE** | | 241 |
| **NOTES** | | 242 |
| **BIBLIOGRAPHY** | | 276 |
| **INDEX** | | 283 |

# 1

# Introduction

The question "Where do we come from?" is one of the really big ones. I guess it stands second to "Where are we going?", but it is still a pretty big issue. And it is a pretty general question too. I could say that I come from my parents, and my grandparents before that. I could try to trace my family tree back as far as I can and many people do just that and find great satisfaction, especially if someone famous turns up somewhere on the line of direct ancestors. Of course, there is a limit to what records can tell us, so I could turn to my broader genetic history. Nowadays it is possible to determine quite a lot about ancestry from various elements of a person's genetic make-up. Perhaps I could even deduce more or less where my forefathers lived thousands of years ago. And, eventually, I could home in on the fact (at least it is now widely recognised as a fact) that the entire human race has developed from a community which lived in Africa somewhere, something like 160000 years ago[1]. So, in a sense, that is where we all come from; genetically, if you go back far enough, we are all Africans. But that really isn't the answer to the whole question. Quite apart from my genetic history, I have a <u>cultural</u> background.

  I would suggest that our language is a very important part of us indeed. It is the vehicle for our culture; it enables us to express ourselves. On a national level, if you ask the question "What makes a Russian person Russian?", the answer is probably "the fact that he/she speaks Russian". It could be a stamp on a birth certificate or passport, but the true essence of Russianness is the fact that a person speaks Russian, as a first language preferably. But why do the people who now speak Russian speak Russian? They did not just wake up one day and start speaking it. In this generation they speak it because their parents spoke it. Or perhaps just one parent spoke it. Or perhaps neither spoke it as a first language – both had to learn it – but schooling in Russian means that it has become the main language for this generation. So, if a modern Russian were to trace their ancestry back far enough, it is quite likely that they would arrive at a generation who spoke quite a different language, perhaps an old Siberian language, but the circumstances of life (for example conquest of the region by the Russian army) meant that the old language had to die.

The point I am trying to make is that, although we may all of us be descended from 'foreigners' if we go back far enough, our current cultural identity is very much determined by the language in which we feel most confident, wherever that language may have come from. Now, I acknowledge that this is not the whole story. Many in America for instance, whose first language is English, are direct descendants of the original Native American inhabitants of the continent, and they do not want to forget that; in one sense they may be United States citizens but in another they feel part of the Sioux nation, for example. However, this sense of belonging to a culture other than the one represented by one's main language will be hard to keep up for very many generations. For example, in various parts of the British Isles Celtic languages are still spoken, though only by a minority, namely Welsh, Irish and Scottish Gaelic. But the importance of the survival of these languages to the way in which the cultures of these three peoples survive can hardly be overstated. In contrast, in Cornwall (south-west England), where another Celtic language was spoken until relatively recently, since the death of the language the Celtic culture has virtually died. I must be careful not to say that it has totally died since there are those who are trying to resurrect both the culture and the language. They will not find it easy though. The number of languages which have been resurrected from the dead to become once again the living language of real people can be counted on the fingers of a hand with most of its fingers amputated; the only one of which I am aware which definitely comes into that category is Hebrew.

So, in general terms, language and culture go hand in hand. I am English because I speak English; well actually because I speak English with an English accent, otherwise I might be from the United States, Canada, the Caribbean, Australia, South Africa, Ireland, Wales, Scotland or New Zealand. However, the current case of English, Arabic, Spanish, Portuguese, French and a handful of other languages, where one language is spoken in a number of different parts of the globe, is unusual in world history terms; usually one language has defined one people and one culture. In my own case, it is probable that, if I go back through enough generations, I would find an ancestor who spoke one of the Celtic languages, spoken before the invasions of England by the Saxons and other peoples in the $5^{th}$ and $6^{th}$ Centuries AD. But I am still English. That is my culture and that is my language.

But the question remains, "Where did the English language come from?" I have just said that 'Saxons' and other peoples invaded the island we now know as Britain at some time in the past, the inference being that they brought the English language with them. But they certainly did not. They brought their own languages with them, Saxon and others, which would have been quite unintelligible to me. The actual language now known as English has sprung up since. It has, if you like, evolved. It must have had roots of course and various parts of this book will be devoted to unearthing those roots. Certainly the Saxon language has played an important role. But then we could ask "Where did that come from?"

So, the history of language tells us something about the history of culture. Languages may be brought from elsewhere, so my cultural ancestry may be completely different from my biological ancestry, if that makes sense. Biologically, mankind has been increasing over the face of the planet for a while now, developing into the various ethnic groups which we see around the world today. But my ethnic origin may not be the same as my linguistic and cultural origin. Both might be important to me but they need not be the same at all. Biologically, my ancestry may reach back to the first colonisers of Europe, the brave individuals who took on the Neanderthals who had called Europe their own for 200000 years (though it also may not!), but my language may have reached me through an altogether different route. If we trace the human race back biologically then we should be able to deduce, more or less, when and where the first community of modern humans (Homo Sapiens[2]) lived, and we are all descended from that community. What about tracing the languages now spoken by the human race and determining when and where our cultural forefathers lived? Philip Lieberman, in his book *On the Origins of Language*, suggests that humans first started to communicate using a complex language something over 100000 years ago, but it may be that our present world languages stem from the much more recent past, reflecting the development of human culture over more recent millennia. The task of rooting out the origins of our present languages is certainly a tough one, but it is well worth attempting.

What I will try to do in this book therefore is to see just how far we can get in giving an answer to the question "Where do our languages and cultures come from?" I shall be probing much deeper into the past than has generally been attempted before, exploring the inter-relationships between languages[3] and seeing where that leads concerning human prehistory. Conventionally, it is often stated that 10000 years is about the limit for discerning relationship between languages. As you will see, I do not believe this to be the case and I shall be drawing conclusions about much earlier times. The story which will unfold is one which has never been told before; parts of it will be completely new and highly controversial. I shall be proposing relationships between language families on a scale hitherto rarely attempted and the conclusions will certainly cut across many of the treasured assumptions of both linguists and prehistorians.

## BUT LANGUAGES ARE SO DIFFERENT

Is it really possible to learn something about human history just by studying the wide variety of languages spoken on the earth today? We might also include those few ancient languages (Latin, ancient Greek, Egyptian, Sanskrit etc.) which are sufficiently well documented to be understood. To most of us English speakers, as soon as we step outside the boundaries of our country into a world where a different language is spoken we can understand nothing at all. Everything is incomprehensible. And the language does not have to be Japanese or Zulu, it could be Spanish or French, languages which are spoken not too far from English. A valid question would be, "Are there different degrees of foreignness?" If I cannot understand a word of French, nor can I understand a word of Zulu, then they are both equally foreign to me, but perhaps a closer study would reveal that French showed more similarities to English than Zulu does. That might tell us something about the way that French and English have developed over the centuries or millennia. The problem would seem to be that all languages appear to be at least 90% different from English and most of them at least 99%, so how on earth can we ever say anything much about the similarities?

Contrast this situation with the work of an anthropologist. Much of the data for historical anthropology, the study of the history, basically the ancient history, of man, has traditionally come from skeletons, or fossil skeletons. Now, if we dig up the skull of a gorilla it has a passing resemblance to a human skull. It is obviously different but it is recognisably related. If we dig up the skull of a Neanderthal man, then it may be quite difficult to tell that it is not the skull of a modern human. Yet Neanderthals are a species of man-like creature which is thought to have lived in Europe and western Asia from around 250000 years ago up until 30000 years ago, and whose genetic relationship to modern humans is not at all close[4]. Of course, to someone who knows the subject, it may not be too hard to distinguish the features of Neanderthal man, the heavy brow ridge for example, much more pronounced than is found in most modern human skulls. But the point I am making is that the human skeleton does not change over night; there may be differences between individuals but there are no rapid changes occurring over our species as a whole. There are traits inherent in different races today, for example high cheek bones in Russians and north Asians, short stature in Pygmy peoples, but these are relatively slight differences, indicating a very slow rate of change indeed. It is interesting to try and calculate the rate at which a human characteristic might change; the gradual variation (for example in height or skin colour) can be modelled by assuming a slight advantage (longer life, more chance of having offspring) for those individuals with the favourable characteristic (for example, increased height). Of course, a large dose of speculation is involved when assigning numbers to the problem, but it would appear that several hundred generations are needed (say 10000 years plus) to achieve really major change[5]. This is quite different from the situation with human language. I guess we all know that the English language did not exist 2000 years ago; nor did French, nor Spanish. And no-one has invented them either! They must have developed from other languages in some way. But what an extraordinarily fast rate of change! Whereas the anthropologist looks for minute changes and measures time scales in hundreds of thousands of years, a linguist has to look for minute similarities and measure changes in hundreds or possibly thousands of years.

Genetics is a key field which is now providing valuable information on the human past. Luigi Cavalli-Sforza and others in universities all around the world have now managed to genetically fingerprint representatives from most of the races of the earth. As you will appreciate, we are all genetically almost identical, so it is necessary to look for those few elements of the genetic code where differences are apparent. This has enabled a type of map to be produced showing the differences between the different races of the earth. If the typical rate of genetic change over the generations is assumed to be broadly constant, it is possible to say, based on a degree of genetic difference, how long ago two individuals shared a common ancestor. The findings of these investigations are fascinating and I recommend Cavalli-Sforza's book *Genes, Peoples and Languages* for a highly readable overview. I can also thoroughly recommend Bryan Sykes' book *The Seven Daughters of Eve* for a parallel study based on the changes in Mitochondrial DNA. If I summarise one of the main points to emerge from both works, both groups found that the diversity was greatest among the races of Africa, leading to the conclusion that the first modern humans lived in Africa for many tens of thousands of years before emerging into the rest of the world. Again, the contrast with the world of the linguist could not be more complete. Tiny genetic variation over many generations has to be compared with huge change in language over very few generations.

So we have a very hard task indeed, looking back in time at relationships, not necessarily between peoples but between cultures, and based solely on the degree of language change found. But, because it is cultural history and not genetic history, it is different and therefore valuable in our understanding of the human race. I say it is different because that is what I expect, but it hasn't stopped numerous researchers, notably Cavalli-Sforza, from drawing parallels, sometimes quite striking parallels, between the distributions of genes and languages. However, since I firmly believe that language is really a cultural matter not a racial one, I certainly do not expect to see strong parallels in every case. In fact, I suggest that the assumption that language and genetics go hand in hand has led many a researcher astray.

I think that is just about enough by way of general introduction to the subject. Let me state up front that you do not have to be a linguist to be able to read this book. I am not a professional linguist myself, although I have studied many languages and I enjoy doing so. Besides, the next chapter is included specifically in order to give an overview of the various languages and language groupings on the earth, as linguists understand them today. If you are already quite familiar with them then move on straight away to the meat of the book which commences in Chapter 3 with some thoughts on the way that languages change over the years, with specific reference to the English language. One of the key aims of the first part of the book is to develop a measurement system with which to express in numbers the change in a language, or the difference between two languages. Here, a parallel with genetics can be drawn once again. The human genome is the most ferociously complex thing you could ever imagine, far beyond my sphere of knowledge; but I do know that one is dealing with an outstandingly large number of individual molecules in a complex pattern and that there is absolutely no simple way of expressing this. Nor is there any simple way of fully expressing the genetic difference between two creatures, for example a man and a mouse. Yet, to enable natural historians to draw meaningful conclusions regarding the differences between species, or between two members of one species, some sort of simplified measurement is necessary – and several such measurement techniques have been proposed and successfully used. Linguists may consider that languages are even more complex beasts than genomes and therefore even harder to express in simple numbers, but I am not sure that this is correct. If a simplified system can be found for genetics then it can't be beyond our ability to devise one for linguistics. So, as I move through Chapters 3 and 4, I shall be progressing towards such a system, a new system and a more complex system (sorry about that) than those commonly in use. It will involve a bit of mathematics I am afraid and, since it differs from currently used methods, I have decided to spell out the gory details. However, you certainly don't need to absorb it fully in order to appreciate the rest of the book.

The remainder of the book is devoted to delving back into history and then pre-history, making deductions about the spread of culture across the face of the globe, based primarily on relationships between languages. It may seem a strange concept but I shall be finding that, for instance, French and English were once the same language! But the years have taken their toll. The community which spoke that common language split and over the course of the millennia the languages, for one reason or another, drifted apart. Each may have been affected in numerous subtle ways since but the upshot is that, if I can measure the difference between modern French and

## Chapter 1  Introduction

modern English, I may be able to say something about the passage of time. Although it may seem quite impossible to you at the moment, I hope you will also come to see that it is possible to say something about the location of the speakers of that common tongue as well! Of course, I cannot afford to ignore the parallel evidence of both written history and archaeology and Chapters 6 to 8, which look at the origin and spread of the language family which includes both English and French, will draw heavily on such evidence. Much of this part of the story is set in the relatively recent past, some of it in times for which written records exist, and this will help in giving an understanding of the factors which affect language change. A study of what has been going on in these few thousand years removes the need to start estimating and guessing right away. After all, it would be rather imprudent to dive straight into the deep end without first learning how to swim!

But, as you probably realise, written history only gets you so far. In modern America, you are looking at 400 years; in England, it gets you back a little over 1000 years; in much of the Roman Empire, we could make that over 2000. Bringing in ancient Greece, we have excellent history back to about 600BC, a little earlier than this for China, and in parts of the Middle East and Egypt there are records of some sort right back to around 3000BC. Archaeology then gives us a window on the development of civilisations around the globe back to the first permanent settlements. In the plains of the Tigris and Euphrates rivers (modern Iraq) and in the surrounding hills, an area thought of by many historians as the cradle of civilisation, this takes us back to about 7000BC. It is a similar story in the valleys of the Yangtze and Yellow rivers in China. In the Jordan valley, the city of Jericho, famous for its walls tumbling down in front of Joshua and the children of Israel, can be traced back to around 9000BC! But before the development of such settlements, before the development of stone or mud brick architecture, before the first use of metals (iron around 1100BC, bronze around 3000BC and copper around 5000BC), before the first pottery (about 6000BC in the Middle East but 11000BC in Japan), even before the first signs of farming (7000BC in China, about 9000BC in Turkey and Syria), in these truly ancient times, there is a limit to what archaeology can be expected to tell us. We have to fall back on the evidence left in the stone and bone tools used by early humans and so a 'culture' tends to be described only by a small part of the tool kit it used.

But these are the times which I am hoping to explore in this book. I want to know where the real root of English culture lies. I want to know the truth about the way civilisation came to America. I am interested in the nature of the great advances in human prehistory. What made the Polynesians such magnificent mariners? How come the early Portuguese explorers found such advanced civilisations around the coasts of Africa, civilisations which they recognised as being on a par with their own?

There are many questions, unfortunately, which I will not be able to get close to answering, questions like "why was Stonehenge built?", but I may be able to take an educated guess at the type of language which the builders spoke (and it wasn't English! – nor Celtic). In Chapters 9 to 15, I will be peering back into the prehistory of each part of the world in turn, going considerably further back than has generally been attempted previously. It will be a story of cultural developments whose impacts spread far and wide across the planet, carried by the languages of the speakers. In part, there will be correlation with the spread of our species from continent to continent. However, most of the story is concerned with the transmission of 'culture' from population to population. I believe it will be a thought-provoking and interesting journey and, to me at least, it raises almost as many questions as it purports to answer. It is not at all easy to answer the question "What happened?"; it is an order of magnitude harder to answer the question "Why did it happen?"

# 2

# The Languages of the Earth

There are thought to be over 5000 languages still 'alive' on the earth today (year 2005). This means that the average number of speakers of each language is over one million. Now, since some languages have hundreds of millions of speakers, this must mean that others have a great deal less than one million. In fact, such is the pace of change on the earth today that languages are dying out at a phenomenal rate all over the world. The immense diversity of language that used to be present in the Americas, for instance, is now being swallowed up by English, Spanish and Portuguese. It is a similar story in Australia, in Russia and, to some extent, in most of the major nations of the earth. In the British Isles, the Celtic languages have been struggling to survive for a long time, and some have failed to make it through to the 21st Century.

So the picture is one of unprecedented change. The effect is that a factual representation of the current distribution of mother tongues around the world would look a little more boring today than it would have done a couple of hundred years ago. It would tell us less about language history. The vast Australian continent would have to be shaded appropriately for 'English', with a footnote to say that there are still a few whose first language is one of the aboriginal tongues, along with other footnotes about those Australians who speak Chinese or other languages. Because this would be rather uninformative, the convention among linguists is to pretty much ignore the last few centuries of colonisation and to paint a picture of the situation as it might have existed before that time. That is what I will try to do in this chapter.

Firstly, it is necessary to realise that languages can indeed be grouped according to their similarities, rather in the same way that we can talk of species of animals and plants. We can talk in terms of a 'language family', where a set of languages are all demonstrably related. We can go further and talk in terms of 'branches' of each family, in a similar fashion to the way human family trees are represented. These groupings have been observed by linguists based on similarities in words, in sound patterns, and in the ways languages are structured. For instance, as I write I am preparing to pay a visit to the Ukraine, one of the countries which emerged from the break-up of the old Soviet Union. I have never been there before and I have little direct knowledge of the Ukrainian language. However I know that Ukrainian is a member of the 'Slavonic' branch of the 'Indo-European' family, like Russian, Polish, Czech and many other eastern European languages, so I am hoping that my somewhat unimpressive knowledge of these other languages will help me to pick up something of Ukrainian reasonably quickly. I know that the structure of the language is much the same and that many words should be instantly recognisable.

## THE INDO-EUROPEAN FAMILY

The geographical extent of the Indo-European family is shown on the following map. As I have just said, the Slavonic languages of eastern Europe belong to this family. So does English. This may be a bit shocking for those of you who have tried to learn Russian or any of the Slavonic languages, but it is undeniably true. It does, however, illustrate the sort of thing we mean when we say that two languages belong to the same family. The differences are always easy to find; the similarities have to be looked for rather carefully! But there are actually some quite strong similarities between English and Russian. For example, human family relationships appear similar: *brother* is *brat*, *sister* is *syostra*, *son* is *syn*, *daughter* is *doch*. When I say 'similar' I mean that it is possible to see how one might mutate into the other after a large number of generations. But the point is that these similarities could not all have arisen by accident. We could take another common word, *water*, for example. The Russian word is *voda* (from which *vodka* is derived, meaning 'little water'). It looks different, but is it? The '*w*' and '*v*' sounds are not all that far apart; nor, if you think about tongue position, are '*t*' and '*d*'. English doesn't pronounce the '*r*' anyway and we pronounce the '*a*' as if it were an '*o*'; so the words are not actually as far apart as you might initially think.

What I am trying to illustrate is the process by which linguists are able to determine just whether two languages are related. Now, it may come as something of a surprise to you just how big the Indo-European family actually is. It includes all the most familiar foreign tongues (to an English speaker) such as French, German, Italian, Spanish, as well as Russian. Even more surprising is the fact that it includes languages in India and Central Asia. Just how that could have come about is a fascinating subject in its own right and one that I shall be tackling in due course. For the moment let us just note that linguists cannot help but observe that there are indeed quite

# Chapter 2  The Languages of the Earth

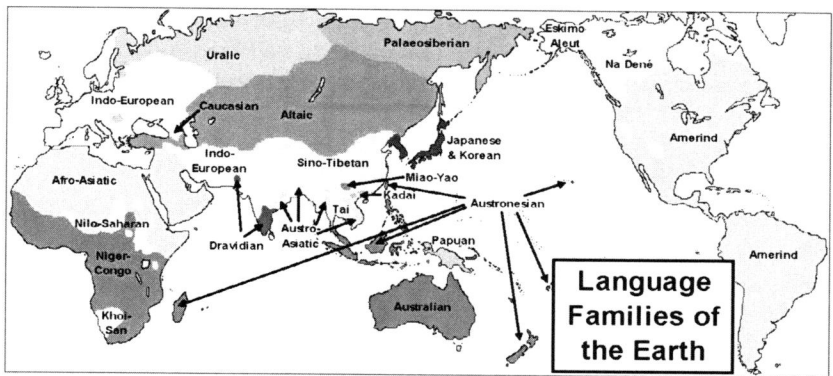

strong similarities, of the sort which I have just illustrated using Russian, among the whole family of languages. They have identified several branches of the family of which the following are the main ones.

Germanic: the branch which includes English as well as German, Dutch and Scandinavian languages;

Italic: this branch was started off by Latin in the time of the Roman Empire, 2000 years ago; it includes French, Italian, Spanish, Portuguese, Romanian;

Slavonic: as I have just illustrated, this includes Russian, Polish, Czech, Serbo-Croat, Bulgarian and other east European languages;

Celtic: now restricted to the Atlantic fringes, it includes Breton, Welsh, Irish and Scottish Gaelic;

Indic: these are the languages of two thirds of the Indian sub-continent, with Kashmiri in the north, Bengali in the east, Sindhi in the west and Sinhala (on the island of Sri Lanka) in the south;

Iranian: this branch includes Persian, Kurdish and other Central Asian languages[1].

In addition to the main branches listed, there are other individual languages which are definitely also part of the family, namely Greek, Albanian and Armenian. Not only so, but there are also other branches of the family known from historical records, but which are now extinct. The most important two are 'Tocharian', once spoken in what is now western China, and 'Anatolian', spoken in what is now Turkey.

So, a glance at the map confirms the impression that this language family has Europe in its grip and has a good hold on India and parts of Central Asia and the Middle East. It was the first family to be recognised and therefore set the standard by which linguists now judge relationships between languages. As far as I know there is absolutely no argument among linguists as to the present composition of the family. The only debates concern certain partially deciphered ancient tongues.

## LANGUAGE FAMILIES OF AFRICA

Unfortunately, as soon as one moves away from Indo-European the harmonious agreement between linguists tends to break down. In Africa, there is no denying it, there are a large number of varied languages, matching the genetic diversity of the continent. And Africa brings us to one of the key areas of disagreement between linguists as to how to think about languages. Just how far can you go in grouping them together? For many years it was acknowledged that the diversity was so great that a large number of families must be present, for example the easily discernible Bantu family, which holds sway over most of the southern part of the continent. Then, in the 1960's, the famous linguist Joseph Greenberg published his views that the entire continent could be divided between just four language families[2], and the agenda changed completely. There was plenty of discussion and disagreement – doubtless there still is – but it would appear that the majority view now supports Greenberg's assertions. His four language families are:

Afro-Asiatic: This family, as its name suggests, spans the two continents of Africa and Asia. It includes such well known languages as Arabic and Hebrew, as well as a whole string of tongues throughout North and East Africa, such as the Berber languages (spoken principally in Morocco and Algeria), Amharic (the official language of Ethiopia), Somali (the official language of Somalia) and Hausa (widely spoken in northern Nigeria). Several important ancient languages were also members of this family, including ancient Egyptian and Akkadian (or Babylonian). For the most part linguists are content with this grouping.

Nilo-Saharan: These languages are much less widely spoken than Afro-Asiatic nowadays. They are mainly spoken by pastoralist peoples in an arc from the southern Sahara in the west, through to the Nile valley and down into East Africa. The Masai people of Kenya and Tanzania are an example of Nilo-Saharan speakers. With the majority of this family there is little disagreement, although a couple of the branches are somewhat tenuously linked.

# Chapter 2   The Languages of the Earth

Khoi-San:
: In the case of the Khoi-San languages, there is very little for anyone to disagree with! Most of the few remaining speakers are to be found in Namibia and are known to the world as Bushmen and Hottentots. Their languages have been disappearing rapidly in the face of Indo-European and Bantu advances. Two languages from Tanzania in East Africa are also placed in the Khoi-San family by many linguists.

Niger-Congo:
: This is the family which most of the fuss was about. It includes the Bantu languages of southern Africa (such as Swahili and Zulu), but also a vast swathe of languages right across central and western Africa to the far west coast. Now, it is easy to see the differences between many of these languages but Greenberg considered that he could see the similarities, and most have followed him.

I have not mentioned the fact that Indo-European languages are spoken in some areas (notably English and Afrikaans in South Africa) because we are ignoring the colonising movements of the last few hundred years.

That is Africa out of the way fairly painlessly, as well as most of Europe and more than a bit of Asia. What about the rest of Asia?

## SOUTH-EAST ASIAN AND AUSTRALASIAN LANGUAGES

We all know that South-East Asian languages (such as Chinese or Vietnamese) sound rather different from most European tongues, but just how many different families are there in the region? I am afraid that there is a lot of disagreement between linguists here, although my impression is that some of it centres around what makes a family distinct enough to be called a family, which, to some extent, is a matter of individual taste. South-East Asia illustrates the differences between those who innately enjoy lumping languages into big groups and those who would rather concentrate on smaller, more definitely related groupings. I apologise if I upset anyone in giving the following list. It represents what I think a majority of linguists would be happy with.

Sino-Tibetan:
: This is the big one in the region. It includes all the Chinese languages (e.g. Mandarin, Cantonese) as well as, not surprisingly, Tibetan. It also contains most of the languages of Burma (and there are many) and quite a large number spoken in the easternmost regions of India. It is therefore an important group with a large number of speakers. Few if any would disagree that

Kadai:
: these languages are indeed related; the disagreement is regarding whether other families should be lumped in with them.

Kadai:
: This is a small group of remnants spoken in south-east China and the island of Hainan. Some linguists believe a link with Sino-Tibetan exists. Most nowadays appear not to.

Tai:
: Tai languages form a modest-sized group, but with two important members (Thai and Lao). They occupy adjacent territory to both Sino-Tibetan and Kadai. Some linguists consider them part of the Kadai family; others part of Sino-Tibetan. I'll keep them separate for now.

Miao-Yao:
: I'm sorry. This one sounds like a cat in pain. It is named after its two principal language branches (Miao and Yao), both spoken in south-western China and neither of which I would expect you to have heard of unless you are either a linguist or from China. It is a very small family indeed. Again, many would suggest that it ought to be included with one of the others.

Austro-Asiatic:
: Do not be deceived. There is nothing Australian about this family; *austro* simply comes from the Latin for *south*. It is a group of languages from Vietnamese and Khmer (the language of Cambodia) in the east, through a few Burmese languages to India, where small pockets of Austro-Asiatic speech exist right into the heart of the subcontinent. The chief dispute here has been whether Vietnamese is really Austro-Asiatic or whether it is Sino-Tibetan, because it has so many Chinese-like features.

Austronesian:
: I am afraid this one isn't Australian either! It is, however, a very widely spoken language family, given the blessing of all linguists I believe, with languages spoken all over Malaysia, Indonesia and the Philippines as well as throughout the Pacific as far as Hawaii, Easter Island and New Zealand. It also has a remarkable outpost, Malagasy, spoken on the island of Madagascar, off the east coast of Africa.

Papuan:
: This family isn't really a family at all; it is more of a loose geographical grouping. An alternative name is 'Indo-Pacific'. It represents the 600 or so languages spoken in New Guinea (the large island just north of Australia) and surrounding islands, some of which are known to be related to each other, many of which have

| | |
|---|---|
| | been insufficiently studied to be sure. Not many speakers are involved (on a world scale). |
| Australian: | Experts have apparently noted a number of different families spoken by the aboriginal inhabitants of Australia. However, many believe them all to be related so, at this stage, I have lumped them all together under a single heading for convenience. |

Perhaps Joseph Greenberg should have had a go at South-East Asia. I am sure he would have simplified the map considerably! Let's head north and west now and take a look at the rest of Asia.

## OTHER ASIAN AND EUROPEAN LANGUAGES

In Asia, even away from the south-east, the picture is still rather a complex one, with a number of different families and a few languages which simply do not fit into any convenient category. And in Europe, although Indo-European languages cover almost the whole continent, there are one or two outposts of other families, as well as a well-known isolated language. It is the classification of these oddities, isolated languages which don't seem to fit in anywhere, which gives rise to the greatest level of disagreement, and which provides ample opportunity for wild theorising. In summary, these are the families, according to the thinking of most linguists.

| | |
|---|---|
| Dravidian: | These languages are clear enough in that they form a neat little group in the southern part of India, including major languages like Tamil. There are also one or two isolated enclaves of Dravidian speech in other parts of India and even in Pakistan. |
| Caucasian: | In linguistic terms 'Caucasian' describes the extremely varied languages of the Caucasus mountain range, between the Black Sea and the Caspian Sea, between Russia, Turkey and Iran. In fact, these languages are so varied that many linguists would assign up to four different families, but unfortunately one is all that will fit on the map, so one we will live with for now! Languages include Chechen and Georgian. |
| Uralic: | In the country known as Russia there are many more languages spoken than just Russian. The Uralic family comprises a group of languages in central and northern Russia (around the Ural Mountains), together with the European languages Hungarian, Finnish, Estonian and Sami (the language of the Lapps). |

Altaic: The Altaic family is sometimes linked with Uralic as a single family, but this is very much a matter for debate. It contains Turkish and similar languages such as Kazakh, Uzbek and others in Central Asia. It also includes Mongolian and languages in the far east of Russia.

Palaeosiberian: This is a tiny group of languages, not really a family but a group of almost extinct remnants, spoken in the farthest northern and eastern extremes of Russia.

These are the recognised groupings. We now come to the 'isolates', languages which just don't fit in. There are seven from this general region which I will mention here. The first is right at the European end. It is Basque, spoken in north-east Spain by a still thriving community. Unfortunately, the Basque name has become synonymous with terrorism and the separatist group ETA in recent years, but the people are an ancient (who knows how ancient?) race, certainly present in their current location during the time of the Romans. There have been many theories over the years about the origins of the Basques, most of them a little far-fetched. Linguistically, Basque is most commonly linked with the Caucasian languages, or with another isolate called Burushaski. I expect you to have heard of the Basques but I would be impressed if you knew so much about the Burusho people and their language Burushaski. They are to be found in a small area of Kashmir, in the high country adjacent to the Himalayas and their language is a delightful mystery to linguists. It is quite different from any of the surrounding language families.

The next three isolates are ancient languages. They are known (to varying degrees) from inscriptions which have been painstakingly deciphered by scholars. They are Etruscan from northern Italy, Sumerian from Iraq, and Elamite from southern Iran. Theories abound, but no agreement has been reached as to which families if any they should be assigned to.

My last two isolates are Korean and Japanese. Some linguists would put them in with the Altaic group; probably more would leave them on their own as being of no proven kin. However, the usual opinion is that they are related to each other. One thing is for certain and that is that they are quite different from Chinese or any of the South-East Asian languages.

## AMERICAN LANGUAGES

In America we can once again express a debt of gratitude to Joseph Greenberg. He it was who rationalised the amazing variety of Native American languages into just three families, two tiny ones and one giant one[3]. Now, many people (myself included) find themselves unable to agree with Greenberg's simplification, but I don't think we need be too worried about that. The main benefit is that he has reduced the number of names to remember when thinking about the world's languages; we just have to remember that some of his families are big enough to be whole tribes, in which it is rather hard to work out just who is related to whom. Anyway, here are his three American language families.

Eskimo-Aleut: These are the languages of Alaska, the far north of Canada and Greenland. There are few speakers and there is no dispute as to the composition of the family.

Na-Dené: This grouping is also small but a little more controversial in one or two of its members. The main language is Navaho, numerically the most spoken remaining native North American language. It has several relatives along the west coast and in Canada, none with many speakers today.

Amerind: This is the one which all the trouble is about. It is basically a catch-all name for the rest of the languages in America, North, Central and South. So it comprises, for example, Cree from Canada and the northern United States, Nahuatl, the language of the Aztecs of Mexico, and Quechua, the language of the Incas of Peru. It is controversial because some of the various branches appear to bear almost no relation to others. Still, let's not worry about that for now; we'll cross that bridge when we come to it.

That completes your world tour. It was intended to give a little background so that when I arrive at each part of the world, you will be moderately prepared. Don't think you have to remember all the details; I just want you to have a picture in your mind of the variety of language groups which are thought to be present today. You can always come back to this list and to the map if you need to, though I will try to give some sort of introduction to each family when I come to it.

## SUPER-FAMILIES

Since Greenberg set the ball rolling by simplifying the map in Africa and America, you could hardly expect people to stop there! Linguists (and plenty of others) began to take a look at the various families and to theorise about the possible linkages between them. After all, the thought was that no two groups could really be totally independent, because they would both be spoken by representatives of the same human family. At some point in the past they must have diverged so, if that point was not too distant, perhaps it was possible to speak in terms of families being related, a sort of second cousin relationship. For example, I have already mentioned Uralic and Altaic, which many people would see as related in some way. This book will be taking a good long look at the whole business of inter-relationships between the language families of the world in the context of the spread of cultures across the planet, so my own views will become clear in due course. Let me introduce for you first, though, some of the theories put forward by others.

Eurasiatic: This super-family comes courtesy of our friend Joseph Greenberg yet again. He suggested not only that Uralic and Altaic are linked but that Indo-European is also related, as are one of the Caucasian families, South Caucasian (basically Georgian), Korean, Japanese, Palaeosiberian and Eskimo-Aleut. The grouping therefore stretches across all of Europe and north Asia, as well as down into the northern half of India. Take a look back at the map and you will see that Eurasiatic forms a sort of 'Northern Alliance' across the top of the world.

Nostratic: This term was originally coined by the Danish linguist Holger Pedersen, but has since been developed further by others, particularly linguists in Russia[4]. It differs somewhat from Greenberg's idea. It also includes Uralic, Altaic and Indo-European, together with South Caucasian, but not the other families. However, most proponents include Afro-Asiatic and Dravidian. The super-family therefore comprises almost all of Europe, North and Central Asia, the Middle East, North Africa and India. Whilst not by any means generally accepted, it is quite evident that many linguists now believe it has some validity.

Austric: This is an eastern grouping, proposed by Merritt Ruhlen[5] (who studied under Greenberg). It includes Austronesian, Austro-Asiatic, Tai, Kadai and Miao-Yao – but not Sino-Tibetan. This would certainly simplify the map in the region although the geographic area is nothing like those proposed for Eurasiatic or Nostratic. It would seem that this super-family is also quite widely accepted nowadays.

Dené-Caucasian: This is a most unlikely sounding super-family, comprising the Na-Dené languages (Navaho etc.), Sino-Tibetan (Chinese etc.) and the northern Caucasian families[6]. The mind boggles slightly as to just how the distribution of this group came to be as it is if these languages do indeed form a unit. It stems from proposals originally put forward in the 1920's by Edward Sapir. It, too, is often referred to nowadays as if it were generally accepted – which it certainly is not.

These are the four main examples from a series of propositions which have been put forward over the years. Browsing through the literature from theorists on historical linguistics, it is quite fascinating how many more or less plausible ideas have been proposed, usually backed up by impressive-looking lists of word similarities. For example, from Turkey comes evidence that many of the major ancient languages of the world (Sumerian, Elamite etc.) are close relatives of Turkish; in India can be found the view that Indo-European languages (and some others) originated in India. From West Africa comes proof that ancient Egyptian, Sumerian, Elamite and modern Indian languages form a group with those in West Africa. Basque is supposed to be related to the Eskimo language Inuit; Japanese owes much to Sumerian; Sumerian is in fact an Austronesian language, etc., etc., etc. Clearly, these theories cannot all be right, though some may well be. However, I believe it is necessary to do some serious thinking about the nature of relationship between languages before passing judgement one way or the other.

## REVIEW

If you were not aware of these things before, I hope you now have some appreciation of the thoughts of linguists, as well as the degree of disagreement between them. I don't think we should be surprised, however, that there is so much disagreement, nor do I think we should jump to the conclusion that linguists are in any way lacking in either ability or common sense. It is just that the problems they are trying to tackle are very complex indeed and, furthermore, linguistics can never be seen simply as a science where, with the right methodology and appropriate investigative techniques, the answer is blindingly obvious. It is not a science. It requires an appreciation of matters which cannot be easily quantified, such as grammar, and any such non-quantifiable element inevitably raises the probability that different experts will reach different conclusions from the same data. It is unfortunate that many people seem not to appreciate that some degree of agreement can always be found between any two languages on earth. In the best-known method by which linguistic difference is currently measured, which I shall be mentioning in due course, it is recognised that about 5% of the most common words in any language will appear to have similar counterparts in any other. For instance, the fact that the Basque word for bird is *txori* and the Japanese word is *tori* does not really imply any close relationship!

Let me say a word or two about the approach which serious linguists take to the problem of judging the relationship between languages. Basically, they look for common 'roots'. There will always be major differences but, if these differences follow a consistent pattern, and if there are enough examples of such a pattern, then it is possible to state that two languages are almost certainly related[7]. The problem is that these are fine words, but what constitutes acceptable proof to one linguist does not convince another! There are no agreed procedures as to how much weight should be given to any particular aspect of similarity.

The approach which I shall, in due course, be taking in this book is to treat the subject semi-scientifically. This is because that is my nature and the way I have been trained. I shall try to bear in mind that, in doing so, I am grossly over-simplifying and so my scientific(ish) analysis will need to be modified from time to time. As I am an engineer by profession rather than a scientist, this is not a problem; we engineers are used to taking exact scientific theory and then adjusting it as we see fit in order to solve real problems. In fact, engineering structures nowadays are so complicated that pure science cannot cope with all the different design elements, so they are in many ways like languages – there are elements of unpredictability alongside other elements which are better understood. My mind goes back to the Millennium Bridge across the river Thames in London, designed by the foremost engineering designers in Britain, analysed and re-analysed in the most scientific ways possible, but which closed after only three days due to 'unforeseen' swaying problems! Similarly, many aspects of language are well understood and conform quite well to laws of one kind or another, for example the ways in which one sound tends to mutate into another over time, but there are also numerous elements which are absolutely unpredictable.

Forgive the digression. One of the key objectives of this book is to introduce a method of language comparison, based on measurable quantities, which can then be used to say something about the relationship between any two languages. That will be the main analysis tool. It will be a little mathematical, but you are quite at liberty to skip the maths if you want to when you reach that part. The maths is only a means to an end, and the end is the aim that we can actually say something, based on language, about the development of the human race, from earliest times right through to the present day.

So, background over, it is time to step right into the business of how language works and, since my mother tongue is English and this book is written in English, I shall be starting with the English language.

# 3

# Language Change

This chapter could have been called 'language development' but for the fact that such a term conjures up the impression that there is some kind of advancement taking place in language, paralleling advances in technology. Certainly we have terms for things nowadays which were not in the vocabulary in times past, things like *laser, dinosaur, virus, microchip*, reflecting our inventions and discoveries, but the structures of the languages in common use today do not appear to be any better suited to expression than those of known ancient languages. In fact, until recently, Latin used to be treated as a type of superior language in Europe, even though it had not been in live use for centuries. There are those who would pick out individual languages and suggest that they are particularly suited to one purpose or another. Italian is often suggested as a language for the expression of love; Celtic languages seem to have a mystic and spiritual quality. These points may have some validity, mainly based on the sound systems used in each case I would guess, but the fact is that love can be expressed in all modern languages without difficulty (other than the fact that it is a hard subject to get across properly at the best of times!).

What cannot be denied, however, is that languages change. It is common to read comments about history which imply that languages spoken in the past were virtually the same as those today. For instance, before the Roman conquest of Britain the dominant culture in what is now England was Celtic. This is known archaeologically from finds of artistic materials, weapons, ornaments, and the like, which parallel those of Celtic cultures in the rest of Europe. It is also attested from reports by Julius Caesar, who was used to fighting Celts in France, and who discovered a people with a similar culture on the English side of the Channel, speaking a similar language[1]. But that language was <u>not</u> Welsh. It is true that early Celtic literature is in a language unmistakably similar to Welsh and that modern Welsh has descended from it, but the language certainly changed significantly during the intervening centuries. We could take the parallel case of Latin, spoken widely throughout the Roman Empire two thousand years ago. It has direct descendants which are still spoken today, namely Italian, French, Spanish, Portuguese, Romanian and others. Yet anyone who knows any of these languages realises that they are quite different from Latin, as well as being considerably different from each other. The conclusion is that changes have taken place over the years, not necessarily sudden changes, but gradual changes which, after two thousand years, mean that the original language is now completely incomprehensible to those speaking a descendant tongue, unless of course they take the trouble to learn it.

So why do languages change? My view is that the main reason, in the absence of direct outside influence such as invasion by a foreign people, is fashion. In the mid 20th Century, it was fashionable in England to speak what was termed the King's English, which meant speaking with a very strange set of vowel sounds indeed. *My* became *may*, *and* became *end*, and the effect is often described as 'having a plum in the mouth'. Nowadays, on hearing this type of accent, in films from the Second World War for example, it seems quite strange and certainly dated. The language spoken in England has moved on since then. It is no better but it has changed. Certain new words and expressions have become fashionable. This is seen most easily in youth culture, where words like *wicked, radical, respect, cool* have all been used in contexts quite different from their original meanings. *Wicked* has even come to mean *amazingly good*, which is 180 degrees from its more traditional meaning. Of course, such fashions change rapidly, but some of the changes inevitably stick and become part of the wider language.

So how quickly do languages change? The answer is, of course, that there is no constant rate, which is a nuisance from the point of view of making deductions about the past. However, over a period of two thousand years, it would appear that the example of Latin and its descendants is by no means an extreme and isolated case. Let's take a look at the English language. Films from the 1940's and 50's are readily understandable. They may sound slightly odd in accent and in the use of certain words (*gay* springs to mind), but the language is not too different from that of today. If I take a glance at Samuel Johnson's famous Dictionary[2], published in 1755, I find that the vast majority of the words included had similar meaning (and spelling) then to today with the notable exception of numerous slang expressions. However, there are examples (*Civilian*: "*one that professes the knowledge of the old Roman law and of general equity*"; *Pompous*: "*splendid, magnificent, grand*") which demonstrate that meaning has certainly drifted over the years. But what if we go back considerably further, to the time of one of the greatest writers in the English language,

# Chapter 3 Language Change

William Shakespeare? The following is a well known extract from his play *Romeo and Juliet*, written just before 1600[3].

| | |
|---|---|
| Juliet: | O Romeo, Romeo! Wherefore art thou Romeo? |
| | Deny thy father and refuse thy name; |
| | Or, if thou wilt not, be but sworn my love, |
| | And I'll no longer be a Capulet. |
| Romeo: | Shall I hear more, or shall I speak at this? |
| Juliet: | 'Tis but thy name that is my enemy; |
| | Thou art thyself though, not a Montague. |
| | What's Montague? It is nor hand, nor foot, |
| | Nor arm, nor face, nor any other part |
| | Belonging to a man. O! be some other name: |
| | What's in a name? That which we call a rose |
| | By any other name would smell as sweet; |
| | So Romeo would, were he not Romeo call'd, |
| | Retain that dear perfection which he owes |
| | Without that title. Romeo, doff thy name; |
| | And for that name, which is no part of thee, |
| | Take all myself. |

Now, I am likely to get into trouble if I look too deeply into the meaning, since I am not an expert on Shakespeare. It is also true that the form of language used is poetic and this means that one should expect some differences in comparison to usual speech. However, I feel that one or two observations are permissible to illustrate the way the language has changed over the centuries. First note the use of the words *thou*, *thee*, *thy*, and the parts of the verb which go with them, *thou art*, *thou wilt*. We all know what they mean but the forms are simply not used in the modern language (and rarely in modern verse). Notice next one or two other unusual words, *wherefore*, *doff*. *Wherefore* is used in a way which is quite foreign to us today, in the sense of 'what are you thinking of?' *Doff* we are familiar with in the sense of removing, of a cap usually, but not for the discarding of a name. These words are recognisable but the usage has changed. Finally, look at the phrase *were he not Romeo call'd*. *Were he* is the 'subjunctive' form which, though it can still be heard today, is relatively uncommon. *Call'd* is written in the way it is for a reason. Shakespeare did not want the '*e*' pronounced, which is interesting, since we never pronounce it nowadays anyway. At that period, however, it would normally have been pronounced as a separate syllable.

It would have been easy to produce other passages from Shakespeare with words which appear even more obscure. For instance, some lines later, Romeo talks of death being *prorogued*, which I (and Samuel Johnson) understand to mean *escaped* or *put off*.

So, the conclusion from this brief look at Shakespeare is that English has changed since 1600 in vocabulary (*prorogued, wherefore, doff*), grammar (subjunctive, *thee-thou* form) and in sound (*call<u>e</u>d-call'd*). The change is modest and does not stop our understanding, at least of the general meaning of the piece, but it is measurable. It is also worth noting that the changes have not led to any noticeable improvement to the language, although one could argue that the grammatical changes have made it simpler.

What about stepping a little further back in time? Geoffrey Chaucer wrote his well known *Canterbury Tales* in the 14<sup>th</sup> Century, over 200 years before Shakespeare. Let's take a look at a piece and see what we can make of it. The following extract is from one of the better-known stories which make up the *Canterbury Tales*, the *Nun's Priest's Tale*[4], which is about a cock, a hen and a fox.

> *And so bifel that as he cast his eye*
> *Among the wortes, on a boterflye,*
> *He was war of this fox that lay ful lowe.*
> *No-thyng ne liste hym thanne for to crowe,*
> *But cride anon, 'Cok, cok!' and up he sterte,*
> *As man that was affrayed in his herte, –*
> *For natureely a beest desireth flee*
> *Fro his contrarie, if he may it see,*
> *Though he nevere erst hadde seyn it with his eye.*

This is clearly more difficult to make out than anything Shakespeare wrote. The first problem is superficial in that the spelling convention which we use nowadays for English had not been established. In fact this makes it easier to see differences in pronunciation, since people tended to write words rather closer to the way they were pronounced than is the case with modern English.

Let's take a look at some of the words which do not seem obvious in meaning. *Wortes* describes a clump of plants and the word *wort* is still in use by botanists today, so no real problem there. *War* needs a little more thought. It clearly doesn't mean *conflict* or *battle*; in fact it replaces our word *aware*, a relatively modest change. The word *liste*, however, is more difficult. It actually means *pleased* or perhaps, in this context, *occurred to*, and I personally have no idea of its origins. *Sterte* simply means *started*. Another difficult word is *contrarie*, which in fact means *adversary*. This is reasonably logical – we might even have deduced it – but it is certainly quite different from today's usage of the word. Finally, *erst* is obvious for anyone who knows German, where it means *first*, and this is interesting in that it suggests a stronger link to the German language the further back in time we go. In the context, however, *before* would be a better translation.

Chapter 3    Language Change                                           25

Other minor changes are apparent, such as *fro* for *from* (recalling Scandinavian languages) and the addition of an '*e*' to the ends of various words (*nevere*, *hadde* etc.). Here is my modern English version.

> And it so happened that as he cast his eye
> Among the weeds, on a butterfly,
> He was aware of this fox lying low.
> He couldn't think of anything to do except crow,
> And cried out, 'Cock, Cock!' and up he started,
> Like someone who was afraid at heart, –
> For naturally an animal wants to flee
> From an adversary, if he sees him,
> Even though he has never seen him before.

Grammatically, the passage looks a little odd to us in places. The line '*No-thyng ne liste hym thanne for to crowe*', meaning '*nothing occurred to him other than to crow*', would not be acceptable today; the *ne* represents a negative whereas today the word *nothing* does the job on its own; the expression *thanne for* has to become *other than* today (or as I translated it, *except*). A little further on, *a beest desireth flee* would nowadays become *a beast desires to* flee.

Finally, the pronunciation was certainly different in those days. This is exemplified by the addition of '*e*' in places and by the spelling of words like *boterflye* and *seyn*.

So, over the course of over 600 years there have been quite serious changes to English, but it is just about understandable still. We could probably have communicated with someone who lived in England in 1400. Quite a few words would have required explanation, but there would have been enough common ground for a halting conversation. My mind wanders to situations around the world where two languages are accepted as being different but where mutual understanding is possible. I had the privilege of spending several months in Slovakia, at that time part of Czechoslovakia. I had prepared myself by learning some Czech since there were no 'teach-yourself-Slovak' books at that time and, as a foreigner, I really noticed the difference between the two languages. Yet there is absolutely no difficulty for a Slovak person in understanding Czech, or *vice versa*. If I compare the difference with that between Chaucer's English and modern English, my estimate would be that the two cases are similar. I will return to the Czech-Slovak example when discussing the way that languages split.

Let's travel a little further back in time now. Students of English history know that a particularly important event took place in the year 1066, namely the conquest of England by William Duke of Normandy, known as William the Conqueror (or William the Bastard). This changed life dramatically. It also would have been expected to have a profound effect on the language, since a new ruling class had arrived, speaking a foreign language, Old Norman French. The great mass of the population would have had to respond by learning to understand this new language and to make themselves understood to their new masters. This would mean using words that the Normans understood and avoiding the use of complicated English expressions. So, if we look at a piece of text from before the conquest, it would not be surprising to find something an order of magnitude different from even Chaucer's English. The following extract is from the *Battle of Maldon*[5]. It was written in about the year 1000 and tells the story of the heroic defeat of the men of Essex in eastern England at the hands of invading Norsemen, which had taken place a few years previously.

*Hi leton þa of folman feolhearde speru,*
*grimme gegrundene garas fleogan.*
*Bogan wæron bysige, bord ord onfeng.*
*Biter wæs se beaduræs. Beornas feollon*
*on gehwæðere hand, hyssas lagon.*

It is pretty clear that we are now dealing with a foreign language. There are even foreign-looking letters, þ and ð, standing for *th* in *thin* and *this* respectively. The odd word looks familiar, such as *hand*, but the general meaning cannot be deduced from a knowledge of modern English. A fairly literal translation would be:

*He let from his palms the file-hard point*
*of the cruelly sharpened spear fly.*
*The bows were busy, shield received point.*
*Bitter was the rush of battle. Warriors fell*
*on either hand, young men lay slain.*

Now it is possible to look and realise that, actually, some of the words are recognisable. *Leton* is *let*, *feolhearde* is *file-hard*, *wæron* is *were*, etc. Other words make some sort of sense because they are close to a word of similar meaning. For example, *grimme* is similar to *grimly*, which is not so distant in meaning from *cruelly*; *gegrundene* is similar to *ground*, and weapons are sharpened by grinding; *bord* is like *board*, and a shield is really a board. There is a distinctly Germanic feel about some words. The *ge-* prefix on *gegrundene* is pure German; *fleogan* is nearer to *fliegen* in German than to *fly* in English. Similarly, in terms of the grammar, the order of the words looks closer to the usual German order than that of English. The verbs *fleogan* (*fly*) and *onfeng* (*received*) appear at the ends of their sentences; *rush of battle* becomes *beaduræs* (*battlerush*). Regarding the sound of the language, we clearly do not know exactly how it was spoken but, so far as it is possible to deduce from the written version, there would certainly have been major differences from the English we know today.

That is just about as far as one can sensibly go back along the ancestral tree of the English language without moving from English soil. In fact, the *Battle of Maldon* is in the language we know as West Saxon, which was just one of several early English variants, although it seems to have been recognised as the 'official language' of the day. There are a few earlier texts, but the only places to look for a significantly earlier version of the language would be in continental Europe or Scandinavia, the places of origin of the invading peoples who brought with them the languages which eventually replaced Celtic all over England. However, this introduces a slightly different topic, 'how languages move', which will be the subject of a later chapter. For an excellent overview of how English came to be, I recommend Tore Janson's book *Speak*.

So what lessons can be learnt from the development of English over a 1000 year period? I would suggest that there are three distinct areas in which it might be possible to measure change, namely <u>vocabulary</u>, <u>grammar</u> and <u>sound</u> and the next few paragraphs will look at each in turn.

## VOCABULARY (i.e. THE WORDS OF A LANGUAGE)

There seem to be two basic ways in which words can change, either suddenly or gradually. Gradual changes are easy to see and understand. There were examples from the passages quoted, such as *bysige* → *busy*, *leton* → *let*, *feollon* → *fell*, *of* → *fro* → *from* etc. Such changes are clearly recognisable at a distance of 1000 years, perhaps many still would be after 2000 years, but there would inevitably come a time when the slow process of change, simply due to the changes in fashion from one generation to another, would result in a word which was completely unrecognisable. Linguists use the word 'cognate' for two words which spring from the same root; they may have developed differently from some point in the past, but they share a common origin.

This type of change is quite a convenient one for purposes of measuring the difference between languages. We could simply compare a list of words, for example modern English words and equivalent words from 1000 years ago, and determine how many of them were obviously 'cognate', how many might be 'probables' but not 'definites', and how many showed no similarity whatsoever. In this way, the closer two languages were, the higher the number of definite and probable cognates would be.

However, other types of change have to be acknowledged. In the examples given, several words appeared that were not simply earlier versions of current English words with equivalent meaning. In many cases, they were indeed earlier versions of English words, but with a slightly dif-

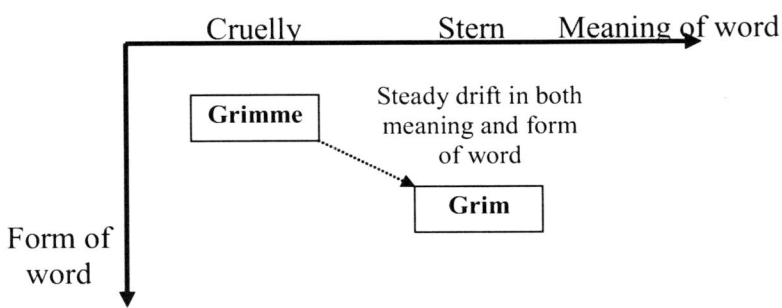

ferent meaning, for example *contrarie* for *adversary*, *bord* for *shield*, *grimme* for *cruelly*. Here, a gradual change has taken place, but it is not a change in the form of the word alone but also in the meaning. This means that, when we compare words of equivalent meaning in two languages, they may appear totally different, but this may still be the result of a gradual effect. This is shown diagrammatically above.

There is yet a further possible cause of word change and that is the coming into use of a new word, or more likely a word borrowed from another language. In the case of English, a whole new raft of words entered the language following the Norman conquest and some of them supplanted the original English. Others simply came into use as an alternative, making English one of the richest languages on earth in terms of vocabulary. Such changes are impossible to legislate for. They are, of course, not random. They are most likely in a situation where two peoples speaking different languages are in close contact. Returning to the passages quoted above, there were no words in the Shakespeare extract which could not be recognised; in Chaucer, the word *liste* does not appear to match any presently used; however, in the *Battle of Maldon*, there were several words (*garas, ord, onfeng, beornas, hyssas*), which would appear to have dropped out of general use since that time, probably as a direct result of the influence of the Norman presence (although my coastal engineering colleague informs me that *ord*, meaning *point* in the passage quoted, is still applied to a promontory on a coast).

## GRAMMAR (i.e. THE STRUCTURE OF A LANGUAGE)

I have suggested that fashion dictates language change and I suggest that this applies to grammar as much as to vocabulary. One of the earliest changes we noted above was the fact that the special form for the second person singular (to use the technical term) *thou* is no longer in common use today. It may come into fashion again. Such a matter is surely a consequence of the social order applying. In a strongly hierarchical society, one would expect a proliferation of terms for *you*, depending upon whether one were speaking to one or more, to superiors, equals or juniors, male or female etc. In English society, and certainly in American society, these distinctions are not considered sufficiently noteworthy for different words to apply, so the single word *you* does for all.

In English, the normal word order is SUBJECT (the doer) – VERB (what he does) – OBJECT (who he does it to). We saw that the order found in the *Battle of Maldon* was closer to the common German order, with the verb at the end. There is no intrinsic advantage to one against the other; it is purely a matter of fashion (or, in the case of English, pleasing the Normans). The language could as easily drift back in a few hundred years. Take another aspect of grammar, the 'genitive' (i.e. where someone possesses something). In Germanic languages this is expressed by changing the ending of the possessor and English, as a Germanic language, follows this by adding '*s* to the end of the word (*his master's voice*). However, the Normans did not take too well to this, so the construction using the word *of* came into fashion (*the voice of his master*). Similarly, there is nothing special about the use of the letter *s* to express the plural (i.e. more than one). As shown in the *Battle of Maldon* extract, the plural was formed in other ways in times past (*folman* for *palms*, *bogan* for *bows*), but fashion changed and the *s* came into general use, with only a few remaining exceptions (*man-men*, *child-children*, *goose-geese*, *mouse-mice* etc). Who can say that this will continue to be the case?

Grammar seems to change by fairly random processes, although there will always be social reasons behind each change. Looking at the English language, the changes noted have been modest. There has been no move to replace prepositions (*in*, *on*, *at* etc) with <u>post</u>positions, just the same thing but coming <u>after</u> the noun, as in Indian languages (so *Dilli mãi* is *in Delhi*), or to do away with them altogether, as in Turkish. These would be more major changes, which would take much longer to occur, and would only be expected to happen by a long series of shifts in fashion.

## SOUND

It is always difficult to make deductions regarding the sound of language in the past because, of course, we have no direct means of finding out. We can make observations such as that made already about the pronunciation of the *-ed* ending, but we cannot really know how the vowels sounded. However, perhaps we can take some educated guesses from the observation that any language, such as English, tends to come in numerous varieties. Within England, a Lancashire accent sounds quite different from a London accent for instance. In some parts, the divergence from the mainstream is significant enough to talk in terms of a dialect rather than simply an accent. Clearly this illustrates the potential for change, as one variation or another comes to dominate others (i.e. to come into fashion) and as further variations initiate. A look at some of the examples from the short passages of ancient literature above shows that it is the vowel sounds which appear to be most prone to change, judging by the way in which they are written. For example, in the Chaucer passage, *bifel* (*befell*), *boterflye* (*butterfly*), *herte* (*heart*) and *seyn* (*seen*) are all cases where there is no change in the consonant sound (ignoring double letters) but where the vowels have changed. It is only when we came to the *Battle of Maldon* that there were significant changes to the consonants as well as the vowels. This is reflected in the differences between accents or dialects; the main divergences are in vowel pronunciation. At least, this seems to be the case with English.

## MEASURING THE CHANGES

A method for measuring the changes in vocabulary has already been suggested, namely evaluating the percentage of words (from an agreed list) which are recognisably similar (cognate). This is exactly the proposal put forward and implemented by Swadesh and Lees[6]. They developed a list of 100 common words (initially 200), and compared languages, assigning a point if the words were cognate. For example, comparing English and German, '*fly*' is '*fliegen*' in German, which is close enough for a point, whereas '*bird*' is '*Vogel*' in German, which is not. The system is simple enough, although it may require a lot of linguistic knowledge to determine whether two words really are cognate or not, that is whether they originate from the same root.

The trick then is to determine a suitable list of words. It doesn't take a genius to realise that some words change more easily than others. If we take a look at German for instance, since it has already become clear that English and German share a common ancestry, perhaps it is possible to pick out a pattern. Let's take a look at a brief passage in modern German[7].

> "*Gibt es an dem Ort, an dem Sie mich auf dem Flugplatz unterbringen werden, ein sicheres telefon, Norm?*"
> "*Ich habe Ihnen gesagt, daβ Sie mich nicht Norm nennen sollen*", brummte Murray verärgert.
> "*Also gibt es eines?*"
> "*Soweit das möglich ist, ja.*" Er grinste Bond an. "*Wir könnten unter Umständen sogar zulassen, daβ Sie es benützen, sobald Sie uns verraten haben, wohin Sie fliegen wollen.*"

I shall now attempt a word for word translation, which will make no sense at all but at least it will be possible to see which German word corresponds to which English equivalent.

# Chapter 3   Language Change                                                           31

> *"Gives it at the place, at which you me at the airport accommodate will, a secure telephone, Norm?"*
> *"I have you said, that you me not Norm name should"*, grumbled Murray angered.
> *"So gives it one?"*
> *"So far as that possible is, yes."* He grinned Bond at. *"We could under circumstances even allow that you it use, as soon as you us disclosed have, where you fly want."*

A better translation would be:

> *"Is there a secure telephone line where you are going to accommodate me at the airport, Norm?"*
> *"I have told you not to call me Norm"*, grumbled Murray angrily.
> *"So is there one?"*
> *"As far as that is possible, yes."* He grinned at Bond. *"In certain circumstances we could even allow you to use it, as soon as you have disclosed to us where you want to fly."*

I would suggest that the following word pairs are reasonably close: *give-gibt, mich-me, sicheres-secure, telefon-telephone, ich-I, habe-have, gesagt-said, nicht-not, eines-one, ist-is, ja-yes, grinste-grinned, wir-we, unter-under, uns-us, fliegen-fly*. Some you might disagree with, such as *gesagt-said*, and I suppose I have taken a liberty in ignoring the *ge-* prefix, which I know is not a permanent fixture. One or two might equally have been added to the list. But is there anything we can say about those particular words where a similarity has been found? My impression is that they tend to be the basic, most common words. Perhaps *sicher-secure* and *grinnste-grinned* may be exceptions. *Telefon-telephone* is also an oddity, since it is obviously not a word traceable to ancestral times; it represents a rather annoying class of words, those which have been introduced into the language (in this case both languages) relatively recently. We should try to avoid such words to prevent erroneous judgements being made.

If we look for words which are <u>completely</u> different, we find the following pairs: *ort-place, dem-which, Sie-you, flugplatz-airport, unterbringen-accommodate, Ihnen-you, brummte-grumbled, möglich-possible, sogar-even, zulassen-allow, benützen-use, sobald-as soon as, verraten-disclose*. (Words included in neither list have some degree of similarity). This list also contains some common words (*place, which, you*) but the majority are not quite so frequently used. In fact, if we examine these three common words, two at least have similar sounding German equivalents (*platz, welche*) which were not used in this context.

My deduction (and that of Swadesh and Lees) is that it is the common words which change the least rapidly. In fact, a sweep of the Indo-

European languages reveals that the most enduring words tend to be the numerals, family relationships, and a few other commonly-used verbs, nouns and adjectives. Since languages seem to change frighteningly fast, it is highly desirable to base any measurement of change on those words which change the least. That way there might just still be something to measure, even after a few thousand years.

To summarise, measurement of vocabulary change can be achieved by:

1. picking a list of common words,
2. working out the proportion of words which are cognate.

What about grammar? First of all, why bother? The examples given demonstrate that both grammar and vocabulary change so why not just measure the change in vocabulary and assume that the change in grammar follows the same pattern? Besides, it is rather difficult to quantify grammatical differences. This is an attractive argument and, so far as I am aware, it has been sufficient to deter researchers from anything other than qualitative observations on grammar. However, it has been remarked by some that grammar appears to be more resistant to change than vocabulary. This might seem an odd thing to say when you look at the difference between the German and English versions of the passage just quoted, where the German verb seems to appear in the strangest of places – from the point of view of an English speaker. But we mustn't let ourselves lose sight of the fact that these differences between English and German, which are from the same branch of the same family, are as nothing compared to the differences which emerge when considering languages outside the Indo-European family. For instance, all Indo-European languages form the plurals of nouns by adding something to the end (-*s* in English) in the vast majority of cases, with only a few exceptions (such as *man-men* in English). But this is quite different from Chinese for instance, which has no plural form at all, requiring the addition of a special extra word if a plural needs to be made explicit. Yet another option is taken by many of the languages of southern Africa, which change the front of the word rather than the end. These differences are highly significant and one wonders how it is possible for a language to change to such an extent that it develops from one type into another, and how long it takes. What seems certain from a look at a selection of the world's languages is that, even after the divergence in vocabulary has become almost complete, it can still take a long time for these fundamental elements of grammar to shift.

So what? Well, this means that, if we can come up with a means of measuring change in grammar, we may be able to say something about the distant relationships between languages, even where there is virtually no apparent similarity in vocabulary. In my view the trick is not to get too hung up on the sorts of difference which most obviously exist between English and German, but to keep the eye fixed on the bigger picture. We could compare languages on a few general points. If two languages both follow the same pattern on any one point then that may be considered in the same way as when two words are found to be 'cognate'. We could say that, with regard to the plural form, English and German grammars are related because they both change the ending in most cases, even though the actual endings used are generally quite different (*house-houses*; *haus-häuser*). The similarity between languages could then be expressed as a percentage, depending on the number of points on which grammatical similarity occurred.

So, a possible set of rules for measuring grammatical change might be:

1. identify a list of grammatical points for comparison of languages,
2. work out the proportion of points where similarity is noted.

Finally, what about changes in sound? Here, measurement should be relatively straightforward. All that has to be done is to compile a list of the possible sounds which the human voice can make and to determine the number which are common to the two languages being compared. It would, however, be a practical step to ignore the vowel sounds since, as we have already seen, they are the first to change and so will give little information on happenings in the distant past. It may also be permitted to shorten the list from the complete range of consonant sounds, if for no other reason than that sounds merge into each other so it is hard to be definite in categorising them too finely.

## SUMMARY

This chapter has taken a look at the ways in which languages change. From the example of English it is evident that it is not necessary for a people to move for language changes to take place, but that outside influences (the Norman conquest for example) are important. There are examples of languages which have changed much less over the last 1000 years, one being Icelandic, and the lack of outside influence would appear to be the main factor.

Changes can be seen in vocabulary, grammar and sound and a sort of rationale has been put forward for measuring these changes, expressing the degree of similarity (or difference) between any two languages. This is the basis for the mathematical comparisons used in this book, which will be explained in the next chapter. I am afraid it will be somewhat technical and a bit mathematical, but you certainly don't need to go through it to appreciate the rest of the book. If maths turns you off, please just skim through to the summary at the end and jump right on to Chapter 5, where I will continue by looking at the way languages divide and spread across the globe.

# 4

# Measuring the Change

The most logical place to start this chapter is with the work of Swadesh and Lees, mentioned already. They introduced a widely-used technique known as 'lexicostatistical glottochronology' – a bit of a mouthful I'm afraid, but if linguists aren't allowed to invent words, who is? They selected a list of 100 common words and looked at the percentage which were 'cognate' (of definitely similar origin) between any two languages. For example, according to my calculations and using the words they proposed, this gives a figure of 74% between English and German. This is an impressively high figure, but what does it mean? According to the calibration carried out by Swadesh and Lees, it means that English and German split from their common parent at least 1000 years ago. Well, this is certainly true; the actual figure for the time since the split is known to be significantly more than 1000 years, probably at least as long as the time since the arrival of the Anglo-Saxons in England in the 5th and 6th Centuries AD.

Let's take a closer look at the calibration proposed by Swadesh and Lees. Mathematically, the law being invoked is known as 'logarithmic decay', a law which applies in any situation where something changes totally randomly. Perhaps the easiest way to understand logarithmic decay is in terms of a 'half-life'[1]. This means that if it takes a certain time for half the words to change, then it will take the same time for the remainder to halve again (leaving just a quarter as recognisably cognate). After the same period again, only one eighth of the words are cognate, and so on. Swadesh and Lees' calibration gave a half-life of about 4600 years. So, if we know the proportion of words which are cognate, it is possible to work out the number of half-lives, and therefore the number of years of language change, which must have passed. If we are dealing with two languages, one of which has developed from the other, such as Latin and its daughter languages of today (French, Spanish, Italian etc.), then the calculation relates directly to the number of years which have passed. The calculation works just as well backwards as forwards. We can trace the roots of a language back through time tracking changes back toward an ancestor language. So we could take French, for example, and trace its development back through mediaeval times and thence back to the language of Roman France and, finally, to the Latin spoken by the Roman invaders of the 1$^{st}$ Century BC. If Swadesh and Lees' calibration is correct, the similarity between modern French and the Latin of those days would be found to be around 75%, equivalent to 2000 years or so. Similarly, we could trace modern Italian back to the same Latin language and the similarity should also be 75%, i.e. 2000 years, but the paths taken by the two languages would be quite different. What if we compared French and Italian directly? Well, if (and it is a big if) the two languages split cleanly 2000 years ago, then the total language development time would be 4000 years, 2000 from French back to Latin and another 2000 forward from Latin to Italian. Actually, if the calculation is carried out it is found that the difference between French and Italian is much less than 4000 years and this is quite correct since the split certainly happened much more recently than 2000 years ago.

'Lexicostatistical glottochronology' may sound horrendous but the principle is actually very simple indeed and very powerful in the deductions it allows. But is it any good? Can it be trusted? Well, its inventors certainly recognised that it was an approximate tool and that it could give erroneous answers. Here are what I feel are the five major issues which have to be addressed.

1. Words change for a variety of reasons; sometimes the change is relatively sudden, sometimes it is gradual.
2. Some words are more resistant to change than others.
3. Language is more than vocabulary; it includes grammar and sound, both of which also change with time.
4. Coincidental similarities are possible.
5. Languages change at greatly differing rates, depending on circumstances.

These are important points and, if I am serious about achieving a really good measurement system, I simply can't avoid taking a good hard look at each.

### Point No 1: Sudden or Gradual?

The logarithmic decay model would be appropriate if words changed suddenly, completely and randomly. This is a mathematical fact. Of course, as with any set of random events, it is impossible to make any precise predictions in an individual case, but what can be said is that, on average, the

Chapter 4    Measuring the Change                                37

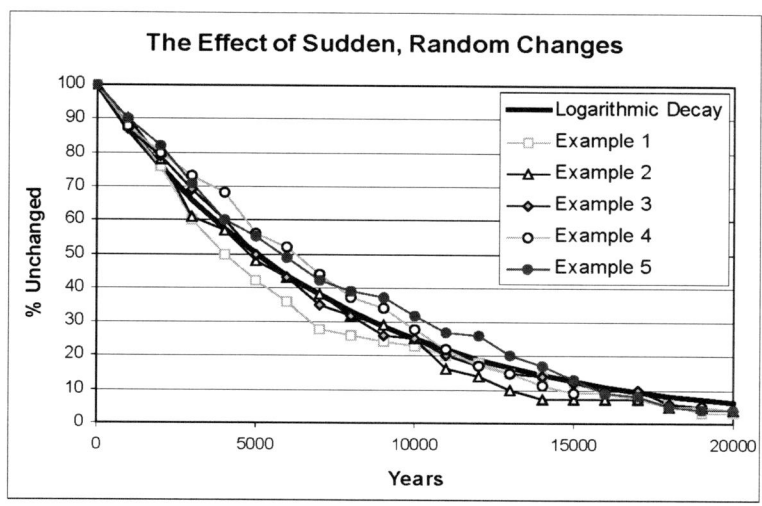

changes would follow the logarithmic decay pattern. This is illustrated in the above figure, where the pure mathematical curve is compared to five different examples of random change. The examples have simply been generated on a computer using a random number function applied to 100 'words', each with an identical chance of changing in any given century.

As we have already seen, seemingly sudden changes can indeed occur, purely due to changes in the meaning of words. For example, in English the words *pig* and *swine* relate to the same animal. However, *pig* has become much the more common word, with *swine* being most usually applied as a term of abuse to a person. The German word however is still *Schwein*. When *swine* was the principal English word, the German and English equivalents were cognate; since *pig* took over they no longer are. Of course, this illustrates a difficulty with this sort of calculation. It is necessary to select a single word each time and there will often be more than one to choose from. Another similar example is the choice between *dog* and *hound*. *Dog* is certainly the dominant English word now but *hound* is cognate with the German word *Hund*. In fact English can present more problems than most because of the additional layer of language which came into being due to the Norman French invasion. We could replace the word *give*, for example, with *donate* or *present* (as used in the previous sentence). Yet *give* is the word which is cognate with the German *geben*. Across the English Channel the usual French word for *give* is *donner*, cognate with *donate*.

I do not wish to overstate the problem. It is usually pretty clear which word is dominant, i.e. most common. I do, however, wish to illustrate the process of change. It isn't really sudden. It is the result of a relatively slow change in word usage, which reveals itself in the seemingly sudden replacement of one word by another. I stated above that German and English came out to be 74% similar according to Swadesh and Lees' list of 100 words. If I scan down the 26 words which were found to be different, in 16 cases I can identify a modern English word cognate with the German word, but with a slightly different meaning. The following table gives these 16 words.

The other sort of change is the slow change which takes place in the form of a word. So long as the process doesn't go too far, it is possible for a linguist to state that two words are cognate, based on the similarity in their sounds. Groups of consonants are found to be so similar that to change from one to another is to be expected. These groups include *t/d/th*, *b/p/f/v*, *h/k/kh/g*, *s/sh/z*, *r/l* and I hope that it is reasonably clear by noticing the positions of the tongue and lips in making each of these sounds that the similarity is one of arrangement of the mouth. So, to take an example from the table, the *tt* in *Blatt* becomes a *d* in *blade*. Linguists can go further than this and, based on observations, make deductions about sounds being either left out of a word or introduced. For example, the English word *father* is cognate with the French *père* (as well as the German *Vater*), yet the *th* of *father* is completely missing in the French word.

So far so good; but what happens when this gradual drifting apart leads to even greater differences? As an example, the respective words for *daughter* in Greek and Polish are *thigatera* and *corka* (pronounced *tsoorka*).

| English Word | German Equivalent | English Cognate Word |
|---|---|---|
| Many | Viele | Very |
| Big | Groß | Gross |
| Small | Klein | Clean? |
| Person | Mensch | Man |
| Dog | Hund | Hound |
| Leaf | Blatt | Blade |
| Root | Wurzel | Mangelwurzel - a vegetable |
| Bark | Rinde | Rind |
| Grease | Fett | Fat |
| Head | Kopf | Cap |
| Neck | Hals | Halter |
| Know | Wissen | Wit |
| Kill | Töten | Dead |
| Walk | zu Fuß gehen | Go on foot |
| Smoke | Rauch | Reek |
| Black | Schwarz | Swarthy |

Chapter 4    Measuring the Change

Are they cognate? *Thigatera* is plausibly related to the English word *daughter*, since the consonants are either the same or close (*th* ≈ *d*, *g* ≈ *gh*). *Daughter* is similarly related to the Dutch *dochter* and thence to the Bulgarian *dycherya* (allowing the omission of a '*t*'). In Czech, this becomes *dcera*, with the diminutive (pet name) form *dcerka*, and it is then only a matter of omitting the '*d*' and changing '*e*' to '*o*' to arrive at the Polish word. However, the similarity would not have been strong enough to say that the Greek and Polish words were cognate without a fuller knowledge of the other Indo-European languages. The point I am trying to make is that a stage will eventually be reached where even the best linguist will not be able to state that two words are cognate because the changes will have been so great, even though the reality may be that the words do actually stem from a common root. How does this affect the assumptions of logarithmic decay?

Take a hypothetical example. Let us say that in any one century every word (from my list of 100) has a 6% chance of changing one quarter of the way to being unrecognisable. Using this rule, five more random computer-generated examples have been calculated and are shown in the next figure – and they certainly don't follow the logarithmic decay curve. It takes quite a time for the first word to actually become unrecognisable but, once that point is reached, the number of such words increases rapidly, leading to a steepening of the curve.

On the face of it, this is bad news for glottochronology. It means that the calibration used by Swadesh and Lees (which was based on a consideration of a range of known ancient languages, including Old English, Latin,

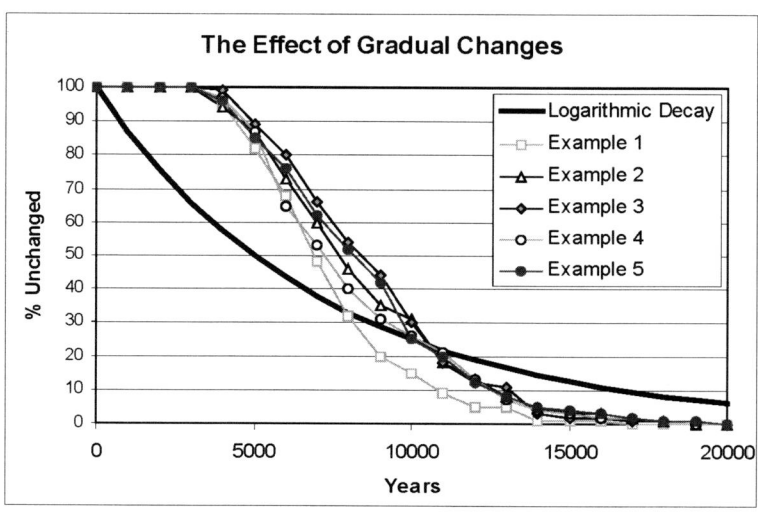

and Ancient Chinese, to an age of about 2000 years) will become increasingly inaccurate the greater the time difference as it becomes great enough for linguists to be unsure whether words are cognate or not[2]. If I am serious about measuring over many thousands of years this problem simply cannot be ignored.

As it happens, however, a mathematical solution exists. The real cause of this problem is the need to make an absolute choice between 'cognate' and 'non-cognate', and as soon as a measure of uncertainty is introduced the problem disappears. This can be achieved by awarding part-scores depending on degree of similarity. If we could manage quarter points then, in my hypothetical example at least, the trend would, once again, follow the logarithmic decay line tolerably well[3].

So, to summarise the position thus far: sudden, random changes, which may appear to occur due to a slow drift in the meaning of words, conform well to the assumption of logarithmic decay; the slow drift in the form of a word, however, will give serious error in the Swadesh and Lees system, but this can be overcome by awarding part-scores according to degree of similarity.

## Point No 2: Differing Rates of Change

Up until now I have assumed that every word has an equal chance of either being replaced or of changing its form. This is never true of course. The fact is that some words change more readily than others and, within any chosen list, there will inevitably be some which are more resistant to change than others. How does that affect the measurement mathematically?

To check out the consequences of this, a further five random change examples have been run on the computer where, out of 100 words, the likelihood of change has been varied. The 100 words have been divided into 10 sets of 10 words each, each set having a different probability of changing (assuming complete and sudden changes again). The results are shown in the next figure.

Once again, there is a significant discrepancy between the simulation and the logarithmic decay line and a definite trend is visible. This is for an increased rate of change in the early stages, compared to the logarithmic decay curve, and then for a slower rate of change later on. And unfortunately, in this case I have no clever trick to bring the trend back to the logarithmic decay line; this type of error is therefore <u>absolutely unavoidable</u> and the logarithmic decay assumption will <u>definitely</u> need to be adjusted if I am serious about matching the real way that languages change. It also means that the Swadesh and Lees measurement system is <u>inevitably</u> incorrect[4].

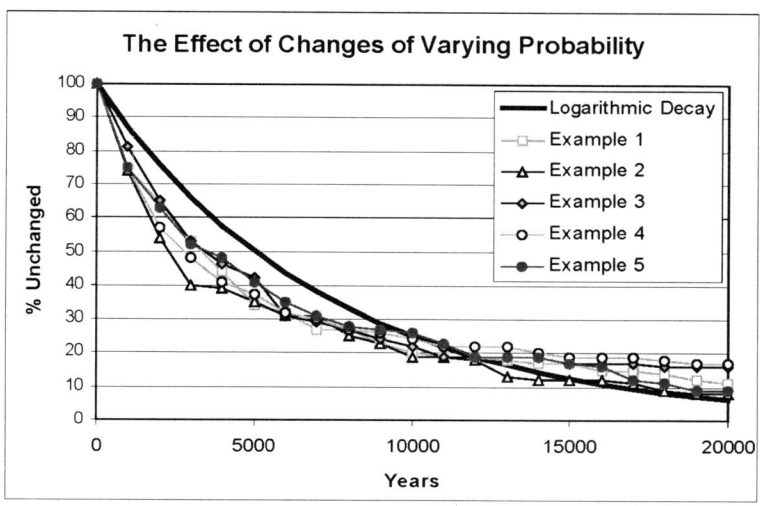

## Point No 3: What about including Grammar and Sound?

In my view, the greatest limitation of Swadesh and Lees' system is that it only takes account of vocabulary, not grammar or sound, whereas grammar in particular opens the door to measurement of language separation over much longer time periods than is possible from vocabulary alone, because the fundamental elements of grammar are more resistant to change. This point is absolutely vital; it is highly desirable to look much further back than the 10000-year limit often quoted by linguists and, indeed, many of the conclusions made later in this book will draw heavily on similarity in grammar. But in what way does grammar change, from a mathematical point of view?

Firstly, is it likely to be sudden? Well, the word 'sudden' is perhaps a little misleading. The actual process may be quite gradual, but the effect would indeed be that an element of grammar which would have been put into a certain category switches to a different category at a particular, if rather indistinct, point in time. I think an example is necessary. In modern Swedish, the verb doesn't change according to person. To put this into words which can be understood, *jag talar* means *I speak*, *du* (or *ni*) *talar* means *you speak*, *han talar* means *he speaks* etc. The word *talar* for *speak* doesn't change (whereas you will notice that English includes a modest change – *speak-speaks*). This was not always so. In the relatively recent past, different endings were used in Swedish according to the 'person' (I, you, he/she, we, they) but these gradually dropped out of the common language. In the past, Swedish would therefore have been classified as using verb endings to indicate 'person', but not today. The classification would, in effect, have changed suddenly. In fact, English presents a categorisation problem at present. The change noted above (*speak-speaks*) is the only one related to person, so one could argue that it should be ignored and English could thus be put into the same category as Swedish. Such issues will always be present when attempting any grammatical 'pigeon-holing'.

To return to the question: although the process of change is not really sudden, the effect on grammar categorisation will be, which means that, if all grammatical changes are equally likely (!!), then the logarithmic decay model <u>is</u> appropriate. Of course, this is far from the case. Certain grammatical differences between English and German have already been highlighted and these have obviously been able to occur over a relatively short time (within 2000 years). However, bigger changes (for example to the southern African system of altering the front ends of words to express the plural) would intuitively take much longer to occur. We are therefore left with a pattern similar to that shown in the most recent figure, i.e. rapid change to the language early on (compared to the logarithmic decay curve) becoming much slower later.

What about the process of sound change? I guess it is essentially random, though the process of language spread into new territory may tend to result in sound changes and I am quite sure that there are differences in the probabilities of change in relation to different sounds. The sounds *m* and *n* appear to be universal; I have not yet come across a language which does not include them both. This all means that sound change should follow a similar pattern to grammar, and therefore a similar error compared to logarithmic decay.

However, for both sound and grammar there will be a rather significant additional issue, that of point 4, discussed in the next section.

## Point No 4: Coincidental Similarities

For better or worse the range of possible sounds emitted by the human mouth is pretty obviously limited. Thus, it would be quite impossible to find two languages with completely different sound ranges. There will always, therefore, be a high residual degree of similarity between languages just by coincidence.

In a similar way, it is always highly likely that grammatical forms repeat themselves. There are only so many ways of forming tenses (past, present, future etc.), for example. Once a language has gone through prefixes (bits tagged onto the front), suffixes (changes to the end), auxiliary verbs (like *will* and *have*), particles (little extra words) and tone changes (pitch of voice), not much is left! It would therefore be unusual to find two languages with completely different grammars (unusual but not impossible – Navaho has an impressive list of languages with which it shows zero grammatical relationship according to the system presented later!).

## Chapter 4   Measuring the Change

Coincidence in vocabulary is rarer but not impossible. When deciding whether two words are cognate, it would be normal to ignore the vowels because they change so rapidly. Then, certain changes in consonants or omitted consonants have to be expected, as outlined above. So, we would find it hard to argue against the Hindi word for tree, *per*, being cognate with the Finnish, *puu*, even though, in reality, the similarity is probably just a coincidence. The fact that Persian has the same word as English for *bad* is also pure coincidence, even though both are Indo-European languages.

What does all this mean? It means that language difference never reaches a zero percent level. There will always be some degree of similarity between languages even in the unlikely event of their being descended from parents which were thought up completely independently. Just how great this residual level of similarity (purely due to coincidence) might be depends on the details of the measurement system used, but Swadesh and Lees reckoned on 5% for their list of 100 words. The figures will certainly be higher for grammar and sound.

### Point No 5: Differing Rates of Language Change

One of the major criticisms often levelled at lexicostatistical glottochronology is that there is no reason on earth for assuming that all languages change at the same rate. This is pretty obvious when the enormous range of social and environmental factors which could apply is considered. It is also a pretty unfair criticism of the concept as a whole. It would be a fair criticism of any user who didn't recognise the fact of differing rates of language change, but I intend to be a user who is perfectly aware of the fact. Indeed, I believe the fact of differing rates of language change will be a distinct advantage to me when it comes to interpreting the data. However, that will have to wait until later.

In summary, therefore, I definitely have to improve on simple logarithmic decay and I also definitely need to broaden the measurement to include grammar and sound; if I don't I stand no real chance of success.

## A NEW LANGUAGE DIFFERENCE CALCULATION

This next section contains details of the way in which the calculations of language difference referred to in the rest of this book have been carried out. It is for information and reference and it is not essential to be aware of all the details. Feel free to speed-read through if you wish.

As suggested, the system includes measurement of difference in vocabulary, grammar and sound. The details of each are open to criticism and I guess that no two people would agree exactly on the best solution, let alone two linguists. However, no progress can be made in the search for the origins of language on the earth without some sort of measurement so, for better or worse, the following one is offered.

### Vocabulary

Rather than the 100 words proposed by Swadesh and Lees, a restricted list of 26 has been chosen, namely:

> Numerals 1-10 (Swadesh and Lees used only *one* and *two*)
> *Father, mother, son, daughter, brother, sister* (not used by Swadesh and Lees)
> *Tree, head, bird, water, white, give, see, fly, eat, not* (all on Swadesh and Lees' list)

The decision to use *son, daughter, brother, sister* was slightly risky. While satisfactory for most languages, the tendency for different words to be used for *elder brother-sister* and *younger brother-sister* and, in some cases, for there to be no separate words for *son* and *daughter* (other than *boy-child* and *girl-child*) means that these words have restricted applicability. It is also true that not all languages have their own separate words for numerals beyond 5 – sometimes not beyond 3 or 4. However, the view was taken that the usefulness of these words in the large majority of cases far outweighed the disadvantages in other cases.

Scores are given as a point for each close relationship and various fractions of a point if the relationship is possible but not clear (thereby overcoming the reason for divergence from logarithmic decay illustrated under 'Point No 1' above). This gives a score out of 26, which is then divided by 26 to give a value from 0 to 1.

EXAMPLE: Comparing Cantonese (spoken in south China) and Vietnamese, a score of 5 out of 26 is obtained[5].

$$\text{Score} = 5/26 = \underline{0.192}$$

### Grammar

Grammar is assessed by means of the following 'yes-no' questions.

> **Nouns** [gender? neuter? class?] – In English, all nouns are of equal standing, but in French they have to be either 'masculine' or 'feminine' (i.e. they have gender) and in many European languages they can also be 'neuter'. The term 'class' was initially added to take account of certain African forms and a 'yes' has only been recorded where noun class forms an important part of the grammar of a language (e.g. affecting verb forms).
> **Person** [separate? prefix? suffix? shows sex? formal form? dual form?] – 'Person' means how to express *I, you, we, they* etc. In English, these are separate words but many languages add something to the front (prefix) or end (suffix) of a verb as well – or instead. In English, we have

# Chapter 4 Measuring the Change

separate words for *he* and *she* (showing sex) but not all languages do. In English, there is no formal form but in French, for instance, *vous* is used for *you* as a formal alternative to *tu*. Finally, some languages have a separate form if only two people are meant (dual form).

**Tense** [internal change? tone? prefix? suffix? auxiliary verb? particle?] – 'Tense' means whether something is in the past, present or future and English shows this by adding extra words like *have*, *is* and *will*, known as 'auxiliary verbs', and by adding endings like *-ing* and *-ed* (suffixes). But other languages can change the verb in the other ways listed or add a particle, a small word usually tacked onto the end of a phrase.

**Case** [prefix? suffix? preposition? postposition? genitive? other case forms?] – English uses prepositions (*in*, *on* etc) but the same ideas can be indicated in numerous ways. Prefixes or suffixes can be added to nouns; postpositions are simply prepositions which follow a noun. A distinction has been made between languages which regularly add a suffix (for example Turkish) and those which make a more subtle change in ending (many Indo-European languages), which comes under 'other case forms'. The 'genitive?' question asks whether any genitive construction (somebody possessing something) exists which involves word changes (either to the possessor or to the possessed or both).

**Number** [internal change? prefix? suffix? classifier?] – This is the way a plural is formed. English adds an *-s* (suffix) but the prefix option is taken by some languages. Others go for an internal change to the word (used occasionally in English: *mouse-mice*). The classifier system, which is principally used in South-East Asia, involves grouping similar types of object (e.g. fruit) into classes.

There are certainly many other aspects of grammar that could have been included. For example, many linguists pay close attention to word order in a sentence but, since this can vary quite a lot within a single language, it was not felt to be a clear enough indicator. The section labelled 'tense' could have been broadened to include other subtleties ('aspect' and 'mood' are the technical terms) but, since these are normally formed using similar techniques to that for tense, it was not considered to be necessary.

For each language, a 'one' is assigned for a *yes* and a 'zero' for a *no*. For example, looking at English nouns, there is no gender, no neuter and no class system, so the 'noun' line would be 0, 0, 0. English uses separate words to express person, but does not use prefixes or suffixes (usually). Sex is shown by the use of different pronouns (*he* and *she*), but there is no formal form and no dual form (only plural). The 'person' line is therefore 1, 0, 0, 1, 0, 0. In all, 25 zeros or ones have to be assigned.

The difference between two languages is then calculated by comparing the answers for each yes-no question. Where both languages have a 'one', a point is scored. The number of points is then divided by the number of elements where at least one of the languages has a 'one'. Perfect correspondence gives a result of 1. Absolute divergence gives a result of zero.

EXAMPLE: Comparing Cantonese and Vietnamese, 6 of the 25 grammar points applied to at least one language but only 4 applied to both.

Score = 4/6 = <u>0.667</u>

<u>Sound</u>
The following 46 sounds have been considered:

b, ch, d, dy, d(retroflex), dh, D(laryngeal), f, g, gb, gh, h, H(laryngeal), j, k, kp, kh, l, ll, m, n, ny, ng, p, q(uvular), r, rz, s, sh, S(laryngeal), t, ty, t(retroflex), th, T(laryngeal), ts, v, z, zh, glottal stop, click, high tone, middle tone, low tone, falling tone, rising tone.

I'm sorry about some of these sounds – a lot of them don't occur in English. 'Retroflex', 'laryngeal' and 'uvular' are descriptions related to tongue and throat position. The glottal stop is used in non-standard English (not pronouncing the *tt* of *butter* for instance) and is a recognised sound in many languages. We use clicks to show disapproval, but not in actual English words – but some languages use them. We vary tone (or pitch) in English but only to indicate a question or an important point; some languages use tone to distinguish between meanings of words.

The list is not a complete one. For instance, no distinction is made between plosive (with a definite release of breath) and non-plosive consonants. The problem is that, while the distinction is clear in some languages, it is not in others. It could also be argued that excessive weight is given to the 'laryngeal' consonants, as used for example by Arabic. It is inevitable that a degree of subjectivity will be present in any such list.

The calculation is similar to that for grammar. Each language is awarded a 'one' or a 'zero' for each sound according to whether it is used or not. Where two languages under comparison both have a 'one', a point is scored. The total number of points is divided by the total number of sounds used by at least one of the languages, giving a final result in the range 0 to 1.

EXAMPLE: Comparing Cantonese and Vietnamese again, 25 of the 46 sounds are used in at least one language but only 19 in both.

Score = 19/25 = <u>0.760</u>

## PUTTING THE SCORES TOGETHER

We now have scores between 0 and 1 for each of vocabulary, grammar and sound. Somehow, it is necessary to combine these into a single measure of the similarity between two languages. This was a hard choice. The Swadesh and Lees system, based entirely on vocabulary, seems to be a pretty good one and it is possible to have a fairly high level of confidence

## Chapter 4  Measuring the Change

in the meaning of a figure for similarity in vocabulary. Vocabulary should therefore form an important element. However, if we are serious about probing the distant past, then changes in grammar will surely have a key role to play. I, personally, would rate sound as much the least reliable element of the three, and a good case could be made for leaving it out completely[6]. I have included it principally because I believe it allows a better measure of language separation during the early years. However, I have given it much less prominence than the other two elements. It is a purely subjective choice, but I have decided to combine the scores for the three elements, vocabulary, grammar and sound, as follows:

$$\text{Combined Score} = 0.6 \times \text{vocabulary score} + 0.3 \times \text{grammar score} + 0.1 \times \text{sound score}$$

<u>EXAMPLE:</u> Comparing Cantonese and Vietnamese again:

Combined Score = $0.6 \times 0.192 + 0.3 \times 0.667 + 0.1 \times 0.760$ = <u>0.391</u>

A score of 1 would mean identical languages; a score of 0 would mean absolutely no similarity in any department, although a small score would always be expected, just by coincidence. But what value should be expected for this coincidence score? This is a very difficult question. Swadesh and Lees suggested that about 5% (i.e. 0.05 on the 0 to 1 scale) was right for their vocabulary list, and I stated earlier that more would be expected for grammar and sound. What I have actually done is to wait until I had the results in for comparisons between numerous languages and then to check just what the scores looked like. Based on this, I have decided to accept Swadesh and Lees' figure of 0.05 for vocabulary and have taken 0.15 for grammar and 0.5 for sound.

The three basic scores are therefore adjusted by subtracting the coincidence score from each (assigning zero if the actual score comes out even lower than coincidence!) and then re-combining. This means that, even if 1 was scored in all three departments, this would be reduced to 0.95, 0.85 and 0.5 for vocabulary, grammar and sound respectively. When recombined, the maximum possible score then works out at 0.875 rather than 1, so I have scaled it back up to give combined scores in the 0 to 1 range again. A zero score means no greater than coincidence in any of the three elements – and there are numerous language pairs which produce such a score!

<u>EXAMPLE:</u> Adjusting the scores for Cantonese and Vietnamese to take account of coincidence:

Vocabulary score of 0.192:   subtract 0.05 → 0.142
Grammar score of 0.667:   subtract 0.15 → 0.517
Sound score of 0.760:   subtract 0.5 → 0.260

New combined score → 0.6 × 0.142 + 0.3 × 0.517 + 0.1 × 0.260 = <u>0.266</u> (out of a maximum of 0.875)

Scaling up → 0.266 / 0.875 = <u>0.304</u> (out of a maximum of 1)

Next, logarithmic decay is applied, giving a measure of the approximate distance between languages in time. Of course, it always has to be appreciated that the measure is not really time because languages change at different rates under different circumstances. In this book, it is called 'linguistic time'. As I hope I have made quite clear, it is also of dubious value without some sort of calibration because we know that logarithmic decay is a very imperfect model. Calibration will be discussed in the next section but for now an arbitrary multiplier of 10000 will be used in order to obtain a number of respectable size. For the mathematically inclined, the equation is[7]:

Linguistic Time = −10000 × Ln [scaled up, combined, adjusted score]

<u>EXAMPLE:</u> Taking Cantonese and Vietnamese again:

Linguistic time difference = −10000 × Ln [0.304]

= <u>11907</u>

For convenience, I will assign units of 'linguistic years'. So, Cantonese and Vietnamese are separated by 11907 linguistic years according to this, as yet uncalibrated, system. However, before even thinking about using such a measurement for real, it is of critical importance to do what we can to improve on the logarithmic decay assumption.

## THE CALIBRATION PROCESS

So much hinges on the correct computation of a number of linguistic years that it makes sense to try every trick in the book to make it as trustworthy as possible. What I need to do now is to find out just how the measurement can best be 'tweaked'; and I believe there is a way to investigate this – at least in theory.

If I only calculate distances between modern languages I have absolutely no reliable way of calibrating my measurements; I simply have to believe them. On the other hand, if I can calculate distances to an ancient language, then this opens up possibilities. Consider the following simple family tree, showing the division of a language at some time in the past.

Language A is an ancient language and it really doesn't matter when it was spoken, since we are dealing purely in linguistic time not real time. Suppose I calculate the distance from A to its direct descendant B as 2000

# Chapter 4   Measuring the Change

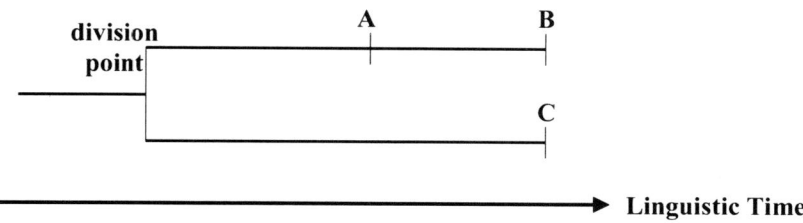

linguistic years. Now I should find that the distance from C to B comes out to be 2000 linguistic years greater than from C to A. If it is, then my calculations are consistent and all my fears are groundless; if <u>not</u> then correction is needed. You see, if language change does not follow the logarithmic decay law perfectly then there <u>will</u> be a discrepancy (i.e. my calculation <u>will</u> be wrong), and this really ought to be corrected to allow further progress.

The ancient languages I have used for this purpose are Latin, as spoken at the time of Julius Caesar (1st Century BC), and ancient Greek, the common east Mediterranean language of the 1st Century AD. The modern 'Italic' languages, comprising Portuguese, Galician, Spanish, Catalan, French, Italian, Romansh and, in the east, Romanian, are all directly descended from Latin. Modern Greek is the direct descendant of ancient Greek. Both branches are from the Indo-European family. At this stage, I have no intention of constructing a proper family tree, so I shall just be averaging the distances from 25 or so modern Indo-European languages from other branches of the family to a selection of 7 modern Italic languages as well as to modern Greek. The situation can be represented as follows.

The direct distances in linguistic years from ancient to modern languages, according to the formula I have just introduced, are:

|  |  |
|---|---|
| Latin to modern Italic | 2811 |
| Ancient Greek to modern Greek | 2182 |

And the distances from an average of the other Indo-European languages:

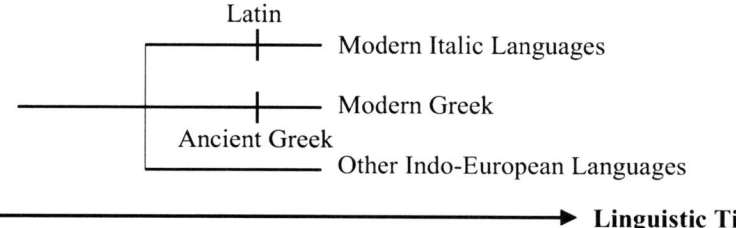

| | |
|---|---|
| Other Indo-European to modern Italic | 8945 |
| Other Indo-European to Latin | 7633 |
| difference: | 1312 |

| | |
|---|---|
| Other Indo-European to modern Greek | 10584 |
| Other Indo-European to ancient Greek | 9944 |
| difference: | 640 |

If no correction was required, then the difference between 'Other Indo-European to modern Italic' and 'Other Indo-European to Latin' (1312) should be the same as the direct distance from Latin to modern Italic (2811) – but it clearly isn't; it is less than half. And the discrepancy is even greater in the case of Greek. The logical deduction from this is that the larger distances (Other Indo-European to Italic etc) are under-registering, which is exactly what would be expected due to different elements of language having different probabilities of change.

It would be possible to go further here and measure to languages outside the Indo-European family but, since I haven't even shown that there is any relationship between Indo-European and other language families yet, I will leave the evidence at that. It is not exactly enough for a fully validated calibration I'm afraid, but I simply have to improve on the pure logarithmic decay assumption if I possibly can and, based on this evidence, I have decided to use an adjustment as follows (please look away now if mathematical symbols make you shudder)[8]. The effect is illustrated in the next figure.

Adjusted distance = Calculated distance $\times\ 2/(1+1.8 \times e^{-(\text{calculated distance}/7000)})$

<u>EXAMPLE:</u> This really is the final calculation for Cantonese and Vietnamese.

Adjusted distance = $11907 \times 2 / (1 + 1.8 \times e^{-(11907/7000)})$
= <u>17925 linguistic years</u>

This is a pretty big adjustment – and I admit that I have indeed taken notice of distances outside the Indo-European family in formulating the equation. If it worries you that this is all a bit approximate, be assured that it is certainly much less approximate than without the adjustment. It is a realistic revision to the rather simplistic assumption of logarithmic decay. In fact I would go so far as to say that simple reliance on the logarithmic decay equation is my greatest single criticism of Swadesh and Lees' widely-used system and it has led to some very inaccurate estimates of the passage of time.

# Chapter 4   Measuring the Change

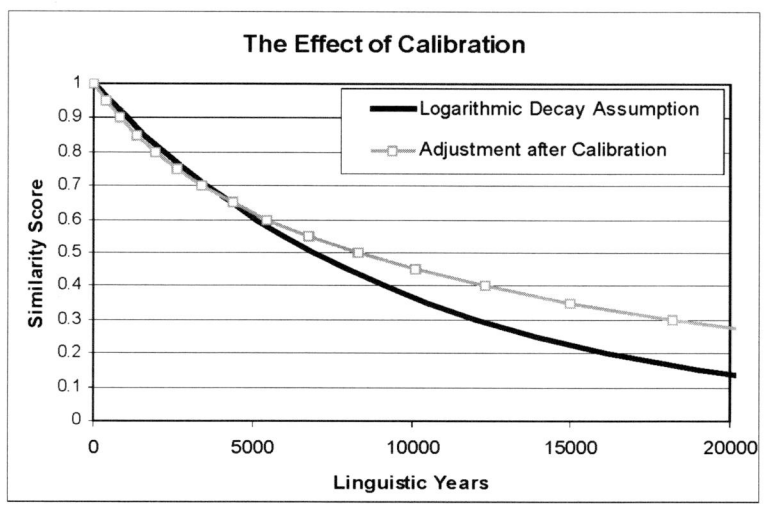

## SUMMARY

This chapter has presented details of a new method for evaluating the difference between two languages, certainly a better measure than can be achieved by means of vocabulary alone, and an improvement on a simple reliance on logarithmic decay. However, it is worth reminding ourselves that a basic assumption behind the use of the model is that language history can be expressed using a family tree type approach. This means that it is assumed that any two languages can be traced back through their respective ancestries to the point where they split from a common ancestor. The split is assumed to be clean and sudden and it is further assumed that there is no interaction thereafter. Of course, these assumptions are known to be incorrect and it has, therefore, to be expected that the lack of a clean break will mean that some confusion exists in the definition of the split point. So, before using this technique for real, I think we should take a good hard look at the way languages divide and spread across the globe. Only by appreciating the mechanisms involved can we hope to come up with a realistic way of peering back through history and making deductions about the past. This, then, is the subject of the next chapter.

# 5

# Divide and Conquer

Up until now, I have dealt mainly with the changes expected in a language simply due to the passage of time, perhaps accepting the effects of outside influence (such as the consequences of the Norman conquest of England in 1066). I tried to make the point that no language remains static, though the rate of change will certainly not be the same in all cases. One could call the language spoken by the Anglo-Saxons before 1066 'English', but we have seen that it was not at all the same language as the one we know as English today. Prior to the coming of the Anglo-Saxons, one could call the language spoken in what is now England (and also Wales) Welsh, but it was not at all the same as the Welsh of today. I could go on. The Greek language of today, when written down, looks just the same as ancient Greek, but only to someone who doesn't know Greek! It is actually significantly different; etc., etc., etc. But we have really only looked at the easy part of the problem of language change. What happens when the territory in which a language is spoken grows? What happens when a language divides? How and why does it happen? These are the questions which are the subject of this chapter and I feel that it is important to be aware of them before continuing with the main business of this book, which is to delve into mankind's history via the language route.

## TERRITORIAL GROWTH

Languages do not themselves move of course; they have to be carried by speakers. If no Anglo-Saxon had crossed over to England, there is no way that the English language could have come into being. If colonists had not arrived in America, no European language would be spoken in the New World. So, it is fundamentally true that the spread of language involves the spread of people, but the question is how many people, over what time scale, under what circumstances?

## Chapter 5  Divide and Conquer

I feel that the best way forward is by looking at some examples. The last few centuries have seen the linguistic face of the globe change as never before, due principally to European influence. Let's take a look at the United States. The principal language is English, with a significant Spanish-speaking minority, and communities of Chinese and many other nationalities. This has come about in two ways as I see it, <u>conquest</u> and then peaceful <u>immigration</u>. During the years of conquest, the English-speaking people physically took and occupied territory previously occupied by speakers of Native American languages, often accompanied by significant slaughter. Some Native Americans survived and had to make a living in the new English-speaking world. There was fairly minimal interaction and, in the short time since these events took place, many Native American languages have disappeared from the map completely and all have been drastically reduced in numbers of speakers. The English of America has not been significantly affected by any of the Native American languages so far as I am aware; the newcomers were culturally dominant and there was absolutely no reason for them to adopt anything from Native American language or culture. In effect, the present population of the United States is almost entirely descended from people who have entered the continent quite recently and so are its languages. Under such circumstances, there is no reason to expect much change in the newcomers' language.

This pattern of conquest and almost complete replacement of population has been repeated in Australia and in the Caribbean, but in few other places to such an extent.

The second effect in relation to the United States is peaceful immigration. Most of the present population has descended from later arrivals from various parts of the world and here the effect on the language has been much more significant. A German colleague of mine thought we had an American on our University staff, until he realised that the English he was hearing was from Ireland. The mistake is not surprising. American English has been profoundly influenced by the large numbers of Irish immigrants in the nineteenth century. Why should this be? Well, unlike the Native American populations, the Irish were seen as important members of society; they were culturally influential and so it is not surprising that the Irish fashion of speaking should become widely adopted. The Italian immigrant community had a similar effect.

Let us look south, to the Spanish and Portuguese speaking parts of the New World. Here the picture is rather different, perhaps partly due to the different attitude taken by the Spanish conquistadors when they took over their new territory, but also because many of the peoples they conquered were culturally and technologically more advanced than those to the north. There is no denying that the process involved was again conquest and the forceful taking over of territory. The difference is, however, that the Spanish and Portuguese never replaced the original inhabitants; they merely added to them and mixed much more freely with them than was the case in the north. They were culturally dominant so their language became the dominant language in the area but the influence of the original American languages was always going to be greater than in the north. Today, there are large numbers of speakers of several South and Central American languages, putting them in a position to challenge and affect the Spanish and Portuguese languages. Yet one has to admit that American Spanish is not so different from that spoken in Spain, perhaps no more different than one would have expected simply due to the time which has passed since independence from Spain; similarly Brazilian Portuguese.

Another influence both north and south was the influx of slaves from Africa. They were at the bottom of the social ladder in all the American societies, so their languages were never going to survive in their new homes; they had no choice but to adopt English, Spanish etc. However, they were still a part of the dominant society, though a lowly part. They were numerically significant and so have been able to bring their own influence to bear on the languages spoken by the ruling peoples in a way that the Native Americans of North America have not. The strongest influence is seen in the Caribbean, where the English spoken has been powerfully affected by the influx from Africa. Caribbean dialects are basically 'creoles', meaning that they are forms of language adopted and adapted by people of different races (slaves were from many parts of Africa) in order to communicate with each other. Now both the descendants of slaves and the descendants of their masters speak the same adapted language. Thus, the contribution of slaves was still of the peaceful immigrant type despite their place in society.

What lessons can we learn from these observations? I think, principally, that it is the degree of <u>cultural</u> importance which affects the contribution a people makes to the language spoken in a particular territory.

Now, no-one would deny that the circumstances of the last few hundred years have been unlike anything the world has seen previously, at least in terms of scale. However, we can see some of the same patterns at work in earlier times. Before the rise of Islam in the 7<sup>th</sup> Century AD, the Arabic language was spoken in much of Arabia but not outside. However, such was the cultural dominance brought by the new religion that, within a few decades, the language had become pre-eminent over a large part of the Middle East and North Africa. The populations in the new areas had not been replaced; they had simply come under the dominance of Arabic speakers and had to submit to the new culture, and with it the new language. Since the people remained physically present, the version of Arabic spoken in each place bore some of the marks, at least in pronunciation, of

Chapter 5    Divide and Conquer                                              55

the languages it had replaced. However, the degree of uniformity still seen across the Arabic speaking world is actually most impressive.

Stepping back a few years, cultural superiority following conquest brought Latin and its descendants to the lands of the Roman Empire, displacing Celtic and other languages spoken previously and replacing them with an impressive completeness. Words of Celtic origin are infrequent in either French or Spanish, both descendants of Latin. In Britain, the situation was a little different since the Celtic language survived the Romans. It was certainly greatly affected but it survived. However, the next serious challenge, that of the Anglo-Saxons, was too much. The first newcomers came peacefully in the early 5th Century, given land in exchange for assistance against the Picts of Scotland, but this did not last long and, after a couple of centuries, Anglo-Saxon culture became the dominant one throughout England, brought about by superior military might. The Celts were not wiped out, however; many would simply have 'become Anglo-Saxons', adopting the new language because it was the only way to make progress in the new society. Within a few generations, most of the population, whatever their true blood line, would have thought of themselves as Anglo-Saxon not Celtic, and the influence of Celtic on the English language was almost zero. Interestingly, the final linguistic challenge, that of the Normans, was resisted and, though English changed considerably, it survived. So did the Celtic language of Wales.

What about stepping much farther back in time, to days when widespread conquest was not so readily achieved? Much has been written about the spread of Indo-European languages (the large group that includes almost all modern European languages including English) across Europe, Central Asia and India. I can certainly recommend Colin Renfrew's book *Archaeology and Language* although I am by no means persuaded by the argument he presents. He suggests that the spread of language can be understood, at least in Europe, as a consequence of the spread of agriculture (starting in Greece in about 7000BC). If correct, this would be not so much military might which caused the spread of language but economic might, albeit on a small scale. The theory goes that the new agriculture would have allowed a far higher population density than could have been supported previously based on a hunting and gathering economy and that this would 'inevitably' have created a continual expansive pressure, resulting in the slow spread of people. Each individual may only have moved a few kilometres during a life-time, to find a new place to plant crops but, added over numbers of generations, a continent can soon be crossed. The existing inhabitants of the land would have had no option but to give way under weight of numbers, although they would perhaps have been more likely to join in with the new prosperity, interbreeding but always adopting the superior culture of the newcomers and with it, so the argument goes, their language. I don't think there is any disputing that agriculture led to a large population increase; language may also have spread with it. My doubt concerns whether that language was Indo-European. However, the spread of agriculture (and other technologies) has certainly been responsible for some instances of language spread. For example, the Bantu peoples of southern Africa are known to have spread relatively recently across more than a third of the continent, partly because of advances in agriculture. Perhaps, here too, it would be more correct to talk in terms of the spread of the culture, adopted by some, at least, of the pre-existing inhabitants, together with newcomers.

Can we look any further back into mankind's past? I guess the answer is: not really! One could speculate that earlier advances in technology, for example in hunting equipment, even in food preparation, perhaps in medicine, could have given one community a significant advantage over others. If such an advance led to more and easier food, longer life, better health etc, then it is pretty much inevitable that the culture represented by this advance would spread across the land, and with the culture the language of the advanced people might also be adopted. The process would be slow, of course, much slower than the more recent language spread processes, but it could account for many or all of the language replacement events which have certainly taken place over the millennia of prehistory.

I think that is enough discussion on the subject. I am persuaded that <u>cultural dominance</u> is the reason for language spread, but that there are many forms which this can take. Let's consider now what causes a language to divide.

## LANGUAGE DIVISION

The fact that languages separate in some way is quite obvious from a glance at today's language map. Groups of similar but not identical languages can be found all over the earth. For example, Portuguese, Castilian Spanish, Galician and Catalan all occupy the Iberian peninsula (modern Spain and Portugal) and they are definitely similar languages. They are just about mutually intelligible and they clearly did not get that way by accident. It is true that two distinctly different languages may actually grow more alike as they come into contact. However, this is mainly restricted to word borrowing, judging from a few examples. The Korean language is full of Chinese words, a mark of the close contact which there has been between the two peoples, but the grammar is still completely different. Welsh bears the battle scars of over 1000 years rubbing shoulders with English, but only in its vocabulary. The grammar (and sound) is distinctly Welsh. So when we come across a case such as the four languages of the Iberian peninsula (ignoring Basque which, though it uses plenty of

Chapter 5    Divide and Conquer                                57

Spanish words, really is different!), the only conclusion is that the similarity is much more than skin deep; they really are closely related. Let's look at a simple sentence in three of the languages (I am afraid my knowledge of Galician is zero).

| | |
|---|---|
| *Este es el dia mas feliz de mi vida* | - Castilian Spanish |
| *Este e o dia mais feliz da minha vida* | - Portuguese |
| *Això és el dia el més feliç de la meva vida* | - Catalan |

I hope you will agree that, when saying *this is the happiest day of my life*, the correspondence between the three languages is close. My conclusion from this, coupled with known history, where Roman control of the peninsula is attested in a multitude of ancient sources, is that the languages were once the same (Latin in fact) and that they have developed separately since. The question is: 'Why did this happen and how did it come about?'

Well, I think we can be sure that it did not happen over night. Language change just doesn't work like that as we saw in Chapter 3. Somehow, different areas of the Iberian peninsula must have developed in different ways; but then what happened at the dividing points? This is a key talking point for linguists, but perhaps it's not really such a great mystery. I believe that what is known as the 'wave theory' is basically a pretty good representation of the sort of thing which must have occurred. Using the following illustrations, I will give my version of the wave theory as I understand it (which may be a little different from that of the theory's originator)[1].

**Stage 1:** The same language is spoken everywhere in a given territory.

**Stage 2:** Accents and dialects emerge, leading to a 'language gradient'.

**Stage 3:** One area becomes culturally dominant, leading to the spread of its version of the language (a language 'wave'). This creates a step change rather than a gradual gradient, which eventually becomes a language division.

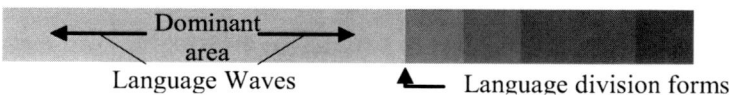

Language Waves         Language division forms

Once a significant step change is created, the theory is that the two areas then develop separately; in effect, a language barrier has formed.

Let's just pause and think for a moment what is going on. We have already noted the tendency for accents and then dialects to appear in any language. In England, there are quite significant differences between the language spoken in Cornwall, say, and that in North-East England but, by and large, there would be no difficulty in people from the two regions communicating. The basic language is still English. Because of the constant interchange of people and communication throughout the country, it is hard to envisage any possibility that any part of England would become so different in its mode of speech that people from other areas could no longer understand it. But this would not always have been the case. Throughout most of mankind's history, the horizon for most people was the next village (or encampment), or not much further. So long as communication existed at that level, life could proceed without difficulty. Such a situation is asking for a language gradient to develop. Each village can communicate with the next village, but the speech in the one after that may seem a little odd and that in the next one odder still. A journey of a few miles might bring the incautious traveller into a region where the language was just about recognisable but where some very strange words were in use, together with some peculiar grammatical twists. Further still, and only the basic meaning can be gleaned from the few words which are still recognisable. This is a language gradient and, in a situation where few people travel far, it is always likely to occur.

There are many parts of the world where such a language gradient clearly exists. In northern India, Hindi is the official language, but just where the boundaries of the Hindi language should be drawn is hard to determine. It changes gradually and merges in the north with Punjabi, in the east with Bhojpuri, Magahi, Maithili and in the west with Rajasthani. In the Slavonic world, Bulgarian changes almost imperceptibly into Macedonian. In a stable world, this situation might persist. But our world is far from stable. In India, the language of Delhi is attaining a local supremacy, extending its range over areas which formerly spoke a slightly different version of the same language. This means that areas outside its range are now the other side of a pronounced language step, if not quite a language barrier.

Perhaps this model of language division is a little oversimplified, but I believe it to be fundamentally correct. It is certainly true to say that other factors also apply, physical separators such as oceans and mountain ranges for instance. A large part of the reason for the separate development of English and German is the fact of a stretch of water in between their two territories.

So just what are the implications from such a model? After each split the territory covered by each separate language becomes smaller. In each area new language gradients will develop, leading to new splits. However,

# Chapter 5  Divide and Conquer

at the same time extinctions will also be occurring as certain languages extend their range due to the temporary cultural dominance of their speakers. The process is continuous. If there is very little expansion due to cultural dominance, because few earth-shattering breakthroughs are being made, and perhaps the geography doesn't make movement easy, then the number of individual languages could in theory become very large indeed, since splitting will still occur as language gradients steepen and then break down. The island of New Guinea is such a place, being home to 600 or so of the 5000+ languages currently spoken on the earth. Where there is massive expansion due to cultural advances, then the number of languages will be fewer, and extinctions more frequent. This can be seen in the Americas, with the recent domination of European languages.

Language division is always likely to be a messy business. Consider the situation described as Stage 2 in the Wave Theory illustration, that of a language gradient. If we were to sample the languages at either end of the gradient, then we could measure a difference between them. Such a case is represented by the Czech and Slovak languages of today. There is an appreciable gradient between 'pure' Czech and 'pure' Slovak (although no language form can really be said to be purer than any other) as one travels through Moravia, the intervening land. Yet the languages are mutually comprehensible so, according to the wave model, no final split has yet taken place. Czech and Slovak still have considerable influence over each other, even after their political separation, because mutual understanding exists. Any shift in the vocabulary or grammar of one is likely to be reflected in the other. It is only with the formation of a true language barrier that one could reasonably expect two languages to go their separate ways. The language border with Polish is, perhaps, great enough to be considered a language barrier. A high degree of mutual understanding certainly exists with both Czech and Slovak, but the communication difficulties are of a much higher order, probably sufficient to mean that future changes in Polish would not be reflected in Czech or Slovak.

What does this rather messy business of language division imply? Well, to me it implies that there is no clean separation point. Taking as an example the relationship between French and Italian via their common ancestor Latin, I might suggest that the distance (in language development time) between the two modern languages should simply be the sum of the distances between each one and the Latin spoken at the time of their separation. But, if this separation actually developed over some period of time, then this rather messes up the calculation. The true picture may be as shown in the following figure.

I don't really have any cunning plan to get round this effect. I think it will simply have to be remembered that the measured distance between two languages is twice the distance back to the last point of mutual intel-

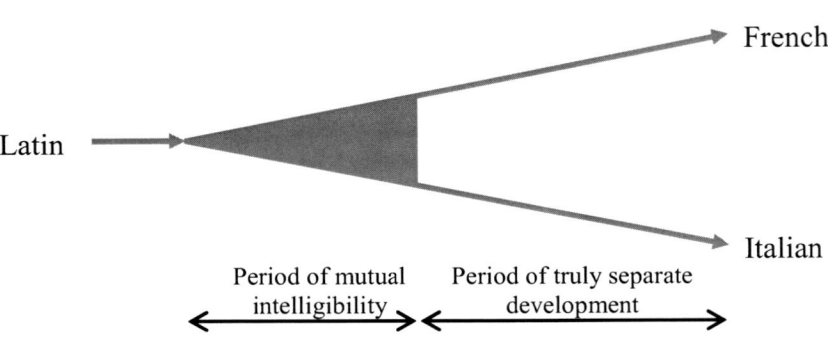

ligibility plus a bit more for the difference which already existed between them at that point. The bottom line is that there is almost certain to be some degree of confusion over the exact split point, particularly when dealing with languages which separated relatively recently, such as French and Italian. When dealing with more remote relationships the error should decrease (at least in relative terms) because the distance will be dominated by a long period of separate development[2].

So, we have visited the subjects of language spread and division. However, there remains one further important matter, which will certainly affect my interpretation of the measured distance between languages, and that is any contact which occurs <u>after</u> separation. I will term this 'secondary contact'.

## SECONDARY CONTACT

This phenomenon is one of the main reasons why many linguists do not hold glottochronology in high regard. There has been considerable debate over the years about the reasons for language change, a little bit like the 'nature versus nurture' debate over the way each of us behaves. On the 'nature' side are those linguists who see a language as essentially a product of the past, a development from a parent (only one required for language birth!). The 'nurture' supporters claim that a language is what it is because of the influences which it has been subject to during its life. I guess you can see that this is quite an important issue for those, like myself, who would like to use language as a tool through which to learn about the past. If 'nurture' is the dominant factor then it is unlikely to be possible to tell much about the past, because every language will be such a mixture of influences that it will not be possible to see its origins any more. If, on the other hand, 'nature' wins, then the opportunity still exists.

By and large, what I have been presenting so far has made the assumption that languages do indeed have an inherent nature, given by a parent

# Chapter 5  Divide and Conquer

and then developed over the years. However, I freely admit that this is only a partial truth. Perhaps, like the 'nature versus nurture' debate over the development of children, there can be no winner (or, to be positive, no loser). Both are right to some extent and I shall try to demonstrate this with reference in the first instance to English. The English language is a particularly useful example because of its varied history. We have already had cause to note that it dates as a separate language approximately from the time of the arrival of the Anglo-Saxons in England from the 5$^{th}$ and 6$^{th}$ Centuries onward and that it was linked before that with the ancestor of modern German. We then noted that the Celtic language which it replaced had virtually no influence on it whatsoever, a consequence of the cultural dominance of the new people. The original population, those who survived, and I feel sure many did, simply forgot their native tongue and adopted the new language, at least within a generation or two. There followed quite serious incursions by people from Denmark and Norway, who came not only to raid but also to settle. These people also spoke a Germanic language, not too different from the early English of those times, if we can indeed call it English. It would certainly have been close enough for a high degree of mutual intelligibility. Having weathered the storm from Danes and Norsemen, there was little time for respite before the famous invasion of William the Conqueror and his Norman French army. They certainly came to settle, and to rule. Amazingly, English survived and it was the Normans who eventually learned to speak the strange tongue of the English, after civilising it a bit. In Chapter 3, I illustrated the significant change which took place around the time of the Norman invasion. Since the Normans, the English language has had it pretty easy, with only a mild amount of outside influence.

    I think the place to start is with a look at a piece of modern English prose and to see what can be gleaned from it. No single piece can be considered typical; the one I have chosen certainly isn't, but I have chosen it because I like it. It is the opening paragraph from J.R.R. Tolkien's *The Hobbit*.

> In a hole in the ground there lived a hobbit. Not a nasty, dirty, wet hole filled with the ends of worms and an oozy smell, nor yet a dry, bare, sandy hole with nothing in it to sit down on or to eat: it was a hobbit-hole and that means comfort.

    I make it that there are 38 different words in this piece, 37 if *a* and *an* are considered to be the same word. The language is pretty ordinary English, with the exception of the word *hobbit*, which has been invented by Tolkien. Let's take a look at the roots of the 36 words remaining (after removing *hobbit*). I am no trained linguist, but I can see that at least 27 of them are Germanic. In many cases, the cognate German word is obvious (*in-in*; *hole-höhle*; *the-die*; *ground-grund*; *there-da*; *lived-lebte*; *not-nicht* etc.). I can find only a single word (*comfort*) which is unequivocally of Norman French (or Latin) origin. Some are fairly typical Indo-European words (*a/an, in, not*); for others the origin is not readily apparent (*nasty, smell, down*). So what about the myth of the effect of secondary contact from the Norman French invasion? Was there really any effect at all? Let's have a look at another passage, this time a piece of technical writing.

> The materials examined were those which the project sponsors considered to be most appropriate. This report gives a brief description of each of these materials and presents the results of initial laboratory tests, carried out on thirteen mixtures of the secondary materials.

This text is completely different in tone and style. It is formal and precise and it uses quite a different language from that used by Tolkien – but it is still English. This time I believe there are 34 different words. I can identify 16 of them as being definitely Germanic (*the, were, those, which, to, be, most, this, gives, of, these, and, out, on, thirteen, mixtures*). However, a further 15 are fairly clearly of Norman French or Latin origin (*materials, examined, project, sponsors, considered, appropriate, report, brief, description, presents, results, initial, laboratory, tests, secondary*). Two others I cannot identify and one could fit either Norman French or Germanic.

One absolutely obvious difference is that the average length of the Germanic words (4 letters) is considerably less than that of the French-related words (8 letters). This may seem irrelevant, but it is the little words which do the real business of the language. As shown by the first passage, it is quite possible to speak English without using any of the Norman French imports; however, we tend to use the longer French-derived words to give a sense of weightiness to what we are saying. Scanning through the pages of a medium-sized dictionary, it may be that well over half of all the words shown are of Norman French origin, but that does not change the fact that English remains, at root, a Germanic language. It is the Germanic words which control the grammar and structure of the language; the French-related words simply provide a rich variety of vocabulary from which to choose. In fact, the larger the dictionary, the greater the proportion of French/Latin-derived words will be.

Now, I am not going to deny that the influence of Norman French on the English language is important. Every sentence I write is full of this influence. But it does not help us to look back into the distant past because it dates from such comparatively recent times. So, to avoid taking account of it, it is important to stick to a consideration of what might be termed the 'core' of the language, that is the short simple words, together with the grammar, which tends to be controlled by those short simple words. In English, these appear to be virtually untouched by the secondary contact of Norman French. It was this observation which guided my choice of the 26 words used in the language comparison calculation described in the last chapter.

A footnote to this consideration of English is that there are quite a number of words which, though of Germanic origin, are actually closer to Scandinavian than to modern German. In the extract from *The Hobbit*, this is true of the words *of* (*av* in Swedish) and *bare* (*bar* in Swedish).

The conclusion, then, is that both nature and nurture apply to a language. The core of the language is endowed by nature (i.e. from its original roots); additional vocabulary and possibly some effect on the grammar is provided by nurture (i.e. from other influencing languages). This means that, if we can isolate the core part, it should be possible to look back deep into time and examine the true family roots which apply. I believe that the method described in the previous chapter does indeed allow the core of the language to be examined and its relation to the core parts of other languages measured. However, the fact of secondary contact has to be remembered and it is possible that not all languages have escaped as lightly as English appears to have done under Norman French influence.

## LANGUAGE FAMILY TREES

Before plunging into real measurements of language difference, it would be useful to review the evidence so far and I feel that the best way to achieve this is by means of a family tree type diagram, albeit one on its side. We have seen that any language, even if left completely isolated, will change with time, if for no other reason than due to changes in fashion. This is illustrated in the next figure by the changing shade of grey, although it is quite impossible to represent the infinite variety of ways in which language can change simply by shades of grey! In this chapter, the evidence for language movement and division has been spelt out, and four separate dividing points are represented in the figure. Most recently, secondary contact has been discussed and this is illustrated in the figure as an effect acting from Language F on Language E. Language E is changed by this experience, but its core remains true to its original roots. Finally, the inevitable fact of language extinction, occurring today at a rate as never before, is also shown.

Now what would we be able to deduce from a measurement of the linguistic difference between the languages still spoken today? Firstly and obviously, we would know nothing about Language G. Next, we should find that the difference between Languages H and I, for instance, is equivalent to the sum of the lengths of the two branches, Length H + Length I. If we could measure this in years, the total would be twice the number of years since the two branches separated. But we have to remember that,

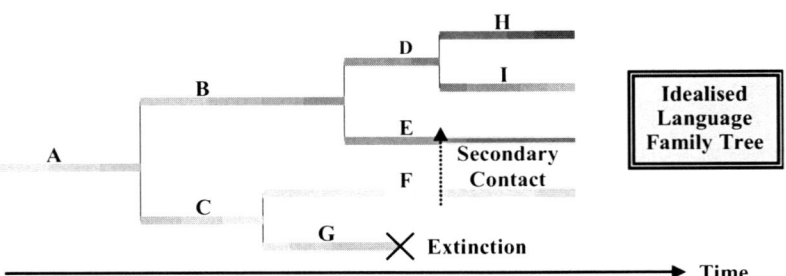

however clever I try to be, there is absolutely no way of measuring this directly in years, only in terms of linguistic difference (linguistic years), so all we can do is to measure the number of linguistic years between modern Language H and modern Language I and to say that a division happened at some intermediate point. It may be that, in linguistic years, one of the branches is actually much longer than the other. Deductions relating to the actual passage of time may then be possible, but there will be no universal calibration factor relating linguistic change to real time.

So what can we know? Well, the same calculation of linguistic difference can be carried out between each of the four remaining modern languages. If, say, the linguistic difference between E and H is 2500 linguistic years, whereas that between E and I is 2700 linguistic years, then we know that branch I has to be 200 linguistic years longer than branch H. We would hope that a similar picture would be given by looking at the distances F to H and F to I. Then, if we calculate that the distance H to I is, say, 1200 linguistic years, this means that branch H has to be 500 linguistic years long and branch I 700, 200 more. The length of branch E could be established in a similar way by comparing the distances F to H (or I) and F to E. Let us assume that F to H is calculated to be 4000 linguistic years and F to I is 4200, but F to E is 4700. So, the E branch has to extend 500 linguistic years further than the I branch and 700 further than the H branch.

In fact, there is only one point which cannot be determined, and that is the initial split point between Languages B and C (apart from the fact that we can know nothing at all of G). The only way to locate the initial split point is go further back in time and to find a more distantly related language, giving distances to each of the four existing modern languages. For purposes of illustration, I shall assume that this has been done and that the distance to F is found to be the same as that to H. The final result could then be represented as in the following figure.

This is a rather odd-looking family tree. But it is nonetheless a faithful representation of the linguistic differences. It simply means that Language E has developed much more rapidly than any of the others in the group, and that in itself is a fact worth knowing. It also faithfully rep-

# Chapter 5 Divide and Conquer

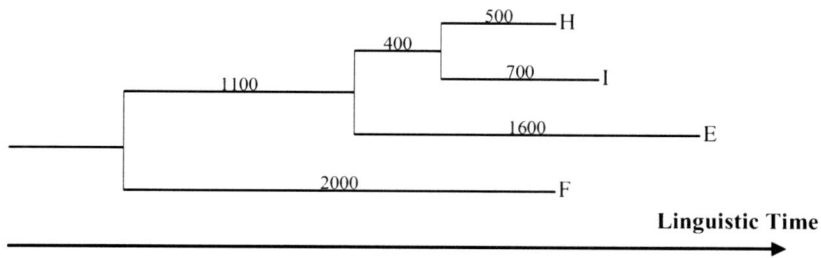

resents the arrangement of language divisions. The only intuitively unsatisfactory thing is that we really have no idea from this of the <u>real</u> time represented by all those linguistic years. But that is a fact of life. We can make some progress by referring to known ancient languages perhaps, but the fact will remain that some languages develop much quicker than others and this means that we will <u>never</u> be able to find a single unique relationship between linguistic years and calendar years.

Enough of discussion and the laying of foundations; we are now fully equipped. We can calculate linguistic difference and we know the theory of how to construct a family tree. Let's put it into practice for real.

# 6

# The Germanic Tribes

For centuries the frontier of the Roman Empire followed the course of the river Rhine, the river which even today divides the French and German speaking worlds. Following Julius Caesar's success in Gaul (i.e. France) in the 1st Century BC, the Romans were in expansionist mood. When Julius Caesar's chosen successor eventually managed to have himself proclaimed as the emperor Augustus, he sought every opportunity to drive forward the frontiers of the empire. The conquest of Spain was completed; likewise Switzerland and most of modern Austria, Slovenia, Croatia and Serbia; the North African tribes were tackled; the border of Egypt was pushed south, and Arabia was attacked. Indeed, the Romans seemed to see it as their duty to bring the light of civilisation to the backward and ignorant peoples of the globe (and to harvest their riches on behalf of Rome). In France, Spain and parts of central Europe, the sometimes less than grateful recipients of Roman culture were the Celts, and the Romans were extremely successful at incorporating them into their empire, but across the river Rhine and north of the river Danube the barbarians were of quite a different kind; they were Germanic. However, Augustus began to lay his plans and, in the year 12BC, the conquest of Germany commenced. For the time, it was a genuine 'Blitzkrieg' with three massive columns of Roman troops smashing through to the river Elbe, toward the east of the country. Over the course of six short years the land was thoroughly pacified and the business of Romanisation commenced. By 6AD the Romans felt so confident about their new province that they began planning their next move, the conquest of Bohemia, now the Czech Republic but then occupied by further Germanic speaking tribes. In fact, their confidence is reflected in their appointment of an administrator rather than a general to govern Germany. There was a little trouble to be dealt with further south, in Croatia, but Germany seemed thoroughly secure.

Chapter 6    The Germanic Tribes                                              67

But then, in the year 9AD, the fate of western Europe took a dramatic turn. Just as the Romans were celebrating their success in quelling the uprising in Croatia, the appalling news reached Rome that the ignorant barbarian Germans had managed to wipe out three whole Roman legions (about 16000 men) and Roman rule over Germany was at an end. The Romans hurriedly reinforced the Rhine and managed to prevent the Germans from invading France but, from that time on until the fall of the western Roman Empire 400 years later, they never managed to control more than a small slice of what is now southern Germany – the Celtic area in fact. The river Rhine remained the frontier of the empire. The Germanic tribes became a feared enemy, the archetypal barbarians. They remained independent of Roman rule and therefore outside the sphere of Roman learning and culture. They remained a backward people. And, like it or not, these backward and uncultured people were the cultural ancestors of the English.

Of course, things have changed since those days, both in England and in Germany! Whatever you think of English culture, the English language has gone on to achieve a pre-eminent position on the planet. This, together with the fact that many of the examples used in generating the model of language development put forward in this book have been taken from English, means that a logical place to start is with the modern Germanic language group, one branch of the Indo-European family. Today it comprises German, Dutch, English and the Scandinavian languages (except Finnish and Sami). It also includes Flemish (from Belgium), Frisian (still spoken in northern Germany and Holland), Afrikaans (descended from the speech of the first Dutch settlers of South Africa) and Yiddish (the language spoken by European Jews). Of this, there is, so far as I am aware, no argument at all among linguists. So, where better to try out my new calculation method?

I have to admit that I have not included all the modern Germanic languages in this study, only German, Dutch, English, Frisian, Danish, Swedish and Icelandic, but I have also included the language known as West Saxon, spoken in England about 1000 years ago. I am confident that this selection will be sufficient to obtain a good understanding of the group and to illustrate just how a family tree can be constructed.

The first step is to work out the difference between each pair of languages, using the calculation (including the calibration) introduced in Chapter 4. This gives us measurements in linguistic years, which we always have to remember cannot be related in any unique way to actual years. The full table of distances (rounded to the nearest hundred) is as follows, except that I have omitted modern English for the time being – thereby postponing what will prove to be a rather contentious issue.

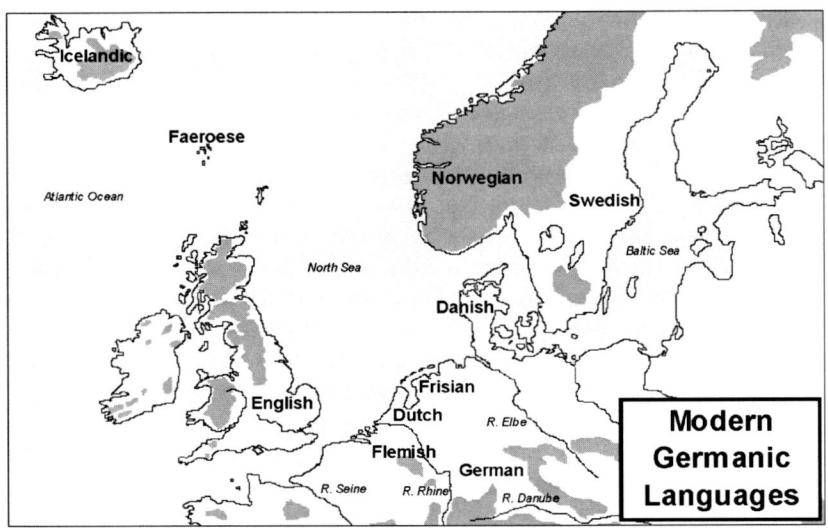

| Linguistic years | W S | Dut | Ger | Fri | Dan | Swe | Ice |
|---|---|---|---|---|---|---|---|
| West Saxon | 0 | 1800 | 1400 | 2800 | 2900 | 2800 | 1500 |
| Dutch | | 0 | 1100 | 800 | 2700 | 1800 | 2000 |
| German | | | 0 | 1900 | 3200 | 2500 | 1400 |
| Frisian | | | | 0 | 3100 | 2300 | 2800 |
| Danish | | | | | 0 | 1000 | 1700 |
| Swedish | | | | | | 0 | 1200 |
| Icelandic | | | | | | | 0 |

## CONSTRUCTING THE FAMILY TREE

So how does one set about constructing a family tree from this information? For me the easiest technique is to forget the tree shape and to construct a route map as if the numbers in the table were distances on the ground. Inevitably it is a little complicated to take full account of the distances between all seven languages at the same time, and there's no way of avoiding a degree of inconsistency between distances. It is logical to start where the confidence is highest and that must mean with the languages which are closest together. The two closest pairs are Frisian and Dutch (800 linguistic years between them) and Danish and Swedish (1000 linguistic years). In each case we can be pretty confident that the two languages in the pair diverged at a late stage, so why not average the distances to each pair from the remaining languages? We can always work out the individual locations for each member of the pair once the overall frame-

## Chapter 6  The Germanic Tribes

| Linguistic years | Dut-Fri | Dan-Swe | Ger | W S | Ice |
|---|---|---|---|---|---|
| **Dutch-Frisian** | 0 | 2500 | 1500 | 2300 | 2400 |
| **Danish-Swedish** |  | 0 | 2900 | 2900 | 1500 |
| **German** |  |  | 0 | 1400 | 1400 |
| **West Saxon** |  |  |  | 0 | 1500 |
| **Icelandic** |  |  |  |  | 0 |

work has been sorted out. This will reduce the problem to one with five 'destinations', namely Dutch-Frisian, Danish-Swedish, German, West Saxon and Icelandic. This gives us a much simpler table of distances (rounded again to the nearest 100 linguistic years).

This is now simple enough for us to start laying out the route map. The best place to start is definitely with the distance between the two pairs of languages, since this distance is actually the average of four individual measurements (Dutch to Danish, Dutch to Swedish, Frisian to Danish, Frisian to Swedish). It should therefore be the most trustworthy. The 2500 linguistic years in the table can be represented on a map as two points joined by a straight line.

Dutch-Frisian ○————2500————○ Danish-Swedish

Next we could add a third language, Icelandic say. It is 2400 linguistic years from Dutch-Frisian and 1500 from Danish-Swedish, 900 closer to Danish-Swedish than Dutch-Frisian. No problem; we just have to join to the right point on the road.

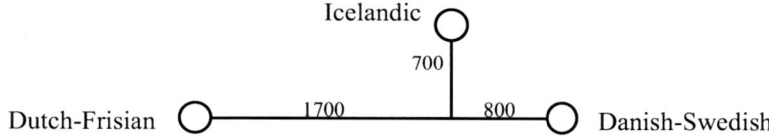

So far so good; let's now take a look at German. It is 1500 linguistic years from Dutch-Frisian, 2900 from Danish-Swedish and only 1400 from Icelandic. If we are going to use a single road, which we must, then there is a bit of a problem here. The distances to Dutch-Frisian and Danish-Swedish mean that we have to hit the Dutch-Frisian to Danish-Swedish road about 600 linguistic years from the Dutch-Frisian end, with a 900 linguistic year long side road to German. Unfortunately this would give 2700 linguistic years from German to Icelandic rather than the 1400 measured! A compromise will obviously be necessary but first let's take a look at the one remaining language, West Saxon. It is 2300 linguistic years from Dutch-Frisian and 2900 from Danish-Swedish, requiring a 1300 long side branch starting about 1000 from the Dutch-Frisian end. This would then give 2300 to German (instead of 1400 measured) and 2700 to Icelandic (1500 measured). For sure, several compromises are required in order to keep errors to a minimum. The next diagram is about the best I can achieve. As you can see, I have slightly extended the distance between Dutch-Frisian and Danish-Swedish and reduced the lengths of the other branches. This spreads the errors out more evenly.

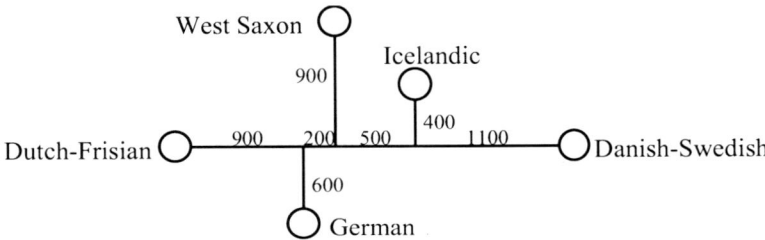

The next step is to work out just where the individual members of the two pairs should be placed. To do this, the technique is to work out a set of average distances from each member of a pair to all the remaining languages (excluding the other member of the pair). These are as follows:

| | | | |
|---|---|---|---|
| Dutch to others: | 1900 | linguistic | years |
| Frisian to others: | 2600 | " | " |
| Danish to others: | 2700 | " | " |
| Swedish to others: | 2100 | " | " |

Thus, Dutch is closer to the rest of the group than Frisian and Swedish is closer than Danish. Since we know the distances between Dutch and Frisian and between Danish and Swedish, we theoretically now have enough data to locate each member of the pair. However, recognizing (from experience) that this technique commonly exaggerates the differences between paired languages, the following is my suggested compromise version of the full route map.

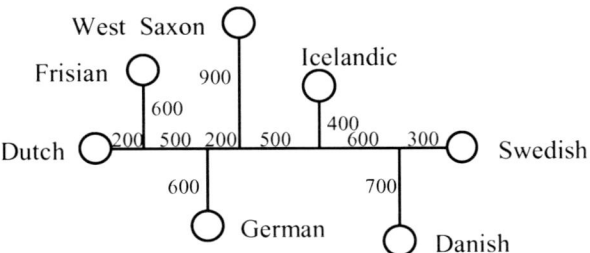

## Chapter 6   The Germanic Tribes

| Error (%)   | W S | Dut | Ger  | Fri   | Dan   | Swe   | Ice   |
|-------------|-----|-----|------|-------|-------|-------|-------|
| **West Saxon** | 0   | 0%  | +21% | −21%  | −7%   | −18%  | +20%  |
| **Dutch**   |     | 0   | +18% | 0%    | 0%    | +28%  | −10%  |
| **German**  |     |     | 0    | −11%  | −19%  | −12%  | +21%  |
| **Frisian** |     |     |      | 0     | −9%   | +19%  | −5%   |
| **Danish**  |     |     |      |       | 0     | 0%    | 0%    |
| **Swedish** |     |     |      |       |       | 0     | +8%   |
| **Icelandic** |   |     |      |       |       |       | 0     |

This all looks very neat. There seems to be a 'continental' group, German, Dutch and Frisian, and we can be certain that Flemish, Afrikaans and Yiddish would have fitted in somewhere pretty close. Then there seems to be a Scandinavian group. West Saxon is clearly closer to the continental end. However, you can be quite sure that there are some pretty hefty errors in distance between individual languages. Let's have a look, comparing the calculated distances with those on the route map. In the above table, a positive error means that the distance on the route map is too large and a negative error means that it is too small. I have converted to percentage error to give a fairer comparison between large and small linguistic distances.

It has to be admitted that some of these errors look a little disappointing. But please remember that this is not an exact science; any measurement system of this type is likely to produce significant uncertainty in individual measurements, as more or less words appear cognate, purely as a function of processes which are essentially random. Also, I must not forget that the assumptions of clean divisions between languages and zero effect from secondary contact are hardly likely to be 100% true. In fact the Germanic languages provide a good example of a group where the past interactions between peoples are known to have been quite complex. So, although I would prefer to see smaller errors (and in much of this book I will), I am quite prepared to live with a result like this.

There is one more important step which has to be taken and that is to find out where the route joins in, which leads from the rest of the Indo-European family to the Germanic group. For this it is necessary to work out in some way the distance from each Germanic language to the rest of the family. Since there are rather a lot of Indo-European languages this could get a bit complicated, so I have averaged the distances to 30 or so other languages to obtain a single distance. It is a little crude but I think you realise by now that this is how it must be. The distances come out as follows:

|  |  |  |
|---|---|---|
| from Icelandic: | 13200 | linguistic years |
| from German: | 13200 | " " |
| from West Saxon: | 13600 | " " |
| from Dutch: | 14100 | " " |
| from Frisian: | 15300 | " " |
| from Swedish: | 15400 | " " |
| from Danish: | 15700 | " " |

Now, the differences between these distances are actually far too great to tie in with the group as it has been constructed, which is hardly surprising since a mere 1% error in any one of them equates to around 150 linguistic years. None the less, Icelandic and German clearly come out to be the closest to the rest of the family, followed by West Saxon, and this strongly suggests that the connection point should lie somewhere on the 700 long straight between the German and Icelandic turn-offs. Just where is a bit of an unknown but we can do no better than maintain equal distance to German and Icelandic since they come out equal closest to the rest of the family. This gives the final version of the route map shown below.

Each line on the map represents the development of a particular language. The point where the path from the rest of the Indo-European family joins represents the ancestor Germanic language, from which all seven of the languages shown are descended. From that ancestral Germanic tongue a split took place, according to the map. One version became an ancestor of the Scandinavian languages; the other gave rise to Dutch, Frisian and German, as well as spawning West Saxon.

Now there was nothing special about the layout chosen for the route map. The direction of a line means nothing – only its length. Therefore it is quite permissible to bend the lines round to give the more familiar shape of a family tree.

With branches of such differing lengths this certainly looks a strange sort of family tree. However, in spite of all the admitted approximations and uncertainties, there is a great deal more than a grain of truth in it – it

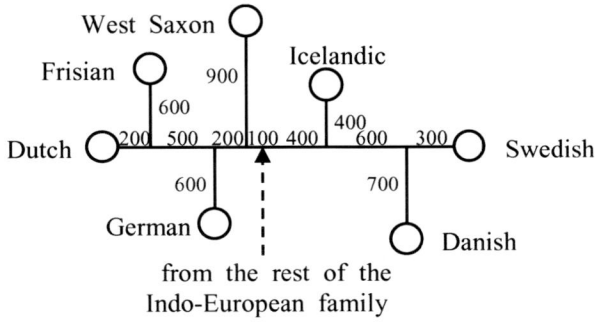

# Chapter 6    The Germanic Tribes

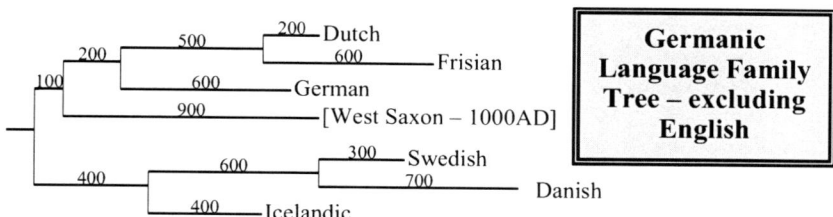

Germanic Language Family Tree – excluding English

is, after all, based on actual properties of the languages. So let's take a look at just what can be learnt from a family tree like this.

## THE HISTORY OF GERMANIC LANGUAGE

The most striking point is that there is a significant difference in the rates of language change represented, Danish having changed more than any of the others, which reinforces the point that measurement in linguistic years cannot possibly be translated simply into real years. This will not stop me trying on numerous occasions, but it has to be remembered that any attempt at such a conversion cannot hope to be more than approximate. Fortunately, in the case of Germanic languages it is possible to say something about actual passage of time from what we know of history. The Germanic conquest of Britain is known to have occurred in several phases. Firstly, Saxon chiefs and their warrior clans from northern Germany were invited to settle in Kent in 410AD to act as a full-time army of protection to ex-Roman (the legions had just left) Britain. Things turned sour in about 440AD and the Saxons then ran amok, grabbing additional lands for themselves; they still only formed a tiny minority of the population however. The second and much more significant phase of settlement got going in around 500AD, with Saxons in the south, Angles in the East and Jutes in the far south-east. All three peoples were Germanic but, whereas the Saxons came from northern Germany and Holland, the Angles and Jutes were both from Denmark. Celtic Britain became restricted to south-west England, Wales and Scotland. The third and final phase commenced in 793AD with the first of the Viking raids, soon to be followed by many, many more.

The Vikings were Norwegian, Norsemen, whose advances in sea-going technology had allowed them to dominate Scandinavia and they were now looking to settle new lands. They conquered northern France (where the resulting culture became known as 'Norman') and, from the year 864, they began serious settlement in Britain. Within a decade they had half the country, and the eastern third remained a semi-autonomous Viking-ruled territory for over a hundred years. And in 1016, after further raids and victories, the Viking king Cnut became king of all England.

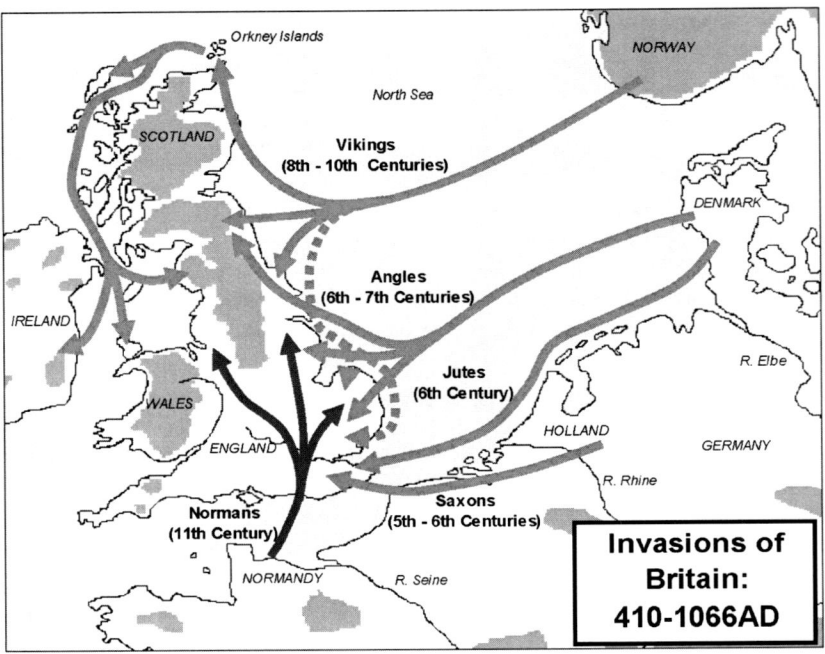

Invasions of Britain: 410-1066AD

Now, turning to the language tree, what can we learn? Well, the first, very clear point is that West Saxon has continental rather than Scandinavian connections, and it is logical to date the divergence of the West Saxon branch to around 500AD, when Saxon settlement in Britain really took off. The 900 linguistic years of change shown on the family tree therefore took place over the following 500 years or so – at 1.8 linguistic years per year. Meanwhile, the continental languages have only averaged about 1000 linguistic years over a 1500 year period, a much slower change rate. Why? What circumstances might be responsible for such a large difference? Well; may I suggest the obvious answer is <u>movement</u>. The West Saxon language physically moved its territory, and must certainly have been adopted by large numbers of Celtic speakers. Children who grew up speaking Celtic will have found themselves turning increasingly to Saxon as the newcomers became ever more powerful and ruled an ever-expanding territory. In contrast, the continental languages are still spoken in the same territories in which the Romans first encountered Germanic tribes. A more settled life has clearly led to slower language change.

However, for seriously slow change, Icelandic takes some beating! The separation of the Icelandic branch can sensibly be dated to the time the island was colonised, in the 9th Century AD, and the rate of change

Chapter 6    The Germanic Tribes                                            75

since that time has therefore been a mere 0.35 linguistic years per year. Lack of movement and lack of outside interference are logical reasons for this stability. In contrast, Swedish and Danish have averaged between 0.7 and 1 linguistic years per year, similar rates to German, Dutch and Frisian.

As for the original, ancestral Germanic tongue, it looks very much as though it must have been spoken somewhere in northern Germany in around 400AD, coinciding with the start of the disintegration of the western part of the Roman Empire – which is logical enough. The trouble is that we know of Germanic languages which were spoken much earlier than this! Putting aside an enigmatic reference by the Greek historian Herodotus (5th Century BC) to "Germanii" as one of the Persian tribes, the first clear mention of Germanic tribes in Europe appears in Roman documents from the 1st Century BC. As we have seen, when the Roman Empire tried to extend its territory east of the river Rhine the barbarian tribes they encountered were Germanic speaking – and there were numerous different tribes, one of which was already known as the 'Frisians'[1]! No-one knows exactly where they came from or when although an earlier Greek author, Pytheas, mentions the Teutoni (from which the word Teutonic derives) as a tribe living somewhere near the Baltic in the 4th Century BC[2].

The point I am trying to make is that there is not necessarily anything special about a particular 'ancestor language'. The ancestor to every one of today's Germanic tongues was just one of several related languages, already Germanic. It just so happens that the vagaries of history have seen

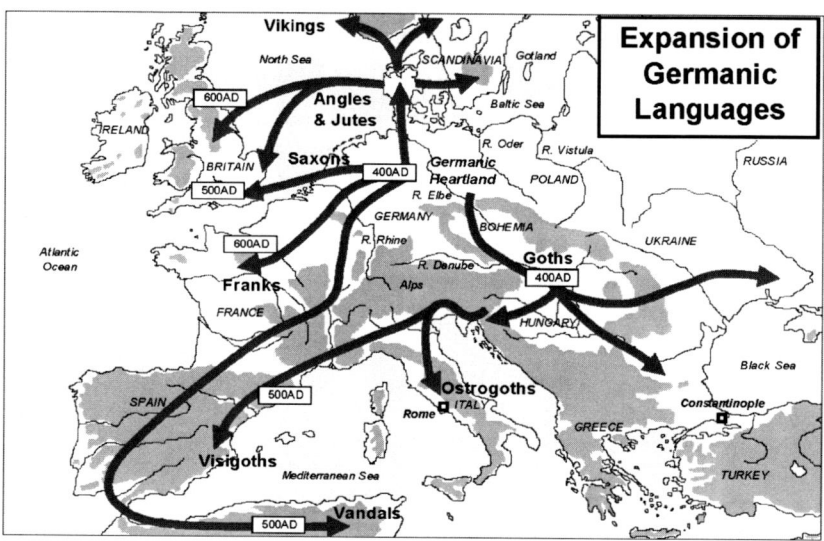

the extinction of all the others and the success of that one particular variant. A study of modern languages alone can of course tell us absolutely nothing about languages which have become extinct. Indeed, there are a number of known Germanic languages which history records and which have no descendants today. 'Gothic' languages were spoken by Germanic tribes who emerged onto the pages of Roman history from eastern Germany and the Baltic region. They were a warlike group of peoples, used as mercenaries by the Romans to shore up their empire, but who then turned and conquered both Italy and Spain in the 5$^{th}$ Century AD, ruling Spain for over 200 years. The Vandals were also a Germanic group; they ruled Spain before the Goths took over, and then conquered North Africa and settled there. The name 'France' comes from the Frankish people, a Germanic tribe which crossed the Rhine and took over much of France in the 6$^{th}$ Century AD, just as 'Burgundy' is named after the Germanic-speaking Burgundians. All the languages spoken by these highly successful conquering peoples died out long ago under the cultural weight of the Latin-derived languages spoken by the earlier inhabitants of the countries where they settled. In the case of the Vandals, their culture was finally extinguished by the Arabic culture of the first Muslim invaders. While the Franks, Burgundians, Goths and Vandals were all submitting (linguistically) to the cultural superiority of Latin, a single north German dialect was spreading its range outside the Latin-speaking world, into lands where Germanic culture could readily dominate. This meant the lands bordering the North Sea and, eventually, the fair island of Britain, now abandoned to its fate by the retreating Roman legions – all of which brings me to the embarrassing subject of modern English.

## THE TRUE ROOTS OF ENGLISH

Modern English should present no problems at all. In all the textbooks, as well as all the myriad popular books on the subject, English is descended from West Saxon and, as we have just seen and as linguists know well, West Saxon stems from the tongue of the Saxon invaders of England from about 500AD. The trouble is that the measurement system in this book, which has so far provided such a logical history of the Germanic languages, does not support this commonly-held view of modern English. Let's take a look at the measurements.

| | | |
|---|---|---|
| English to Danish: | 1500 | linguistic years |
| English to Swedish: | 1900 | " " |
| English to West Saxon: | 2000 | " " |
| English to Icelandic: | 2500 | " " |
| English to Dutch: | 2600 | " " |
| English to German: | 2800 | " " |
| English to Frisian: | 2900 | " " |

Chapter 6    The Germanic Tribes

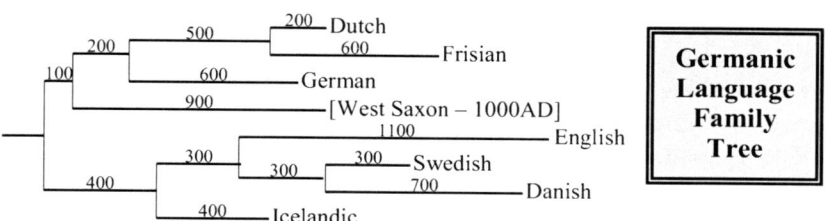

Now admittedly these measures are not exact; however there is absolutely no way that they allow me to place modern English as a direct descendant of West Saxon. In fact, it comes out distinctly closer to the Scandinavian languages[3]! If I take the same approach as previously and minimise the errors as far as possible, then I have no choice. English branched from the Scandinavian side of the family some time after Icelandic, say in around 1000AD, and the only possible interpretation is that English stems not from the Saxon language of southern England but from the speech of the east and north.

As far as I can see, the most likely explanation is that modern English has developed principally from 'Anglish', the tongue of the Angles, and that final separation from the languages of Denmark and Sweden probably only occurred following the collapse of Viking rule in the 11th Century AD[4]. In the 1000 years since the rule of king Cnut, English shows 1100 linguistic years of development, and it's a reasonable bet that the lion's share of this change occurred in the century or so following the Norman conquest in 1066AD. Note that there is a relatively large discrepancy between the measured distance from West Saxon to modern English (2000 linguistic years) and the value suggested by the family tree (2800) and I would certainly concede that this indicates significant 'secondary contact'. To put it another way, while the root of modern English is shown here to be Scandinavian, it is true that many elements of West Saxon speech have made their way into the language. This concession will not of course satisfy those who have for so long believed in the direct line of descent from West Saxon to English, but I refuse to disbelieve the evidence of the measurements. It is quite possible that the bulk of the population may have been speaking Anglish even during the years when West Saxon was the official tongue and the language of government. With the demise of Saxon power, first under Viking dominance, then under Norman rule, so the Saxon language would have lost its previously prestigious status, liberating Anglish for its starring role!

## SUMMARY

I trust that the Germanic branch has been an interesting one with which to start. As you have seen, it has not been a model group; it has revealed more than its fair share of difficulties in reconciling the various linguistic difference measurements into a family tree. It does however show the potential of this analysis method very clearly indeed. While most of the results have been fully in line with traditional thinking, based on existing methods of language analysis, those for modern English are most definitely not; and this immediately sends out a warning to prepare for more surprises to come. I am afraid this will be by no means the last occasion on which conventional thinking is challenged!

Be that as it may, the Germanic branch illustrates two absolutely fundamental characteristics which will prove of immense worth in interpreting the results for other language groups. The first, most important, but slightly controversial point is that physical movement of a language (generally including adoption by new people) causes rapid change. Amongst Germanic languages this is exemplified by West Saxon and Anglish. I use the word 'controversial' because there are two diametrically opposed schools of thought on the subject. Many linguists would agree with my statement linking movement with rapid change, but there is a second theory (the 'Lateral Theory') that sees languages on the extremity of a particular language zone as being the most conservative, i.e. changing the least[5]. We'll have to keep an eye out as to which way the evidence leans. Although the evidence of West Saxon and Anglish weighs in against the Lateral Theory, the case of Icelandic undoubtedly lends it support. The second point which I take from the Germanic languages is that strong influence from another group also causes a higher than normal level of change. Again, it is Anglish/English which makes the point. In round numbers, it seems that 1.5 or more linguistic years of change per year can be expected from a language on the move or in difficulty in some way, but that 0.7 linguistic years per year or less is typical of the change rate in the language of a settled people.

I think the groundwork has now been laid sufficiently well for an all out assault to be made on the rest of the Indo-European family. This language family is surely the most completely studied of any on the face of the earth, simply because such a high percentage of the better-off inhabitants of the earth speak Indo-European languages. It has been a highly successful language family, spreading over almost all of Europe and into Central Asia, the Middle East and most of the Indian subcontinent. In more recent times it has thrived in both North and South America and Australia, together with numerous other locations all over the world. Having been introduced to the Germanic branch, now let's meet its brothers and sisters.

# 7

# The Indo-Europeans

You may never have realised that there was such a thing as the Indo-European language family. Perhaps even a relatively closely related language such as German seems quite foreign enough. To suggest that Russian is in any way related to English may seem a little crazy. To go further and make the same claims for Persian or Pashto (the main language of Afghanistan) is even more far fetched; but to go even to Sri Lanka or to Bangladesh and be told that Sinhala and Bengali are also Indo-European may be just too much. And you would have a point. According to the calculation method presented in Chapter 4, the score for similarity between English and Bengali is 0.32, i.e. 32%, but this is found by considering only the few most common words in the language and by awarding points for similarity even when some of the words may initially appear quite different. Thus *father* and *pita* are considered to be the same! So are *mother* and *mata*, and *ten* is close enough to *dosh* for at least half a point. Similarly, grammatical closeness is judged according to only the most general features. So, for 32% similarity read only a tiny fraction of this in practice. But this is just the beauty of comparative linguistics; it is possible to extract from two seemingly quite different languages the essential pointers to their common ancestry. Don't imagine you are the only one who sees all foreign languages as completely alien; the reality is that such similarity as exists is only to be found right at the core.

To return to the Indo-European family: it was the discovery of this family by Europeans that first brought the question of how languages arose to public attention. People had, of course, noticed some degree of similarity between many of the languages of Europe, though this may have been attributed to the influence of one language on another rather than any true family relationship. What really drew the matter to the attention of European scholars was the fact that travellers to India also noted a certain if distant similarity[1]. Attention is often drawn to the similarity between the names for family members, such as those for *mother* and *father* mentioned above. What could this mean? How could languages from such different parts of the world be related?

Since then, we have had the startling revelation that ancient Hittite, spoken in Turkey in the 2$^{nd}$ Millennium BC, and Tocharian, spoken in western China in the 1$^{st}$ Millennium AD, were both Indo-European. These discoveries caused a sensation in linguistic circles and of course spread even more confusion about the origins of the Indo-European family. In all, therefore, there are a lot of pieces to the Indo-European jigsaw, all of which have to fit into the picture somewhere. However, my principal aim in this chapter is to construct language family trees for each branch of the family in turn and to compare them with known history. I'll leave the vexed question of Indo-European origins until the next chapter.

So now let me introduce you to one of Germanic's most powerful neighbours.

## ITALIC LANGUAGES

The Italic languages comprise those spoken in the Iberian peninsula, i.e. Portuguese, Galician, Spanish and Catalan, also French, Italian, Romansh (spoken in Switzerland) and, in the east, Romanian. Portuguese, Spanish and French are also spoken in various far away parts of the world, but the homeland for each language lies within the borders of the old Roman Empire, the region where Latin was once the common tongue. The following table gives calculated distances between a selection of the lan-

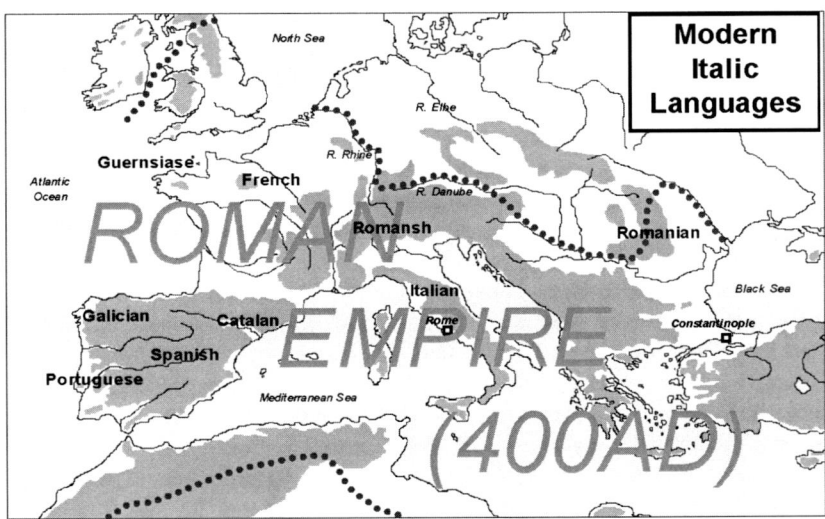

Chapter 7    The Indo-Europeans    81

| Linguistic years | Cat | Fre | Gue | Ita | Por | Rom | Spa |
|---|---|---|---|---|---|---|---|
| Catalan | 0 | 1400 | 1600 | 1200 | 800 | 3300 | 2000 |
| French | | 0 | 300 | 600 | 1200 | 3400 | 2700 |
| Guernsiase | | | 0 | 600 | 1900 | 3800 | 2600 |
| Italian | | | | 0 | 1400 | 2700 | 2200 |
| Portuguese | | | | | 0 | 3300 | 700 |
| Romanian | | | | | | 0 | 4800 |
| Spanish | | | | | | | 0 |

guages. I have omitted Galician (I admitted earlier that I had no knowledge of it at all) and Romansh, but I have added a 'non-standard' French patois (or dialect), that spoken on the island of Guernsey, between France and England. The language is called Guernsiase and it is thought to descend from Norman French.

The other piece of information required is the average distance from each Italic language to the rest of the Indo-European family. These are as follows.

| | |
|---|---|
| Romanian | 12800 linguistic years |
| French | 12800 linguistic years |
| Italian | 13300 linguistic years |
| Guernsiase | 13500 linguistic years |
| Portuguese | 13700 linguistic years |
| Catalan | 14300 linguistic years |
| Spanish | 14300 linguistic years |

I think it's fair to say that Romanian stands out as being different from the rest. It is nearest (equal with French) to the other members of the Indo-European family, which should mean that it has changed relatively slowly, but it is not particularly close to any of the other Italic languages. Spanish is also interestingly distant from most of the rest. These traits should therefore appear in the family tree and indeed they do. The following figure is the best fit I can find to the data.

The errors are similar to those for the Germanic branch; you can check them out for yourself if so inclined. In percentage terms, the

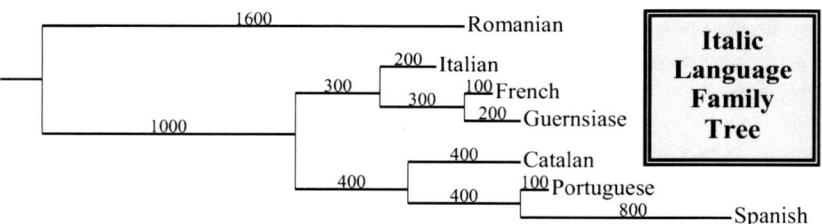

worst is 33%, between French and Portuguese, equivalent to 400 linguistic years.

So what can we learn? Firstly, the start point, representing the ancestral Italic language, is not too difficult to guess at from a knowledge of history. The Roman Empire ruled over the entire Mediterranean area until the early years of the 5th Century AD. But, in the year 406AD, the Germanic tribes east of the Rhine finally broke through the Roman lines and the process of collapse began. By 410AD Rome had been sacked by the Goths and the empire was effectively divided into a reasonably stable Greek-dominated eastern part, governed from Constantinople (modern Istanbul), which included Romania, and a highly volatile western part dominated by the Germanic invaders (Franks, Burgunds, Goths and Vandals). The year 410AD therefore represents the approximate date of the political separation of Romania from the rest of the Latin-speaking lands and a logical date for the ancestral language to today's Italic branch. We can check this out by referring to the Latin language itself and measuring the distances to the various modern Italic languages. Taking the Latin at the time of Julius Caesar (1st Century BC), the unambiguous message from the measurements is that it sits about 700 linguistic years <u>before</u> the division between Romanian and the rest, which is pretty much where it should be. This gives no more than 8% error compared to the calculated distances from Latin to each of the seven modern languages.

The second key dividing point on the family tree can surely be identified with the break-up of the Holy Roman Empire (basically the old Frankish empire of France) in the early 10th Century and the growing independence of the rulers of northern Spain, although Latin would still have been the official language since it was the language of the Christian church.

Let's take a look at the change rates involved. The rate of change to Latin between the 1st Century BC and 410AD works out at about 1.5 linguistic years per year. This is a high rate, which is interesting since there was no movement involved and no external domination. It raises the possibility that we should add being a 'language of empire' as a further cause of rapid change, which perhaps is unsurprising when the influence of numerous subordinate nations is considered. When we come to the next 500 years or so, the time of the Frankish empire, which then became the Holy Roman Empire under its greatest ruler Charlemagne, the rate of change rises further, to over 2 linguistic years per year. Clearly being the language of a highly volatile and unstable empire causes even faster change! In contrast, Romanian has changed by an average of just 1 linguistic year per year since being cut off from its brothers and sisters. Although it has had to endure significant influences from Slavonic (there are numerous Slavonic words in modern Romanian vocabulary), Turkish, German and Hungarian, it has never been a language of empire, nor has it been under serious threat.

Since the end of the Holy Roman Empire in the early 10th Century AD, French and Italian have settled to a modest 0.5 to 0.7 linguistic years per year. No-one could claim that the times have been uniformly peaceful but it appears that lack of movement, lack of significant empire and only occasional and partial domination by outsiders has been sufficient to allow relatively slow change. The same is true of Catalan and Portuguese, both of which grew from territory already independent of Arab rule. Spanish, however, is a rather striking anomaly. It has seen 1600 linguistic years of change during the same 1100 years; why on earth should this be? The answer is surely political domination by the Arabs. Much of central southern Spain was under continuous Arab control from the time of the initial Muslim invasion (711AD) until the 15th Century and it is therefore no wonder to see the degree of change to the language; modern Spanish has large numbers of Arabic loan words. In many ways, it is surprising that it survived at all. One should also remember that the language has expanded geographically more than any of the others. It was at one time just one of several variants in northern Spain but has gone on to spread itself across most of the country over the course of the centuries.

The Italic language branch clearly makes the point that being a language of empire leads to rapid change. The experience of Spanish also reinforces the point, made when looking at the Germanic languages, that both domination by outsiders and movement contribute strongly. These are important points; they may seem of dubious relevance here, but they will prove invaluable aids to interpretation when we arrive at times for which historical records are scarce or non-existent.

Anyway, having dealt with the linguistic fall-out from the Roman Empire, a highly successful empire which ensured the important position of Italic languages today, let's move to a certain other Indo-European branch which, on account of that empire, has a much less important position today than it otherwise might have.

## CELTIC LANGUAGES

Celtic languages, spoken by the Druids of old, once reigned supreme over a large part of central Europe, not merely the western fringes to which they are now confined. The ancient Gauls of France were Celtic; there were Celts in Spain and Portugal, in southern Germany, Austria and Hungary. Saint Paul even wrote one of his letters, now one of the Books of the Bible, to the Celts of Turkey (known to us as Galatians). But today the Celtic world has shrunk to a mere shadow of its former self, hammered into relative obscurity by the Italic-speaking Romans and then by the Germanic-speaking Anglo-Saxons. Welsh is still thriving reasonably well. Irish, too, remains in several areas and is making something of a comeback.

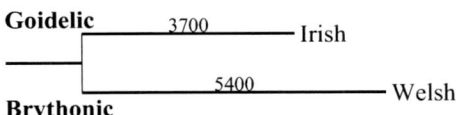

But Scottish Gaelic now has a lot of ground to make up and Breton is also finding life decidedly tough. However, Celtic languages are important to an overall understanding of the Indo-European riddle.

I have selected Irish and Welsh, since they are the most widely spoken modern Celtic tongues; they also represent two quite different sub-branches of Celtic, known as 'Goidelic' and 'Brythonic'. With only two languages, the relationship between them is a trivial matter. It is simply the distance between the two. Using the formula, this distance is 9100 linguistic years which, you may note, is rather a lot compared to what we have seen so far from Germanic or Italic languages. Comparing distances to other Indo-European tongues, Irish comes out much closer and the result is the above family tree.

It is rather a bare tree I am afraid. It would certainly be possible to add Scottish Gaelic as a late branch from the Goidelic arm (when Irish colonists moved into western Scotland during the late 1st Millennium AD), and also Breton and Cornish as rather earlier offshoots from the Brythonic arm. However, what cannot be seen today is the undoubtedly large number of extinctions of Celtic tongues from all over Europe. There is really very little evidence as to how these ancient languages would have fitted into the Celtic family tree, and this means, unfortunately, that there is little scope for confident interpretation. The reason that Welsh has changed so rapidly compared to Irish must surely be the quite different experiences of the two languages. Irish has been less disturbed for much of the last 2000 years, enduring just a period of Viking pressure and, more recently, the hated English rule. Welsh, on the other hand, has suffered two millennia of continuous foreign domination.

Regarding origins, I believe we can quite confidently link Welsh to the language of Britain immediately prior to the Roman invasion and, thence, to the La Tène culture of northern France and western Germany, which flourished in the 5th Century BC. Although archaeologists see little evidence for a Celtic 'invasion' of Britain, there is no doubt that the La Tène culture, identified by exquisite examples of metalwork such as swords and brooches, arrived in Britain somehow. Irish, on the other hand, seems to represent an earlier wave of Celtic language. The best evidence for this comes from place names, the ending *–magus* being found in Ireland, Britain, France and Italy, whereas *–dunum* apparently never made it to Ireland. The earlier wave of language (and culture) should probably be identified archaeologically with a development of the 'Urnfield' culture,

Chapter 7    The Indo-Europeans    85

so called after the practice of burying cremation urns. This widely dispersed archaeological culture can be traced spreading west through Europe and reaching Britain in the first half of the 1st Millennium BC[2]. The later La Tène culture of France and western Germany represents a specific and successful development from the well-known Hallstatt culture of Austria (800-500BC), itself also a development of the Urnfield tradition[3]. All of this means that the Goidelic and Brythonic sub-branches of Celtic may well have diverged in early Hallstatt times, around 800BC, somewhere in Central Europe. The average rates of change would therefore be 1.3 and 1.9 linguistic years per year for Irish and Welsh respectively. One would expect the early years of Celtic expansion to have produced very high rates of change in both, with a much slower rate for Irish for the succeeding, more settled period.

And what of the Celtic languages of Spain and Portugal, known to have been spoken in the north and west of the Iberian peninsula when the Romans arrived (2nd Century BC)? They would probably have been of yet another sub-branch, identifiable with the place ending –*briga*, found only in Portugal, Spain and France, but with absolutely no hard evidence the details appear now to be quite beyond recovery and the arrows shown on the map can be no more than informed speculation.

## GREEK

If you had visited Europe in 400BC, you would never have picked Italic or Germanic speech as being destined to play a dominant role. Celtic would

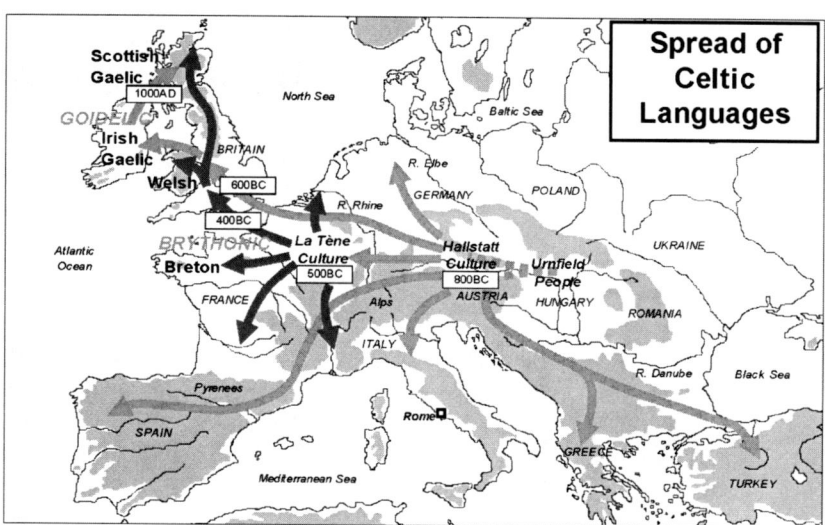

certainly have been a very strong candidate (increasingly so after the Celtic invasion of northern Italy and their sack of Rome in 390BC), but your favourite would almost certainly have been a quite different Indo-European tongue, based in the eastern Mediterranean, namely Greek. At that time, Greek culture dominated much of the Mediterranean. The Greeks colonised far and wide, competing with Phoenicians and Etruscans for mastery of the high seas. Greek colonies sprang up in southern Italy and Sicily, southern France (Marseilles was a Greek city once), Spain and North Africa, not to mention numerous locations around the Black Sea. Variants of Greek language were spoken until recently both in southern Italy and in southern Russia. Then, in 336-328BC, Alexander the Great took Greek culture right across the known world, to the Middle East, Central Asia, India, Egypt, places where the Greek language thrived for centuries. Queen Cleopatra's death brought to an end some 300 years of Greek-speaking rule in Egypt. Alexandria was as important a Greek city as Athens. The New Testament of the Bible was deliberately written in the world language of the day, namely Greek. But the plain fact is that modern Greek is now once more restricted to the place where it all began, Greece. Romans, Persians, Slavs, Arabs and Turks have all contributed to the decline of the once proud Greek world.

So, although both Greek and Celtic started the race well, neither has stayed the course, giving way in the face of upstarts like Italic and Germanic. But the real dark horse in the field, a beast of relative insignificance until quite recently, was quietly going about its business in the east.

## SLAVONIC AND BALTIC LANGUAGES

The Slavonic branch has today become one of the most important pieces in the Indo-European mosaic in terms of numbers of speakers. Russian is the best known Slavonic language, but many of the languages of eastern Europe, such as Czech and Serbo-Croat, also fall into the group. Many linguists would also include the so-called 'Baltic' group (Latvian, Lithuanian and the now extinct Prussian language) within the same branch and there is no denying that there are strong similarities. Both use similar systems of noun declension (different endings for nouns depending on their role in a sentence) and treat verbs in the same distinctive fashion. Furthermore, there are very obvious similarities in vocabulary. I have therefore included a Baltic representative, Latvian, in my analysis as well as seven selected Slavonic languages. The measured distances are given in the following table.

To these distances must be added the fact that Ukrainian comes out to be much the closest language to the rest of the Indo-European family. Putting all this information together, I have constructed the family tree shown. The errors are all small within the Slavonic side of the family (i.e. excluding Latvian), few exceeding 200 linguistic years, so there seems to be no room for doubt that the family tree reasonably accurately expresses the relative positions of all the Slavonic languages. The errors involved with Latvian are, I admit, much greater.

So what can be deduced here? Well, the thing that strikes me above all is the very small change which there appears to have been in the Ukrainian language. Now, I would not dream of claiming that the linguistic distances shown should be taken as exact truth, but I would maintain the basic message that Ukrainian has changed much less than the other languages. Based on what we know from the Germanic and Italic branches, this can only mean one thing – Ukrainian has hardly moved, at least not since the other Slavonic languages separated from it; but when was that?

| Linguistic years | Lat | Bul | Ukr | Rus | Pol | Cze | Sl'k | Sl'ne |
|---|---|---|---|---|---|---|---|---|
| Latvian | 0 | 6300 | 2800 | 4000 | 2500 | 3300 | 4500 | 4100 |
| Bulgarian | | 0 | 1400 | 1700 | 2300 | 2200 | 2200 | 2500 |
| Ukrainian | | | 0 | 800 | 1100 | 1300 | 1700 | 1700 |
| Russian | | | | 0 | 800 | 500 | 700 | 1100 |
| Polish | | | | | 0 | 500 | 800 | 1800 |
| Czech | | | | | | 0 | 300 | 1500 |
| Slovak | | | | | | | 0 | 1500 |
| Slovene | | | | | | | | 0 |

88　　　　　　　　　　　　　Chapter 7　　The Indo-Europeans

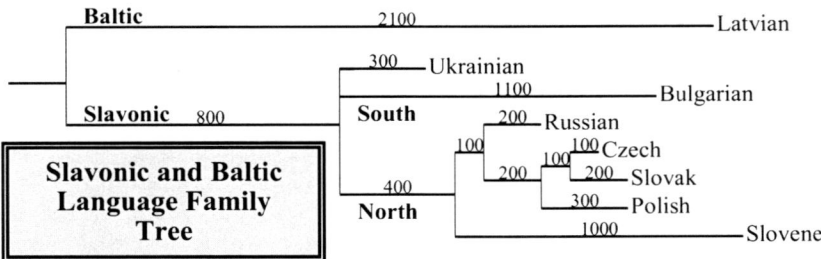

Slavonic and Baltic Language Family Tree

The Slavs appear in history from the 5th Century AD as thorns in the side of the Eastern Roman Empire, spreading down from the north into the Balkans. They allied themselves with the Avars (see Chapter 11) and eventually settled throughout the Balkans, including Greece, where Slavonic originating place names can still be found. As they settled, the language they spoke 'did battle' with those spoken by the earlier inhabitants, whether Greek, Latin or, in places, Albanian. In some cases it lost, leaving Greek in Greece, Latin in the country which is now Romania, and Albanian in Albania. However, elsewhere it was victorious, leading to the modern languages of Serbo-Croat, Macedonian and Bulgarian. Please remember that a victory by a language is quite different from a victory by a people; it does not necessarily mean the extermination or expulsion of those speaking other languages, but rather that following generations adopted the language of the dominant group in place of that of their own forefathers. This southward movement is represented in my family tree by Bulgarian, and 400AD is therefore a sensible approximate date for the separation of the so-called 'South Slavonic' languages.

In the north, we first hear mention of Slavonic tribes in Poland, Bohemia, Hungary and even eastern Germany during the 6th Century[4] and, by 862, the ancient Russian city of Novgorod ('New Town' in Slavonic) had been founded south of the much later capital, St Petersburg. It seems safe to assume therefore that northern Slavonic tribes (traditionally twelve in number) headed out in several directions from the Ukraine during the mid 1st Millennium AD, settling broadly in their current locations over the course of a few hundred years. Just what prompted this dispersal is far from clear, but it may have been pressure from the Avars and, later, the Khazars[5] (both Turkic speaking) and the military technology they brought. Archaeologically, the Slavs of the Ukraine have to be identified with the Chernyakhovo culture of the first half of the 1st Millennium AD[6].

The rates of change to Slavonic languages therefore range from an admittedly unlikely 0.2 linguistic years per year for Ukrainian to nearly 1 linguistic year per year for Slovene[7]. None are particularly high, reflecting reasonably settled conditions. Overall, it is fair to say that the language

Chapter 7   The Indo-Europeans                                89

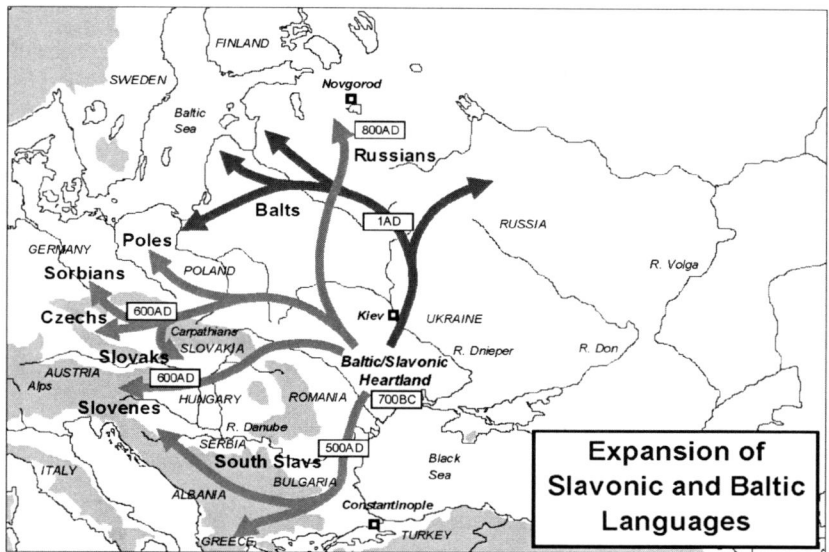

**Expansion of Slavonic and Baltic Languages**

family tree tells pretty much the same story as known history and archaeology, including the Ukrainian origin of the family as a whole.

Unfortunately, the early history of Baltic speakers is rather vaguer than that of the Slavs but it is clear that their languages developed from one spoken by a group of 'Balto-Slavs' whose language and culture must have spread north during the 1st Millennium BC, perhaps identifiable with the Zarubintsi culture[8], known from northern Ukraine and Russia. Evidence for Baltic speech has been found as far east as the Volga River[9]. The current distance between Latvian and Lithuanian comes out at some 2600 linguistic years, which suggests that Baltic languages have probably been spoken on the shores of the Baltic Sea for the best part of 2000 years, and we know that there were once Baltic speakers further west still (where Prussian was formerly spoken[10]). As to the location of the initial parent language to Slavonic and Baltic, the family tree is silent; however, it is unlikely to have been far from the Ukraine. I'll be able to be more definite in the next chapter when we see how the different Indo-European branches inter-relate. My estimate for the date is around 700BC[11].

## INDIC LANGUAGES

With the exception of the single language Albanian, which I will leave until the next chapter, that completes the round-up of European members of the Indo-European club. However, much the most remarkable aspect of

| Linguistic years | Hindi | Punjabi | Bengali | Sanskrit |
|---|---|---|---|---|
| Hindi | 0 | 1700 | 3100 | 6800 |
| Punjabi |  | 0 | 4500 | 6300 |
| Bengali |  |  | 0 | 6300 |
| Sanskrit |  |  |  | 0 |

Indo-European is that it has two quite separate centres with no direct connection between them today. European languages are certainly interesting and important but, for serious numbers of speakers, we need to look east to the billion plus whose first language is Indic. From Pakistan to Bangladesh, from the Himalayas to Sri Lanka, the Indian subcontinent is dominated by a single Indo-European branch, today boasting a couple of dozen or more individual languages, and it gives me the excuse to introduce a further, almost ridiculously simple, method of language comparison. However, first let me show you the results of distances (calculated in the usual way) between three modern Indic languages, Punjabi, Hindi and Bengali, and one famous ancient language, Sanskrit.

The Indic languages illustrate the phenomenon of a language gradient, introduced in Chapter 5, in this case with Punjabi at one end, Hindi in the middle and Bengali at the other end. I should perhaps have drawn your attention to similar situations between Swedish and Norwegian, Spanish and Portuguese, Czech and Slovak, and it makes constructing a family tree slightly more problematic since the distance between languages on the 'gradient' tends to measure rather less than it might be expected to. Never mind; the following figure is my best estimate in this case. The root point has been deduced from the fact that Sanskrit is well over 1000 linguistic years closer to the rest of the Indo-European family than the modern languages.

Now let's try and put a bit of meat on these bare bones of a family tree. Although I have argued that it is best to take account of grammar and sound as well as vocabulary, I would now like to introduce a purely vocabulary-based system. The vocabulary in question consists of the numerals from 1 to 10 and, by comparing these ten words, it is extremely easy to look at inter-relationships within a single family. Basically, what I am trying to do is to add detail once the overall framework has been put in place using the full measurement system. Let's look at an example calculation.

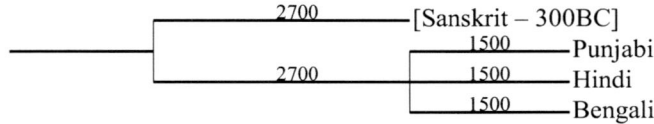

## Chapter 7  The Indo-Europeans

English: one, two, three, four, five, six, seven, eight, nine, ten
Bengali: ek, dui, tin, char, panch, choy, sat, at, noy, dosh

I hope you can see some strong common themes. If we first ignore the vowels and then take into account the ways in which relatively similar sounds can be equated, the matches are actually not too bad. *Two* and *dui* are pretty similar, since *t* and *d* are really the same letter as far as mouth position goes. *Three* and *tin* start with what is effectively the same letter also; so do *seven* and *sat*, *nine* and *noy*, *ten* and *dosh*. In fact, in all ten cases the words are actually 'cognate', i.e. from the same root, but that isn't really the point; what we are interested in here is a measure of the way that the forms of the words have drifted apart over the centuries and millennia. So, if I award scores of 0, ¼, ½, ¾ or 1 depending on the degree of closeness (inevitably a subjective decision) then I come up with a score out of 10 (5¾ in this case). This can then be translated into linguistic years using a logarithmic decay law in a similar way to the more complicated method I have been using so far, but with one crucial advantage; using only the numerals means that there is little difference in the probabilities of each word changing. This neatly avoids most of the problems I had with the main system and means that the logarithmic decay equation should be able to do the job pretty well. The actual equation I have used in this case is:

Linguistic distance     =     $16000 \times \text{Ln}\,[10/(\text{score} - 0.75)]$

The score of 5¾ translates to 11100 linguistic years, which compares with 10900 according to the main measurement system. Without the grammar element, the method will not work so well between distant languages, but I find it ideal for adding 'foliage' to a family tree. The full result for the Indic languages is given in the next figure[12].

And the picture which emerges reveals a great deal about Indian history. For a start, Sanskrit is shown as having developed quite independently from all today's Indic languages. It was the spoken language of the far north-west, centred on the city of Taxila in Pakistan, and the Sanskrit we know today crystallised into its official form with the writing of Panini's grammar in the 4th Century BC. It died out as a living language during subsequent centuries.

Turning to the rest of the family, the point where Sinhala and Divehi (spoken in the Maldive Islands) separated from the rest can be dated to the time (perhaps 1000BC) described in the semi-mythical tales of the Hindu 'Puranas', when the Yadava clan moved south to Gujurat and, thence, to Sri Lanka. This ties in well with archaeology and also Sri Lankan tradition[13]. The next, three-way, split neatly corresponds to the break-up of the first great North Indian empire, centred on the middle Ganges city of Pataliputra, in the late 3rd Century BC which, under king Asoka, had

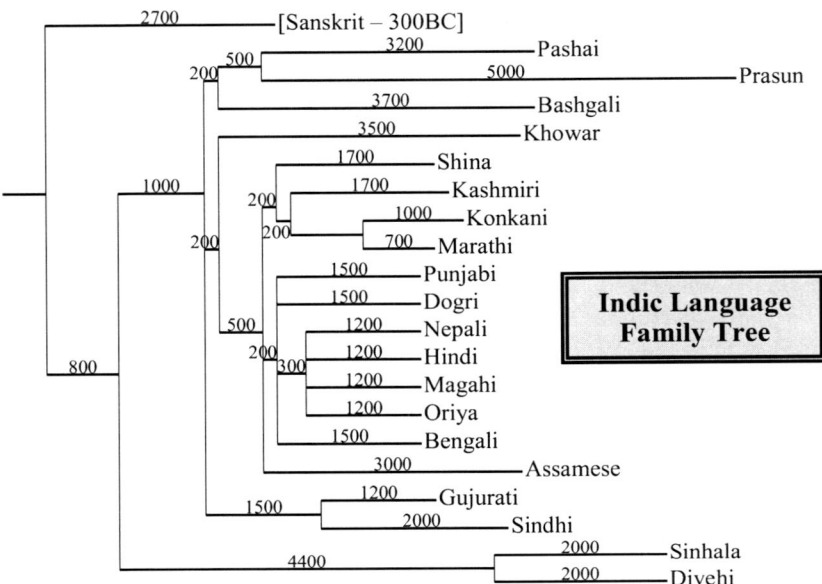

spread the culture and language of the middle Ganges from Assam to Gujurat and Afghanistan[14]. Yet another major three-way split occurs 700 linguistic years later and it matches perfectly the rise and fall of the Gupta dynasty, which re-united northern India from Kashmir to Assam for nearly 200 years, bringing unity of language, followed in about 500AD by fragmentation[15]. These absolutely clear parallels with known (or partially known) history, including the final fragmentation (languages from Punjabi to Bengali) following the last Ganges emperor, king Harsha, prove that, at least in the case of India, linguistic history genuinely ties in with political and cultural history.

Regarding change rate, the north central languages from Punjabi to Bengali have averaged just over 1 linguistic year per year since the death of Harsha in 647AD, with similar rates applying at every stage from about 1000BC. Those languages that moved further from the Ganges heartland changed more, particularly those planted in the far north (Pashai to Khowar) and in the west (Sindhi and Gujurati) following Asoka's empire in the 3rd Century BC, 1.5 linguistic years per year being typical, well over 2 in the case of Prasun. Sinhala and Divehi are also greatly altered, demonstrating once more a relationship between distance travelled and degree of change.

But what about the origin of Indic? The ancestor to today's languages split from Sanskrit 800 linguistic years before the separation of the Sinhala-Divehi arm, which I have just dated to around 1000BC. Sanskrit

Chapter 7    The Indo-Europeans    93

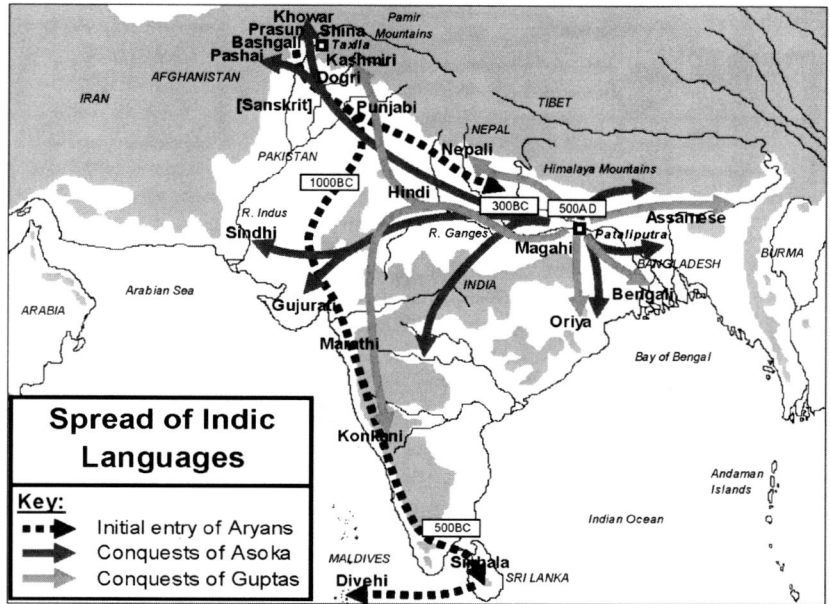

itself, which suffered 200 years of Persian domination[16], had 2700 linguistic years on the clock by the time Panini wrote his grammar in the 4th Century BC. Based on this evidence, it looks suspiciously as if the origin of Indic more or less coincides with the end of the so-called Indus Valley civilisation and the coming of the mysterious Aryans, a key theme of the Indian epic, the 'Rigveda', and also a key area of dispute between scholars[17]. If this identification is correct, we are looking at the early 2nd Millennium BC and the location was northern Pakistan.

## IRANIAN LANGUAGES

And so to the last and possibly the most complex major branch of the Indo-European tree, Iranian: Iranian languages are found in Iran (unsurprisingly), parts of Turkey, Pakistan, Afghanistan and Tajikistan, together with Ossete, a language of the Caucasus Mountains. But they have ranged much more widely in the past. To construct the family tree, I have adopted the same technique as for the Indic branch, using Kurdish, Persian and Pashto to generate the basic shape and then filling it out by means of the numerals 1 to 10. The result is shown in the next figure.

First, the easy bit: Iranian-type languages are known from Iran since the time of the great Persian Empire, carved out by Cyrus the Great in 540BC, and the peoples associated with those languages (Medes and

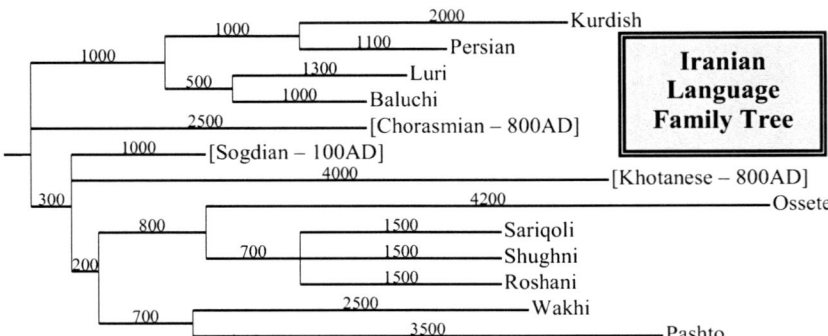

Persians) are known from 9th Century BC records[18]. The common ancestor of Kurdish, Persian, Luri and Baluchi, today's languages of Iran, must surely have been spoken during these times and I suggest that the split between the Kurdish-Persian and Luri-Baluchi arms is most likely to have occurred in 330BC when Alexander the Great destroyed the Persian Empire. The Kurdish-Persian split probably occurred following the break-up of the Parthian Empire in 226AD[19].

Now the tricky bit: what can we make of the rest of the tree? You will notice that I have included three ancient languages and, of these, I am impressed by the lack of change to Sogdian. It suggests that the ancestral Iranian language may well have been spoken in or near the ancient land of Sogdiana, which today means eastern Uzbekistan and northern Tajikistan. Besides, the geography then ties in nicely with the family tree. From Sogdiana, languages could readily spread north-west to the Aral Sea region (ancient Chorasmia), south-west to Iran, south to Afghanistan (languages from Sariqoli to Pashto) and east to the Chinese province of Xinjiang where the city of Khotan (and its ancient language Khotanese) is located on the old Silk Road from China to the west. I suggest that this great spread of language – and therefore culture – must have commenced very roughly in 1500BC which, coincidentally, was just about the date that people first started riding horses somewhere in Central Asia[20]. Horse riding represented a massive cultural breakthrough and it seems to have propelled Iranian language to great things. Within a millennium the Persian Empire stretched from Europe to India and from Egypt to the Aral Sea. Archaeologically, this explosion of Iranian language can also be identified with the widespread 'Andronovo' culture of Central Asia and the Steppe, spreading the phenomenon of 'timber graves' or 'pit graves' westward into southern Russia[21].

But all this leaves one modern Iranian language unexplained, Ossete, spoken in the middle of the Caucasus Mountains between Russia and Georgia. How on earth did it get there?

Chapter 7    The Indo-Europeans                                    95

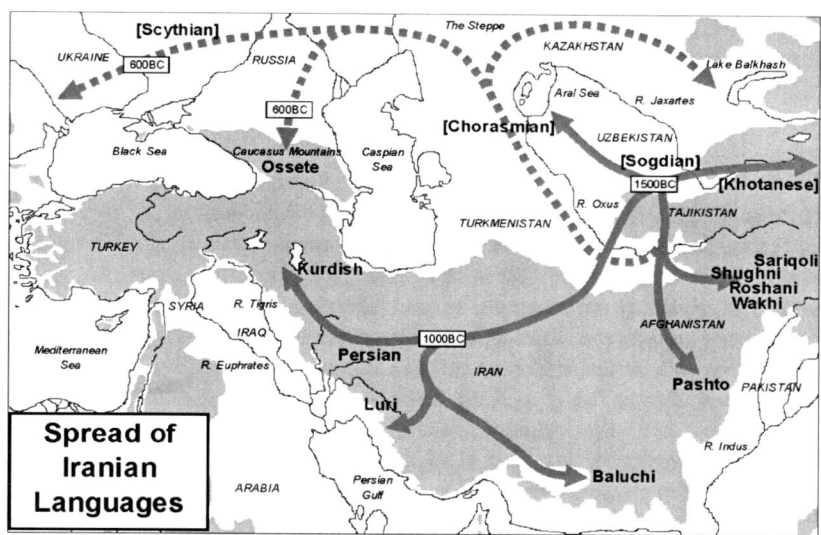

The family tree shows it branching from some of what would become languages of Afghanistan, but since that time it has changed massively. In fact, historians agree that today's Ossete people represent the last remnant of a once mighty nation known as the 'Scythians', who burst onto the plains of southern Russia and the Ukraine from about 600BC. The great Greek historian Herodotus, writing in the 5th Century BC, describes their country as extending across all of what are now the Ukraine, Poland and Russia, and east into Kazakhstan, to the edge of the known world, and Scythian finds have been made as far east as the Altai Mountains, east of Lake Balkhash[22]. They were skilled horsemen and we know from archaeology that they raided deep into Europe, reaching Germany and even France. They also crossed the Caucasus Mountains into Turkey. Their art had a profound influence on that of the Celts – as did their warlike society[23]. And from those few scraps of Scythian language which others recorded we can be quite certain that it was an Iranian language. Finally, after several hundred years of dominance, the Scythians were first tamed and then slowly squeezed into oblivion. Doubtless the people survived but their languages vanished with the single exception of Ossete. The 4200 linguistic years of change shown for Ossete is just what would be expected bearing in mind the remarkable history of the Scythians and their martial society. A change rate of 3 linguistic years per year is quite plausible between about 800BC and 200AD.

Once again, information gleaned from the languages corresponds closely with both history and archaeology. Indeed, it goes further since neither history nor archaeology could have told us that the great Iranian adventure initially stemmed from the region of ancient Sogdiana.

## SUMMARY

To recap: we have seven major branches (Germanic, Italic, Celtic, Greek, Slavonic-Baltic, Indic, Iranian), seven individual pieces of the Indo-European puzzle, and I have also noted Albanian, an individual language which has to slot in somewhere. The final living Indo-European tongue is Armenian, spoken to the south of the Caucasus Mountains. But history tells us of at least two further branches, now extinct, for which we have plenty of evidence and which must also fit into the overall picture. These are known as Anatolian and Tocharian.

The discovery that ancient Hittite was an Indo-European tongue was a total surprise to scholars. It is known from large numbers of inscriptions written in the cuneiform script, discovered in various locations in modern Turkey, most notably near the central Turkish village of Bogazköy, which was once Hattusas, the capital of the Hittite Empire. This language dates from the 2$^{nd}$ Millennium BC[24]. Much more fragmentary evidence has also been found of other clearly related languages, which were spoken in Turkey until long after the conquest of the region by the Greeks under Alexander the Great. These languages comprise the Anatolian branch, Anatolia being the geographical term for Turkey.

The Tocharian branch is represented by evidence of two quite closely related languages known somewhat unimaginatively as Tocharian A and Tocharian B. The inscriptions we have are from western China and Central Asia, mainly comprising Buddhist religious texts, and it is thought that the languages died out in the late 1$^{st}$ Millennium AD[25]. Both Tocharian and Anatolian have the potential to be very useful as evidence for the way that Indo-European arose and then spread; both were spoken in lands which are now the province of a quite different language family, namely Altaic.

Inevitably, the story so far is a little incoherent. We have a series of pieces of a jigsaw but no attempt has yet been made to put them together. Somehow, a chain of events has seen individual Indo-European languages come to be spoken in northern Germany (Germanic), Italy (Italic), Austria (Celtic), Ukraine (Slavonic-Baltic), Greece (Greek), northern Pakistan (Indic) and Central Asia (Iranian), each of which has gone on to form a branch of the modern Indo-European family. Regarding timescale and the relationship between linguistic time and real time, things are getting clearer. We have seen that a rate of change of 0.5 linguistic years per year is slow and that such rates of change are associated with languages which do not move and which do not suffer the problems either of being at the centre of an empire or of being seriously dominated by other languages.

# Chapter 7   The Indo-Europeans

Ukrainian is a prime example. Conversely, a change rate of over 2 linguistic years per year, such as is evidenced by Welsh and Ossete, usually indicates either severe domination or extensive movement or both.

But when and where did it all begin? In the next chapter I will try to fit all the different pieces of the Indo-European jigsaw together, and for this it will be necessary to rely much more heavily on the language evidence, with much less help from recorded history, though we may still expect assistance from archaeology. Unfortunately, I shall be stepping straight into a minefield, since opposing opinions on Indo-European origins have become very firmly entrenched over the years. Never mind; the truth is always worth discovering and I believe that, by letting the languages speak for themselves, the truth is actually not too hard to find in this case.

# 8

# Indo-European Origins

Before diving into the detail, let's just stand back for a moment and consider why the various Indo-European branches have been so successful. Was it all due to horse-riding skills? This might explain the success of the Scythians. What about use of the horse in chariot warfare? This was a key part of Celtic life; and the Vedas, the most ancient of the Indian tales, have plenty to say about use of chariots by the Aryan people, usually (though with vociferous dissent[1]) identified as the first Indic speakers in India. We also possess a fascinating treatise on chariotry dating from the mid 2$^{nd}$ Millennium BC, written in the non-Indo-European Hurrian language (see Chapter 11) and found in central Turkey, which uses several identifiably Indic terms. In fact some Chinese terms connected with horsemanship have also been shown to have an Indo-European origin. But mastery of the horse, important though it undoubtedly was, is inadequate to explain the ongoing success of the languages over several millennia. Horsemanship was surely just a tool in achieving that success rather than a root cause.

The real common factor looks more likely to be one of society. Wherever we first come across Indo-European speakers, they appear as warrior clans. They live by conquering and their continuing prosperity therefore depends on their ability to dominate other populations, living off the agricultural base of others. This is apparent in Britain where archaeology tells of a fairly sudden adoption of chieftain-based society in the first half of the 1$^{st}$ Millennium BC. In Greece we have the example of the Spartans treating their neighbours the Helots as a slave class. In India, rule by the Aryans resulted in a highly stratified society geared to supporting the new nobility. And parallels could be drawn with the expansion of the Roman Empire, the Germanic tribes and the Slavs. I suggest that it has been this propensity to thoroughly dominate other populations which has been responsible for the rapid replacement of the languages of the vanquished by those of the conquerors. The first generation of children fol-

# Chapter 8  Indo-European Origins

lowing conquest may have grown up bilingual; succeeding generations will have adopted the tongue of the new ruling class. Surely this is the true root of the success of Indo-European cultures across the globe. It has meant that the children of Etruscans 'became Romans'; children of the civilised pre-Indo-Europeans of the Indus Valley culture (known as 'Dasyas' in the Vedas) 'became Aryan'. One could argue that the process has continued throughout the ages, with many Native American societies almost 'becoming Spanish' for example and inhabitants right across northern Asia 'becoming Russian'.

But when and where did it all start? There is more than one theory concerning Indo-European origins. I have already mentioned the case made by Professor Colin Renfrew that Indo-European languages may have spread across Europe with the introduction of new agricultural practices during the Neolithic (New Stone Age) period. This would imply a steady wave of advance from Greece in about 7000BC to northern Scotland by 3000BC[2]. In contrast, Marija Gimbutas is the best known of those who have considered the 'Kurgan' culture of southern Russia, known from around 4000BC or a little earlier, as the true origin[3]. Others continue to suggest northern Europe, Central Asia or northern India. These proposals tend to be made chiefly on archaeological grounds, as similarities in such things as burial practices (a 'kurgan' is a burial mound), pottery forms etc. are noted. There is even a body of opinion which claims that Indo-European language has been spread across Europe and southern Asia since Palaeolithic times, that is since prior to 10000BC[4]. However, what I would like to do is to ignore all such theories for now and take a look at what can be deduced from the languages themselves.

## INTER-RELATIONSHIP BETWEEN INDO-EUROPEAN BRANCHES

In looking at the inter-relationship between the different branches of Indo-European, the process is really just the same as for the languages of each individual branch, except that the distances involved are the average distances from each language in one branch to each language in another. All the branches will have to be included, not forgetting Albanian, Armenian and the ancient branches of Anatolian (represented by the Hittite language) and Tocharian. The results are shown in the next table.

You will notice that some of the branches are much closer than others, for example Celtic and Italic. Some are relatively far apart, such as almost anything and Armenian! However, we are now faced with a problem; in theory it should be possible to draw a 'route map' between the branches but, in order to draw up a family tree, it will be necessary to measure distances to some language or languages <u>outside the family</u>.

| Linguistic Years | Ge | It | Ce | Gr | Sl | Al | Ir | In | Ar | An | To |
|---|---|---|---|---|---|---|---|---|---|---|---|
| Germanic | 0 | 12200 | 13300 | 15200 | 10400 | 12500 | 16300 | 10400 | 21100 | 13700 | 11800 |
| Italic |  | 0 | 9200 | 14800 | 9500 | 10200 | 15900 | 12900 | 20800 | 16100 | 13400 |
| Celtic |  |  | 0 | 16500 | 15600 | 16800 | 18600 | 16800 | 21400 | 16600 | 16300 |
| Greek |  |  |  | 0 | 13400 | 17800 | 14900 | 18100 | 24900 | 13200 | 17400 |
| Slavonic |  |  |  |  | 0 | 11400 | 16200 | 14800 | 23200 | 12300 | 13700 |
| Albanian |  |  |  |  |  | 0 | 16600 | 17100 | 28400 | 14100 | 20600 |
| Iranian |  |  |  |  |  |  | 0 | 12100 | 16600 | 17200 | 17500 |
| Indic |  |  |  |  |  |  |  | 0 | 20800 | 16000 | 14800 |
| Armenian |  |  |  |  |  |  |  |  | 0 | 24900 | 22300 |
| Anatolian |  |  |  |  |  |  |  |  |  | 0 | 18000 |
| Tocharian |  |  |  |  |  |  |  |  |  |  | 0 |

Without this I have no real idea where on my route map the initial split point lies. Up until now this has not presented any difficulty. Because the membership of the Indo-European family is recognised by all linguists, I have always been able to measure distances to the rest of the family when drawing up the family tree for each individual branch. Never mind; let's tackle one problem at a time and draw up the route map first.

I have done my best to minimise the errors. The large majority are less than 10%; only six (out of 55 individual measurements) are over 20% out and these are all distances involving single languages (Greek, Albanian, Armenian, Anatolian, Tocharian) so errors are expected. And, as I have said before, this is not an exact science, so I am pretty satisfied with the overall result.

But where is that all-important initial split point – representing the ancestral Indo-European tongue? It is just not possible to know for sure by studying the Indo-European languages alone, although it would be a reasonable guess to suggest that it was somewhere in the middle of the group. However, to do the job properly, there is no alternative but to check out the distances to languages <u>outside</u> the family.

## THE NEAR NEIGHBOURS OF INDO-EUROPEAN

It is a bit like talking in terms of near neighbours to our galaxy! All things are relative though. There are already some pretty large linguistic distances between individual languages of Indo-European and there's absolutely no reason why we shouldn't check out the distances to languages outside the family. After all, if there really is no discernible relationship then that should show up as a string of scores no better than the coincidence level.

# Chapter 8 Indo-European Origins

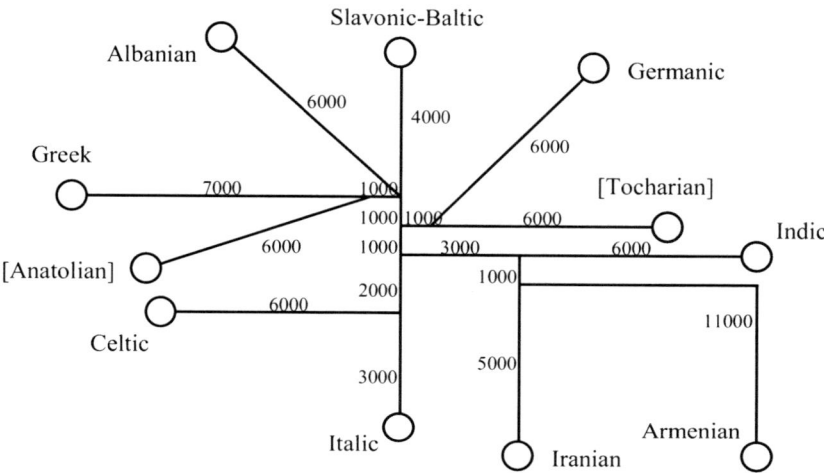

The question is, which other language families are we talking about here? Well, logically, the ones which are adjacent geographically are most likely to be closest linguistically. These are Afro-Asiatic (to the South), Uralic (to the North-East), Altaic (to the East), Caucasian (from within), Dravidian (to the South), Sino-Tibetan (to the East), and I could add in isolates like Basque and Burushaski, and pockets of Austro-Asiatic in India. All of this means that there are quite a few to choose from.

And here I had better admit that I have inevitably only been able to take a limited sample from each family although I believe I have included representatives of all the likely groups involved. Accepting, therefore, that the list is not a complete one, I have managed to find fourteen of the world's languages, eleven modern and three ancient, whose average distances to over 30 Indo-European languages come out to be 40000 linguistic years or less. As will become increasingly apparent, I consider 40000 linguistic years to be just about the limit for reasonable confidence that a genuine relationship exists. I can illustrate what this means in practice by taking the case of English and Arabic (40000 linguistic years apart); the scores for vocabulary, grammar and sound are 0.08, 0.33 and 0.55, which can be compared with those expected purely due to coincidence, 0.05, 0.15 and 0.50. You can see that the only score which is significantly above the coincidence level is the one for grammar, which of course is why I considered the inclusion of grammar in the measurement system to be so important. Anyway, my list of fourteen is as follows:

1. Hungarian   (Uralic family)              32000   linguistic yrs
2. Amharic     (Afro-Asiatic family)        33000        ″          ″
3. Burushaski  (no recognised affiliation)  34000        ″          ″

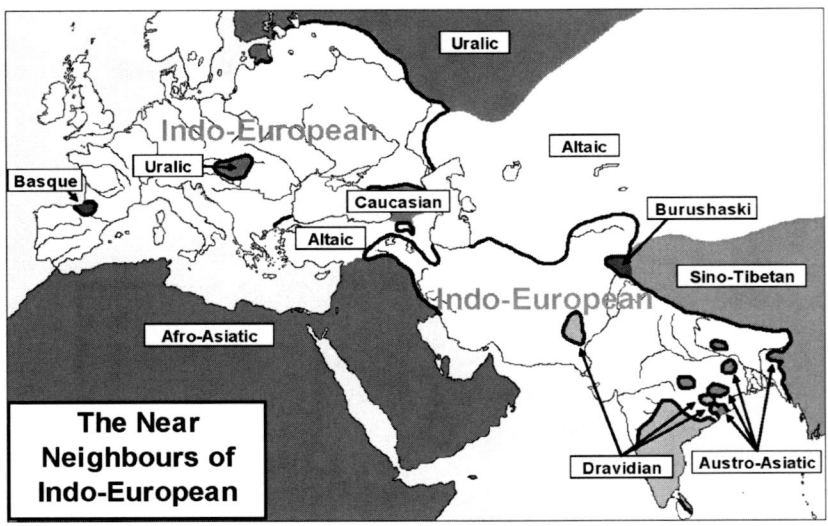

The Near Neighbours of Indo-European

| 4. Telugu | (Dravidian family) | 34000 | " | " |
| 5. [Egyptian] | (Afro-Asiatic family) | 35000 | " | " |
| 6. Finnish | (Uralic family) | 35000 | " | " |
| 7. Hebrew | (Afro-Asiatic family) | 36000 | " | " |
| 8. Basque | (no recognised affiliation) | 36000 | " | " |
| 9. [Etruscan] | (no recognised affiliation) | 36000 | " | " |
| 10. Brahui | (Dravidian family) | 37000 | " | " |
| 11. Tamil | (Dravidian family) | 37000 | " | " |
| 12. Somali | (Afro-Asiatic family) | 39000 | " | " |
| 13. Arabic | (Afro-Asiatic family) | 40000 | " | " |
| 14. [Akkadian] | (Afro-Asiatic family) | 40000 | " | " |

This list is really quite shocking, and on the face of it hard to believe. Notice the complete mixture of different language families involved. Afro-Asiatic is very well represented but top slot goes to Uralic – although not by much. The top four languages include three different language families and one isolate! But, if these measurements can really be trusted, if so many languages and language groups really are linked to Indo-European, then this opens up tremendous possibilities, possibilities which I shall certainly start to explore in the next chapter. For now, though, what we need is the start point for the Indo-European family itself and for that we need to compare distances from outside the family to each individual Indo-European branch. I would ask you therefore to suspend any disbelief you might have until the next chapter and accept my list of fourteen purely as a tool for this purpose. Using them as a representative set of probably

Chapter 8    Indo-European Origins

related languages, I can calculate average distances to each branch of Indo-European in turn.

| to Tocharian: | 31000 | linguistic | years |
| --- | --- | --- | --- |
| to Albanian: | 33000 | " | " |
| to Anatolian: | 34000 | " | " |
| to Iranian: | 36000 | " | " |
| to Slavonic-Baltic: | 36000 | " | " |
| to Germanic: | 36000 | " | " |
| to Italic: | 36000 | " | " |
| to Indic: | 37000 | " | " |
| to Greek: | 38000 | " | " |
| to Celtic: | 39000 | " | " |
| to Armenian: | 41000 | " | " |

Unsurprisingly there is no point on the Indo-European route map which matches these distances perfectly, particularly the relative closeness of Tocharian and Albanian. However, a point about 1000 linguistic years along the 3000 long stretch from the Slavonic-Italic vertical towards Indic is pretty much as close as we can get. This point, therefore, is my best estimate for the ancestral Indo-European tongue and it gives us enough information to construct a full Indo-European family tree.

I would say that this result looks reasonably promising. I am pleased to see that it has some similarity to those constructed by others. Even as early as 1863, Augustus Schleicher proposed a family tree of Indo-European languages with many of the same features, in particular the relative closeness of Italic and Celtic, of Germanic and Slavonic and of Indic and Iranian. At that date of course he had no knowledge of Anatolian or Tocharian. Admittedly, not every researcher since has come up with the same features, and many today do not even agree with the family tree model. Of course, what makes this family tree different from others you may have seen is the difference in length of the different arms and it is this property, meaning

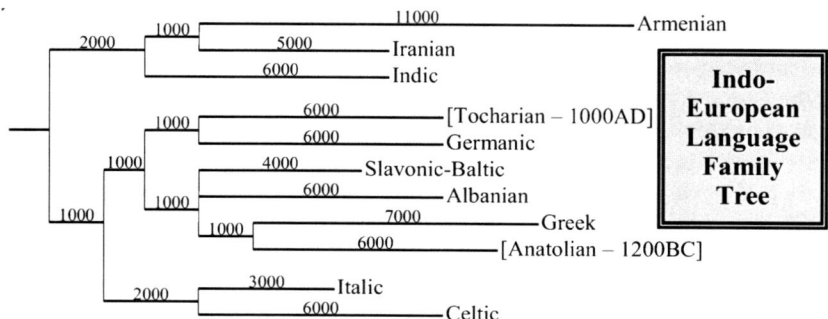

different rates of change, which I will now try to use to deduce something about the history of the language family in space and time.

## THE INDO-EUROPEAN STORY

We have seen when looking at some of the individual branches that language change has sometimes occurred slowly, at less than half a linguistic year per year, and sometimes much more rapidly, at well over two linguistic years per year. We have seen that movement of a language tends to result in fast change (as new populations have to learn to speak it), as does being the centre of an empire and, also, domination by speakers of another language. Only the quiet settled life allows a slow rate of change. Of course, all this has been deduced from cases within the last three thousand years or so and conditions of human society have been continuously changing since much earlier times. The influence of writing should be taken into account. One could argue that a language will tend to be more stable where a written version of it exists, which would speak for a more rapid rate of change in earlier times; but then again, literacy has only achieved high levels comparatively recently. In the end, there are so many factors which may or may not have had a significant influence that it seems impossible to use pure logic to suggest rates of language change in the distant past. We need more evidence.

Let's turn to archaeology. In the 3rd Millennium BC the cultures of the eastern Mediterranean were much more advanced than those of most of Europe, and they included the earliest Bronze Age civilisations of the Aegean, datable back to around 3000BC. Of course, what cannot be known prior to about 1400BC, when the first writing definitely in the Greek language (though not in the modern Greek script) appears[5], is just what language these people spoke. It would be nice to identify this early Aegean culture, with its advanced architecture and art, as early Greek. Unfortunately for Indo-European pride, this is most unlikely. Early Aegean culture shows undeniable similarities to early Minoan (from the island of Crete), which most would identify as non-Indo-European[6]. However, a most striking change took place around 2200BC; settlements were torched and laid waste right across Greece and the culture reverted almost to that of the Stone Age. I'm afraid it is this episode of wanton destruction which is most likely to mark the arrival of the ancestral Greeks from the European hinterland. Turning to the family tree, the Greek branch is 7000 linguistic years in length, of which we have already found that about 2000 occurred within the last 2000 years. Previous to this were centuries of great empire, international trade and travel, during which the Greek language was spread from Italy to India and doubtless many of the foreign influences found their way back to Greece. This was certainly a recipe for fast language change.

# Chapter 8  Indo-European Origins

The flowering of Classical Greek culture from around 700BC was preceded by a 'dark age', an age whose length no-one has reliably established[7]; earlier still, there were centuries of Mycenaean civilisation, the times of Agamemnon and the war against Troy, remembered in Homer's epic tale the *Iliad*. This takes us back to perhaps 1400BC. This all followed the volatile period during which Greek society dragged itself out of the Stone Age culture of the people who ransacked the settlements of the Aegean in 2200BC. All of these periods, except perhaps that of the 'dark age', should logically have seen rapid language change.

The family tree shows Greek separating from the Anatolian branch. Anatolian languages are fascinating to linguists simply because they are extinct. To some they are proof of theories regarding the make-up of what linguists call 'proto Indo-European', the original Indo-European language. Linguists had theorised regarding the existence of certain laryngeal sounds in proto Indo-European and were delighted when they turned up in ancient Hittite. The natural reaction of many has been to place the Anatolian branch as the earliest division of all from the Indo-European stem. As you can see in the family tree, based on cold, hard mathematical measurement, I cannot subscribe to that view. I have no doubt that the laryngeal sounds mean something[8], but the evidence I have is that the Anatolian branch represents a division from prehistoric Greek, a language which must have been spoken by people who crossed the Bosphorus from Europe into what is now Turkey. In fact, the destructions of 2200BC, which I have just attributed to Greek speakers, are mirrored across western and central Turkey (for example the end of Level II at Troy) and it is logical to attribute these to Anatolian-speaking invaders[9]. The earliest evidence of ancient Hittite itself comes from cuneiform tablets, some of which are tentatively dated to around 1700BC[10]. The language was then and for the next several hundred years the official tongue of the Hittite Empire. Now, as in the case of Greek, a very high rate of language change must surely have occurred during those turbulent times, first during the centuries in which Anatolian languages were carried east through Turkey and then during the time of the appallingly unstable Hittite Empire[11]. Considering the change rates deduced for the Scythians and Celts during their periods of expansion, and taking into account the archaeological evidence, I suggest that Greek and Anatolian separated in roughly 3000BC, probably somewhere in the vicinity of modern Bulgaria[12].

Taking a further 1000 linguistic year step back through the family tree, we come to a three-way split between Slavonic-Baltic, Albanian and Greek-Anatolian. The geography certainly makes sense here; the logical assumption must be that the language at this point was spoken somewhere around the lower Danube area, probably modern Romania. Allowing a continuing high rate of change of 2 linguistic years per year to Greek-Anatolian, the

date would have been around 3500BC. Concerning Albanian, there is limited historical light available. The Albanians have never, so far as we know, built an empire or colonised significantly outside the Balkans. The rate of change in Albanian has averaged about 1 linguistic year per year since 3500BC, much less than in Greek or in Anatolian, which is exactly as it should be due to its more settled history[13]. In fact during the same 5500 years (since 3500BC) Slavonic has changed even less. In Chapter 7 the average change to Slavonic (and Baltic) from about 700BC to the present day was found to be about 2000 linguistic years, which leaves just 2000 over the previous 2800 years or so (3500BC to 700BC), at a very modest 0.7 linguistic years per year, and the implication is that Slavonic didn't travel too far during those 2800 years. In fact, the Thracian language spoken in Bulgaria and Romania in about 500BC fits the bill nicely as an ancestor, or at least a very close relative, of today's Slavonic and Baltic branches. Such evidence as has been found from inscriptions is fragmentary, but strong similarities with the Slavonic and Baltic languages are apparent[14].

And this brings in one further extinct Indo-European tongue from Turkey, namely Phrygian. Phrygia was the land of king Midas, whose touch, according to Greek myth, turned everything to gold, and Phrygia thrived during the early 1st Millennium BC following the collapse of the Hittite Empire – but Phrygian was not an Anatolian language. Its closest affinities (according to several linguists and supported by my own observations) are with the modern Slavonic and Baltic languages and with Thracian. Phrygian therefore represents a further wave of Indo-European speech which must have entered Turkey at the end of the 2nd Millennium

## Chapter 8  Indo-European Origins

BC (in time for Phrygians to assist Troy in its war with Greece – if Homer is to be believed).

Good; the pieces are beginning to fit together nicely. Winding the clock back another 1000 linguistic years brings us to the time when the ancestor of all the languages discussed to date separated from the ancestor of the Germanic and Tocharian branches. Continuing at 2 linguistic years per year (assuming a mobile society), the separation date would have been around 4000BC. In the case of the Germanic languages, Chapter 6 found that only about 1300 linguistic years of change (on average) had taken place since about 400AD which means that the remaining 5700 linguistic years of change occurred over the previous 4400 years. In the case of Tocharian, 7000 linguistic years of change took place over about 5000 actual years, prior to the language becoming extinct. The two branches were therefore both averaging 1.3-1.4 linguistic years per year and they would have parted company from each other in about 3300BC. Unfortunately, it is very difficult to find firm evidence concerning the early history of either Germanic or Tocharian. Elizabeth Barber, in her book *The Mummies of Ürümchi*, presents highly persuasive evidence that the language we know as Tocharian first entered the Tarim Basin area in the far west of China in about 1200BC, brought by people from the Russian steppe. The evidence, apart from the physical remains of the people, remarkably preserved by the climate of the Taklimakan Desert, comes from Chinese records. At one stage the Chinese sought to ally themselves with the Tocharians against the northern nomads, only to find that they had (temporarily) abandoned the Tarim for a more comfortable life on the Oxus river. If Elizabeth Barber is correct it seems highly likely that the Tocharian branch should be associated with the Afanasievo culture, a culture which extended from the Urals to the Altai Mountains and which produced the spoked wheel in about 2000BC[15]. It seems that the Tocharians then went on to displace Iranian speakers in western China. At one stage (2nd Century AD) they conquered and ruled all of Afghanistan and northern Pakistan as well as their slice of western China, greatly contributing to the spread of Buddhism into China[16].

As for Germanic, having separated from Tocharian somewhere in Russia in 3300BC, all we really know is that the languages turned up in northern Germany some 3000 years later. It is just possible, for instance, that the spread of the so-called 'Corded Ware' culture into the Baltic region, bringing the first settled agriculture in about 3300BC, should be attributed to Germanic speakers – although I doubt it[17]. I feel more confident that the Lusatian culture of Poland, eastern Germany and the Czech Republic (1500BC-500BC) was Germanic speaking; the area ties in with what I consider to be the most likely home of the 'Gotones' and 'Teutoni' mentioned by the Greek explorer Pytheas[18]. In general terms, I would sug-

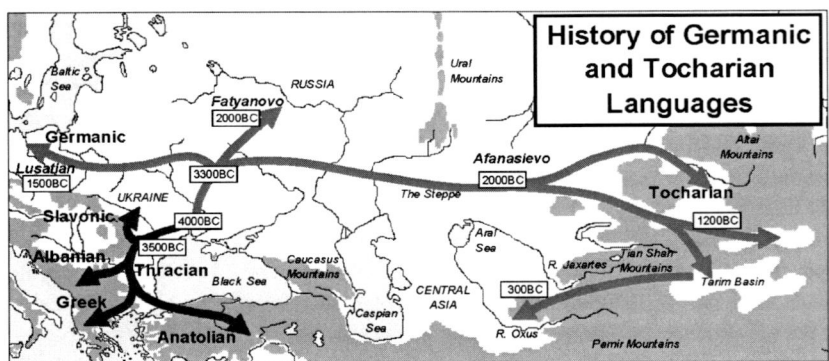

gest that the tremendous expansion of Germanic and Tocharian speech should be associated with the first domestication of the horse (not at that stage for riding) in about 4000BC in the Ukraine, closely followed by development of the cart and successful breeding of wool-producing sheep, leading to a strongly nomadic pastoralist society.

I should admit here that others have come to the conclusion that Tocharian is just as close to Italic and Celtic as to Germanic, the material culture (to archaeologists the Tocharians are known for their incredibly well preserved tartan clothing) being particularly reminiscent of the Celtic cultures of central Europe. In my opinion, however, a connection with Germanic fits the data well and is not in the least surprising. I don't really like using particular examples of cognate words because I know they can be used (and unfortunately often are used) to prove or disprove almost anything, but let me mention one in support of this linking of Germanic, Tocharian, Greek, Anatolian, Slavonic and Albanian; it is the word for *water*.

| Germanic | *water* (English) |
| Tocharian | *war* |
| Greek (ancient) | *udor* |
| Anatolian | *wadar* (Hittite) |
| Slavonic | *voda* (Russian and others) |
| Albanian | *uje* |

I hope the strong resemblance between the first five is reasonably clear. The Anatolian word may well be closest to an original. In Greek, the *w* has gone; in Tocharian, there is no *d*; in Germanic, the *d* is a *t*; in Slavonic, *v* replaces *w* and there is no *r*. The difficult one is Albanian, but actually a *j* (pronounced in the same way as English) is a sort of composite sound, *dy*, so the word is actually not unlike the ancient Greek. In contrast the other Indo-European branches all have somewhat different words:

## Chapter 8  Indo-European Origins

Italic has *aqua*, Celtic has *uisce* (pronounced *whisky*), Indic has *jol* or *pani*, Armenian has *jur* and Iranian has *ab*.

Let's continue another step back up the family tree. Celtic culture has already been mentioned as one of the most significant in Europe prior to the time of the Roman Empire. The culture known as 'Hallstatt' after its initial discovery in Austria can be linked with later known Celtic cultures (notably La Tène) by its art, for example the particular decorative motifs and styles of metalwork. In language terms, Hallstatt represents a stage on the Celtic branch of the language tree whose origins can be dated to around 800BC, the approximate date suggested in the previous chapter for the division between the Goidelic and Brythonic sub-branches of Celtic. This leaves 1500 linguistic years of change between the time that Celtic and Italic parted and 800BC, which probably brings me back to a Celtic-Italic division very roughly in 2000BC. Archaeologically, Hallstatt culture seems to have arisen following the clear movement of people (or at least culture) from the east, as evidenced by burial customs (the previously mentioned Urnfield culture). So it would seem a fair bet that the language of about 2000BC, which then divided and became Celtic and Italic, was spoken by the immediate ancestors of these Urnfield folk, at that time living in western Romania. The family tree then tells us that there have only been 3000 linguistic years of change to the Italic branch since that time, most of which we have already assigned to the last 2000 years! Of course, the family tree is only an approximate construction but it strongly implies that the peoples who spoke Italic languages between 2000BC and Roman Empire days were living relatively settled lives, and this nicely matches the presence right across western Romania and Hungary of a stable and peaceful town-dwelling people throughout the 2nd Millennium BC[19]. Italic language must have arrived in northern Italy in around 1000BC, as did the Urnfield culture[20]. By the time of the Roman Republic (founded in 509BC), Latin was one of several closely related Italic tongues spoken in Italy[21].

Working back from the Celtic-Italic split (about 2000BC), the family tree has 2000 more linguistic years back to a separation from the ancestor of Germanic, Slavonic, Greek etc., which probably took place in around 4500BC. It seems highly probable that this early Celtic-Italic period should be identified with the well-known 'Tripolye' culture of western Ukraine and northern Romania, a stable society with a mixed arable and pastoral economy which lasted from 3000BC to 1500BC[22]. Prior to 3000BC, the Dnieper-Donetz farming culture, which filled the northern Ukraine, logically represents the earliest stage of Celtic-Italic language. Certainly, at a change rate of just 0.8 linguistic years per year, ancestral Celtic-Italic speakers must have been in a much more stable state than most other Indo-Europeans, suggesting settled arable farming rather than pure pastoralism[23].

So, by 4500BC or thereabouts, a parent language to most of today's European languages would have been spoken somewhere in southern Russia or the Ukraine. Regarding location, the weight of evidence is overwhelming. The way that the family tree shows the branches connecting has drawn me inexorably north and then east, from the Aegean to the Ukraine. There is simply no other location which could possibly fit the combination of language and archaeological data. From about 4500BC I suggest that a division grew between the settled Dnieper-Donetz farmers in the more heavily wooded north and the less settled peoples of the south. It was in the southern part of the Ukraine and in adjacent Russian territory that the so-called 'Kurgan' culture arose, a kurgan being a burial mound, some of which have been found to contain significant wealth. It would have been early Kurgan culture which was ancestral to Germanic, Tocharian, Slavonic-Baltic, Albanian, Greek and Anatolian.

However, to arrive back at the point where the ancestor of Indic and Iranian diverged, a further 1000 linguistic years have to be travelled, through times prior even to Kurgan culture, times for which evidence for language change rate is hard to obtain. For these less mobile times (the horse was still nothing more than an item on the menu), I suggest a more moderate change rate of 1 linguistic year per year would be a reasonable estimate, giving a date of around 5500BC for the original Indo-European language, presumably spoken in or to the east of the Kurgan zone, just north of the Caucasus Mountains.

In fact, some independent light can be thrown on the timing, and indeed the location, of the ancestral Indo-European language by looking at the range of words for which a common root is evident. Two particular

# Chapter 8   Indo-European Origins

points I believe to be relevant. The first stems from detailed work by linguists, looking at those Indo-European words which most probably survive from earliest times, and these studies have found that the range of words (e.g. tree types) is suited to a broad territory which includes southern Russia. This evidence is still disputed, but I have not yet been convinced by any counter-arguments[24]. The second is that the warp-weighted loom was in common use throughout Europe west of the Dnieper river from about 5500BC (evidenced by warp weights found by archaeologists), yet Indo-European languages have no common vocabulary for this technology[25]. This suggests either that the first Indo-European language was spoken significantly earlier than 5500BC or that the origin lay to the east of the Dnieper (the Dnieper runs through the middle of the Ukraine). I would definitely go with the second option. As far as I can see, archaeology and language speak with one voice and that voice does not accord with Colin Renfrew's book of that title[26]. It does however broadly support Marija Gimbutas and her theory of Kurgan culture origins, at least for a significant part of the European side of the family. In stating as much, I am following a well-trodden path, for example J.P. Mallory's *In Search of the Indo-Europeans*.

Let's now take a quick look at the Indic and Iranian branches. During discussion of the Indic branch, the likely presence of Indo-European speakers in northern Pakistan in the early 2nd Millennium BC was noted and the separation of the ancestor of the modern Indic languages from Sanskrit was deduced to have taken place at approximately that time. According to the family tree, the 3½ to 4 millennia from 5500BC to the time the language appeared in India saw just over 4000 linguistic years of change, not a slow rate, yet not fast enough to suggest anything other than steady movement. The arrival of the first Indic speakers in northern Iran is almost certainly evidenced by a clear change (new weapons, pottery styles) at settlements such as Anau and Hissar in about 2500BC[27], followed by a similar major change at sites in Afghanistan a couple of centuries later[28]. In fact, the Indic-sounding names of the kings (and Gods) of the Mitannian and Kassite empires of eastern Turkey and Iraq[29], suggest that Indic speakers thrived in the Middle East region for well over a thousand years. Before 2500BC, Indic language can reasonably be associated with the spread of a predominantly pastoralist culture right across Central Asia. The Iranian branch must have separated in about 3500BC somewhere near the Aral Sea, just one of several divisions which presumably occurred but the only one to survive to the present day. By 2000BC, there would have been a vast spectrum of Indic-Iranian language from the river Volga in the west to the mountains of western China, Afghanistan and Iran.

Finally we come to the enigmatic case of Armenian. It stands out from the rest of the family like a sore thumb. The point of its separation from

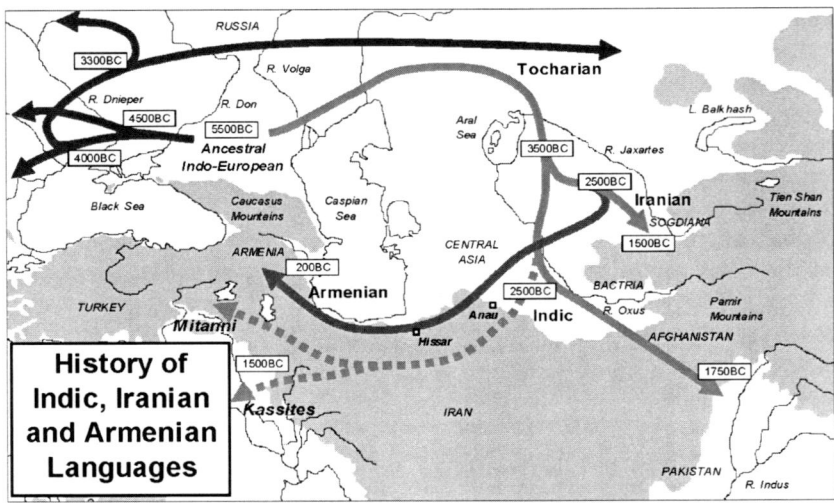

History of Indic, Iranian and Armenian Languages

Iranian would have to have been around 2500BC, probably somewhere south-east of the Aral Sea, yet the change in the years since has been a massive 11000 linguistic years, an average of about 2.5 linguistic years per year. Certainly, situated as it now is, and has been since at least 200BC[30], just to the south of the Caucasus Mountains, it is spoken in an area of the world which has seen a lot of action during recorded history. Assyrians, Hittites, Persians, Greeks, Romans, Arabs, Turks and Russians have all shared in dominating the region. Only in relatively brief spells has significant independence been achieved. It is also fair to point out that Armenian has rubbed shoulders with a very wide variety of other languages, few of which have been Indo-European. The Caucasus, as we shall see in a later chapter, is one of the most linguistically varied regions on earth. So, surprising though the sustained high rate of change is, the ingredients are certainly there to explain it.

## DID THE PEOPLE MOVE OR WAS IT JUST THE LANGUAGE?

This is always a tough area to understand. It is so obvious that language cannot move on its own but has to be carried by people. But how many people does it take to change the language of a region? In the 9th Century AD, the Magyars invaded modern Hungary, dominating the population, who previously spoke an Indo-European (Slavonic) language[31]. But within a generation or two the whole population was speaking the Magyar tongue, from which modern Hungarian is descended. I have also illustrat-

# Chapter 8   Indo-European Origins

ed the case of England, where the adoption of English did not mean the wholesale slaughter of the Celtic-speaking population – it merely meant that the next generation adopted Anglo-Saxon language and, within a generation, only the old people would have known Celtic. Over a thousand years earlier, the population of Britain first started speaking a Celtic tongue. Why? Was there a great invasion of Celtic warriors? It is true that there were real changes, as evidenced by increased use of defensive fortifications (hill forts, fortified farmsteads) and that many archaeologists see evidence for a more stratified society, ruled by local chieftains. It is also true that the pottery ensemble changed significantly. However, the majority view among British archaeologists is that there never was any Celtic invasion. Yet Celtic languages clearly arrived somehow! The conclusion seems inescapable to me; it took very few individuals to change the speech of an entire country. Indo-European warrior clans may have been few in number but they dominated others with tremendous success.

In a similar way, a battle is raging between those who see the self-evident truth that Indo-European language has 'invaded' India from the north-west and archaeologists who confidently state that there is no evidence at all for any such invasion! Yet it seems that a small number of Indo-European speaking warrior groups, making full use of the latest chariot technology, were clearly able to dominate, control and, most remarkably of all, effect a complete change in language within just a few generations. A major reason why archaeologists are so insistent that there was no invasion is the degree of cultural continuity, both in India and in Britain. And it is true; the bulk of the population may have changed their language, but they certainly didn't change all their beliefs over night! In many of the lands which the Indo-Europeans took over, India, Turkey, Greece, Italy, Britain, they were culturally inferior in most respects other than in warfare, so it is hardly surprising that many aspects of the preceding culture continued to flourish.

Nowadays, the rapid advances in the study of DNA, the molecule which determines all our various physical characteristics, mean that we are in a position to know something of the genetic history of peoples across the globe. In particular, Mitochondrial DNA, a relatively short molecular chain with the useful characteristic that it is passed down from mother to daughter unchanged – well almost unchanged – has been found to be particularly revealing. If it really was completely unchanged every time then we could learn nothing, but it seems that every thousand or so female births there is a slight mutation of the DNA, meaning that the DNA characteristics of a population change steadily through the centuries. After a few thousand years of separation, two populations develop quite distinct traits within the Mitochondrial DNA string. Now, I am certainly no geneticist, but the potential for determining the relative closeness of populations is pretty clear. In his fascinating and highly readable book *The Seven Daughters of Eve*, Bryan Sykes has explained the technique and also applied it to the population of Europe, taking samples from inhabitants of every corner of the continent.

And what was the result? Are all Europeans descended from a southern Russian population living 7500 years ago? Absolutely not! What about being descended from the first agriculturalists, spreading up from Greece? Some certainly, but a minority. In fact, Bryan Sykes and his team have determined that most of the population of Europe can trace their ancestry (or could if they were DNA tested) to one of seven individual women and, based on current population concentrations, it is even possible to say where these women lived, approximately. Not only so, but the relatively constant rate of genetic mutation means that the time at which each lived is also known, approximately. And it appears that around 17% of Europeans are descended from a particular individual who lived in or around Turkey about 10000 years ago and it would be reasonable to suggest that the descendants of this woman were the first European agriculturalists. In fact, the distribution of her European descendants today is concentrated across the lands of the southern Mediterranean and up the valley of the river Danube, the very areas through which agriculture was first to spread.

And 17% (or 20% based on Y Chromosome studies of male ancestry[32]) is actually very impressive indeed. The so-called Neolithic revolution, by which ancient historians mean the spread of agriculture, lasted some 4500 years as it travelled from Turkey to the western fringes of Europe, say 180 generations[33]. If we simplify the process to one of steady linear progression and assume that equal new territory was taken over in each new generation (far from the truth I realise), then it is possible to calculate the degree of interbreeding which must have taken place between populations as territorial expansion occurred, in order to leave 17% of the population as a whole of pure 'Turkish' descent. And the result, remarkable though it may seem, is that the agriculturalists at the leading edge of the revolutionary wave must have remained 96-97% pure in each generation[34]! By the way, a similar picture has now been obtained from India where studies of Mitochondrial DNA[35] reveal that about 17% of the gene pool is of Iranian or Middle Eastern type, two thirds of which seems to have arrived in the subcontinent during the last 10000 years. This seems very likely to be associated with the spread of agriculture (starting prior to 6000BC in Pakistan[36]) and most unlikely to be associated with the spread of Indo-European language.

Agriculture really heralded a momentous change in both European and Indian DNA as well as in society. In contrast, neither Mitochondrial DNA nor Y Chromosome studies reveal any clear trace of a separate influx from Russia 7500 years ago so, while Indo-European culture certainly

## Chapter 8　Indo-European Origins

spread, and our evidence is that its language did likewise, the same cannot be said for its genes[37]! I cannot emphasize the implications of this too highly. It means that language spread does not necessarily have much to do with population spread. It also, in the case of Indo-European, had very little to do with the spread of agriculture[38]. Language spread simply means cultural dominance, achieved (some might say still being achieved) by Indo-European by means of warfare. It may be a rather depressing conclusion, but the evidence admits no other.

So, the history of Indo-European has taken us back about 7500 years, which is impressive but nothing like as impressive as the length of time that Homo Sapiens is thought to have walked the earth, perhaps 160000 years. It is not even particularly impressive compared to the 40000 years or so during which Europe has been inhabited. To look deeper into the mists of time it is necessary to tackle languages which are much more foreign to an English speaker than Russian or Hindi. If we want to know more about our true cultural roots we will have to step outside the cosy Indo-European world and the most logical place to start is with some of the fourteen 'near neighbours' introduced earlier in this chapter.

# 9

# Out of Africa

Before jumping into really deep water, let me review the assumptions which underlie the way in which relationship between languages is presented in this book. The family tree model has been discussed at length in earlier chapters and, though limitations have been highlighted, I personally see it as a <u>fundamentally correct</u> view of the way that language changes over the millennia, so long as it is used sensibly. The process at work today of spread, division and extinction is the same process as has occurred throughout the history of mankind's speech, though the rate of change has already been seen to vary enormously according to circumstances. This means that the situation in 5500BC, when the ancestral Indo-European language was spoken, was not so different from that applying now, so far as language development goes. Nowadays there are, in Europe, a large number of related languages as well as an immense variety of dialects. In addition, there are a few other languages which are not obviously related (Basque, Hungarian etc). There is no reason to suppose the situation was radically different at the time that the ancestor of Indo-European was being spoken. There were probably many related languages, of which 'proto Indo-European' was but one, spreading, dividing and suffering extinction in a similar manner to today. Now, if any of the very closely related languages had survived to have descendants today, we would be able to recognise them and we would naturally group them in with an expanded Indo-European family. The fact that there seems to be a clear break between the modern Indo-European languages and the other language families of the world implies that no such survivals occurred; all closely related languages have been swallowed up over the course of the intervening 7500 years by the ever-expanding Indo-European family. This is not surprising or in any way special; it is just the ongoing process of spread, division and extinction which is occurring throughout the world. There will always be some languages which are expanding at the expense

Chapter 9   Out of Africa                                                      117

of others; nowadays English is the supreme example. There will always be a cultural reason for this expansion, though the range of possible cultural factors is surely greater than any list I might be able to dream up.

But, if a linguist were to have studied the languages of southern Russia in 5500BC, what would he or she have found? It is possible, for example, that proto Indo-European was actually part of a distinct family, with closely related languages (with no current descendants) and languages which, though definitely related, might be considered as being in other branches of the family. But would we be able to recognise the descendants of such languages today? To reverse the question: today we can see that English and Hindi are related. In the unlikely event that descendants of both survive to the year 9500AD, 7500 years into the future, would we still be able to recognise them as being from the same family? Perhaps, but it certainly wouldn't be easy.

So, when I talk in terms of language families which may be related to Indo-European, all I mean is that there are likely to be groups of languages today descended from a language which, 7500 years ago, would have been recognised as being in the same family as proto Indo-European. This is not an outrageous concept, nor is it at all illogical; indeed it would be remarkable if no such languages existed.

I hope you will forgive this little discussion, but I want to make the point that there is nothing magical in the unit which we, today, call a language family; all it really means is the biggest grouping possible where most experts are agreed that relationship exists. There is every reason to look for further relationships, from further back in time, but we should not expect that the same agreement of experts is found! OK; having cleared the ground, let's get to it.

## INTRODUCING AFRO-ASIATIC LANGUAGES

If you remember, of the fourteen languages listed in the last chapter as 40000 linguistic years or less from Indo-European, six were Afro-Asiatic, namely Arabic, Hebrew, Amharic, Somali, Egyptian and Akkadian, the last two being ancient languages. The other families represented were Uralic and Dravidian, together with three language isolates, an amazing range really. However, rather than biting off more than we can chew, let's start with the most obvious, which is the Afro-Asiatic family. By the way, I only subjected a total of eight Afro-Asiatic languages to my measurement system, so six out of eight isn't bad.

The whole area of the southern part of the Middle East, Arabia and North Africa is today dominated by a single language, Arabic. The last speakers of Aramaic, the *lingua franca* of the Middle East for centuries, are dying out; most of the other languages of Arabia have disappeared, leaving just a few remnants in the Yemen and Oman from the language group that once included Sabean, the language of the Queen of Sheba who, according to the Bible, visited king Solomon in Israel; ancient Egyptian only survives as Coptic, used in Christian church services in Egypt. The expansion of Arabic is one of the clearest historical examples of the effect of cultural dominance. However, it is far from the only Afro-Asiatic language. Hebrew survives as the language of the Jewish people; in North Africa, the Berber languages are spoken in several countries and are still strong in the mountains of Morocco and Algeria. To the south of the Sahara are the Chadic languages, the most important of which is Hausa, spoken in the northern half of Nigeria. Across the other side of Africa, in Ethiopia, Amharic is the national language and is one of several Afro-Asiatic tongues in that country. Finally, the so-called Cushitic and Omotic languages are spoken mainly in Somalia and parts of Ethiopia, with a group known as South Cushitic being spoken as far south as Tanzania.

The main features of most of these languages are not really so different from Indo-European. Many use masculine and feminine gender for different words, like French, German, Russian and most other Indo-European languages (but not English of course). They also use prepositions (words like *in*, *on*, *for*, *with*); the verb forms (past, present, future) tend to be rather different, making greater use of varying the form of the word rather than relying on suffixes and auxiliary verbs (words like *will*, *have*, *are*). In general, the grammar is not too difficult for an Indo-European speaker to take on, but the vocabulary is quite different.

In analysing the Afro-Asiatic family, I have taken the same approach as for Indic and Iranian; that is I have conducted the full vocabulary, gram-

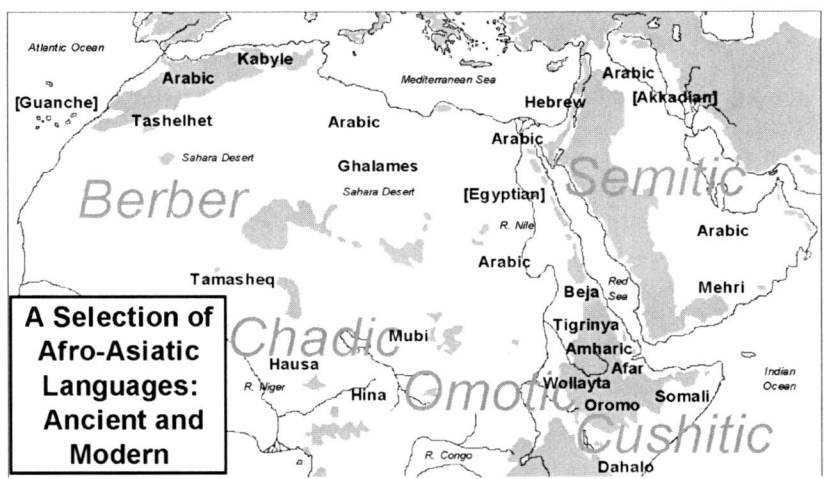

# Chapter 9  Out of Africa

| Linguistic years | Ara | Heb | Ber | Amh | Hau | Som | Egy | Akk |
|---|---|---|---|---|---|---|---|---|
| Arabic | 0 | 5000 | 13000 | 15000 | 29000 | 37000 | 19000 | 8000 |
| Hebrew | | 0 | 16000 | 15000 | 36000 | 43000 | 21000 | 6000 |
| Berber | | | 0 | 27000 | 29000 | 41000 | 16000 | 19000 |
| Amharic | | | | 0 | 37000 | 31000 | 35000 | 17000 |
| Hausa | | | | | 0 | 45000 | 46000 | 32000 |
| Somali | | | | | | 0 | 40000 | 43000 |
| Egyptian | | | | | | | 0 | 23000 |
| Akkadian | | | | | | | | 0 |

mar and sound comparison on just eight languages, deriving the basic structure of a family tree, and have then used the numerals 1 to 10 to add bulk. The above table shows the distances between the eight primary languages selected.

If you glance back to the equivalent table for the Indo-European branches, you can see that this family is an order of magnitude 'bigger' in terms of the distances between some of its members. In fact, you might note that several languages were reported in the last chapter as being closer (on average) to the Indo-European family than they are to others within their own Afro-Asiatic family! That should be enough for most traditionally schooled linguists to throw this book into the fire as heresy, but I hope that you will take a slightly more indulgent view and stay with me.

First, some reminders: the system used here is exactly the same as that for the Indo-European family, so it is not obvious why the measurements, which seemed so sensible for Indo-European, should be any less so here. But can I produce a family tree? Regretfully, not easily. Ideally, I need to refer to some language (or preferably group of languages) outside this family, one with joint roots even further back in time and, since this could be tricky, I am afraid I shall be forced to cheat! What I have had to do is to construct a route map figure for the eight languages in the table – no cheating necessary there – and then add in the locations of additional languages based on a comparison of the numerals. I have then selected a root point such that it gives similar minimum overall changes to several languages (Arabic, Tamasheq, Tashelhet, Beja), producing the family tree shown. It's really just educated guesswork, but it's also a pretty sensible working hypothesis. The family tree probably looks horrendously complicated and full of names which you are unfamiliar with – so I don't wish to trawl through it unnecessarily. However, it is well worth taking a look at the overall picture, since the clues to cultural history contained in this family tree go way beyond what can be known using more conventional approaches (historical documents and archaeology). I shall therefore

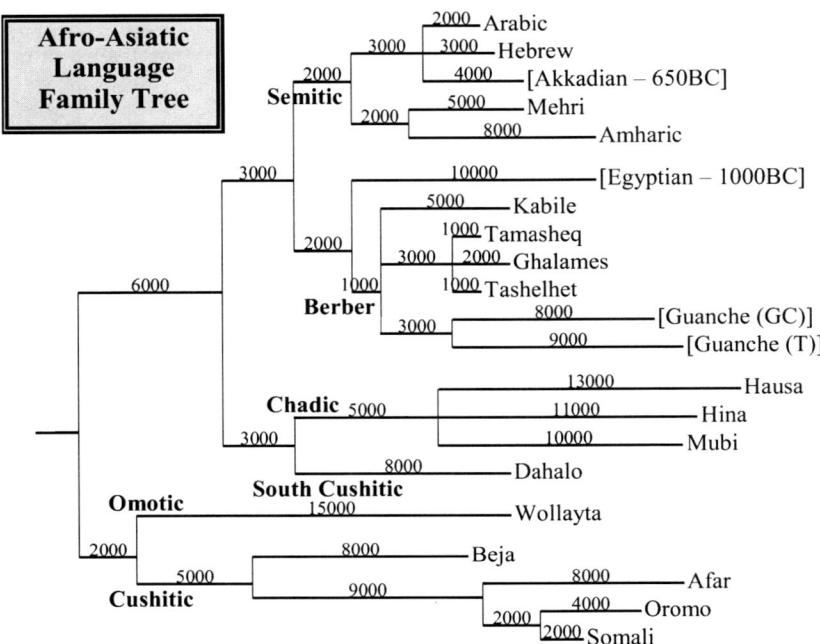

try to pick what I hope will be a meaningful path back through Afro-Asiatic history.

## SEMITIC LANGUAGES

Arabic and Hebrew may be languages spoken by political enemies today but they are closely related, having changed by just 2000 and 3000 linguistic years respectively since separation, and betray strong cultural links. Hebrew is known to have changed negligibly over the last 2000 years, partly because of the key role played by the language in the religious life of the Jewish people, but mainly due to the fact that it died out completely as a spoken tongue before being resurrected as the language of the modern state of Israel. However, in earlier times, as the language of the people of Israel and, before that, as one of the variant Semitic languages of Palestine and Syria[1], it is likely to have changed more significantly, probably at 1 linguistic year per year or more. Arabic has also been restrained greatly by the importance of the language in religious life and, in the 1350 years since the explosion of Arabic under Islam, it is amazing the degree to which the modern language remains a single unit. To be sure, it is not always easy for an Arabic speaker from one part of the Arab world to understand someone from elsewhere, but contrast that with the fact that

Chapter 9    Out of Africa                                                     121

1350 years ago there wasn't a language anything like modern English. Prior to the coming of Islam in the 7th Century AD, Arabic was something of a backwater in language terms, so a slow rate of change, perhaps as little as half a linguistic year per year, would be expected then too. Putting all this together, Arabic and Hebrew both descend from a language which was probably spoken some time during the 3rd Millennium BC.

But the family tree also shows that Akkadian, which here means the language of Babylon in about 650BC, had already changed by a massive 4000 linguistic years since a three-way split with Arabic and Hebrew. However, from the days of Sargon the Great in the 3rd Millennium BC through to the defeat of the Neo-Babylonian Empire in 539BC, Akkadian was the main administrative language of empire (sometimes empires[2]) so a sustained high rate of change is expected. The three-way split date looks to me to have been in the first half of the 3rd Millennium BC. Actually, this ties in nicely with archaeological finds of old Akkadian texts (on clay tablets) from Iraq, and other very closely related Semitic languages from northern Syria (from the ancient cities of Ebla, Mari and Nabada[3]), which imply that the whole of this part of the Semitic branch is descended from a parent tongue that was brought into the Syria-Iraq region in the early 3rd Millennium BC[4]. It seems logical to relate this parent tongue to the 'Proto-Urban' archaeological culture (or cultures), intrusive to Palestine in the late 4th Millennium BC[5].

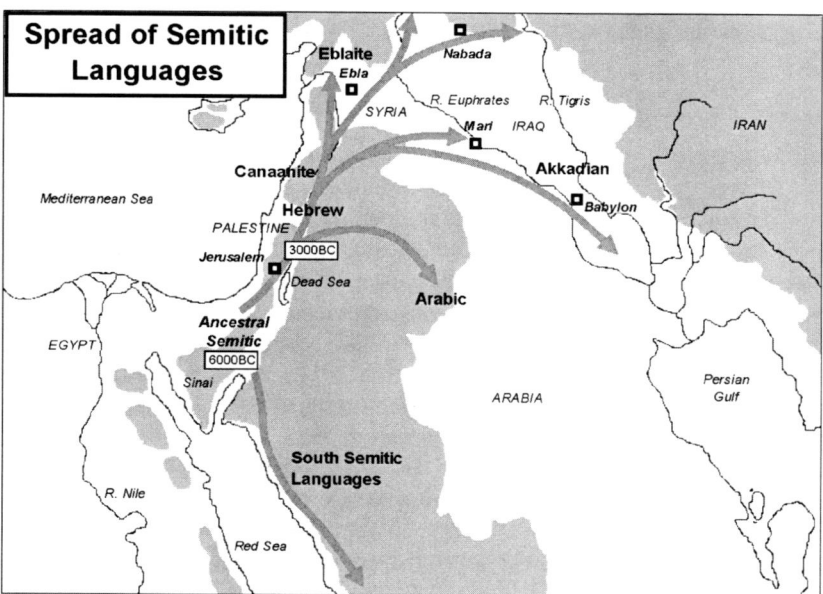

Working back, we come to the junction with the ancestor of the South Semitic languages Mehri and Amharic and, bearing in mind the path taken by South Semitic speech, the location was probably the Sinai region, between Egypt and Palestine. The obvious inference is that Semitic culture was spilling out of Africa. These were times during which the society of Egypt and southern Palestine was making the transition from settled Stone Age hunter-gatherer to metal-using farmer[6]. Cattle-raising is evident from the 6$^{th}$ Millennium BC, but at that stage there was no significant town or city development[7]. The lack of movement in North Semitic culture during these times suggests a change rate of no more than about 1 linguistic year per year; 6000BC is therefore a reasonable date for the ancestral Semitic tongue.

Mehri, one of a very few southern Semitic remnants still spoken in Yemen and Oman, has therefore averaged just under 1 linguistic year per year since 6000BC. On the other hand Amharic, which must have separated from Mehri in about 3500BC, has since changed much more rapidly, but then Amharic has been a language of empire. It almost certainly descends from 'Sabean', the language of Sheba, now Yemen. Sheba was a powerful and literate society, ruling over both African and Arabian territories in the 1$^{st}$ Millennium BC[8]; when the Sabean empire collapsed, the languages either side of the Red Sea went their separate ways. Ancestral Amharic eventually became the language of an Ethiopian kingdom centred on the city of Axum[9], and modern Amharic is now one of a small group of closely related South Semitic tongues in Ethiopia and Eritrea, Tigrinya being another important member.

## BERBER LANGUAGES AND EGYPTIAN

The next junction, 2000 linguistic years back up the family tree, sees the link between the Semitic and Berber branches. These were times before empires ruled and when the technology of war was happily insufficient to allow one population to dominate in the way that Indo-European and Arabic were able to in later times so, despite the fact that the languages have clearly moved, I am unwilling to assign more than about 1 linguistic year per year. A separation date of 8000BC seems likely. While Semitic language spread north down the Nile, Berber-Egyptian speech must have moved steadily west into the then fertile and productive Sahara, and this is nicely matched by the archaeological culture known as 'Capsian'[10]. Egyptian and Berber would have parted company in about 6000BC.

The four Berber languages shown in the family tree have since changed only slowly, at about 0.6 to 0.8 linguistic years per year, as befits languages which have led a relatively quiet existence for much of the last 8000 years. Based on the similarity between the three Saharan Berber lan-

Chapter 9    Out of Africa                                                          123

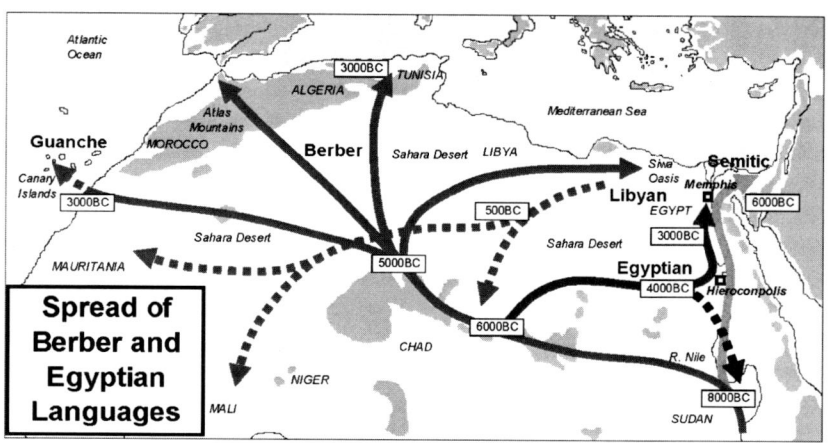

guages (Tamasheq, Ghalames and Tashelhet), it can only be very recently, probably since the introduction of the camel to North Africa[11] about 2000 years ago, that they have come to be spread across the Sahara region, from the inhabitants of the Siwa oasis in Egypt to the Tuareg peoples of Mali. And the Berber branch is also where the mysterious Guanche people of the Canary Islands fit in, a predominantly fair-haired race who vigorously defended their islands from the Spanish in the early 15th Century. Now, let me be honest; no-one knows any Guanche language today. In placing the two variants shown on the family tree (from Gran Canaria and Tenerife) I have used a significant proportion of the words we still know, namely the numerals from 1 to 10, but the point is that even that meagre knowledge is enough to assign these long-dead languages their true place in history – and to reveal a very high rate of change. And the crystal-clear picture is that the Canary Islands were colonised in about 3000BC but that – and this defies all logic – there was negligible interaction between the inhabitants of Gran Canaria and Tenerife following colonisation. It is a complete mystery how the islands could possibly have been colonised by a people who then forgot how to travel even quite short distances by sea[12]!

The position of ancient Egyptian in the family tree reveals two things, one totally unsurprising, the other perhaps more so. The unsurprising point is the high change rate, expected in the language of a great empire with such a long and rich history. The rather more surprising point is that the origin of Egyptian culture is shown to lie out in the Sahara desert – this is demanded by the link to Berber. In fact, this has been an area of some controversy among prehistorians, some preferring to see an origin in the Nile region[13], but the language evidence is absolutely clear; and that evidence implies that Saharan language and culture replaced early Semitic in Egypt[14].

## ORIGINS

Prior to 8000BC, the date at which Semitic and Berber parted company, probably on the banks of the Nile somewhere in Sudan, we move into truly prehistoric times, and I freely admit that it is difficult to make informed judgement regarding rate of language change. However, I suggest that the baseline rate of change in a language which doesn't move far would be rather higher for a hunter-gatherer society than for those practising arable farming because of its less settled nature. Thus, if 0.5 linguistic years per year is considered typical of settled farmers, this might be more like 0.7 linguistic years per year for hunter-gatherers[15]. The effect of movement would be to raise this further of course, and I suggest that around 1 linguistic year per year is therefore reasonable for the ancestor of Semitic and Berber as it spread steadily north. This gives a separation from the ancestor of Chadic and South Cushitic in about 11000BC – rather a long time ago! To put this into some sort of perspective, the last Ice Age was only just beginning to lose its grip in 11000BC; the Pacific and Arctic oceans were just meeting again after an interval of some 12000 years to form the Bering Strait, and all of human society was firmly in the pre-agricultural Stone Age. The family tree shows a continuing slow rate of language change in my South Cushitic representative, Dahalo (0.85 linguistic years per year on average), whose speakers remained in the Stone Age until comparatively recently, and this implies that the South Cushitic languages have not travelled far. At that rate, the South Cushitic-Chadic division would have taken place in about 7500BC[16]. However, a much faster rate of change (1.6 to 1.8 linguistic years per year) is evident in the Chadic languages, effectively proving that it is Chadic that has moved rather than South Cushitic. This illustrates nicely the power of this sort of language analysis; there is no way that history or even archaeology could possibly tell us so much about the ancient origins of north Nigerian culture. It is true that there is archaeological evidence for the spread of a remarkably uniform fishing-based society (during times of much higher rainfall than today) from northern Kenya and Uganda through Sudan and across the southern Sahel to Lake Chad during the 7th and 6th Millennia BC, but the archaeology cannot tell us which language group was involved[17].

Let me say once again: none of this means that modern Hausa speakers are descended from East Africans of 11000BC! But their language is. And this means that an important part of their culture is too.

But 11000BC is recent compared to the date of the first Afro-Asiatic language! For this we have to travel back a further 6000 linguistic years, presumably in East Africa and presumably during times when language change rates would have been slow; at 0.7 linguistic years per year, a date of around 20000BC is called for, with an estimated location somewhere in

## Chapter 9    Out of Africa

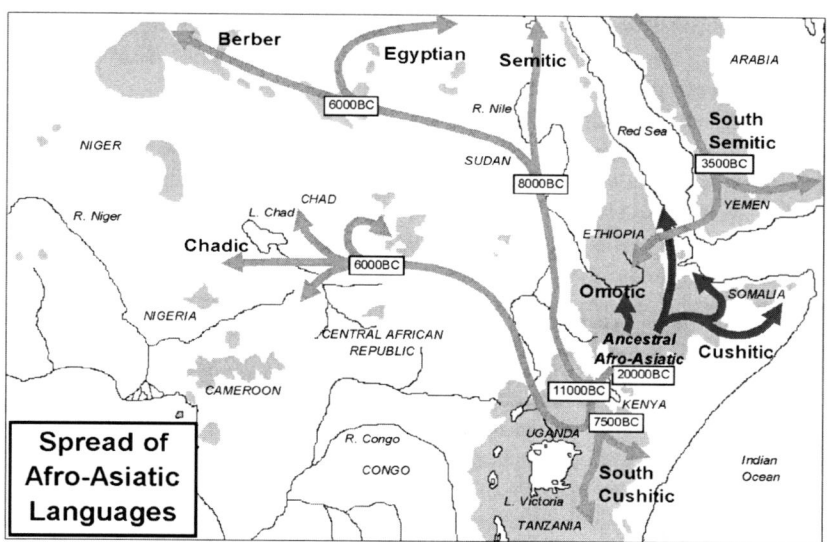

northern Kenya or Ethiopia[18]. Since that time Omotic and Cushitic speakers have slowly spread their cultures across the horn of Africa but it has been a gradual process. The Omotic languages stayed in Ethiopia where Wollayta has changed by around 17000 linguistic years (averaging 0.8 linguistic years per year). Beja represents those Cushitic languages which also remained in or close to Ethiopia; it has maintained 0.7 linguistic years per year. Those Cushitic languages which moved further east have changed more, reflecting greater movement. Afar has changed the most but, even though it is now spoken in Ethiopia, it is a relatively recent import to that country, carried north from Somalia.

An excellent question would be: "What was going on in East Africa in 20000BC which might have led to this highly successful outpouring of culture?" Well, the archaeological culture known as 'Nachikufian', which appears to have commenced in Zambia in about 30000BC, spread north across Tanzania and into Kenya, and it had reached true microlithic (meaning *small stone*) status by about 17000BC[19]. This means that the technology of stone working had by then attained a level where complex tools (spears, harpoons, arrows) could be created by gluing small razor-sharp pieces of stone onto a wooden shaft, and although I use the word 'tool' I could as easily have said 'weapon'. Clearly microlithic technology didn't just arise over night and there would have been a gradual improvement in techniques from well before 17000BC. Archaeologists suggest that these developments were driven by changes in the environment and the need to hunt smaller game but it is undeniable that such improved weaponry could also be used against human beings from other tribes! The inhabitants of northern Kenya in 20000BC would have held a considerable advantage over many of their neighbours.

And these distinctly plausible ties between Afro-Asiatic language and archaeology would appear to bring this analysis of the Afro-Asiatic family to a reasonably neat and logical conclusion – or they would do if it weren't for one rather controversial branch, a branch which all linguists seem to regard as so important that they treat it as a separate family. I speak of course of the Indo-European family which, if my measurements are to be believed, is actually just one more branch of Afro-Asiatic! Can this be true?

## THE INDO-EUROPEAN BRANCH?

It is all very well to carry out exhaustive research and then to claim that the Indo-European question has been solved by assigning its origin to 5500BC in the steppe land of southern Russia, but the human race certainly did not originate then or there – neither did human language! So it is perfectly reasonable to look for even earlier origins and to ask the question: "how did the original Indo-European language reach Russia in the first place?"

Well, according to the measurements, Indo-European is a 19000 linguistic year long branch of Afro-Asiatic, splitting from the Semitic-Berber-Chadic-South Cushitic side of the family just 1000 linguistic years after the ancestral Afro-Asiatic tongue was spoken, i.e. in about 18500BC. Bearing in mind what we know happened after 5500BC, this leaves something like 11000 linguistic years of change over 13000 actual years between 18500BC and 5500BC (at 0.85 linguistic years per year). Is this really possible bearing in mind the distance involved?

I believe it is possible – indeed I believe the language evidence demands it. However, I can think of only one mechanism. To achieve such a journey with such a modest rate of change to the language, these pre-Indo-European speakers simply have to have been Nile river dwellers. A boat-based, presumably fishing-based, economy is the only possible explanation I can come up with for such a rapid journey[20]. I suggest that speakers of the Indo-European branch of Afro-Asiatic could even have reached the Nile delta as early as 15000BC. Once there, the more usual slow land-based spread would have occurred, through Palestine and towards the north and east. Genuine archaeological support for this is seen in the fact that microlithic technology took off in Egypt, Palestine, Syria and Turkey in about 14000BC, as evidenced by the so-called 'Kebaran' culture in Israel and 'Helwan' in Egypt[21].

Of course, just because it could be true that doesn't make it true! But in my view the case for Indo-European's inclusion within the greater Afro-

Chapter 9    Out of Africa                                                127

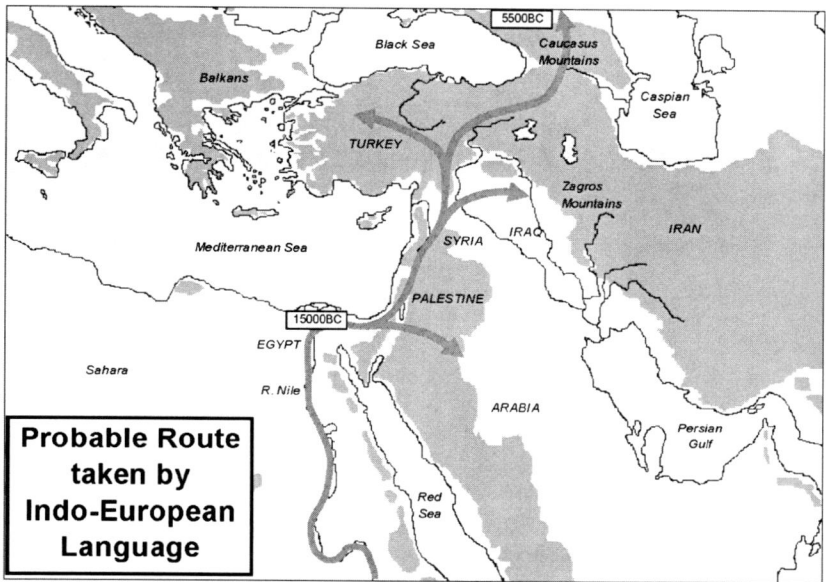

Asiatic family is almost as strong as that of the Chadic languages for example and, as you can probably tell, I am now fully persuaded of the truth of it. For me, the strange coincidence that both families use a masculine-feminine system for their nouns, when this is seen almost nowhere else in the world, practically forces the issue. You might wonder about the lack of any intermediate language evidence, languages which remained along the route from East Africa to southern Russia; on the other hand there is no intermediate language evidence between East Africa and the region where Chadic languages are now spoken. The truth is that language evidence is being obliterated all the time, and with the greatest of ease. Both Egyptian and Semitic have contributed to covering the traces of Indo-European's passage north.

However, I think you would be right to be a little cautious about sharing my conviction of Indo-European's origins. As you have seen, the relationship between Indo-European and Afro-Asiatic is not a particularly close one and the archaeological evidence of the progress of microlithic technology, though supportive, certainly doesn't represent cast iron proof. What we need to do is to collect more evidence. This study of Afro-Asiatic has led to a reasonable theory; we need to check out whether the theory still looks reasonable even after considering how all the other languages measurably close to Indo-European fit in. After all, there can only be one truth, and we want to be quite sure that this is it!

# 10

# To the Urals and Beyond

I admit that I haven't really addressed the question as to what prompted and sustained Afro-Asiatic and then Indo-European expansion. Certainly microlithic technology allowed it to develop in the first place, but similar technologies also appeared in contemporary Europe for example[1] and, in my opinion at least, no trace of that ancient European language remains. I am forced back, therefore, into suggesting that the true root cause was a function of the way society developed. The tendency already seen for Indo-European speakers to dominate others is paralleled by the way Semitic took over the Middle East and by the Chadic 'conquest' of half of Nigeria. It's hard to put one's finger on it, but it seems that a remarkably enduring self-belief somehow got into these people, perhaps a natural consequence of the development of a tribal or class-based structure with chiefs whose principal job it was to 'lead their people to glory'. I have to say I find it most intriguing, since whatever development it was, it has seen 22 consecutive millennia of continuous success – although often of one branch of the family at the expense of another!

Anyway, as you have seen, I believe there is a very strong case for Indo-European to be viewed within the greater fold of the Afro-Asiatic family. By placing it there, I am merely illustrating and putting numbers to the belief of many linguists that some sort of connection exists, though by suggesting an outline history for the spread of the language family, down the Nile valley, through Palestine and Syria to Turkey and then southern Russia, I am going much further than most would. But a question may be in your mind. What if I had looked not at the Afro-Asiatic family but at one of the others represented in the list of languages 40000 linguistic years or less from Indo-European? Would I have come up with completely different conclusions? This is a serious question and needs addressing. If these other languages really are relatively close to Indo-

European, then they have to fit into the picture somewhere, and it is the task of this chapter to find out just where that is.

The remaining eight languages listed in Chapter 8 as within 40000 linguistic years (on average) of Indo-European include some of the waifs and strays of the language world, those in the general Indo-European region. In Europe, they comprise Basque, Etruscan, Finnish and Hungarian, and if I had included other Uralic languages, such as Estonian and Sami, they would also have been listed. In India, three Dravidian languages, Brahui, Tamil and Telugu appeared on the list and others such as Malayalam and Kannada would also have made it if I had included them; the final position went to Burushaski, from Kashmir. Could it be that these waifs and strays are in fact the remains of one or more earlier waves of language, which have since been largely obliterated by Indo-European? By even asking the question, I am inviting controversy but, since I have a measurement system at my disposal, there is nothing stopping me from at least taking a look and coming to an opinion. However, before looking at the bigger picture, let me introduce you to each element in turn.

## DRAVIDIAN LANGUAGES

Today the main centre of Dravidian speaking is southern India, where four very widely spoken languages exist, namely Tamil, Telugu, Kannada and Malayalam. However, there are several other languages which are recognised as being in the same family. Tulu completes the southern Indian set; Gondi and Kurukh are two of a cluster of languages spoken in east central India by isolated tribes in areas now dominated by Indo-European tongues; and Brahui is spoken in far away Pakistan. To investigate Dravidian, I have supplemented a full analysis of Tamil, Telugu and Brahui with a comparison of the numerals from 1 to 10 for the other languages, in exactly the same way as previously, generating the following family tree.

The root point for the family has been determined by comparing distances to the average of the 11 Indo-European branches. By the way, Brahui brings me to a particular problem, namely an incomplete set of words for comparison purposes, in the case of Brahui due to its use of Indo-European numerals for *four* and upwards. Wherever this problem occurs I have simply scaled everything up from a reduced word set, 19 words instead of 26 in this case.

Let's try a little interpretation. Firstly, the least changed languages are Gondi and Kurukh, spoken by hill tribes in east central India. They have been relatively isolated from the Indo-European civilisation of India and a fairly basic but settled economy has been the norm. As is now absolutely clear, a settled existence means a slow rate of language change and, accepting that 0.7 linguistic years per year is a typical minimum rate of change

Chapter 10   To the Urals and Beyond

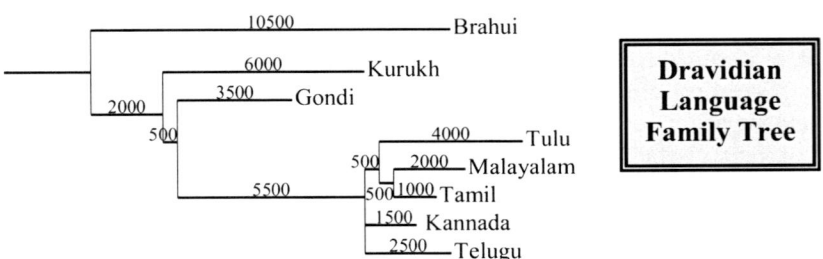

Dravidian Language Family Tree

in settled but non-agrarian societies, the common ancestor of Gondi and Kurukh (and therefore of the five south Indian languages as well) would probably have been spoken about 6000 years ago, in 4000BC. The ancestral language for the whole family looks likely to date from around 6500BC – plus or minus a millennium or so. The relatively large change in Brahui probably implies movement but could also be partly due to the fact that pastoralist agriculture has been practised in that region for all of the 8500 years since 6500BC[2].

The south Indian group are really very close indeed, on a smaller scale even than the Indic branch of Indo-European. Malayalam and Tamil are known from historical sources to have separated no more than about 1000 years ago[3] and the inescapable conclusion is that all five south Indian languages stem from an ancestor spoken no earlier than about 500BC. Logically, this ancestral south Indian tongue had spread south during the millennia between 4000BC and 500BC; equally logically, the vigorous

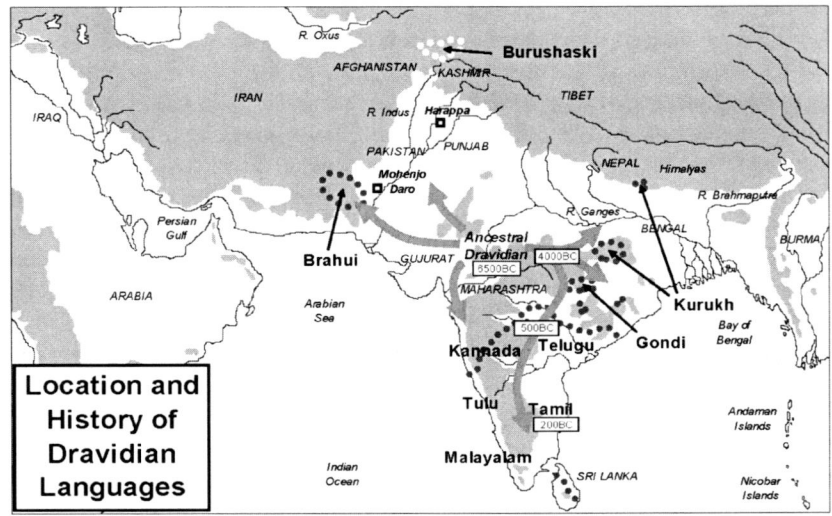

Location and History of Dravidian Languages

# Chapter 10  To the Urals and Beyond

expansion since 500BC owed much to interaction with the newly-arrived Indo-European civilisation to the north, particularly during king Asoka's reign in the 3$^{rd}$ Century BC[4]. The language had certainly arrived in Tamil Nadu by the 2$^{nd}$ Century BC when the first poems in old Tamil appear.

As for the location of the ancestral Dravidian tongue, the relatively significant change to Brahui compared to Gondi and Kurukh suggests central India. However, the fact that there is a clear substratum of Dravidian words in the Indo-European languages of Maharashtra, Gujarat and southern Pakistan implies that Brahui is simply the sole survivor from what was once a considerable expanse of Dravidian speech, stretching from central India right across the lower Indus plain. Whether the Indus Valley civilisation of the 3$^{rd}$ and early 2$^{nd}$ Millennia BC, known from two great city sites (Mohenjo Daro and Harappa – a city referred to in the Vedas[5]) as well as hundreds of smaller towns and villages, was Dravidian speaking is debatable. It clearly could have been – but the family tree provides insufficient evidence to be sure[6].

Perhaps I should say something about Dravidian languages themselves. There are actually quite a lot of similarities with Indo-European, which has led to a tendency to look for links between the two families. For example, both make use of quite similar 'case structures', meaning that the endings of words are changed according to the position in the sentence. English is an exception to this, so let me illustrate using Russian to represent Indo-European and Telugu to represent the Dravidian languages. The Russian for *with a pen* is *perom*, the *-m* meaning *with*; in a similar way, Telugu uses *kalamuto*, the *-to* meaning with. However, the Telugu use of cases, or perhaps one should simply term them suffixes, is much the more extensive. And this brings me to a particular point regarding the relationship between Dravidian languages and Indo-European. You may remember that I tried to be very careful to avoid the effects of secondary contact between languages in my measurement of linguistic difference; well, I am afraid I have not been totally successful and this is highlighted by the situation in India. One of the distinguishing features of the Indic branch of Indo-European is that the languages make use of postpositions rather than prepositions; this means that to say *in London* in Hindi, for example, one has to say *London mãi*. They are the only Indo-European languages to use postpositions but the usage is shared with the Dravidian language family, and the logical explanation is that the fashion was 'transferred' from the Dravidian languages at the time of the Indo-European incursion into the region. A similar 'transferring' effect can be seen in the use of 'retroflex' consonants in both Dravidian and Indo-European languages throughout the Indian subcontinent. If you have never heard of retroflex consonants then you should try pronouncing one. For example, an English '*t*' is formed by placing the tip of the tongue against the back of the teeth or sometimes a little way up the palette. But there is no reason why the 't' sound should not be produced with the tongue anywhere from the ends of the teeth right back to as far back as the tongue can reach, somewhere in the roof of the mouth. This last position, with the tongue turned back against the roof of the mouth, produces the retroflex 't' and this is one of the characteristic sounds of India. Other Indo-European branches make no use of the sound, implying that it has recently been acquired by Indic languages.

I don't wish to make a big thing of this, but it serves as a timely warning that the measured distance between languages may sometimes be artificially lowered by such secondary contact effects. I don't think the effect would be too great in this case but it might amount to a couple of thousand linguistic years or so.

I'll leave Dravidian for the moment. Clearly, the fact that its languages are within measurable distance of Indo-European according to the system in this book means that I shall shortly be looking for a connection. However, before embarking down that road, let me introduce some more of the languages and language families within striking distance of Indo-European.

## BURUSHASKI

Burushaski (accent on the *ush*) is spoken by a still-thriving community in two valleys in the extreme north of Kashmir, now in territory administered by Pakistan. Until the recent construction of the Karakoram Highway from Pakistan to China, there was only one road in and out, and this has given the people and their culture a degree of isolation and therefore protection from the outside world. The language they speak is another which makes use of postpositions and suffixes, like the Dravidian languages. The verb structure is also not so different. To cap it all, Burushaski uses a masculine-feminine-neuter system like German and many other Indo-European languages. However, there is little sign of similarity in basic vocabulary with either Dravidian or Indo-European, so clearly the relationships cannot be close.

Inevitably, the presence of an isolated language invites speculation, which then leads to wild theorising, followed by semi-mythical status! In Chapter 2, I introduced the Dené-Caucasian super-family and Burushaski has tended to be branded as a member of this legendary grouping for reasons that I have not explored and have little desire to. In truth, although Burushaski is considerably different from the other languages of India in its vocabulary, it is far from dramatically different in grammatical form, which suggests to me that there is no need to look too far to see where its closest relatives may lie.

Chapter 10    To the Urals and Beyond                               133

I would also suggest that geography is relevant here. The valleys where Burushaski is now spoken connect down into the Indus river system and so to the rest of Pakistan. That is therefore the direction from which the language came. Until a few years ago there was no Karakoram Highway; travel to or from Tibet and China was not for the faint-hearted. So it does not take a genius to work out that the immediate origin of Burushaski has to be looked for in modern Pakistan.

## BASQUE

The Basque language is spoken in north-east Spain and south-west France and is another isolate, unrelated (to most people's eyes) to any other language, although relationship has been claimed with the Caucasian languages (see next chapter), Burushaski and sometimes the Dené-Caucasian super-family. The language is quite different from the Indo-European tongues spoken all around today. It is another language which makes extensive use of suffixes on nouns as replacements for prepositions (so *to the beach* becomes *hondartzara*, the *-ra* suffix meaning *to*). It also has a phenomenally complicated set of verb forms. Needless to say the basic vocabulary is also quite different; there are nowadays large numbers of Latin-derived loan words, but these do not affect the core of the language.

Much has been written, not all of it well informed, concerning the Basque language. Many have suggested that it represents the remains of the language spoken by the earliest Europeans who reached Spain about 30000 years ago. Some have stated that they have detected words whose roots can be traced back to cave-dwelling times, although that would hardly be so very amazing in any language since cave-dwelling was a worldwide phenomenon! Certainly the Basques have been a distinct people throughout recorded history, noted by the Romans and never fully assimilated into the Roman Empire. However, the fact remains that the measured distance between Basque and an average of the 11 Indo-European branches is 'only' 36000 linguistic years and this relative closeness has to be explained in a plausible way. Perhaps secondary contact explains some of it but this is not obviously the case. To some it is almost an article of faith that Basque is unique, that it is absolutely and totally different from any other language (except perhaps the almost unknown ancient languages, Iberian and Aquitanian[7]). I expect you will realise by now that I have no sympathy with such views. Besides, I have studied Basque and was struck straight away by how non-unique it is – and the languages which appeared to me to be the closest were those you are about to meet, the Uralic family.

## URALIC LANGUAGES – FINNO-UGRIC BRANCH

Basque does not stand quite alone in Europe, amidst the sea of Indo-European tongues. To the far north, the Lapps, Finns and Estonians all speak non-Indo-European languages, called Uralic after the Ural Mountains. These languages certainly have superficial similarities to Basque. They also make use of suffixes and postpositions, so *uimarannalle* is *to the beach* in Finnish, the *-lle* replacing our preposition *to* in the same way that *-ra* does in Basque. There are also similarities, though not particularly close, in the way the verbs are formed.

Also, right in the heart of Europe are the Hungarian-speaking people, and Hungarian is another Uralic language. It too uses suffixes so that *to the beach* is *strandra* (suffix *-ra*, the same as in Basque). However, as I have mentioned already, the present Hungarian nation is known to be the result of an invasion from the east by the Magyars in the 9th Century AD, i.e. quite recently. Were they perhaps, without realising it, reclaiming the territory which had belonged to their ancient relatives thousands of years earlier, before the Celts, Slavs and other Indo-Europeans made the area their home? This is the sort of question which needs answering if a proper understanding of European pre-history is to be achieved.

And there are other Uralic languages still spoken in various regions of central and northern Russia. The central Russian languages, some still with hundreds of thousands of speakers, are clearly related to Finnish, Sami (the language of the Lapps) and Estonian. Finally, there is a further, northern branch, Samoyedic, which is considerably different but is still

Chapter 10    To the Urals and Beyond

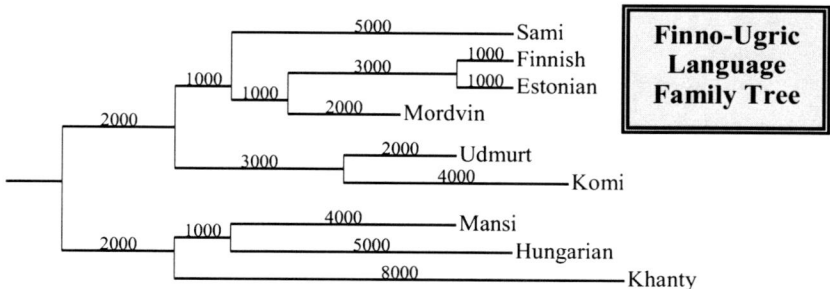

thought of by most linguists as Uralic. However, according to the calculation method used in this book, it is highly debatable whether Samoyedic languages should really be bracketed in the same family and, if you don't mind, I will ignore them for the moment and pick them up in the next chapter. The family tree shown is therefore restricted to the so-called 'Finno-Ugric' side of the family, and has been constructed first by applying the full vocabulary, grammar and sound analysis to Finnish and Hungarian, then establishing the initial split point by looking at the relative distances of Finnish and Hungarian to Indo-European, Dravidian, Burushaski, Basque and Afro-Asiatic, and finally adding the other languages using the numerals from 1 to 10.

It really isn't too difficult to see what this family tree means. The shortest arms are those to Mordvin, Udmurt and Mansi, languages from central Russia, either side of the Ural Mountains, and experience thus far suggests that these languages have therefore moved least. First Sami then Finnish and Estonian have diverged from Mordvin, the most westerly of the central Russian languages, and all have changed more than Mordvin. Many researchers believe (and I fully agree) that this language spread is mirrored by the development of a uniform hunting and fishing culture stretching from the Urals to modern Latvia and up into Finland, a culture recognised by its use of so-called 'pit-comb ware' pottery[8].

Hungarian is a bit of an oddity; its roots lie to the <u>east</u> of the Urals, where its closest relative Mansi is spoken, with Khanty rather further to the north-east. Hungarian was carried into the heart of Europe by migration and conquest, reaching the 'promised land' in the 9th Century AD.

Taking the evidence together, I would suggest a change rate of a little under 1 linguistic year per year for Mordvin, Udmurt and Mansi – the economy of the speakers has been that of relatively settled hunter-gatherers and then farmers – and rather higher change rates for the other languages. This gives a date of about 6000BC for the ancestor Finno-Ugric language. The most likely point of origin has to be the Ural Mountain region.

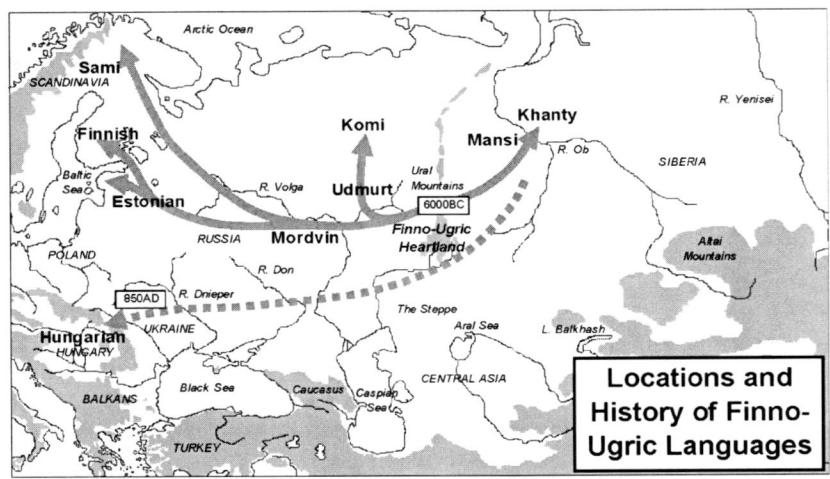

Locations and History of Finno-Ugric Languages

## ETRUSCAN

One really useful thing about the method for comparing languages presented in this book is that we hardly have to know them! The Guanche languages were placed appropriately within the Berber group simply based on the numerals 1 to 10 – and we know much more than that about ancient Etruscan, the language of the first great civilisation of Italy. Etruscan stands as one of the great remaining challenges to decipherers of ancient languages. We have reasonably extensive texts; we can read the script since it uses the same letters as that of the Phoenicians and early Greeks; but we still can't understand it that well. There are several parallel texts, written in both Etruscan and Greek, which give a good starting point, and it is this knowledge which makes the inclusion of Etruscan possible here. There is sufficient to provide a fair proportion of the 26 key words, and to characterise both grammar and sound with reasonable confidence. We know that the language is another of those which adds suffixes to nouns instead of using prepositions, and also to verbs in forming tenses and to show who is doing what, and it therefore has some similarity to the other languages mentioned in this chapter. That doesn't prove relationship but it suggests we could look for one. My principal source for the language comes from the work of Professor Beekes and Dr van der Meer of the University of Leiden[9].

So who were these mysterious Etruscans? They were a people who lived in northern and western Italy during the 1st Millennium BC. At the time the Greeks started colonising the western Mediterranean in the 7th Century BC, the Etruscans constituted one of the serious rival peoples. It was the Etruscans who founded Rome as their colony; the Latin speakers merely rose up in rebellion and took over some time later. Yet, by the end of the millennium, Etruscan language and culture was dying, soon to be forgotten entirely. The Romans did not record the language of their erstwhile masters; they left us just a handful of comments about its strangeness, suggesting that it was not closely related to Latin. In fact the only clearly related language known has been found in a fragmentary inscription from the island of Lemnos in the Aegean and both legend and reputable historical evidence suggest that the Aegean, specifically the Turkish side of the Aegean, was the original home of the Etruscans rather than Italy[10].

## MAKING THE CONNECTION

So, we have two recognised families, Dravidian and Uralic, and three language isolates, all of which have been found to be a similar linguistic distance from Indo-European. The time has come to look at the distances between them all, as well as those to Indo-European and Afro-Asiatic. I have averaged the distances to the Dravidian languages Brahui, Tamil and Telugu, to the Uralic languages Finnish and Hungarian, to eight Afro-Asiatic languages, as well as, of course, to all the Indo-European branches. The following table gives the results.

Since I already have a perfectly good family tree for Afro-Asiatic, with Indo-European as a branch, I should simply be able to bolt on the other five arms. Inevitably there are errors, particularly in the distances to Etruscan. However this is to be expected given the degree of uncertainty in classification of the Etruscan language but, other than minor adjustments, it is hard to see any alternative to the general arrangement given in the following family tree.

Notice the rather close relationship which is revealed between Basque, Etruscan and the Uralic languages; heresy to many, I know, but the measurements do not lie.

Looking at the bigger picture, it would appear that all the languages introduced in this chapter are, in reality, offshoots from the Indo-

| Linguistic years | I-E | Dra | Ura | Bur | Bas | Etr | A-A |
|---|---|---|---|---|---|---|---|
| **Indo-European** | 0 | 36000 | 34000 | 34000 | 36000 | 36000 | 39000 |
| **Dravidian** | | 0 | 40000 | 33000 | 38000 | 31000 | 51000 |
| **Uralic (Finno-Ugric)** | | | 0 | 39000 | 25000 | 24000 | 51000 |
| **Burushaski** | | | | 0 | 31000 | 44000 | 38000 |
| **Basque** | | | | | 0 | 26000 | 39000 |
| **Etruscan** | | | | | | 0 | 46000 |
| **Afro-Asiatic** | | | | | | | 0 |

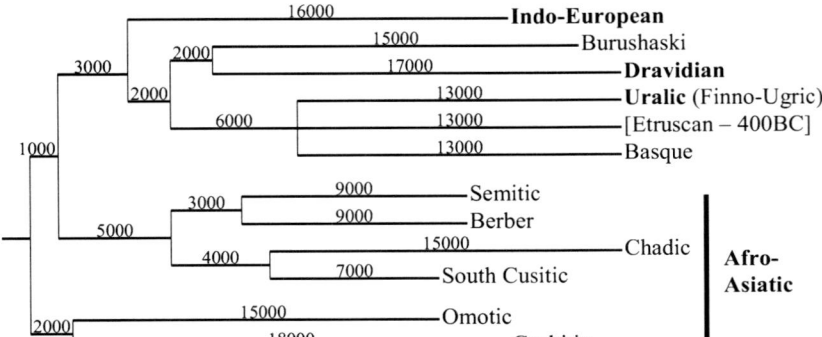

European branch of a greater Afro-Asiatic tree, and happily this solution in no way upsets the view of Indo-European roots built up in the last chapter. But is it true? Is it logical? Let's try and deduce what this really means in historical terms.

## HISTORICAL DEDUCTIONS

In the last chapter we saw how Indo-European separated from the rest of Afro-Asiatic in about 18500BC and was brought down the Nile valley, progressing through Palestine and Syria and eventually turning up in southern Russia in about 5500BC. Looking at the family tree, it seems that a key division occurred at some point during this period, leading to the separation of an ancestor to every one of the languages covered in this chapter, and the only sensible location for this division is southern Palestine. There is no reason to suppose that the successful Indo-European language branch (associated with the successful Kebaran culture) would confine itself to a northward route to Turkey, so one would naturally expect to find that it had also fanned out into the rest of the Middle East[11]. And remember that we are not necessarily talking of the physical spread of a population – or only to a limited extent; it is the spread of the culture, of the technology, which would have been occurring. No matter who first developed it, the ideas would have been adopted by other racial groups in a sort of wave of progress north, south, east and west. And the wave would logically continue until it either reached a natural barrier (ocean, jungle, desert, mountain range or ice sheet) or came up against a culture which was not impressed by the advance, i.e. one which had done just as well or better itself. Assuming a steady rate of change to Indo-European through the millennia, the separation date should have been about 15000BC, just about the time that the language reached northern Egypt.

Chapter 10    To the Urals and Beyond                                139

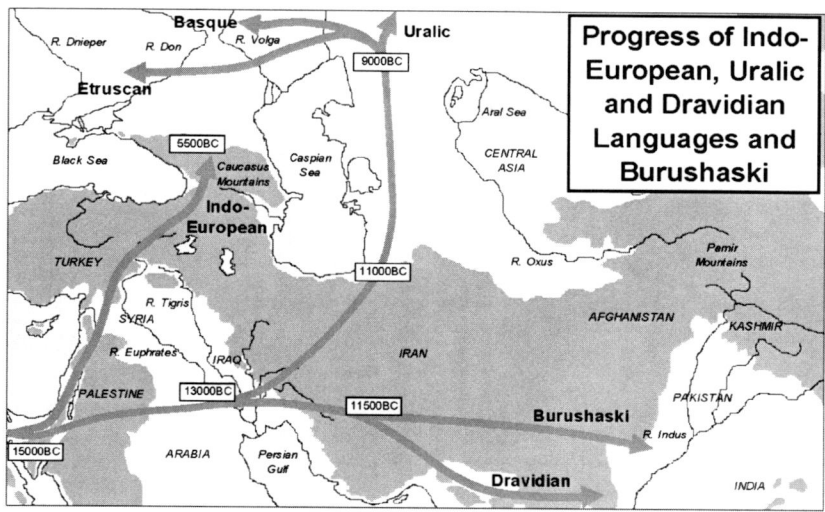

Over the course of the next 8500 years or so, a version of this successful hunter-gatherer culture must then have spread east, a descendent language turning up in central India in 6500BC as the ancestral Dravidian tongue. The rate of change during those 8500 years works out at 1.2 linguistic years per year on average, reasonable in view of the movement involved.

The division between Dravidian and Uralic would have occurred in about 13000BC, probably in Iraq. By 11000BC, pre-Uralic speakers would have reached the edge of the Central Asian plain, now the Kara Kum desert but then temperate grassland. In fact, by 11000BC ice was beginning to melt all over the northern world, releasing its grip on Europe and on the mountains of Asia and positively inviting a northward migration into territory until then very sparsely populated. By about 9000BC, when the Ice Age was finally over, the advance had reached the northern end of the Caspian Sea, opening up a choice of routes, and this is the point indicated on the family tree where the ancestors of Basque and Etruscan separated from Uralic.

Let me speculate a little here. I believe the earliest pre-Basque speakers should almost certainly be identified with the Svidrian culture, which spread up the Dnieper river to the Baltic states and Poland[12]. This Mesolithic (Middle Stone Age) hunter-gatherer culture then gave way to the Linear Band Pottery culture of Poland, Germany and Holland, the first agricultural society of northern Europe, which commenced around 5600BC, and which I also suspect spoke ancestral Basque. If these deductions are correct then the next stage was the 5th Millennium BC Rössen

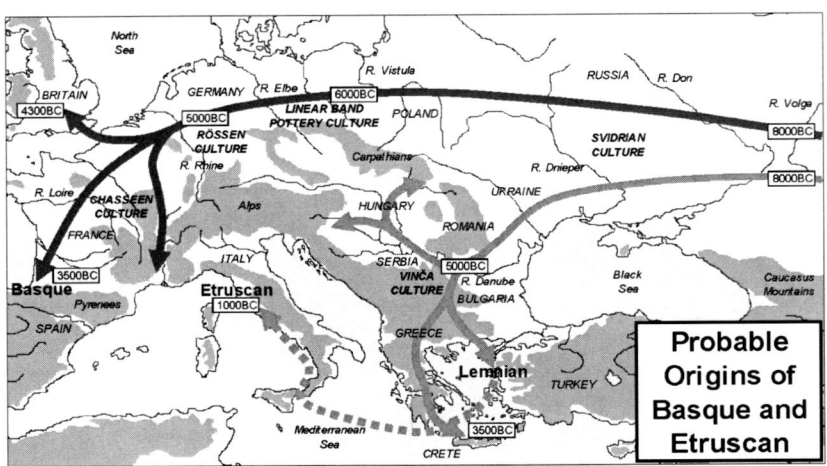

**Probable Origins of Basque and Etruscan**

culture of Germany and eastern France, a direct successor of Linear Band, leading then to the 4th Millennium BC Chasseen culture which covered most of France. The sudden arrival of agriculture in Britain in about 4300BC must logically be ascribed to the same cultural impulse[13].

Furthermore, I would suggest that the now extinct Etruscan branch can also be traced archaeologically. It would have been the language of the southern stream of Svidrian culture, spoken in the Ukraine, its speakers embracing agriculture when they reached Romania in about 6000BC. It then became the speech of the 5th Millennium BC Vinča culture[14], which stretched from Hungary down into the Balkans and Greece. At that date Vinča led the world. In addition to agriculture and a knowledge of copper production, finds from Vinča itself and other associated sites have revealed the use of signs (on tablets) which look very much like an early form of writing, long before the development of anything comparable in the Middle East or Egypt. Indeed more than half of the letters used in the still undeciphered Linear A script of Bronze Age (2nd Millennium BC) Crete have direct equivalents in Vinča signs[15]. It very much looks as though Etruscan, Lemnian and possibly ancient Cretan[16] represent end products of this wave of language and culture, since squeezed into oblivion by the more warlike Indo-European tribes.

Forgive me for going into some detail on Basque and Etruscan; I find it simply fascinating what can be deduced by tying language history into the evidence from archaeology, and I hope you will agree that in both cases the tie-up is distinctly plausible. However, let me return briefly to the one remaining language, Burushaski. It must have separated from the Dravidian branch in about 11500BC, presumably somewhere in Iran. Just what happened during the next 13500 years who can say? Like Dravidian, ancestral Burushaski clearly spread into Pakistan, presumably to the north of the Dravidian zone, and it may once have ranged far across the Indian subcontinent. However, all we can say for sure is that, for some reason, it has since been replaced everywhere except the far north of Pakistan by other languages and cultures.

## SUMMARY

I have painted a picture of a spread of language, fanning out from southern Palestine from around 15000BC. The picture appears to be an entirely logical one; it fits in with geographical constraints, with climatic factors (the end of the Ice Age) and with archaeology. One could even name this whole group of families 'Nostratic', the super-family introduced in Chapter 2, although I have never seen a history of Nostratic proposed in this way[17]. Just why this language wave should have continued to make progress and to devour all before it is still debatable but it is surely certain that it was no accident. The details as to which branches became the more successful, these may be ascribed to accidents of history and geography, but the fact of a continuing advance right across southern Asia, into central and northern Asia and then back west into Europe, implies a very real cause. It has to mean that a cultural development had reached southern Palestine in 15000BC which gave significant advantage over surrounding communities. But whereas Indo-European language is associated with a clan-based society, which makes warfare a virtue, indeed almost a necessity for continuing success, the Dravidian cultures of India are different; similarly the Uralic cultures of Russia and Scandinavia and the ancient civilisations of the Indus Valley, Vinča, Crete and Etruria. There is plenty of evidence for strong centralised authority but warfare seems to have been an occasional necessity rather than a virtue, and society seems to have been much less stratified. If I had to pick a key characteristic, therefore, responsible for the phenomenal spread of these cultures, it would be that of strong central authority. It would be superior social organisation which allowed these cultures to steadily take over everything in their path. The fact that they all had to give way in the end to clan-based Indo-European society is probably as much as anything due to accident of history, notably the fact that it was an Indo-European-speaking genius who first domesticated the horse rather than an Uralic speaker.

But just how far did this massive cultural movement go? Did it stop in India, Europe and northern Asia?

# 11

# Huns, Mongols and Tatars

I have now exhausted all the language groups with representatives within 40000 linguistic years of Indo-European – so where to turn next? Well, you may remember that right at the outset, in Chapter 2, I said that many linguists talk in terms of an Uralic-Altaic family, which implies that the Altaic languages are, in the opinion of some at least, quite closely linked to the Uralic family, which I have already found to be a cousin of Indo-European. Not only so but, when we were looking at the Uralic family, I deliberately left out one branch of that family, Samoyedic, on the grounds that it was just too distant. So here are a couple of leads to follow. I think the time has now come to explore the whole region where Altaic and Samoyedic languages are spoken and to see what can be made of the plethora of tongues to be found in the vast expanses of northern Asia.

## THE ALTAIC SPEAKING PEOPLES

In the European subconscious the memory of events from centuries ago is preserved by the meaning now given in everyday speech to such ethnic terms as the 'Huns'. Through the years of recorded history there has been a succession of invasions of Europe from the east by warlike groups and the Huns under their famous leader Atilla were one of them. They stepped into history (meaning written history) in the 4$^{th}$ Century AD when they appeared on the north-east frontier of the Roman Empire, yet another barbarian horde, like the Celtic and Germanic tribes, eager for a share in the riches of Rome. The Huns of Europe are generally identified by ancient historians with the 'Xiongnu', recorded by the Chinese as a people who had become a significant nuisance to the newly established Chinese Empire, such a nuisance in fact that the greatest artificial defence system ever created was built to keep them out, namely the Great Wall of China. Such fragments of their language as the Chinese records show can, apparently, be assigned as being Turkic in origin[1], i.e. related to Turkish, Kazakh, Uighur, Uzbek and several other Central Asian tongues. These languages are all Altaic, named after the far off Altai Mountains on the Russian-Chinese border.

The Huns ravaged Europe, China and northern India. Their relatives, the Tatars, then effectively ruled China north of the Yangtze river for the best part of 300 years. In Europe the Huns were followed in the 6th Century by the Avars. They also came out of distant Asia, from the Chinese frontier, and carved out for themselves an empire in south-east Europe, teaming up with the Slavs and battling the Eastern Roman Empire right to the gates of Constantinople. They also spoke an Altaic language, probably also Turkic. The Turkic-speaking Khazar Empire then dominated the Ukraine and southern Russia from the 7th to the 10th Century[2]. At the same time, other Turkic groups were setting up their empires in Central Asia and eventually ruling Iran and northern India, finally penetrating in the 11th Century into the land which is now Turkey.

Finally, and most traumatically of all, Genghiz Khan and the Mongols entered the scene in the 13th Century, easily defeating the best armies of Europe and of the Islamic world. Under Genghiz, they swept through Central Asia and northern China; the next wave reached Poland and Hungary, stopping on the news of the death of their great Khan. The third great attack reached the borders of Egypt, and this was then followed by the conquest of all China and the rule of emperor Kublai Khan. The Mongols too spoke an Altaic language and they too came from the same general region of northern Asia.

So, it would be fair to say that the world has gained a certain impression of Altaic speakers over the years and that impression is not one of a sedentary peace-loving people! The migrations of the last 2000 years have occurred over amazing distances and in all directions. I think it is clear that the lifestyle which was typical of those Altaic speakers was a mobile lifestyle (an inevitable function of the environment they inhabited), such that a population could suddenly uproot themselves, travel thousands of miles *en masse* and take up residence in a different corner of the planet. So a language spoken by such a group might shift about the place quite a bit! We must therefore bear this lifestyle in mind when interpreting matters to do with Altaic languages.

## THE ALTAIC LANGUAGES

As I have mentioned already, there has been considerable discussion amongst linguists as to just whether and to what extent the Uralic and Altaic families are related, because they undeniably have similar structure, making use of suffixes and building words up rather than using lots of smaller words as we tend to do in English. There are other more detailed similarities, for example in the use of what is called 'vowel harmony', where only certain combinations of vowels are allowed in any given word. So, *plaja* means *to the beach* in Turkish, using the *-a* suffix for *to*, whereas *denize* means *to the sea*, the suffix now being *-e* because the word *deniz* contains *e*'s and *i*'s and not *a*'s. The same expressions in the Uralic language, Hungarian, are *strandra* (suffix *-ra* as we have seen already) and *tengerre* (suffix *-re*). I am sorry if I am boring you with details, but I want to get across the fact that there are real similarities between Uralic and Altaic languages which are hard to explain unless there is some sort of reasonably close relationship between the families.

To get an impression of the position of the family relative to Uralic and others, I have calculated distances from an average of four Altaic languages, Turkish, Uzbek (from Central Asia), Mongolian and Manchu (from north-east China), to the various other languages and language families dealt with so far, and they come out as follows:

| to Etruscan: | 31000 | linguistic | years |
|---|---|---|---|
| to Uralic (Finno-Ugric): | 32000 | " | " |
| to Basque: | 32000 | " | " |
| to Dravidian: | 33000 | " | " |
| to Burushaski: | 36000 | " | " |
| to Indo-European: | 46000 | " | " |
| to Afro-Asiatic: | 59000 | " | " |

Now, the distance to Indo-European is at the level where confidence is very shaky and that to Afro-Asiatic is well off the scale. However, it is difficult to dismiss the apparently much closer relationships with Uralic, Dravidian, Etruscan and Basque. And the conclusion is as clear as daylight. The Altaic languages represent yet another branch of the same tree, with an approximate position as shown in the next figure. A split from the main Uralic stem must have occurred, in roughly 10500BC, and the Altaic languages have since changed at an average of 1.4 linguistic years per year. If my interpretation was right in the last chapter then the geographical location was Central Asia, somewhere east of the Caspian Sea. In fact, given that the Uralic language wave swept north to the Urals, with Basque and Etruscan being carried west into Europe, it would be most remarkable if related languages had not also been taken east, and the Altaic family logically represents that eastward movement.

Turning next to the distances between the four individual Altaic languages, Turkish, Uzbek, Mongolian and Manchu, and supplementing this information with data on four further languages using the numerals 1 to 10, the following family tree emerges.

The languages from Chuvash to Kazakh are clearly closely related. Furthermore, I know that I could have added Uighur, Turkmen, Azeri and others and found that they all lay in the same part of the family tree. These

Chapter 11    Huns, Mongols and Tatars                               145

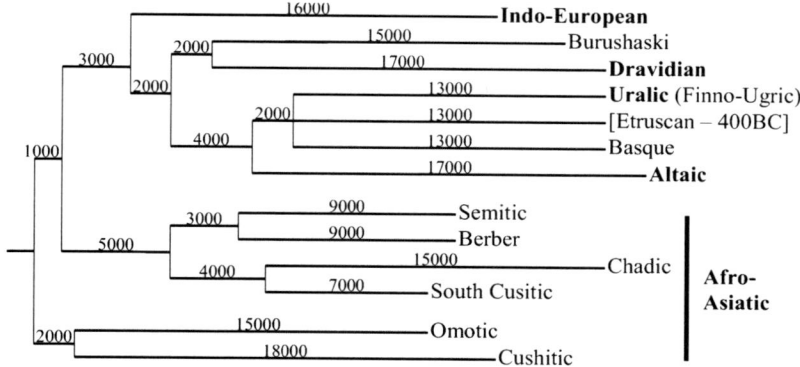

are the Turkic languages and most of them stem from the time of the great Turkic migrations across Asia from about the 7th Century AD to the 14th. Chuvash probably dates from the time of the Huns or the Avars. These migrations are known historically; they all stemmed from the Lake Baikal region of Siberia, as did the Hun and Tatar assaults on China.

However, the Mongolian and Turkic sides of the family clearly separated in the very distant past – about 8500BC if I assume an approximately constant language change rate through the millennia – and they have since gone their separate ways. The speech of the Khinsky culture of Lake Baikal from about 4000BC was almost certainly Turkic. Geography strongly suggests that the Mongolian branch spread south of the Altai Mountains through Dzungaria and into Mongolia, while Turkic took the more northerly route through Siberia. With the possible exception of some who reached China (see Chapter 12), speakers of neither branch knew agriculture until the Indo-Europeans (Iranian and Tocharian speakers) arrived in the region in around 1500BC[3], also bringing with them their knowledge of horsemanship, a knowledge which the Altaics first adopted and then improved, giving them the military edge and paving the way for future conquest. In fact, I suggested in the last chapter that an ability to centralise authority was a key to the success of Dravidian, Uralic and related cultures, and the evidence of Hun, Mongol, Ottoman Turk, Manchu and several other giant and unwieldy Altaic-speaking empires certainly reinforces this suggestion.

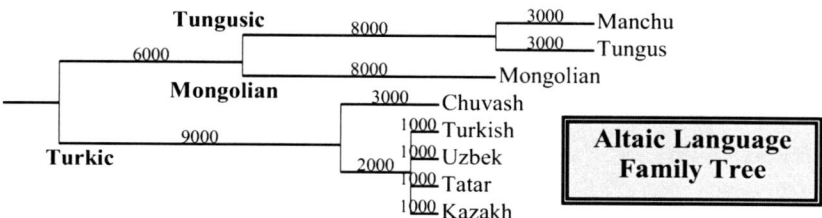

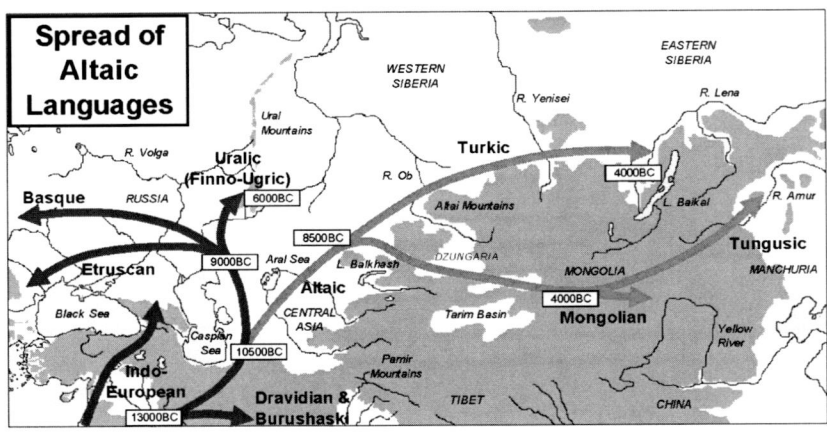

The other important language division shown, the separation of the Tungusic branch, must have taken place in about 4000BC. Tungusic speakers pushed ever eastwards and are now located in Manchuria (northern China) and the Russian far east, once again making the point that language change tends to correlate with distance moved. The current distance between Tungus and Manchu suggests an arrival in Manchuria at least 2000 years ago.

## OTHER NORTHERN TONGUES

But there's a lot more to northern Russia than the Uralic and Altaic languages encountered so far. I have already mentioned the Samoyedic branch of Uralic, spoken to the north of the Finno-Ugric zone. Then there are several other languages which would be classed under the umbrella name 'Palaeosiberian' (i.e. Old Siberian), which is really nothing more than a geographical description, since there is no uniformity among them. Nowadays, those few speakers who remain live in widely scattered communities, many still nomadic, across the far north and east of Russia.

Let's tackle the Samoyedic branch first. Nenets is the major member of the group. According to my measurement system, it comes out 31000 linguistic years from the Finno-Ugric languages and 32000 from Altaic, 35000 from Dravidian and well over 40000 from Indo-European, and the implication is that the Samoyedic languages branched off not long after the time that Uralic and Altaic themselves parted company. In fact, I have Nenets branching off the Altaic rather than the Uralic side – in about 9500BC. Speakers clearly moved north from Central Asia as global climate warmed rapidly after the Ice Age, finally ending up along the Russian north coast.

Chapter 11   Huns, Mongols and Tatars   147

Turning to the Palaeosiberian languages, there are basically four elements to consider. The first is Yukaghir, dialects of which were spoken until recently over a vast swathe of eastern Siberia, and which bears unmistakable similarity to Nenets (21000 linguistic years distant). The only feasible placement is as a division of Samoyedic, separating in around 6500BC; distances to Finno-Ugric and the Altaic family are quite consistent with this. You might note that this link with the Samoyedic branch of Uralic is not in the least controversial nowadays and many linguists speak of an Uralic-Yukaghir family.

Now for something much more controversial! On the shores of the Bering Sea we find Chukchi, Koryak and Itelmen, comprising the second element of Palaeosiberian, often known as the 'Chukchi-Kamchatkan' family. Here, Chukchi itself measures 29000 linguistic years from Samoyedic (i.e. Nenets and Yukaghir), 30000 from Finno-Ugric, 35000 from Altaic and 36000 from Dravidian, and on this evidence Chukchi-Kamchatkan must have branched off the Uralic stem even earlier than Altaic, in about 11500BC. But the problem is that this places its origins five thousand miles south-west of its current range! Yet in my view the measurements are close enough and numerous enough to allow no other conclusion. As Uralic speech headed north and Altaic went north-east, I am forced to conclude that speakers of an early Chukchi-Kamchatkan language took yet another route east. By a simple process of elimination, this had to be through the Tien Shan Mountains and into the Tarim basin, following the line of the Silk Road into China. And if this is true, the language spoken by the inhabitants of China's oldest village, Xinglong Wa in Inner Mongolia, dated to 6200BC, was probably ancestral Chukchi-Kamchatkan. In fact, this may also be the case for the whole millet-growing culture known as Peiligang (6500-5000BC) centred on the middle reaches of the Yellow River[4]. The language family and its culture must then have spread north-east into Manchuria and further still, right up to Kamchatka and the Bering Strait. The comparative lack of variation between today's Chukchi-Kamchatkan languages suggests that they have only quite recently arrived in their current location, probably within the last 2000 years[5]. Of course, this proposed route for the spread of Chukchi-Kamchatkan language, which represents a massive departure from conventional thought, has enormous implications for ancient Chinese history and this will be explored further in the next chapter.

Anyway, let's now turn to the third Palaeosiberian element, Nivkh, a language spoken on the Pacific coast and the island of Sakhalin north of Japan. On (painfully) working through my first and only piece of Nivkh literature, I was immediately struck by how close the grammar was to that of Chukchi with, according to my system of comparison, a significant similarity in vocabulary also. In fact, it measures just 14000 linguistic years

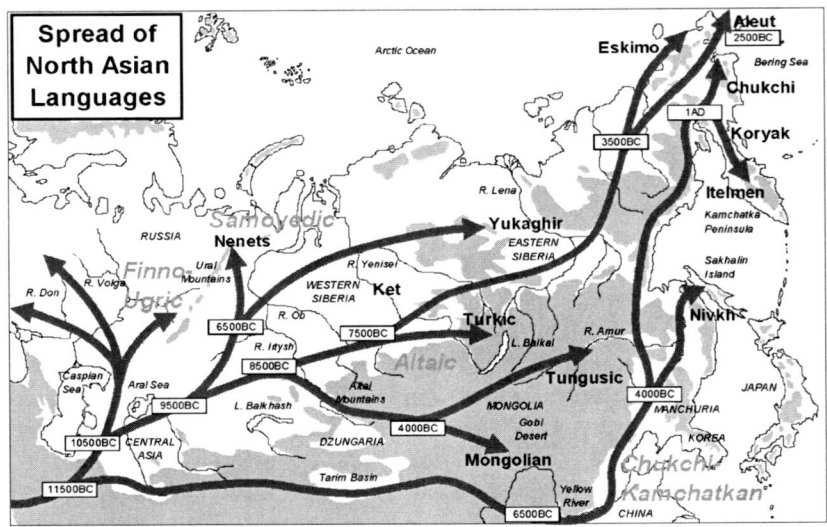

from Chukchi and has distances to the other families very slightly greater than those of Chukchi. I therefore have absolutely no doubt that Nivkh should be considered as a Chukchi-Kamchatkan language, and that it separated in about 4000BC, probably in central Manchuria. Indeed, I am slightly surprised not to see this connection more widely accepted. And this link between Nivkh and Chukchi-Kamchatkan at least provides some support for my suggestion that Chukchi-Kamchatkan was once spoken far to the south, in northern China, although I am slightly embarrassed at the greater change to Nivkh compared to Chukchi, for which I have no ready explanation.

The final Palaeosiberian group is known as the 'Yeniseian' family. Ket[6] is the sole survivor today, if not for many days more, although plenty of evidence has been found (place names, sub-strata in other languages) that the family was once much more widespread, covering a vast area of central and western Siberia. Several suggestions have been made linking Ket to Burushaski or to the Caucasian languages (see later in this chapter) and

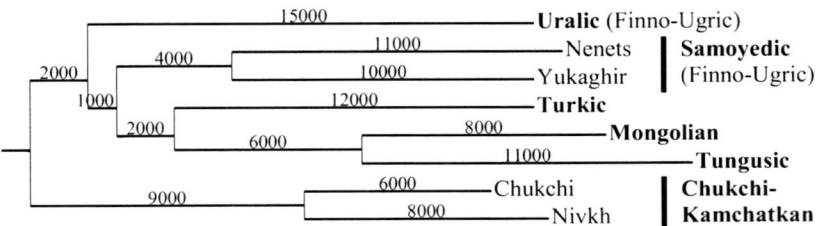

recently some distinguished linguists have presented evidence (based on vocabulary comparison) for relationship with the Na Dené family from North America[7]. Ket is therefore an intriguing oddity. And Ket genuinely is different from Uralic, Altaic and the rest of Palaeosiberian. For a start it is a tonal language, like Chinese, absolutely unique in the region. It agglutinates (adds numerous prefixes and suffixes), but in quite a different manner from the other north Asian languages. And by the system used in this book it is over 40000 linguistic years from Uralic, Samoyedic, Altaic and Chukchi-Kamchatkan. It is much further still from Dravidian, Indo-European and Afro-Asiatic. In fact, Ket stands as the first language encountered so far which, in my opinion at least, definitely cannot have been part of the great language wave which originated in East Africa in about 20000BC. Whatever the history of Ket culture, and I shall be returning to Ket later on, it is quite different from that of all the surrounding peoples.

## ESKIMO-ALEUT

But there is one further north-east Asian language which scores much closer to the Altaic family, to some extent even in its vocabulary but particularly in its grammar, and that is the absolute last language on the north-east corner of the Asian continent, namely Inuit, the language of the Eskimos. The range of the language nowadays is mainly Alaska, the islands of the Canadian Arctic and the giant island of Greenland, but a few speakers still remain in Asia. To complete the story of north-east Asia, it is essential to include Inuit, which then brings in the rest of a small family of languages called Eskimo-Aleut.

Eskimo-Aleut languages take agglutination to new heights. A single long Inuit word can easily translate into a sentence of 10 or more English words; such is the amazing diversity of language on planet Earth! The Eskimo languages are spoken on the mainland of Alaska as well as the high Arctic, where Inuit dominates; the Aleut languages are spoken on the Aleutian Islands, the chain of islands which reaches out from the coast of Alaska most of the way across the northern Pacific towards the Kamchatka Peninsula in Russia. The archaeological record tells us that colonisation of the Aleutian Island chain commenced, from Alaska, in about 2000BC[8], which implies that Aleut language had by then already reached Alaska. Colonisation of the high Arctic also commenced in around 2000BC, probably also by Aleut speakers[9], whereas we know from archaeology that the modern Eskimo culture originated much more recently, in about 1000AD, from the Asian side of the Bering Strait. Eskimo languages then went on to supersede Aleut throughout Alaska and the Arctic, and there is quite a noticeable difference between the culture of the earliest colonisers of the high Arctic and that of the more recent Inuit.

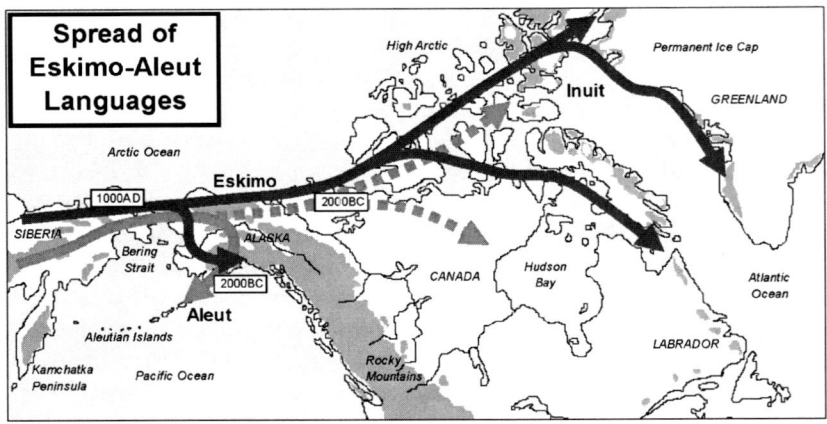

But this is all recent history; where did Eskimo-Aleut culture come from in the first place? According to my measurement system, Inuit averages only 27000 linguistic years from the Altaic family as a whole, and just 22000 from the Turkic branch; it is 23000 from Samoyedic, 29000 from Dravidian, 32000 from Finno-Ugric and 34000 from Chukchi-Kamchatkan. From this data, much the most likely interpretation is that the Eskimo-Aleut family originated as an offshoot of the Turkic branch of the Altaic family in around 7500BC somewhere in western Siberia. Bearing in mind the significant difference today between the Eskimo and Aleut branches, they must have parted company in about 3500BC in eastern Siberia, and it took a further 1000 years or so for Aleut language to reach Alaska.

By now it must appear to you that Siberia was unnaturally crowded during these ancient times! However, there are two good reasons for this. The first is that the millennia between about 8000BC and 3000BC were significantly warmer than today, allowing a much greater population. The second is that the only way to survive in the far north has always been to lead a nomadic existence, either following herds of wild animals (reindeer, elk) or else pasturing semi-domesticated herds. This inevitably means small mobile communities with vast distances between, and the possibility for groups of more than one language to share the same territory with little danger of ever coming into conflict. Siberia is a vast land. It may have a relatively low overall population but that population may be linguistically diverse.

For better or worse, I have stepped well beyond the bounds of conventional linguistic thought in this chapter, and in the next section I shall step further still! Perhaps it all seems logical enough to you – it certainly does to me – but I doubt very much whether you will read elsewhere of most of the connections I am suggesting. I am convinced that the main reason for this is that a vocabulary comparison is simply not sensitive enough to pick up many of these inter-relationships; they only appear when grammatical similarity is measured. Anyway, I hope you can now appreciate that a knowledge of these connections unlocks the door to a much fuller understanding of human history, and the particular door I now wish to unlock has traditionally been one of the most tightly shut of all.

## THE CAUCASUS MOUNTAINS

The Caucasus mountain range, located between the Black Sea and the Caspian, between Russia and the Middle East, is a remarkably diverse treasure trove of languages. Russian is spoken in the northern parts and Armenian in the south, both Indo-European languages. Turkish is spoken to the south-west and Azeri to the south-east, both Altaic languages. And we have also met the Iranian language Ossete, spoken right in the centre of the region. However, the word 'Caucasian' in the linguistic sense applies to the large number of other languages lying in between. They all share one common feature (and little else according to most commentators) and that is that they are all agglutinating languages, making extensive usage of suffixes. Many of them also share the distinction of being in the top rank for the sheer number of consonant sounds employed. But what could possibly lead to such a strange and varied set of languages right in the middle of what has been a pretty hectic zone of activity over the millennia? Joanna Nichols in her book *Linguistic Diversity in Space and Time* speaks of the Caucasus as a "residual area", a place where languages wash up and then remain. Her point is that language spread rarely seems to have washed right over the Caucasus but to have lapped around the edges, leaving traces but not obliterating what was there before.

Inevitably the Caucasian languages have tended to take on an air of mystery, particularly since the concept of a Dené-Caucasian super-family has been peddled, and this has hardly helped our understanding of their true place. Be that as it may, linguists usually manage to identify four different families within the small stretch of land which is the Caucasus; these are known as North-East, North-Central, North-West and South Caucasian. Let's visit them one at a time.

## SOUTH CAUCASIAN

The South Caucasian (also known as Kartvelian) family as it stands today is a small, closely inter-related group. Georgian, the principal language, has the following set of distance measurements to other families.

| to Dravidian: | 28000 | linguistic | years |
| to Burushaski: | 30000 | " | " |
| to Altaic: | 31000 | " | " |

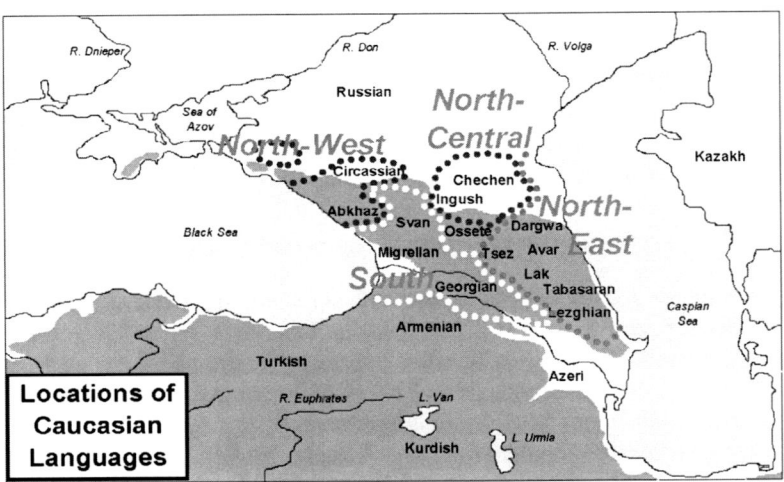

Locations of Caucasian Languages

| | | | |
|---|---|---|---|
| to Uralic-Basque-Etruscan: | 33000 | " | " |
| to Samoyedic-Yukaghir: | 33000 | " | " |
| to Chukchi-Kamchatkan: | 34000 | " | " |
| to Indo-European: | 43000 | " | " |

These distances are pretty unambiguous and can only sensibly fit one location. If you are a linguist then (unless you subscribe to the Nostratic super-family) you may be surprised to learn that South Caucasian is yet another offshoot of the great wave of Uralic-Altaic-Dravidian speech, separating as the wave progressed eastward through the Middle East. More specifically, it is a 13000 linguistic year long branch from the Dravidian stem and it separated in about 10500BC. The location was western Iran. At about 1 linguistic year per year, South Caucasian has since changed rather less than Dravidian, as befits a language family which has travelled less far. It seems that one of the languages which was 'left behind' in Iran as Dravidian speech expanded eastwards thrived and spread. It is not unlikely that peoples such as the Lullubi and Guti[10], known from Akkadian records to have inhabited the Zagros Mountains of western Iran in the 3rd and 2nd Millennia BC may have spoken South Caucasian languages. Judging by the current difference between Georgian and the other South Caucasian languages (Migrelian, Svan, Laz), the family has been spoken in its present location since roughly 1000BC[11].

## NORTH-CENTRAL CAUCASIAN

Moving north across the Caucasus range we find Chechen and the small North-Central Caucasian family. Chechen has the following distances to the other families.

## Chapter 11 Huns, Mongols and Tatars

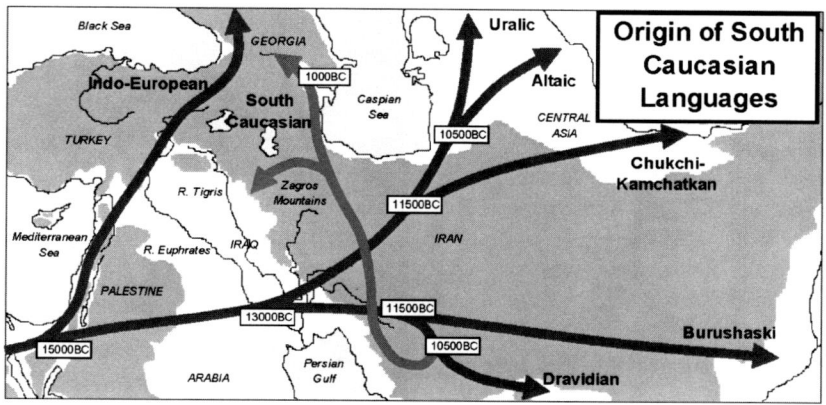

| | | | |
|---|---|---|---|
| to Altaic: | 30000 | linguistic | years |
| to Samoyedic-Yukhagir: | 36000 | " | " |
| to Uralic-Basque-Etruscan: | 38000 | " | " |
| to Burushaski: | 38000 | " | " |
| to Chukchi-Kamchatkan: | 43000 | " | " |
| to Dravidian: | 43000 | " | " |
| to Indo-European: | 48000 | " | " |

These distances are of the same sort of magnitude as those from Georgian but you will notice that they come in quite a different order – and they too give little room for manoeuvre regarding the placement of Chechen in relation to the other families. There is one location and one location only which fits the data and that is as an offshoot from the Altaic family, specifically from the Mongolian branch, and it separated in about 7000BC, at which time the language had probably reached the region east of Lake Balkhash, on the Kazakh-Chinese border. Since this time the North-Central Caucasian languages have changed by 18000 linguistic years, at a remarkable 2 linguistic years per year. This implies movement – and movement there must have been, from the Chinese border, back around the Caspian Sea to the Caucasus. Judging from the differences between the three languages which make up North-Central Caucasian, namely Chechen, Ingush and Bats, the family has been spoken in its current location for no more than about 2000 years, perhaps less.

## NORTH-WEST CAUCASIAN

My main North-West Caucasian representative is Circassian, spoken in pockets of Russian territory just north of the mountain range itself. Here, the calculated distances average 3000 linguistic years further than Chechen to all the families listed previously. It is a pretty consistent picture, and it strongly suggests that North-West Caucasian stems from the

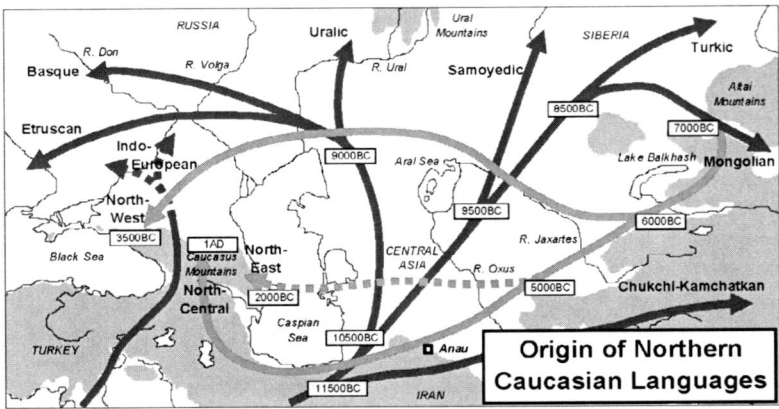

Origin of Northern Caucasian Languages

same offshoot of Altaic as North-Central. However, the two branches must have gone their separate ways in around 6000BC, while the language would still have been spoken far to the east of the Caspian Sea. So far as I can see, there is only one possible explanation: as North Caucasian culture spread west across the Central Asian plain, it flowed both north and south of the Caspian. Geography leads me to propose that North-West Caucasian probably represents the northern stream and North-Central the southern. The large difference between the two most important North-West Caucasian members, Circassian and Abkhaz, means that the ancestors of these two separated quite some time ago – my estimate is 3500BC – which implies that the language family reached the Caucasus at about that time. What is particularly interesting is that it must have displaced early Indo-European in order to get there, which suggests (logically enough) that Indo-Europeans only really managed to achieve serious dominance after their successful domestication of the horse[12]. Of course, since achieving dominance, they have been able to obliterate all trace of northern Caucasian speech right across the Central Asian plain.

## NORTH-EAST CAUCASIAN

So, if North-Central and North-West Caucasian are actually branches of Altaic then might North-East be yet another branch? As it happens, most linguists have come to the conclusion that North-Central and North-East are related and I would certainly agree; the two families probably separated in about 5000BC, judging by current differences. The present level of divergence suggests that they have been boxed into their corner of the Caucasus for quite a while now, probably at least since 2000BC, and the only remaining route they could have taken to get there would appear to be across the Caspian Sea itself – quite feasible by 2000BC.

# Chapter 11    Huns, Mongols and Tatars

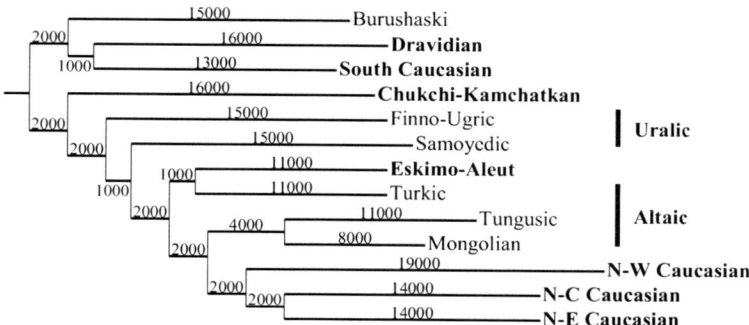

And so ends the story of Caucasian language. It's a bit of an anticlimax really! There is no Dené-Caucasian super-family, and no particularly special relationship with Basque or Burushaski. Once sober measurements are taken which include grammar, it becomes evident that all four Caucasian families are offshoots of the great Dravidian-Uralic-Altaic language wave. To me the most thought-provoking issue is the reason why speakers of the North Caucasian languages should suddenly have been able to spread their culture back across the Central Asian plain. Archaeologically, I believe that the ancestral North-Central Caucasian speakers can be identified with the inhabitants of the earliest crop-growing settlement levels at Anau and similar sites in Turkmenistan, visible from the 6th Millennium BC which, by the way, adds to the accumulating evidence that there is absolutely no general correlation between the spread of agriculture and that of language; Central Asian crops originated in Turkey or Iran.

## ANCIENT TONGUES

Having found a plausible answer to the Caucasian problem, let's now apply the same measurement system to some equally intractable problems posed by a set of four extinct languages from the Middle East area, the first and most problematic of which is Hattian (also known as Hattic). Unfortunately, however, I have to admit that our knowledge of this particular language is so limited that I doubt whether it will ever be possible to assign it a place with confidence and there certainly isn't sufficient material to carry out a full measurement here. We know of it from the records of the Hittite Empire, which occupied much of modern Turkey during the 2nd Millennium BC. The Hittite language, as we have seen, was Indo-European, but the Hittites gave a special recognition to Hattian as an already venerable language[13], presumably the former language of the region, and indeed the language which shared its name with that of the region, Hatti, and our term Hittite (the Hittites actually called their own language "Nesili"). Several experts have provisionally placed Hattian in the North-West Caucasian group; however I can't help noting that those words from my list of 26 which are known appear closest to Chechen, and therefore to the North-Central Caucasian family, which I have to say makes better sense geographically[14]. The placement shown in the next family tree is, however, no more than speculative.

Hurrian, my next language, was spoken over quite a wide area of the upper Euphrates and Tigris valleys through to western Iran in the 2$^{nd}$ Millennium BC, important enough to be the official language of the empire of 'Mitanni'[15], one of the rivals to ancient Egypt and Babylon. Much of our still very imperfect knowledge of the language comes from letters sent by one of the kings of Mitanni to the Egyptian pharaoh of the day. Fortunately, we know enough of Hurrian to carry out the necessary measurements and these confirm that its closest living relatives are those of the northern Caucasian families. Once more, the North-Central Caucasian language Chechen turns out to be closest, at 19000 linguistic years, and the distance implies that Hurrian split off in about 4500BC, while the language was still spoken in northern Iran. This agrees with archaeological evidence, which suggests that Hurrian culture arrived from the east, reaching northern Syria in about 3000BC[16]. It was eventually squeezed into extinction during the 1$^{st}$ Millennium BC by the massed forces of Persian, Greek, Armenian and Georgian.

However, there is another language, now long dead but much better known than either Hurrian or Hattian, which we should definitely take a look at. It is Sumerian[17]. Sumerian was the language of the first great Tigris-Euphrates civilisation, the language which, shortly before 3000BC, generated the first truly successful writing system in the world. Cuneiform, 'written' by impressing signs into a wet tablet of clay, opened the door which led a couple of thousand years later to the development of a true alphabet. What can be said then about the family connections of Sumerian? My closest measurements are to North-Central Caucasian (35000), Altaic (36000), Chukchi-Kamchatkan (36000), South Caucasian (37000), Burushaski (39000), North-West Caucasian (40000), Dravidian (41000), Afro-Asiatic (41000), Uralic-Basque-Etruscan (42000) and Indo-European (42000). In short, Sumerian seems to be about equidistant from all the families considered so far! There is certainly no placement possible which matches this well (perhaps partly because of the greater error present when categorising a dead or incompletely known language) and in fact it leaves me with two options. Either I must accept that the measurements to Uralic and Altaic are too high for some reason (by some 7000 linguistic years), or else those to the northern Caucasian families are too low. The first option sees Sumerian as an offshoot from Altaic in about 9000BC somewhere in Central Asia; the second as an earlier branch, from about 12000BC, while the parent language was still in western Iran. Given that the Sumerian-speaking civilisation of the Tigris and Euphrates plain originated in the

## Chapter 11  Huns, Mongols and Tatars

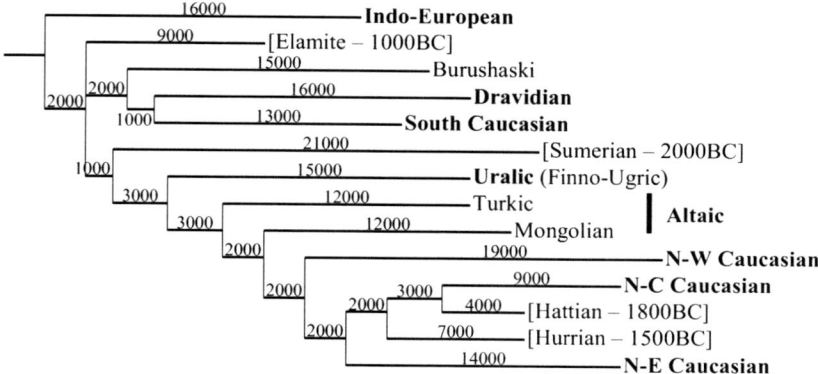

Zagros Mountains of Iran in about 6000BC, and given that the Zagros Mountains had been home to early agriculturalists since about 10000BC[18], the second option definitely looks favourite to me. The unexpectedly close measurement to North-Central Caucasian could then be put down to secondary contact since North-Central Caucasian culture spread through the northern Zagros from about 4000BC. Sumerian-speakers must have spilled out onto the Tigris-Euphrates plain in the 6th Millennium BC, before going on to create the world's first truly urban society, founding cities such as Eridu, Uruk and Ur[19]. The average rate of change from 12000BC to 2000BC (when Sumerian ceased to be a spoken language) was a surprising 2 linguistic years per year, perhaps a consequence of being for so long at the cutting edge of an ongoing technological revolution.

Three down; one to go! My final ancient tongue is Elamite, a language from southern Iran which many linguists have confidently linked to the Dravidian family[20]. It was the language of an important civilisation, centred on the city of Susa, which existed right through the 3rd and 2nd Millennia BC and into the 1st. The earliest scripts from Elam cannot yet be read, but those from the latter part of the 2nd Millennium and from the 1st have been deciphered and, although our knowledge is much less complete than it is for Sumerian, there is sufficient to categorize the language according to grammar and sound and to obtain at least some of the necessary vocabulary comparison. And the result is that Elamite is indeed found to be within striking distance of Dravidian, at 26000 linguistic years. It also comes out only 28000 from Uralic, Basque, Etruscan, Altaic and South Caucasian with slightly greater distances to the north Asian and northern Caucasian languages. It is also just 33000 linguistic years from Sumerian. And in this case there can be absolutely no doubt about the position of best fit. Elamite branched from the Dravidian-Uralic-Altaic wave in approximately 13000BC, just as it reached southern Iraq. Since that time it has changed only slowly, at about 0.8 linguistic years per year, which is exactly as it should be considering the lack of movement involved.

Chapter 11  Huns, Mongols and Tatars

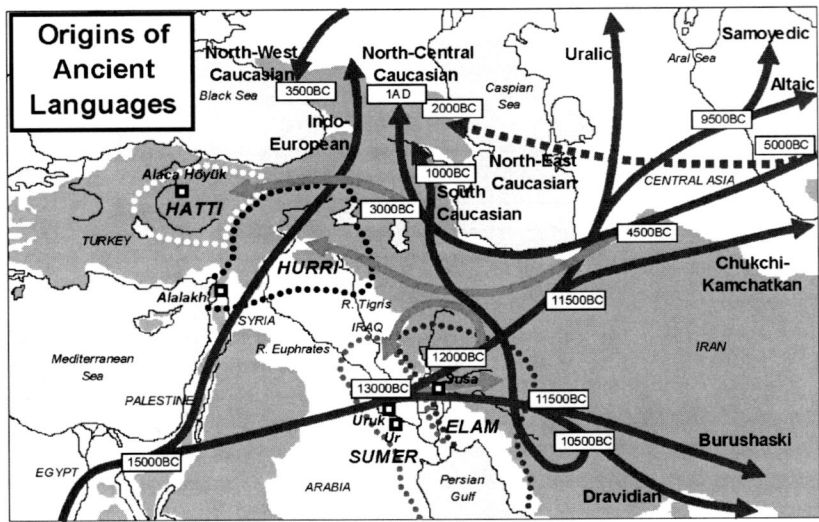

Let's take stock for a moment. Surely the most compelling reason for believing in the measurement method used in this book is that everything suddenly seems to make sense. No longer do we have four mysterious ancient Middle Eastern tongues but we have a sound-looking explanation for when and where each originated; no longer do we have inexplicable isolates like Burushaski, Basque and Nivkh but all are found to fit in perfectly logically; no longer do we have to concoct wild theories about the Caucasian languages or admit ignorance of the parentage of Eskimo-Aleut. In fact no longer need we talk in vague terms of a Nostratic super-family; we now know that it really exists and we can see how the members relate together. Even the fact that no relationship could be found for the Yeniseian language Ket might be seen as 'the exception that proves the rule'. Each individual finding might be considered questionable; taken together the picture is so consistent as to demand to be taken seriously. It even fits well with climatic factors, seeing a northward wave of language just as the planet suddenly warmed (in the 10$^{th}$ Millennium BC) following the last Ice Age. To be sure, it raises new questions, questions such as just when and why Chukchi-Kamchatkan language was displaced from northern China and just why the North Caucasian languages spread so readily westward. But at least the data is there to allow these questions to be asked!

However, I am now about to take you well beyond any scheme dreamed up by the most ambitious proponent of super-families. We are still left with a large chunk of east and south-east Asia unaccounted for, containing over a quarter of the world's population. Could they also be part of the same general picture? No linguist I know of would say other than "definitely not". Let's see.

# 12

# Behind The Great Wall

It has always been an irritant to proponents of European civilisation and the innate superiority of western thinking that the Chinese often got there first! Similarly, those who believe that the path to true civilisation could only have been taken once in human history and that it must have been transferred from that time and place to the rest of the world would also rather ignore eastern Asia. Europe can stake no claim to the discovery of agriculture – that honour is usually conferred on Turkey, Syria or Iran – but it is mildly annoying to some that the Chinese and other eastern peoples seem to have come up with the idea too, pretty much independently. They used their own native plants and animals and came up with an alternative agricultural system – in fact three, one based on rice, another on millet and a third on taro. Even in warfare where, it has to be admitted, Europe has excelled, we owe the discovery of explosives to the Chinese; at least, if the Greeks knew of them, the knowledge was lost for centuries. So how come China got there?

## INTRODUCING SINO-TIBETAN LANGUAGE

Few languages can be stranger to an English ear than those of the Far East. Chinese is so different in its sound that the majority reaction in English-speaking countries is not even to consider the possibility that an outsider could actually learn it. Perhaps part of the reason for this is the Chinese script, which is undeniably off-putting though intriguing and beautiful. The language itself has a certain sound quality, the tone rising and falling for no apparent reason at all. But these exotic languages are spoken by humans who are no different from the rest of the world in their ability to form sounds; the population is certainly related to that of the rest of the world, and so is the language. Besides, Chinese is not really so mysterious. The principal difference, which gives it its special sound quality, is that it is, like the majority of African and American languages, a tonal language. This means that it matters not only what consonants and vowels you pronounce but also whether your voice is at a high or low pitch and whether it is rising or falling. For instance, in Mandarin, *mei* means *beautiful* when spoken with a slight fall in the voice leading to a rise, but it means *not* if spoken with a continuously rising tone. There is a particularly well known example in the Thai language: *glai* means *far* in a level medium tone but *near* in a falling tone! You can see how confusing it can be for someone who is not used to tone control.

But, when all is said and done, use of tone in this way is simply a means to distinguish words in the same way that consonants and vowels are used (or click sounds in parts of Africa). However, you may be sure that use of tone would not simply be adopted or abandoned over night. It represents a considerably different way of speaking from any in Europe. In English we make some limited use of stress to distinguish a few words. For instance, *perfect* is an adjective meaning *flawless* when it is stressed on the first syllable but a verb meaning to *make flawless* if stressed on the second syllable, but we could still vary the tone (rising or falling) in either case without changing the meaning, other than to denote a question or an exclamation. In almost all the languages of Europe, northern Asia and the Indian subcontinent, tone plays no part or only a minor part in either distinguishing between words of different meaning or between different grammatical constructions. In fact Ket, the last surviving Yeniseian language, is the only exception we've met so far. But this is by no means the case for the majority of east Asian languages. By the way, I can thoroughly recommend John McWhorter's book *The Power of Babel* for a fascinating explanation of the reasons why languages tend to drift from one type into another, including suggested reasons for the development of tones.

So I hope I have prepared you for something different. But, if these languages are quite different from any in Europe, just how widely separated are they from each other? Chinese is by far the most widely spoken Asian language, being the mother tongue of about one fifth of the entire population of the world, if one includes variants such as Cantonese. However, it is but one member of the group of languages known by linguists as Sino-Tibetan. Linked to Sino-Tibetan by some, the Tai family includes Thai, as well as quite closely related languages stretching through Burma and Laos, and up into China. As there is clearly considerable disagreement among linguists as to whether these two families are really distinct, and some disagreement as to the composition of the Tai family, and as my own subjective experiences with both Chinese and Thai lead me to believe that they are most definitely related, I have decided to take them together here. After all, I have a measurement system and, for better or worse, I will be able to derive a measure of the linguistic distance between

# Chapter 12    Behind The Great Wall    161

| Linguistic years | Tib | Bur | Man | Can | Tha | Lao |
|---|---|---|---|---|---|---|
| Tibetan | 0 | 21000 | 39000 | 30000 | 35000 | 36000 |
| Burmese | | 0 | 34000 | 25000 | 32000 | 31000 |
| Mandarin | | | 0 | 3000 | 10000 | 9000 |
| Cantonese | | | | 0 | 6000 | 8000 |
| Thai | | | | | 0 | 600 |
| Lao | | | | | | 0 |

them. The grammar is undeniably very close indeed; many of the most common words seem to be related (for example *mei*, introduced above as *not* in Mandarin, is paralleled by *mai* in Thai) and I do not believe that the evidence from other parts of the world supports the view that such similarity can be explained purely by secondary contact.

So much for the introduction; the first step in evaluating the family (or families) is to carry out a full vocabulary, grammar and sound analysis on selected individual languages and, for this, I have chosen Tibetan and Burmese, often listed as being in the same sub-group, Mandarin and Cantonese, representing the Chinese sub-group, and Thai and Lao, representing the Tai languages. The above table gives the calculated distances between them.

Now, I am sure that those who consider Tai and Sino-Tibetan as quite distinct have correctly identified traits which distinguish them, and I shall suggest a possible reason why this should be a little later on. However, if I am right in considering my measurement system as related to the true root of a language, then there can be absolutely no doubt that the two Tai languages shown, Thai and Lao, share a close family relationship with Mandarin and Cantonese, with an average separation of just 8000 linguistic years. Burmese and Tibetan are obviously much more distant.

## CHINESE AND TAI LANGUAGES

Rather than tackling the whole Sino-Tibetan family in one go, let's adopt a slightly more cautious approach and check out what has become the most successful part of the family, the Chinese-Tai element. Besides Mandarin, Cantonese, Thai and Lao, I have added a further ten languages using the method of comparing numerals, and reworked the whole group into a family tree. The root point has been deduced by looking at distances to Tibetan and Burmese.

When the arrangement of this family tree is compared to the locations in which these languages are spoken, then the geographic origin of the whole group becomes very clear indeed, as shown on the next map. The dates are also quite tightly constrained. The start date of 3000BC

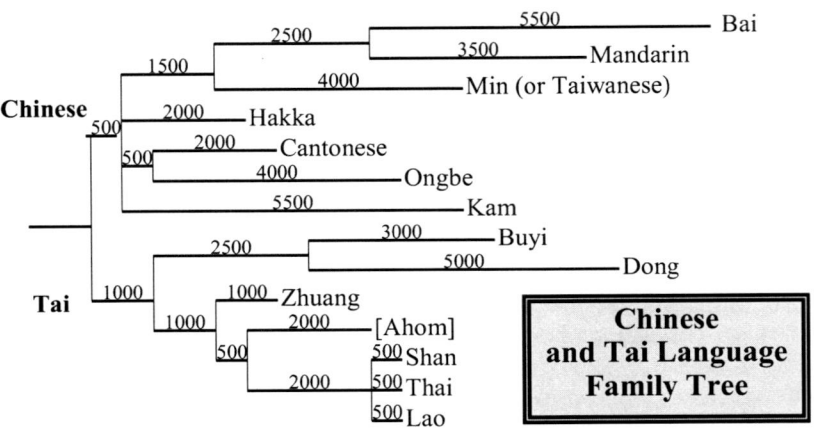

gives a slow change rate of 0.5 linguistic years per year for the least changed language, Hakka; in contrast, Bai must have changed at well over 2 linguistic years per year during its long journey west. Although the history of Bai speakers is a complete mystery, Bai culture is one of lowland rice cultivation and is therefore closer to that of Mandarin speakers than to that of surrounding tribes. The location of the language is probably the result of a migration up the Yangtze River during the 1st Millennium AD. In the south, the expansion of Thai and Lao, known from historical sources to have occurred within the last 1500 years or so, can be seen to have been paralled by movements of closely related speech into Burma (Shan) and north-east India (Ahom – now extinct).

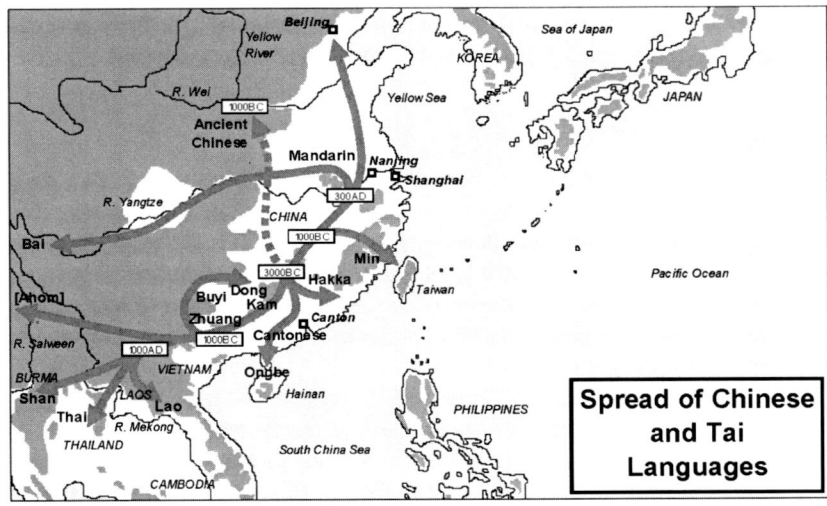

Chapter 12    Behind The Great Wall                                    163

Quite simply, these results turn Chinese cultural history on its head. In the last chapter I stated (highly controversially) that I doubted whether the millet growing Peiligang culture of the Wei and Yellow River area (6500-5000BC) was Sino-Tibetan-speaking, since the region appeared to lie on the path taken by Chukchi-Kamchatkan during its long march east. If the dates shown on the map are correct, then the succeeding Yang Shao culture (5000-3000BC) was also much too early to have been Chinese-speaking. A different branch of Sino-Tibetan would be a possibility, but the similarities which experts have noted between Yang Shao and the cultures of Central Asia[1] imply to me that it is much more likely to have been Altaic speaking, from the Mongolian-Tungusic branch; after all, Central Asia would by then have hosted North Caucasian tongues and the separation of North Caucasian from Mongolian-Tungusic had taken place as recently as 7000BC[2]. Furthermore, neither Lung Shan culture (3000-1500BC), nor the Shang dynasty (1500-1050BC), nor even the Chou period (1050-221BC) could possibly have seen languages ancestral to modern Chinese since all were civilisations of northern China, while modern Chinese was yet to cross the Yangtze River! We can read characters from Chou dynasty times (after 1050BC) easily enough because Chinese characters denote concepts rather than sounds[3], but the actual sounds would have been significantly different from those of today. Now, as it happens, linguists have been able to reconstruct the likely sounds of ancient Chinese numerals[4] from around 2000 years ago, based partly on the evidence of rhyming poetry, and this allows a direct check to be carried out. The result: ancient Chinese lies about 4000 linguistic years distant from the original Chinese-Tai language of 3000BC, but <u>not</u> on any of the modern sub-branches. Chou language and culture must certainly have reached the Yellow River region from the south, but quite independently from ancestral Mandarin. The language of Confucius (551-479BC) could be said to be 'Chinese' but it was not a direct ancestor of modern Chinese!

Yet it is undeniable that the principal early developments in Chinese civilisation took place in <u>northern</u> China. Yang Shao civilisation was pushed aside in about 3000BC by the culture we call 'Lung Shan', stemming from the region north of Shanghai. And Lung Shan speech was almost certainly Sino-Tibetan, as was that of the succeeding Shang dynasty – but the language was not a member of the modern Chinese-Tai branch[5]. The Shang emperors were, in their turn, ousted by the Chou[6], and the centre of gravity shifted once more to the Yellow River valley. The Chou dynasty slowly faded into the 'warring states' period, but the cultural centre during these times remained in the north. When the first emperor ruled in 221BC his homeland was the Wei river valley and so it continued throughout the succeeding Han Dynasty until the traumatic time between about 317 and 589AD during which Altaic speaking Tatars dominated the north of China. Recovery was followed by invasions by another Altaic people, the Kin, and then, in the 13th Century, came Kublai Khan and the Mongols. With each destructive wave of conquest from the north, the economic and cultural heart of China shifted south, to the major cities of Shanghai, Nanjing and Canton, particularly during the Southern Sung Dynasty, which ruled in parallel with the Kin. It was only during the Ming Dynasty (early 15th Century) that the capital moved north again, to Beijing, taking the Mandarin language with it. The written language had changed hardly at all since Chou times, but the spoken language of the Chou was at least as different from Mandarin as Cantonese is today (and I can assure you Mandarin and Cantonese are quite different languages despite the written versions being identical).

I make no apology for spending a little time on Chinese history. It provides a perfect example of the role of the study of language in allowing a proper appreciation of cultural history. The cultural history it reveals may not accord with what is traditionally taught, particularly the lack of a direct line of descent from ancient to modern Chinese, but it is based on fact. The placement of the Tai languages within the Sino-Tibetan family is also seen to be inescapable[7].

## THE WIDER SINO-TIBETAN FAMILY

But if we are to have any hope of discovering where the whole Sino-Tibetan family comes from, we need to look much wider afield than China, Laos and Thailand. There are Sino-Tibetan languages in Tibet, Nepal, eastern India and Burma. Now it is blindingly obvious from a scan of the literature that there is no agreement whatsoever between linguists as to just where this family's roots lie[8]. Southern China is often proposed; as you have seen it fits the bill for the Chinese and Tai languages. Some opt for northern China, although this seems to be based on nothing more than the realisation that many elements in modern Chinese culture (notably cuisine) can be traced back to Yang Shao civilisation. However, I am strongly of the opinion that eastern India or Bangladesh is much the most likely source, and I will try to explain why.

First, it is necessary to divide the family up into branches, and I am afraid there is no unanimity among linguists on that issue either. Nevertheless, progress is impossible without a decision and, based on my own measurements, I suggest that the following seven groupings can be discerned.

a) Chinese-Tai: as presented already;
b) Burmese: including the so-called Lolo languages of northern Burma and western China, the Kuki Chin languages of western Burma and also the Karen languages of south-east Burma;

# Chapter 12 Behind The Great Wall

c) Bodo-Garo: languages of Assam in eastern India;
d) Naga: languages from the extreme north-east of India;
e) Mikir-Meithei: from just south of the Naga languages;
f) Bodic: from Nepal and Tibet;
g) Kadai: from south-east China and Hainan Island.

Many (probably most) would disagree with my inclusion of the Kadai languages here, but, though they are undeniably distant, they have measurable similarities to some at least of the other Sino-Tibetan branches. Anyway, to investigate the inter-relationship between these seven groups of languages, I have compared a number of representatives (14 Chinese-Tai, 9 Burmese, 3 Bodo-Garo, 1 Naga, 1 Mikir-Meithei, 2 Bodic and 4 Kadai), resulting in the route map diagram shown. The distances derive from comparison of the numerals, but they compare reasonably with those from the full vocabulary-grammar-sound system where I have carried out both types of measurement.

Notice the fact that the Kadai and Chinese-Tai branches are the longest, yet Kadai languages are spoken in exactly the same region of southern China as we have just deduced for the source of Chinese-Tai speech. This is not at all what we would expect if that was the location of the original Sino-Tibetan tongue; the lengths of the branches should be shorter, reflecting lack of movement. On the other hand, the shortest branches, Bodic, Naga, Burmese and Bodo-Garo point very firmly to the north-east India region as the most likely point of origin. The lengths of the Kadai and Chinese-Tai branches might then be explained by the distance travelled to reach southern China.

Exactly which point on the route map represents the origin is much less certain. However, the connection shown between the Kadai and Bodo-Garo branches, geographically at opposite extremes, would be hard to explain unless the point of origin was somewhere near that junction, and indeed the following family tree and map assume that the origin is exactly

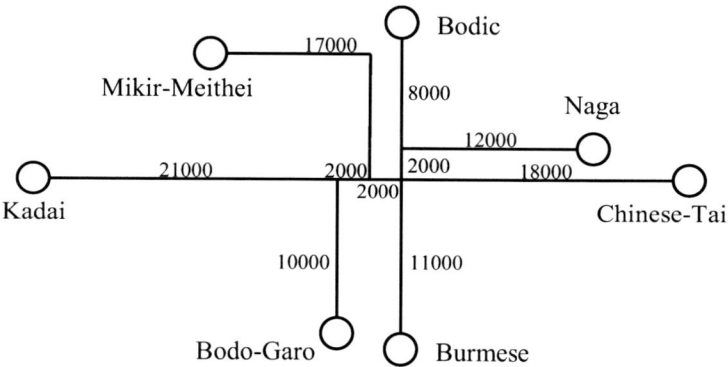

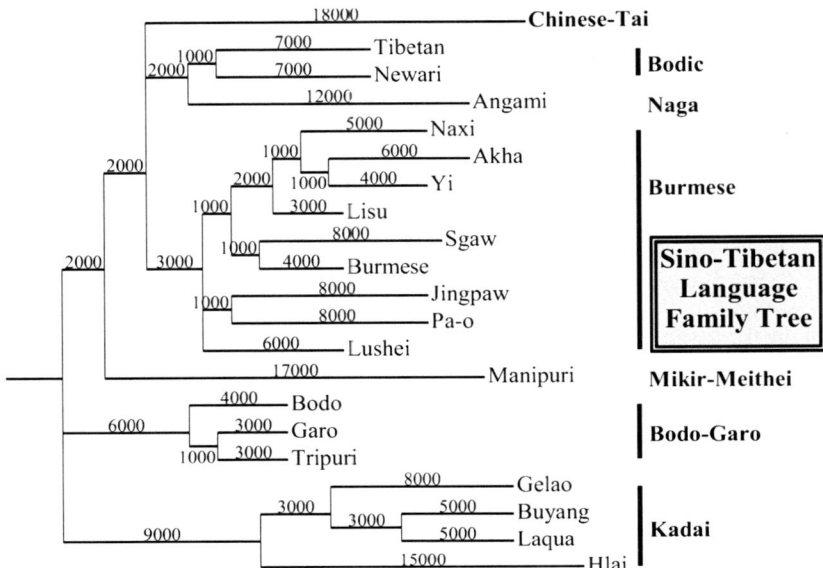

at the junction. This means that the Bodo-Garo languages become the least changed of all and it implies that the location of the original Sino-Tibetan tongue was probably in or around modern Bangladesh.

## AN EARLY HISTORY OF SINO-TIBETAN

As you can see on the map, I am suggesting 12000BC as an approximate date for the original Sino-Tibetan tongue. This allows the Bodo-Garo lan-

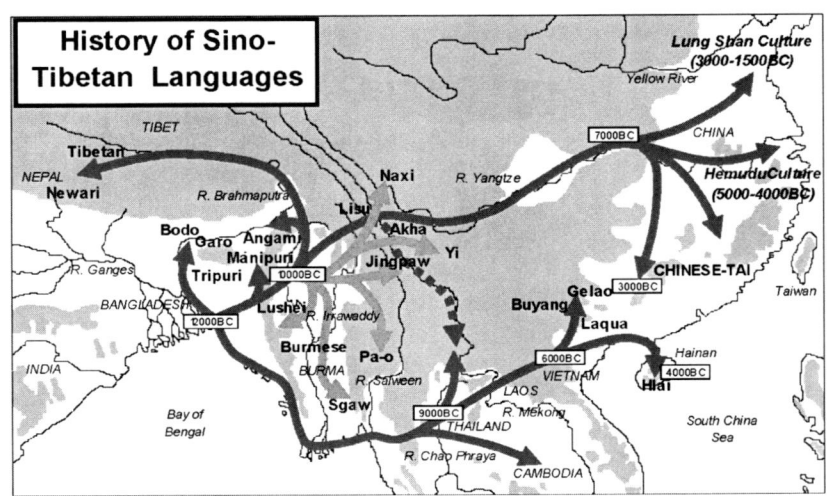

Chapter 12   Behind The Great Wall                                    167

guages to have averaged 0.7 linguistic years per year, the sort of rate we expect in settled hunter-gatherer societies. For whatever reason, the message is that a highly successful culture had either developed or arrived in Bangladesh by 12000BC, a culture which then spread in all directions. By 10000BC, the language was splitting into the ancestors of the Burmese, Chinese-Tai, Bodic and Naga languages, leaving ancestral Bodo-Garo in Bangladesh. And Kadai languages were already on their way to China. The most spoken Kadai language remaining today is Hlai (or Li), heard in the southern region of Hainan Island, off the Chinese coast; other related languages are spoken in the hills of south-east China and across the border in Vietnam. However, the difference between Hlai and the other members of the Kadai group is a massive 26000 linguistic years, and it is hard to envisage a separation date any later than about 6000BC, giving rates of change of 1.4 to 1.9 linguistic years per year since (and a rate of 1.5 linguistic years per year during earlier millennia, from 12000 to 6000BC). In northern Thailand and Laos, the culture known as Hoabinhiam, famous for its cave art, is discernible from about 9000BC, with the development of pottery and, probably, gourd cultivation from the 7$^{th}$ Millennium BC. Hoabinhiam surely represents this spread of Kadai culture across the Chao Phraya and Mekong river basins. In Hainan, clear evidence for human habitation has been found from about 4000BC and I would suggest that this was the approximate date at which the ancestors of the Hlai speakers first arrived.

And east of the Mekong in western China flows the Yangtze, leading directly into central China, and it is on the middle reaches of the Yangtze river in about 9000BC that the first disputed evidence for rice growing appears in the form of husk impressions on ceramics; by 7000BC, it is claimed that Yangtze valley sites such as Pengtoushan and Jia Lake show evidence for paddy fields[9]. Rice is thought to have first been domesticated from the wild Indica rice plant, which grows over a wide region from north-east India to the upper Yangtze valley in China. Thus Sino-Tibetan speakers, moving down the Yangtze valley, would appear to be prime candidates for initiators of this crucial step in mankind's development. Rice agriculture, presumably accompanied by Sino-Tibetan language, then spread across all of central and southern China; rice farming also spread to South-East Asia, probably down the Mekong river[10].

The final twist to the language story came in about 3000BC when the Chinese-Tai and Kadai branches met once more, in the hills of southern China. It was a showdown which the Chinese-Tai languages won handsomely and the Tai sub-branch eventually spread south right across Kadai territory. This is surely the reason why the languages which I have termed 'Tai' have been bracketed by so many linguists with those for which I have reserved the term 'Kadai', even though the computations presented here imply that their true relationship is actually very distant. Undoubtedly secondary contact has seen many of the traits of Kadai speech rubbing off onto the Tai languages, to the confusion of many[11].

## SINO-TIBETAN ORIGINS

Now that a date (12000BC) and a place (Bangladesh) have emerged, it's time to ask the big question. Did the Bangladeshis of 12000BC achieve the advances which led to Sino-Tibetan culture themselves, or did the ideas come from somewhere else? In language terms, can Sino-Tibetan be linked with any other family? Well, the measured distances from most of the Sino-Tibetan languages to most of the other languages of the world are undeniably large and it forces one to admit the possibility that Sino-Tibetan may have evolved independently, perhaps from the very first human languages ever to reach eastern India some 50000 years ago, in which case we could never realistically hope to see any connection with the language families covered in previous chapters. But is this really the case? I can't help noticing that at least one Sino-Tibetan language, Tibetan, measures significantly closer (using the full vocabulary-grammar-sound system) to two of the other families, namely:

> Tibetan to Afro-Asiatic:      41000 linguistic years
> Tibetan to Indo-European:      42000    ″      ″

Burmese measures just a few thousand linguistic years further away than Tibetan. These measurements are certainly compatible with the existence of a connection, albeit a very distant one, with the Afro-Asiatic/Indo-European tree; but where? Is there any part of the great super-family described as 'Nostratic' in the last chapter which measures significantly closer than 40000 linguistic years?

The answer, I am pleased to say, is a clear "yes" and, unlikely though it may seem, the closest languages are to be found in the Cushitic branch of Afro-Asiatic (a branch which, incidentally, includes tonal languages), with a short 30000 linguistic years between Tibetan and Somali. As a check on this, a comparison of the numerals gives me 35000 linguistic years between an average of 4 Cushitic languages and 3 Bodo-Garo languages (the Bodo-Garo languages being the least changed from the Sino-Tibetan family). Needless to say, this connection is not one which you will see proposed outside this book.

Now, while I am certainly not going to stake my life on the relationship between Cushitic and Sino-Tibetan being genuine, the acid test is surely whether it makes any sense. So, what about the timescale involved and the geographical implications? Well, geographically, the two fixed points are the Red Sea coast of East Africa and Bangladesh, separated by a distance of about 3500 miles, more if the coastal route around India is

Chapter 12    Behind The Great Wall                                    169

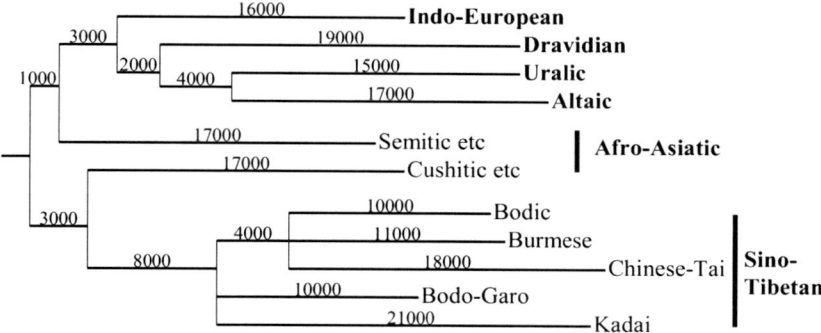

taken. Regarding timescale, separation from the Cushitic branch would have to have taken place in about 17000BC (if earlier deductions for Afro-Asiatic were correct). Thus, the language would have taken just 5000 years to reach Bangladesh, averaging 15 to 20 miles per generation, very rapid movement reflected in rapid language change (1.6 linguistic years per year). However, by the standards seen elsewhere neither the speed of travel nor the change rate is particularly unusual – which of course means that it could all be true!

Now one thing is crystal clear. If this language spread actually occurred, someone somewhere could build boats, otherwise the Red Sea could never be crossed – although it would have been much narrower than today because of the much lower sea levels in 17000BC, close to the coldest part of the Ice Age. But once boat travel is introduced, it becomes easy to envisage a rapid spread of fishing culture[12] along the Arabian coasts, across the then narrow and shallow Persian Gulf, basically just a river

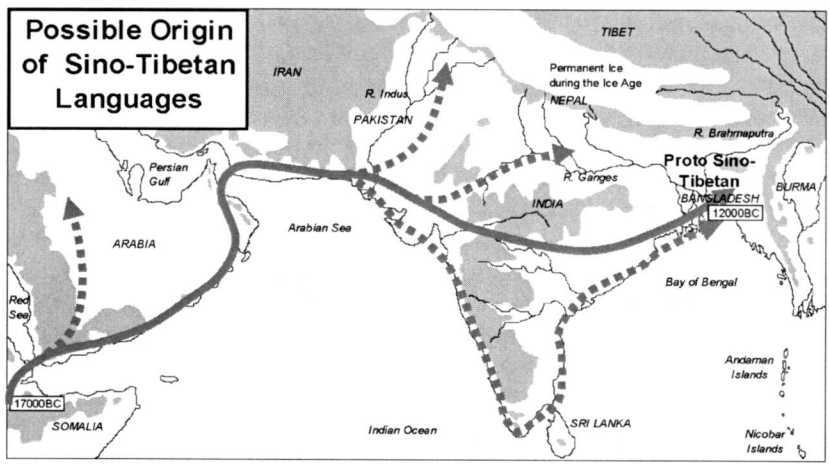

mouth in those days, and along the Makran coast to India. All along these coasts, the prevailing ocean current is eastward, toward India[13], and it could easily have been that 'progress' resulted from accidental sea journeys on more than one occasion.

I think all I can do here is to put the proposal on the table. There is every reason to suspect that the advanced culture of East Africa would not only spread north down the Nile but would also spill across the Red Sea; after all, the Arabian coast would have been clearly visible just 15 miles away, and curiosity is hardly an uncommon human trait! And if it did cross, there is good reason to expect that it would have spread rapidly east. Archaeologically, we know that microlithic technologies had reached the Indus valley no later than 10000BC, although it is of course impossible to be sure whether early Sino-Tibetan speakers had a hand in these developments.

I confess to being happy to have stirred up a hornets' nest in China. It's about time Chinese prehistorians freed themselves from the straightjacket of politically correct thinking! However, let's now leave China and head south, to one of the trickiest language families of all, Austro-Asiatic, a family whose history will prove to be crucial to a proper understanding of the spread of civilisation within South-East Asia and far beyond.

## THE AUSTRO-ASIATIC CONUNDRUM

You may remember that the example I gave back in Chapter 4 was the measurement of distance from Vietnamese to Cantonese, and it wasn't particularly large. It was a mere 17925 linguistic years, similar to the distance between two branches of Indo-European. And that was no isolated result. The average from Vietnamese to Mandarin, Cantonese, Thai and Lao comes out to be only a little over 21000 linguistic years. Yet Vietnamese is supposed, according to all the books, to be in quite a different family, the Austro-Asiatic (meaning south Asiatic) family. So just what is going on? Are the experts wrong? Is Austro-Asiatic just another branch of Sino-Tibetan?

Take a look at the next map. This is clearly a rather widely dispersed family and it does not look at all straightforward to explain its current distribution; so far as I am aware, no-one has. There are pockets of Austro-Asiatic in India (and Nepal) amounting to a few million speakers, in discrete areas stretching from the east coast right into the centre of the subcontinent; these are generally referred to as the 'Munda' languages. In north-east India, the Khasi speakers are best known for inhabiting the wettest place on earth, the Khasi Hills. Further east there are Austro-Asiatic speaking tribes in eastern Burma (speaking 'Wa' languages). Next comes the 'Mon-Khmer' branch; the once powerful Mon people straddle the Burmese-Thai border, while Vietnamese and Khmer are still impor-

## Chapter 12  Behind The Great Wall

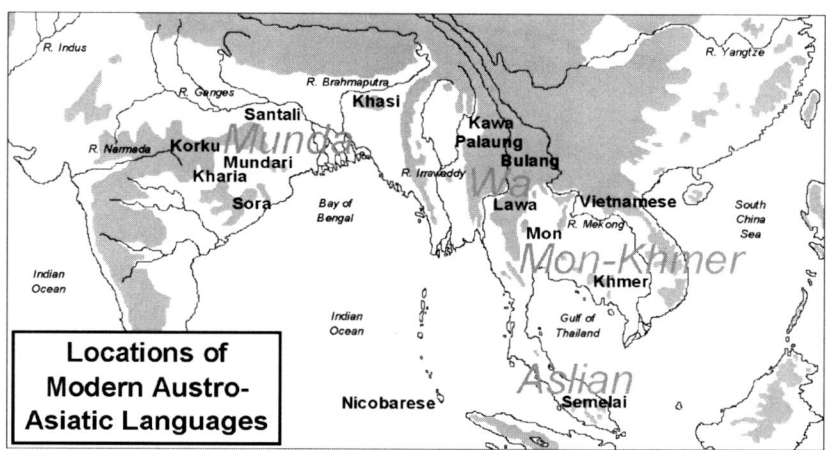

Locations of Modern Austro-Asiatic Languages

tant national languages. Unlikeliest of all are the Austro-Asiatic speaking hill peoples in the southern part of the Malaysian peninsula (speaking 'Aslian' languages) and those on the Nicobar Islands in the Indian Ocean.

So is this family simply part of Sino-Tibetan? As we have seen, at an average of 21000 linguistic years Vietnamese is relatively close to the Chinese and Tai languages. So is Mon. So, if I carried out the measurements, would Khmer and all the Wa and Aslian languages be. It looks like pretty strong evidence – except that, on closer inspection, a most peculiar pattern emerges. Normally two languages just 21000 linguistic years apart (for example Tibetan and Burmese) have a significant score for vocabulary similarity (0.308 on the 0 to 1 scale in the case of Tibetan and Burmese) and also for grammar (0.385 for Tibetan and Burmese). Turning to the average for Mon and Vietnamese relative to the Chinese and Tai languages on the other hand, we find just 0.106 for vocabulary (not far above the coincidence level) but a massive 0.734 for grammar! Now this may seem like a trifling detail to you but it is actually so unusual that there is absolutely no way this relationship is that of a normal family. It exists, there's no denying it; but it is most certainly not a normal family tie.

OK; are there any other possible connections? Well, not for the Mon-Khmer languages; all other families score significantly more than 40000 linguistic years. However, it is quite a different story at the other end of the Austro-Asiatic world. The Indian language Santali, also spoken in parts of Nepal, comes out only 27000 linguistic years from the Samoyedic languages, 29000 from the rest of the Uralic family (including Basque and Etruscan) and also from Chukchi-Kamchatkan, and between 30000 and 35000 linguistic years from Altaic, Dravidian, Burushaski and Elamite. And this time the relative vocabulary and grammar measurements are more or less of the expected pattern. If we didn't know that Santali was an

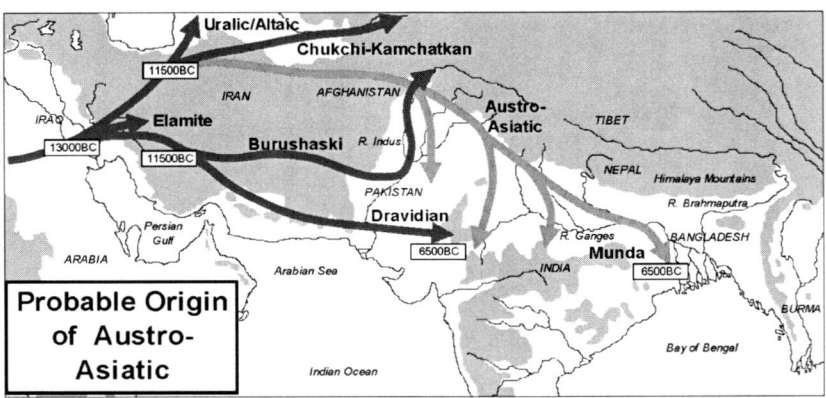

Austro-Asiatic language, we would have no hesitation in assigning it a place as yet another offshoot from the remarkable Uralic-Altaic-Dravidian language wave, separating in about 11500BC somewhere in Iran[14]. This would mean that, while Dravidian and Burushaski were spreading across southern Iran, ancestral Munda (and therefore ancestral Austro-Asiatic) speech would have been heard in northern Iran, spreading east through Afghanistan, northern Pakistan and the North Indian plain[15].

This is clearly a most complex family! It is hard to deny that the Munda branch has *bona fide* ancestry as a member of the Nostratic clan; yet the Mon-Khmer languages are grammatically close to Sino-Tibetan for some reason. What about the relationship between Munda and Mon-Khmer? Perhaps unsurprisingly, things look decidedly odd here too. The average vocabulary score between Santali and Vietnamese-Mon is 0.212. There's nothing particularly wrong with that; it suggests a separation of 20000-25000 linguistic years. However, the corresponding grammar score is just 0.074, well <u>below</u> the coincidence level! It seems that, for some reason, the non-Munda Austro-Asiatic languages are a blend of Munda vocabulary and Sino-Tibetan grammar! Never mind; let's be practical about it. If I can't trust the grammar scores, I'll just have to construct a family tree based on vocabulary alone (the sound element counts for very little anyway), and I might as well bring in other family members using the numerals 1 to 10. Admittedly, the root point is far from certain, but the family tree shown represents my best assessment of the data.

## A SUGGESTED HISTORY OF
## THE AUSTRO-ASIATIC FAMILY

I personally am now pretty confident that the picture I am about to paint is the solution to a conundrum on which the linguistic community has not

# Chapter 12  Behind The Great Wall

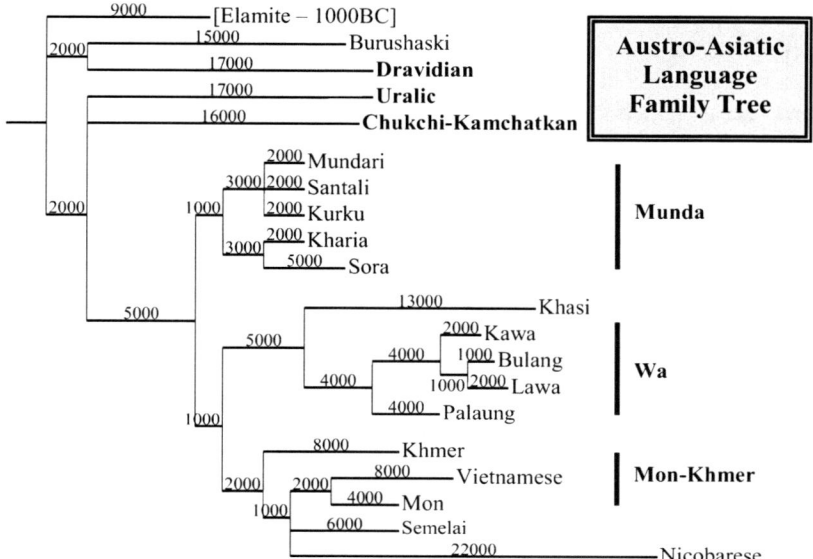

yet come remotely close to any conclusion. In fact, the linguistic community only relatively recently convinced itself that the Munda languages were actually related to the rest of the Austro-Asiatic family.

Let me start at the end of the story, the Mon-Khmer end. Today, Khmer and Vietnamese are widely-spoken national languages, while Mon has suffered under the hand of Thai and the Burmese languages. But only a few centuries ago Mon was king, both in large parts of modern Thailand and also in Burma. The picture in South-East Asia has changed both radically and rapidly. The dominance of Thai and Lao is a very recent phenomenon. There is every reason to suppose that the greater part of modern Vietnam, Laos, Cambodia and Thailand was under the Austro-Asiatic banner only a millennium ago. Turning to the language tree, Vietnamese seems to have left Mon rather than the other way round, simply judging by the lengths of the branches. This would make most sense if the two languages had parted company somewhere in Thailand, with Mon more or less staying put while Vietnamese continued on to the north, towards northern Vietnam. If I estimate that Mon has averaged 1 linguistic year per year – it didn't move but it has had a rough time in recent centuries – this puts the split with Vietnamese at roughly 2000BC. Vietnamese would have changed at a rapid 2 linguistic years per year, first because of movement into northern Vietnam and then south down the coast, and secondly because it has been dominated by Chinese culture for much of the last 2000 years[16].

And how can we be sure that Vietnamese didn't simply spread directly east from Thailand? Because the ancestor of Khmer was already being spoken in eastern Thailand and Cambodia. It would probably have separated from the ancestor of Mon and Vietnamese in around 4500BC, giving a moderate 1.2 linguistic years per year of change in both branches. It would seem that these Austro-Asiatics readily managed to dominate the previous cultures of South-East Asia (probably the Kadai branch of Sino-Tibetan). Archaeologically, Ban Chiang and related sites in Thailand indicate a sophisticated rice-based economy from the mid 4<sup>th</sup> Millennium BC, with evidence for use of bronze at a relatively early though still disputed date. The enduring success of this culture may be at least partly due to speakers of Mon-Khmer language[17].

But where did these Mon-Khmer people come from? The answer has to be Malaysia, or at least the peninsula which leads to Malaysia. The Malaysian language Semelai (a representative of the Aslian branch of the family) is shown as dividing from Vietnamese and Mon at a date which must be around 4000BC. Yet Aslian languages are spoken far to the south, across the Gulf of Thailand. Not only so but Nicobarese also diverged at about the same time. This can only mean one thing; the Austro-Asiatics were seafarers, and were establishing settlements around the coasts and islands of South-East Asia by the 5<sup>th</sup> Millennium BC. In fact, without sea travel I can see no way to explain the Austro-Asiatic family, wherever their point of origin. A remnant of that seafaring tradition can be seen in the 'Oran Laut' people of the Indonesian coasts[18], a people who literally live their lives on board their distinctly primitive ships. It was probably their ancestors who, in more prosperous times, were responsible for the spread of Austro-Asiatic culture around the South-East Asian coasts. It seems highly likely that they settled, traded and transmitted their language and culture in numerous locations throughout Malaysia and Indonesia. Nicobarese, with a change rate of over 3 linguistic years per year since 4000BC, has clearly had a disturbed history; it is probably the last remnant of the ancient Austro-Asiatic speech of the island of Sumatra[19].

So, a picture is emerging of an international trade language of the coasts of the Gulf of Thailand and the Andaman Sea, spoken by practitioners of the top culture of the day, a people who had mastered the art of seafaring. Judging by the family tree, the early 6<sup>th</sup> Millennium BC saw the establishment of a colony on the southern coast of Burma, a colony whose culture then spread inland, up the Salween river. By about 3000BC they had settled the lower Salween valley and the languages had started dividing into the ancestors of Palaung and the other Wa languages.

The division between the Munda languages of India and the rest of the family must have taken place in about 6500BC, somewhere in eastern India or Bangladesh. Munda-speaking culture had by then spent 5000 years spreading steadily across northern Iran, Pakistan and India at some 12 miles per generation and changing at 1.4 linguistic years per year. But, some time between 6500 and 6000BC, a most dramatic event must have

Chapter 12   Behind The Great Wall                                            175

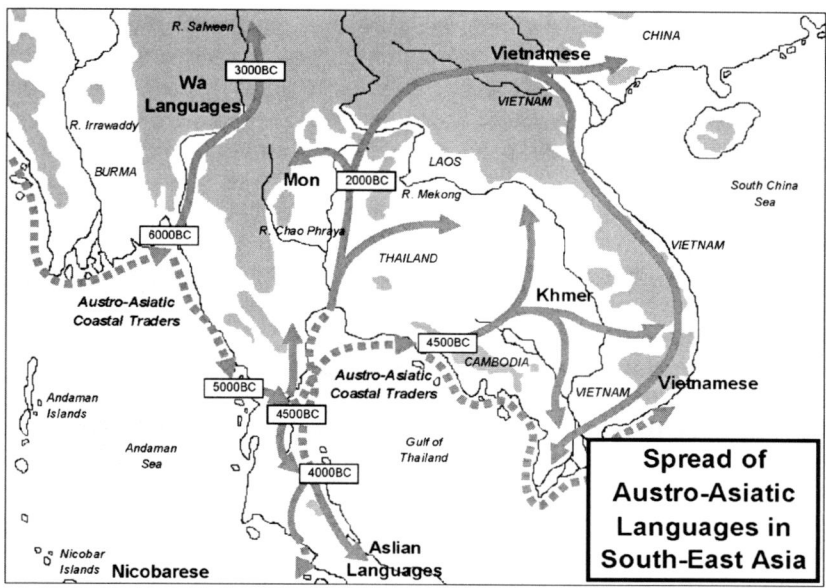

occurred. For some reason a particular group started speaking a version of the language in which the basic vocabulary was left intact but the grammar was altered out of all recognition. Only one explanation fits the evidence. Controversial though the suggestion may be, the language of the Austro-Asiatic seafarers was a 'pidgin'.

Pidgin languages arise when two or more peoples with different languages need to communicate. The slave trade produced pidgins all over the world, as slaves from different races found means to communicate; they tended to take the words from the dominant language, often English or French, but then to use those words in an initially almost grammarless way. Of course certain grammatical conventions would have to evolve in order to allow proper understanding, but the grammar of the pidgin might bear little resemblance to that of the donor language. Pidgins have also developed in order to facilitate trade; Bazaar Malay, the trade language used throughout the islands of Indonesia, is a good example. In the case of Austro-Asiatic, not only does 'pidginising' explain the remarkable difference in grammar between the Munda languages and the rest of the family but it also explains the grammatical closeness of the rest of the family to Sino-Tibetan. Assuming the analysis of Sino-Tibetan presented earlier in this chapter to be broadly correct, it is quite certain that the inhabitants of eastern India, Bangladesh and the coasts of Burma prior to the arrival of the Austro-Asiatics were Sino-Tibetan speakers. Of course, we can only guess at the circumstances which gave rise to the pidgin but, once this explanation is accepted, it becomes not in the least surprising to find that both

Mon and Vietnamese are grammatically close to Chinese. However, this has less to do with the last 2000 years of Chinese influence (a commonly quoted cause, and admittedly a contributory factor) than with events some eight millennia ago. Pidginising seems to me to be a plausible, commonsense, answer to what I called the Austro-Asiatic conundrum.

The fusion of Munda and Sino-Tibetan cultures produced a strong community with a high level of technology and it was this community who learnt to master the sea. Sino-Tibetans, the cultural descendants of those who first crossed the Red Sea, had used boats for millennia, and doubtless already travelled the coasts of the Bay of Bengal. However, the speakers of pidginised Austro-Asiatic were clearly willing to take seafaring to a new level. They ventured ever further from coastal security, making their way rapidly around the lands of South-East Asia. And the impact of this particular culture would eventually be felt much farther afield, as we shall see in the next couple of chapters.

While this explosion of seafaring Austro-Asiatic culture was taking place, the Munda languages of India steadily went their own way, changing at about 0.7 linguistic years per year, as expected for a settled hunter-gatherer society. One has to suppose that Munda-related speech dominated all of northern India for several thousand years, and linguists have indeed found evidence for a substratum of Munda words in both northern India and Pakistan[20]. Munda languages now form a remnant in an Indo-European sea.

But Khasi, though an Austro-Asiatic language spoken in India, is most certainly not a Munda language. Its roots are quite clear from the family tree. As Wa languages filled the Salween valley, some speakers spread their culture much further north and they eventually reached the extreme north-east of India and the Brahmaputra valley. And today, even after the arrival of the Indo-Europeans with their military might, that culture still survives high in the Khasi hills.

## THE FINAL PIECE IN THE JIGSAW

And there is yet one small piece outstanding in the language mosaic which makes up inland South-East Asia; it is what linguists usually term the Miao-Yao family (although variant names are used), spoken in southern China and now also in Vietnam, and I have the impression that quite a large number of linguists would now group Miao-Yao with the Austro-Asiatic family. Its principal language, Hmong, comes out just about the same distance from the Chinese and Tai languages as do Vietnamese and Mon. However, as with Vietnamese and Mon, the greater closeness in vocabulary is with the Austro-Asiatic family, including the Munda languages. And the greatest closeness of all is with the Wa branch of the family, at distances of some 25000 linguistic years. In fact, I have absolutely no

Chapter 12    Behind The Great Wall                                177

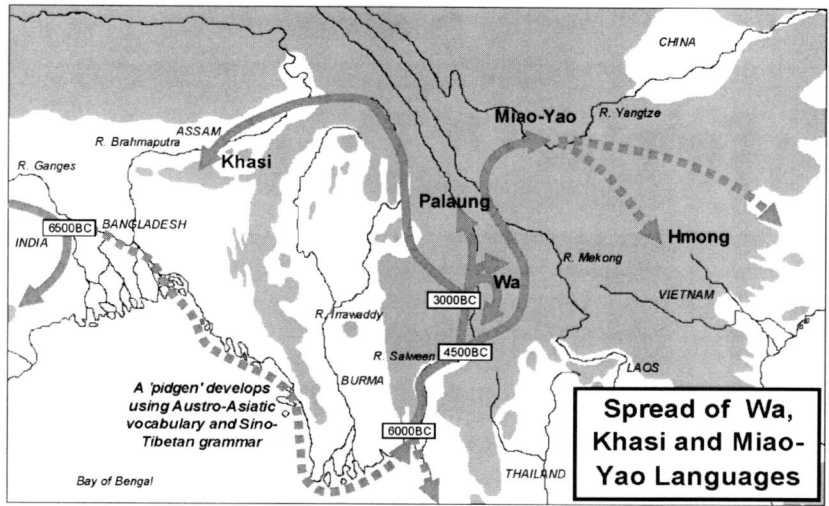

doubt that, while Austro-Asiatic culture was making its way up the Salween river valley, it divided several times. Not only did one group end up in north-east India, now being found only in the Khasi hills, but another group travelled north to the river valleys of southern China. As with Khasi, the rate of change to the language would have been considerable due to the distance travelled; as with the Khasi people, it would be extremely difficult to hazard a guess as to how extensive their territory once was. All that is certain is that the rejuvenated Sino-Tibetan-speaking peoples have, for well over 1000 years, been pressing Hmong and its relatives back into the hills (and south into Vietnam).

And so ends a remarkable tale. It is certainly the story of the spread of a culture or cultures. In some instances it would have involved the migration of a people, certainly where overseas travel was concerned. But the bottom line is that both Austro-Asiatic (including Miao-Yao) and, probably, Sino-Tibetan (including Tai and Kadai) stem from the same ancestral East African tongue as all the other language families dealt with so far. They took different routes, both physically and in terms of language ancestry, but ended up sharing South-East Asia between them. At this stage, it looks as though all the world apart from the small patch of Siberia where Ket is still spoken is culturally descended from the same East African community!

But let's now push eastward another notch. For whatever the early seafaring achievements of Austro-Asiatic culture, they pale into insignificance compared with those of the real masters of the sea. It may sound impressive to criss-cross the Bay of Bengal and the Gulf of Thailand, but our next group have gone a great deal further than that. It is time to meet the Austronesians.

# 13

# Peoples Of The Pacific

We have now traced the great, seemingly unstoppable 'Nostratic' language wave from Africa to the Pacific and even (in the case of Eskimo-Aleut languages) across the Bering Strait to America. In the last chapter we encountered the precocious seafaring Austro-Asiatic culture as it steamed down the Malaysian peninsula as early as 5000BC, and one could reasonably ask why it seems to have ground to a halt rather than progressing victoriously along the Indonesian island chain. In fact, I suggest that it didn't stop at all – but that a new and even stronger culture has since swept through. In Malaysia, the remnants of the once proud Austro-Asiatic cultures cling on in remote regions, but the dominant language of the dominant culture is now of a different kind. Malay is actually one of very few mainland-based languages from the enormously successful Austronesian family.

## AUSTRONESIAN LANGUAGES

Austronesian language is spoken on almost every island in the Pacific Ocean, though not on the continent of Australia, and it does not take an outstanding intellect to guess that the cultural advance which gave this language group the ability to spread across such a wide area was an even greater knowledge of the craft of seafaring than that of the Austro-Asiatics. That, together with an ability to use the land to produce food, would seem to be explanation enough for the quite astonishing spread which we see today.

The main members of the family are Malay, the languages of Indonesia and the Philippines, and the Polynesian languages of the Pacific. There are also Austronesian languages in Vietnam, on Taiwan and Hainan, and on the island of Madagascar in the Indian Ocean. And the speakers of these languages have been the bearers of an advanced culture. Not only does the art of seamanship speak for a high degree of development, but

### Chapter 13  Peoples Of The Pacific

agriculture has been practised since long before the time that the first westerners reached these parts, before even the first Chinese[1].

Taking a look at the languages themselves, it is quite striking what a coherent group they form. They are not particularly complex in structure; there are no tones, no horrible verb endings (*I have, he has; they do, we did*), no masculine or feminine, no majestic agglutinations so that a whole sentence runs into a single word. There are a few pretty regular prefixes, the occasional 'infix' (a syllable appearing in the middle of a word) but nothing too taxing. Of course, that doesn't mean that it is particularly easy to speak any of the languages well, but it makes it not too hard for a beginner to pick up enough to be useful. Malay has been described as a language you think you know after studying it for 2 weeks, but which you realise you never will after studying it for 2 years. One of the peculiarities of the family is the prominence given to vowel sounds, not the number or complexity of vowel sounds but their stability, their resistance to change. When looking at the way that vocabulary differs from language to language, it is frequently the consonants that vary while the vowels remain the same. For example, the word for *seven* is variously *ficu, pitu, hiku, hitu*. This is quite different from the way English and the Indo-European languages have tended to behave, where I suggested we may as well ignore the vowel sounds completely. In fact so important are the vowels in Austronesian languages that the number of consonants used is sometimes very small indeed, Hawaiian taking the prize for the least of all.

By many counts there are over a thousand Austronesian languages. However, by all counts many are very similar indeed! Sometimes each small island is ascribed its own language, whereas the reality is that whole groups of islands are really speaking dialects which can be mutually understood with ease. I believe those shown on the map will serve to illustrate the family as a whole.

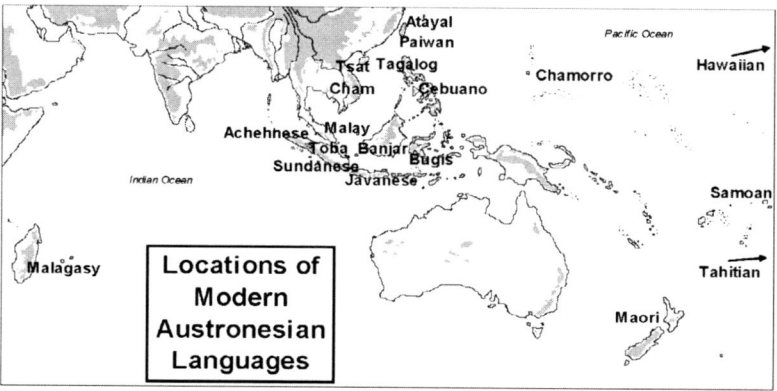

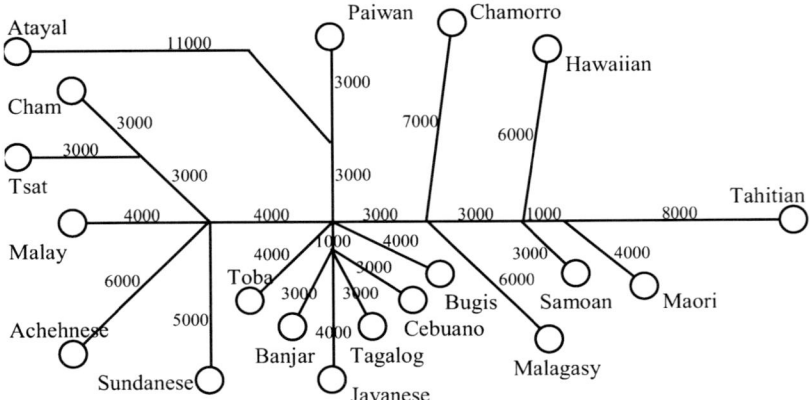

Without any idea of the origin of this family, the best thing to do is to draw up a route map connecting the individual languages. This is shown in the above figure, based on a comparison of the numerals, together with use of the full vocabulary-grammar-sound system on Malay, Tagalog and Maori.

As it happens, there are good reasons to place the origin of Austronesian speech in Taiwan simply by looking at the route map. Let me explain. If Taiwan is not the origin, then it must have been a destination, reached from elsewhere, and the two Taiwanese languages shown, Atayal and Paiwan, must then have developed separately. But this would mean that Atayal had changed by 11000 linguistic years in the same time it took Paiwan to change by just 3000 and it is highly unlikely that circumstances could lead to such a difference on the same small island. So, if Taiwan was not a destination point for Austronesian then the only alternative is that it was the origin. If the root point for the whole group turned out to be somewhere on the line to Atayal, then it could be that the two Taiwanese languages have actually changed by similar amounts. Of course it makes life a lot easier when you realise that archaeologists have picked out Taiwan as the place of origin of Indonesian and Polynesian culture and that geneticists have now traced back the typical Polynesian DNA, first to Indonesia and then to Taiwan[2]. But it is still nice to be able to show that a study of the languages can actually support these findings. So, there is not one controversial shred in all this; linguists are now unanimous in their opinion that Taiwan is the place of origin. That being the case, let me draw up a family tree, making the assumption that the two Taiwanese languages shown, Atayal and Paiwan (which have been selected from a dozen or so indigenous Taiwanese languages, spoken today by minority tribes dominated by Chinese culture), have been changing at similar rates.

# Chapter 13   Peoples Of The Pacific

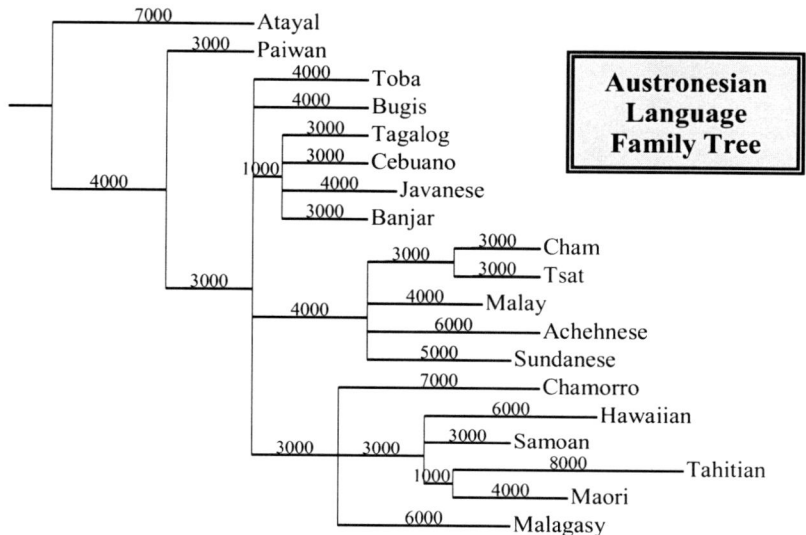

## THE HISTORY OF AUSTRONESIAN

But just how old is this family? How long is it since the ancestral Austronesian language was spoken? Now, the first thing that strikes me is that there have been very widely differing rates of language change for the different branches of this family. In the time that Paiwan has changed by 3000 linguistic years, several other members of the family have changed by well over 10000. Yet experience is that even settled agricultural communities are unlikely to undergo language change at less than about 0.5 linguistic years per year. I would therefore place the division between Paiwan and the bulk of the family no earlier than 4000BC[3]. Prior to about 5000BC, the economy of Taiwan was that of hunter-gatherers and the change rate might be expected to have been a little higher. The original Austronesian tongue was therefore probably spoken in about 9000BC, somewhere on Taiwan[4].

But it was in about 4000BC (plus or minus a few hundred years) that the truly spectacular events surrounding this language family began to unfold. Somehow, someone must have acquired or developed the know-how to design ships capable of ocean voyages. It's about 250 miles from southern Taiwan (where Paiwan is spoken) to the nearest point on the Philippines with one or two small islands on the way, but this is the journey which must have been undertaken in 4000BC, with a genuine settlement party.

Looking at the family tree, it is clear that the various phases of sea-borne colonisation typically induced language change at or above 2

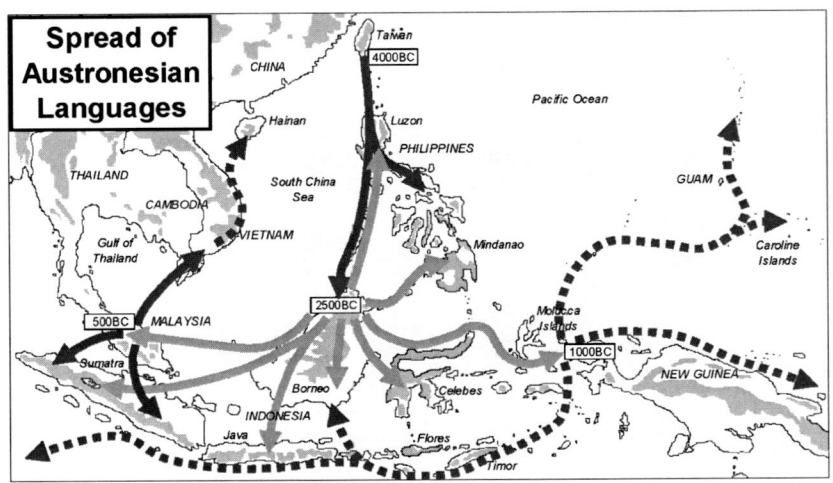

linguistic years per year, which means that the next big expansion commenced in about 2500BC, where the family tree shows a five-way split. Clearly something had happened, almost certainly a technological development, probably in connection with seafaring. I suggest it was either in boat construction technology, control or navigation. As for location, I have shown this phase to have commenced on north Borneo, although I have no independent evidence for this.

From Borneo, colonisation parties took languages back to the Philippines (Tagalog and Cebuano), to Sumatra (Toba), Java (Javanese) and Celebes (Bugis). These languages (and their many close relations) have all since experienced the slow change of settled peoples. A further colonisation wave reached mainland Malaysia (Malay), and this was followed by a second phase of settlement in Sumatra (Achehnese and Sundanese) as well as Vietnam (Cham[5]) and, eventually, Hainan, where Tsat arrived about 1300 years ago. In these cases the languages changed much more rapidly, partly due to distance travelled but perhaps also because they were subject to much greater influence from the Austro-Asiatic languages they encountered. In human terms, there is no escaping the fact that all this activity implies conquests involving serious and prolonged warfare.

But it was in the east, starting in the Molucca Islands in about 1000BC, that the most remarkable journeys of all took place. One group headed north, eventually reaching the Caroline Islands and Guam; another headed south and west, settling some of the southern Indonesian islands; the third group headed past New Guinea and neighbouring islands down to the Solomon Island chain. An amazing boldness then led these

Chapter 13    **Peoples Of The Pacific**

adventurers to explore and settle islands right out in the Pacific Ocean. Vanuatu represents the start of these Polynesian trans-Pacific movements. Fiji and Samoa, far to the east, were the next major staging posts; Fiji is about 500 miles east of Vanuatu, Samoa 500 miles further still, with the Tongan group 300 miles south of Samoa. Up until Samoa, there are quite large numbers of small intervening islands, so errors in navigation may not have been immediately fatal, but what happened next was truly breathtaking. Journeys must have been made 2500 miles north to Hawaii, 1500 miles east to Tahiti and 1000 miles south (from Tonga) to New Zealand. They discovered and colonised pretty much every available island group right across the Pacific. And the most remarkable journey of all was to one of the remotest islands in the world, Easter Island, 2500 miles further east than Tahiti. Their 100 foot double-hulled canoes represented technology which gave them a quite outstanding ability to transport both themselves and the essentials needed for a new life on a new island (seeds, animals) and to be able to navigate with considerable precision. And as they travelled from island to island, often in small independent parties, their languages mutated at a quite extraordinary rate, up to 4 or 5 linguistic years per year in the case of Tahitian[6].

And then there is the amazing story of Malagasy. The language evidence is quite clear; the colonists of Madagascar were closely related to the Polynesians, having travelled south and west from the Molucca Islands while the Polynesians travelled east. After island-hopping for a while within southern Indonesia and leaving the closely related 'Barito' languages in south-east Borneo, a party then set out right across the Indian Ocean. They may have managed one or two stops, in Sri Lanka, the Maldives or the Seychelles[7], but the feat is still quite remarkable. The date (immediately recognisable by the start of the progressive extinction of all the large

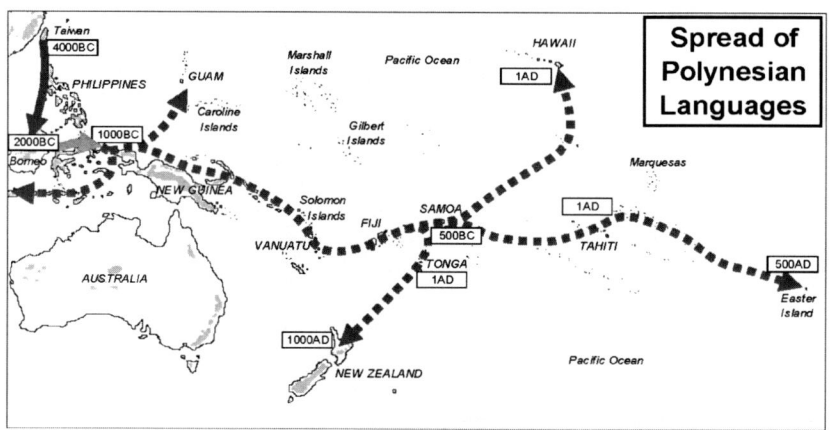

fauna on Madagascar[8]) was about 200AD; their close relatives were at that time making themselves at home on Hawaii, almost exactly on the opposite side of the world!

But is it really only 6000 years since the first Austronesians left Taiwan? Is there any corroborating evidence? Fortunately there is plenty! It's relatively straightforward to date the first human presence in previously uninhabited lands, such as the Pacific islands, New Zealand and Madagascar. A further key piece of archaeological evidence is that of the pottery type known as 'Lapita'. It suddenly appears all over Indonesia and then the Pacific 3000 to 4000 years ago. It is found in Samoa from the 1st Millennium BC, effectively proving the time that this particular stage of the Polynesian journey took place. I also note that Bryan Sykes has made a calculation of the approximate time since the first Polynesians left the Moluccas, based on the genetic mutations which have taken place since in Mitochondrial DNA[9]. His estimate is 3500 years, 1500BC – which is close enough.

It is interesting to consider for a moment the places which Austronesians did not colonise. Australia and the island of New Guinea stand out (lowland New Guinea was colonised but not the interior). A people who can reach Easter Island and Madagascar would obviously have no difficulty in reaching Australia. It lies across quite a modest stretch of water and so I think we can assume that Austronesian speakers found it[10]. My feeling is that the reason they failed to colonise is to do with the role of seafaring, the hallmark of the Austronesian-speaking peoples. The other islands are smaller; the advantage represented by rapid travel between islands would have enabled the newcomers to move quickly and mass numbers where necessary, thereby maintaining dominance. This would not have applied to large land masses however; they would have required some other cultural advantage, not merely seamanship, in order to take on central New Guinea and Australia. The same argument obviously also applies to any colonisation of the mainland of Asia itself. The main continental area which they did manage to reclaim, the Malaysian peninsula, is the nearest thing to an island which it is possible to imagine without it actually being one; and southern Vietnam, where Cham achieved dominance, largely comprises the Mekong delta – with almost as much water as land!

## AUSTRONESIAN ORIGINS

But what about the true roots of the family? Was Austronesian culture an independent Taiwanese achievement? To many linguists it is as good as proven that Austronesian and Austro-Asiatic are directly related. Many speak of 'Austric', the super-family introduced in Chapter 2, whose two

## Chapter 13   Peoples Of The Pacific

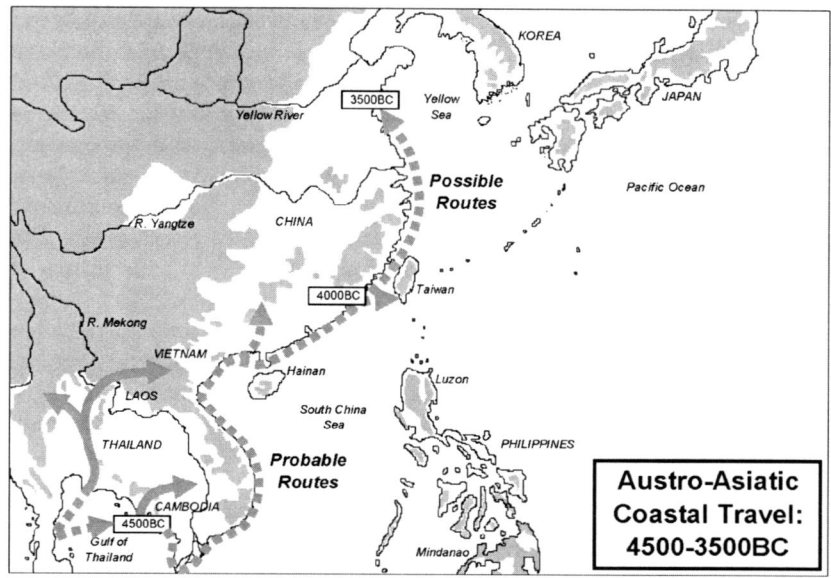

principal members are Austro-Asiatic and Austronesian. On the other hand, I have just deduced that Austronesian originated in Taiwan in 9000BC, at which time Austro-Asiatic was only just entering northern Pakistan! If there really is a family relationship I'll have to go straight back to the drawing board. But there isn't. The average distance between the families (three languages representing each family[11]) works out at 47000 linguistic years. Admittedly Malay is much closer, but then Malay has had over two millennia of close contact with Austro-Asiatic as the two families 'fought it out' for lordship of the Malaysian peninsula.

So why do so many linguists persist in relating Austro-Asiatic and Austronesian? I believe the clues are there both in the dates and the geography. By 4500BC, a phase of Austro-Asiatic language spread had commenced, by boat, across the Gulf of Thailand from Malaysia to modern Thailand and Cambodia, leading to the Mon-Khmer varieties of Austro-Asiatic speech and culture. About 500 years later, a particular community in Taiwan, on the southern tip of Taiwan as it happens, suddenly acquired the capability for oceanic travel. Coincidence? I think not. The obvious deduction is that the Austro-Asiatics voyaged, traded and probably settled right around the coasts of South-East Asia and that at least one group reached Taiwan[12]. It may not have been a large group, it certainly was not a strong enough group to obliterate the local language, but it looks as though they were strong enough to be a serious influence culturally[13]. Parallel cases elsewhere in the world would be the Norman invasion of

England in 1066 – the Normans ruled but the English language won – and the Mongol domination of China – the Chinese language won that one with ease. The Austro-Asiatic settlers on Taiwan were absorbed, but their know-how was not lost. Within a few short years the Taiwanese themselves, though only those of the Paiwan language group, were also setting out across the high seas. And the language of those Austronesian adventurers, though it was Taiwanese at root, must have been significantly affected by contact with the Austro-Asiatic of the newcomers – as English was strongly affected by the Normans, and Chinese bears the marks of Mongol domination. The system used here doesn't detect it strongly because I have deliberately tried to exclude such secondary effects, but it provides some justification to those linguists who have detected strong resemblances between the two families[14]. The fact that much of the subsequent Austronesian expansion into Indonesia, Malaysia and Vietnam would have been at the expense of Austro-Asiatic speech would only have added to the resemblance.

Incidentally, the deduction that Austro-Asiatics voyaged right around the coasts of China also appears to explain elements of Chinese prehistory. Suddenly, a logical explanation presents itself for the development of Lung Shan civilisation, originating in north-east coastal China[15] in about 3000BC. Contact with Austro-Asiatic colonists surely also occurred at a similar date in south-east China, the point (and time) of origin for all today's Chinese languages[16]. It very much looks as though, while Sino-Tibetan may have donated its grammar to the original Austro-Asiatic pidgin, it then reaped the reward and benefited greatly from subsequent Austro-Asiatic influence.

But, to return to Austronesian: where do its real roots lie? And how did the first Taiwanese arrive? Easy: they walked across from China, as the Chinese army wish they could today! 9000BC represents the end of the last Ice Age; the melting of glaciers around the world had recently seen sea levels rise high enough to separate Taiwan from the mainland[17], marooning the Taiwanese until that day, some 5000 years later, when a strange Austro-Asiatic ship arrived. I bet those Austro-Asiatics were worshipped as gods! The Taiwanese must, by then, have thought their island was all there was in the universe since the beginning of time. But, regarding their earliest roots, all that can be said is that humans have been in eastern Asia for about 40000 years, speaking in some manner, and that the Taiwanese must have descended from one such group[18]. By the time Sino-Tibetan culture arrived in China, reaching the shores of the Taiwan Strait no earlier than about 3000BC, the sea offered the Taiwanese the protection they needed – just as it does today.

All of this means that Ket no longer stands alone! Austronesian civilisation may be massively indebted to Austro-Asiatic technology, but the language family most certainly does not stem from an East African parent spoken in 20000BC any more than Ket does. I have finally found an entire family which, though it may still quite possibly have originated in Africa, dates from much earlier times.

## THOSE WHO CAME BEFORE

Let's consider for a moment that very first human exodus from Africa. The archaeological evidence is that it took place at least 65000 years ago (from my reading of the various conflicting views) – perhaps as early as 100000 years ago[19]. At that time the route north into Europe was blocked by other 'hominid' inhabitants, the well-known Neanderthals. The same was true of the route into Central Asia[20]. The only relatively 'easy' area for further expansion would have been to the east, into India and then eastern Asia[21]. Of course the reality is that it would have been far from easy. Our ancestors were not yet confirmed as top predator; they were competing with bears, lions and tigers armed only with wood and stone tools, so it is not surprising that the spread of our species was a slow one. It may also be that they were competing with another hominid type in the east as well. Homo Erectus is the general name given to several related types of human, evidence for which has been found from Africa to China and Indonesia, and Homo Erectus may still have been on the scene when our forefathers first spread east. The recent remarkable find of skeletal remains of dwarf hominids on the island of Flores in Indonesia, dating to just 16000BC, has certainly re-ignited debate over the disappearance of Homo Erectus[22]. Whatever the truth, it is easy to sympathise with the slow rate of mankind's progress across Asia. They apparently made the 8000 mile journey from Africa to Australia in about 30000 years, at a sedate 6 miles per generation.

The question now arises as to whether we can find any further linguistic reminders of that first journey east, to add to Ket and the Austronesian family. Logically, the places to look are islands and out-of-the-way places, locations which may have escaped the influence of the more recent 'Nostratic' cultures. The Andaman Islands, out in the Indian Ocean, fit the bill nicely. They are home to a primitive hunter-gatherer people who speak a language apparently unrelated to any other language group on earth. These people must surely be a remnant from this first wave of colonisation, probably moving to the security of their island home at the height of the last Ice Age (18000BC) when low sea levels reduced the sea crossing to just a few miles[23]. Since then they have been cut off from the rest of the world by the rising waters of the post Ice Age global warming, just as the inhabitants of Taiwan were. In fact, as you look around the coasts of Asia, you can't help noticing other groups of islands which are well placed to harbour further language remnants. Indonesia

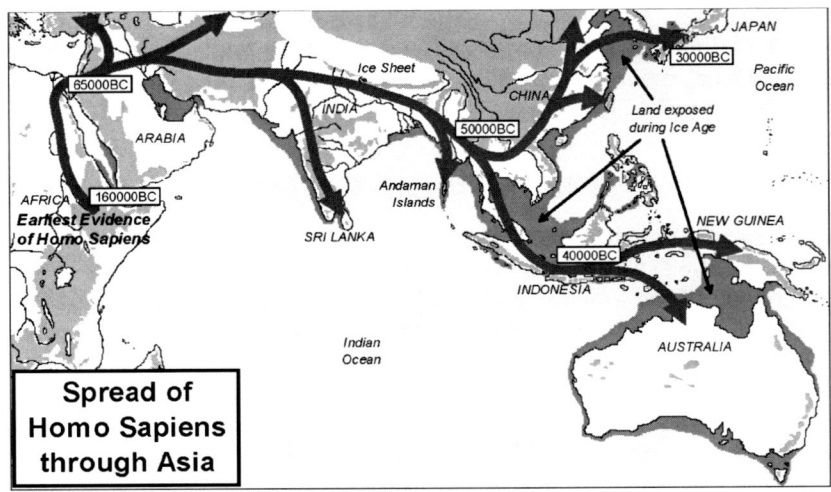

Spread of Homo Sapiens through Asia

was swept pretty clean by the passage of Austronesian, but central parts of the island of New Guinea remained untouched; and beyond New Guinea lies the largest off-shore island of them all, the continent of Australia. And far to the north, the Japanese archipelago has been separated from the Asian mainland for some 15000 years. You would have to suspect that some or all of these lands contain languages which predate the flood of Afro-Asiatic-originating culture that seems to have covered so much of the world over the last 22000 years. Let's look and see.

## PAPUAN LANGUAGES

The island of New Guinea is chock full of different languages, known as 'Papuan', or 'Indo-Pacific'. Excluding the Austronesian languages of the coastal plains, there are about 600 in an island three times the size of the British Isles, many being spoken by only one or two villages. Clearly, with so many languages to study this is a work for which specialist knowledge is required. In a moment I will introduce you to one language from the 600 but first, can anything be deduced purely from the fact that so many different languages exist? It is a situation quite unlike any yet encountered. Over most of the world, movement of people has resulted in large areas with clearly related speech. Even without large scale movement of people, each cultural advance has resulted in a wave of new language as existing populations adopted a new culture. This has obviously not occurred in New Guinea, at least not for a very long time. The island was touched by the Austronesian speakers, who managed to establish their culture on the coasts, but not inland in the central highlands. Inland, the slow passage of the centuries gave rise to minimal cultural change and no large-scale infusion of new people. This is surely the only possible explanation for there being such a profusion of different languages. In each small area of the island the culture must have developed separately and its language would have developed with it. And yet these people were agriculturalists! Even as the first Europeans were being introduced to wheat and barley farming and the earliest Chinese experiments with rice agriculture were taking place, fields of taro were already being cultivated in central New Guinea and the practice spread throughout the island. It is a telling point, though, that there is no sign of any corresponding spread of language. It appears that the idea of taro cultivation jumped readily from language group to language group, reinforcing the point that there is no certain link between the spread of agriculture and the spread of language.

In as far as any language can be considered typical, the Yimas language is typical of New Guinea in that it is only spoken by a couple of villages, with a total number of speakers in the low hundreds. It is noticeably related to some of the surrounding languages (the Lower Sepik group) but not others. It was extensively studied by Professor William Foley of the University of Sydney[24], who spent many months living amongst the Yimas people, and my impression is that the form of the language would not seem too strange to an Indo-European speaker. There is a greater usage of suffixes and case forms, together with postpositions, and word order may appear unusual. But the key question is: "Do the measurements reveal relationship with any language outside New Guinea?"

And the answer is "none at all"; well over 40000 linguistic years to all other families. The languages of New Guinea (and one or two much smaller adjacent islands such as the Solomon Island chain) have apparently been isolated for a very long time, a time which could easily be 40000 years or more and, like Ket and the Austronesian family, they certainly owe nothing to the much later 'Nostratic' language wave.

But what of Australia, the vast continent to the south, which has been accessible by dry land from New Guinea for at least some of the last 40000 years?

## AUSTRALIAN LANGUAGES

Not surprisingly the Aboriginal inhabitants of Australia know no more of their origins than any other race on earth. From beyond the short span of recorded history every people has its myths and legends, sagas of heroes and miraculous occurrences and, though some may contain kernels of truth, there is certainly much which is the product of generations of imagination and story-telling. In Australia the mythological period is known (by some groups at least) as the time of the 'dreaming', when the world and its human population were formed by spirit beings. Now, it is perfectly understandable that memories of the earliest origins of the Aboriginal Australians are a little hazy since, while estimates vary considerably, it appears that most anthropologists and archaeologists put the date of the arrival of the first Australians no later than 35000 years ago, with many arguing for a date as early as 60000 years ago[25].

Unfortunately the Aboriginal languages of Australia have been decimated by the impact of English, though current measures may at least prolong the life of a few of them. Before the arrival of Europeans there were perhaps 500 Aboriginal languages; now relatively few remain. Linguists are able to determine that there are a number of language families on the continent, but that a single family (Pama-Nyungan) dominates 80% of the land area. The other languages are restricted to the north-west, particularly Arnhem Land in the Northern Territory. To get a flavour of Australian language, I have selected Kamilaroi, a Pama-Nyungan language from New South Wales (south-east Australia), Wagiman, an almost extinct language from the Daly river area of the Northern Territory, and Yangula, a more widely spoken Northern Territory language. In my view, neither Kamilaroi nor Wagiman looks too shocking for an Indo-European speaker. Suffixes are liberally used to express verb forms and cases (as in Latin); there are complexities to do with whether verbs are 'transitive' (doing something to someone) or 'intransitive' (just doing something), but nothing radically different from examples in Indo-European speech. Expression of the plural is a bit subtle (certainly too subtle for me!). Yangula, on the other hand, is clearly quite different and reminds me more than anything of southern African speech forms.

Anyway, applying the system used in this book, none of the three shows any significant resemblance to any other language family on earth which, of course, supports the view that Australian language, like that of New Guinea, has developed independently from the rest of the world for a long but quite unquantifiable time. Kamilaroi and Wagiman are just 21000 linguistic years from each other, with Yangula measuring 49000 and 39000 linguistic years respectively from the other two. It therefore looks as though Kamilaroi and Wagiman are of the same family (although Wagiman is supposed to be non-Pama-Nyungan in the literature!), but that Yangula is virtually unrelated.

Let's broaden things out. In Australia a comparison of numerals is useless since the normal counting system appears to have been *one*, *two*, *two-one* (or *one-two*), *two-two*, *many*! Even for those languages which did use different words for *three* and *four* (and in a few cases *five*), that was the limit. In this case, therefore, I have decided to compare the different regions of Australia by listing as many words as possible from each region[26] from my list of 26 (referring back to Chapter 4). If every word

Chapter 13    Peoples Of The Pacific                                      191

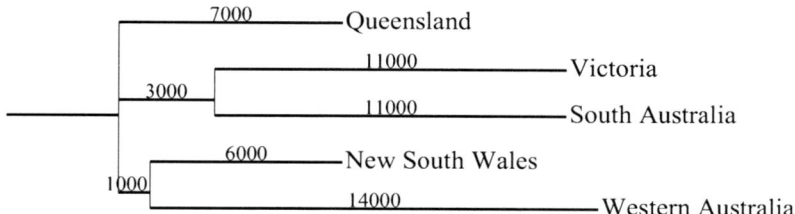

listed with a given meaning, for example *tree*, in one region has a counterpart in another region, then 1 is scored. If only half are recognisably cognate, 0.5 is scored etc. The score for similarity between any two regions is then processed as in Chapter 4, except without the grammar and sound elements, and factored slightly because of the omission of most of the (usually relatively slow-changing) numerals. This gives a distance which is admittedly crude, but is more than adequate for an overview. And the result is that the languages of Queensland, New South Wales, Victoria and South Australia are all found to lie within 32000 linguistic years of each other. Western Australian speech is a little further away, linguistically. The languages of the Northern Territory on the other hand are much more distant, well outside my measurement range. With the omission of the Northern Territory, I could even express this as a family tree, making an educated guess as to where the root point lies.

Judging by the relative lengths of the branches, it looks very much as though the point of origin of this family lies in eastern Australia, and assigning a low 0.7-0.8 linguistic years per year to the Queensland and New South Wales languages, the start date works out at a surprisingly recent 7000BC. Languages from the other regions show much greater change, consistent with a greater distance travelled. So, we have a large area with definitely related languages (the Pama-Nyungan family in fact), stretching all around the east, south and west of the continent, and a smaller area, the north-west and the central interior, with apparently unrelated languages.

Although there is nothing new or controversial in all this, the interpretation is actually quite startling. The 'politically correct' view of Aboriginal Australia is that man has lived in harmony with both his fellow man and nature since the dawn of time (i.e. for at least 35000 years, perhaps 60000 years). Yet the message from the Pama-Nyungan language family is that something rather radical occurred in about 7000BC (plus or minus at least 2000 years I would guess), leading to a great wave of language and culture which swept 80% of the continent. Now, so far as I can ascertain, there is nothing in the archaeological record to explain this. In fact, the greatest technical advances, microlithic tools and the taming of the dingo, occurred in the north-west (i.e. non-Pama-Nyungan territory)

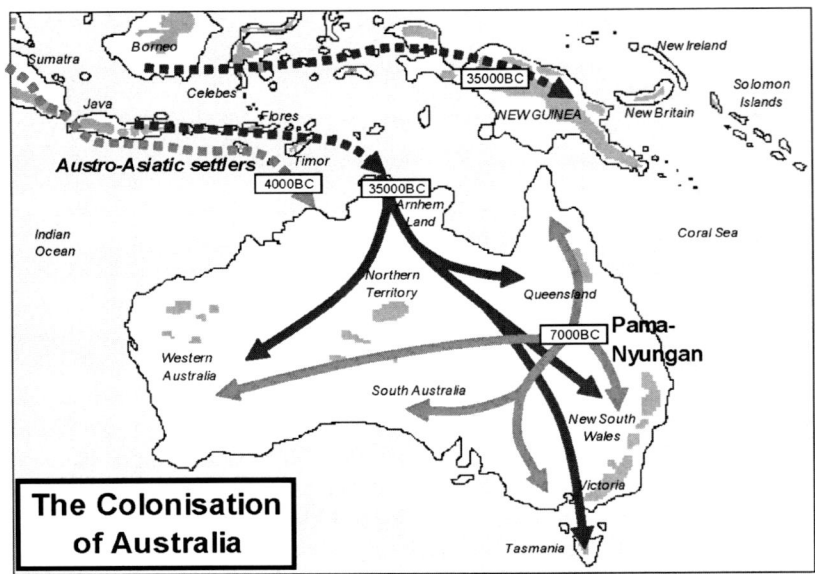

The Colonisation of Australia

in about 4000BC[27]. I am afraid my explanation for the spread of Pama-Nyungan language is much too controversial for this book, but I am certainly prepared to suggest a source for the stone tool developments of the north-west. I suggest that Austro-Asiatic seafarers, who had reached Malaysia by 5000BC, continued to voyage and settle throughout southern Indonesia as far as Timor and that they were then (in about 4000BC) bold enough to cross the Timor Sea and explore the Australian coast. Their languages didn't survive, just as they didn't in China or Taiwan, but Austro-Asiatic technology represents much the most probable source for the sudden advancement of Australian stone-working knowledge.

However, the bottom line is that Australian languages join those of New Guinea and the Andaman Islands, plus the Austronesian family, as remnants from very distant times, protected from later cultures by kindly stretches of water. You would therefore hardly be surprised to learn that the waters separating Japan from mainland Asia have fulfilled a similar function.

## THE LANGUAGES OF KOREA AND JAPAN

I have so far avoided much mention of Japanese and Korean, as well as the little known and now extinct language Ainu from northern Japan, despite the fact that several linguists have linked them all with the Altaic family. But, with average measurements to Altaic of 62000, 48000 and 51000 lin-

## Chapter 13    Peoples Of The Pacific

guistic years respectively, I am certainly not going to take this proposed link seriously! In fact, I can find no significantly close relative to either Japanese or Korean, although they are a measurable 25000 linguistic years from each other. Ainu, recently spoken by a racially distinct people[28] on the northern Japanese island of Hokkaido, on Sakhalin and on the neighbouring Kuril Islands, also bears no significant similarity to any of the language families introduced so far with one notable exception, Ket, at 32000 linguistic years[29]. This is an important exception, however, and one that I will be referring to again in the next chapter. However, Ainu bears not the remotest similarity to either Japanese or Korean (over 50000 linguistic years in each case). There can be no doubt about it; we are looking once again at languages from the very distant past. Japanese and Korean probably separated following the last Ice Age, say in about 12000BC, when rising sea levels formed a physical barrier between them.

However, ancient Japanese culture was in quite a different league from that of New Guinea and Australia. A relatively advanced people, known as the 'Jomon', inhabited Japan as early as 11000BC, long before the appearance of Chukchi-Kamchatkan, Altaic or any other 'Nostratic' culture, leaving evidence in their settlements, their stone artefacts and, particularly, their pottery, the earliest known on earth[30]. Remarkably, Jomon culture appears to have blossomed as a totally independent Japanese achievement, only being superseded by the Iron Age 'Yayoi' culture, which swept through Japan in about 400BC. There is no mystery about the impetus for the Yayoi culture however; it was contact with the advanced civilisation of China.

While the ancestors of the Jomon people presumably first reached the main Japanese islands from Korea, some 30000 years ago based on archaeological evidence, a quite different group, ancestors of the Ainu, must have made the crossing further north, from the Asian mainland to the island of Sakhalin and from there to the northern Japanese island of Hokkaido. Here, the arrival of Siberian-type stone tool technology in around 8000BC seems likely to mark the coming of Ainu culture (and language). During the Ice Age these sea crossings could have been made on dry land, whereas the short distance from Hokkaido to the largest Japanese island, Honshu, would have remained very wet and very dangerous; during the depth of the Ice Age it would have represented the sole outlet from the Sea of Japan into the Pacific Ocean, and a natural frontier between the Jomon Japanese and Ainu worlds. In fact, the Japanese conquest of Hokkaido only took place as recently as the 17th Century.

So, by the time Chukchi-Kamchatkan speakers reached the far northeast of China and then Manchuria, in perhaps 5000BC, both Japanese and Ainu would have been secure behind their protective stretches of water. As we have seen, Nivkh, which separated from Chukchi-Kamchatkan in

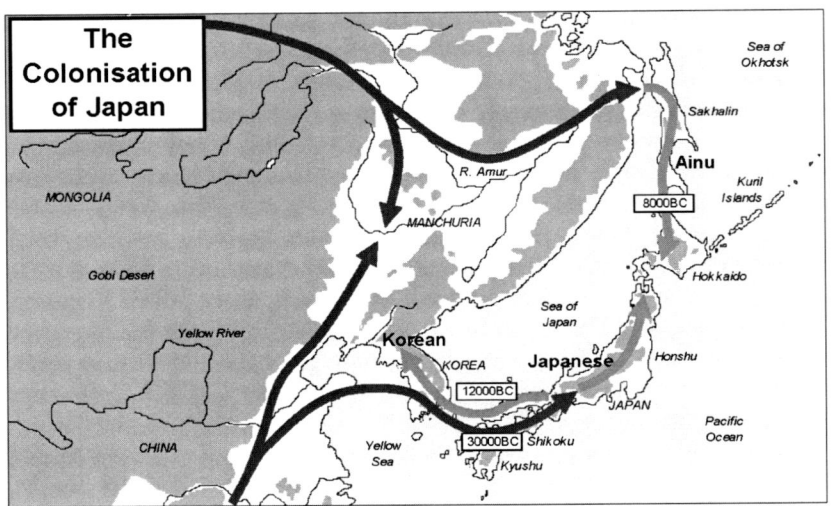

around 4000BC, eventually managed to cross the narrow strait to Sakhalin, but Ainu remained the live spoken tongue of a distinct culture until a few decades ago. Meanwhile, Japanese has gone from strength to strength. The impact of Sino-Tibetan civilisation in the form of the Yayoi culture was tremendous, and it is very clearly visible in the language; Japanese uses countless thousands of Chinese-related words, a Chinese-related script and Chinese numerals – but the core of the language is still directly descended from that of the indigenous Jomon people.

But Korean is the real marvel. Its survival cannot be attributed to any convenient stretch of water. When the millet-growing Chukchi-Kamchatkan speakers appeared on the border, their language should logically have swept right down the Korean peninsula. Yet, while the idea of millet-growing may have done so[31], the language it seems did not. Perhaps the culture of Korea at the time, related to the Jomon culture of Japan, was simply strong enough; it may have been unimpressed by Chukchi-Kamchatkan ways. It could even have been strengthened by having to defend itself, ready for even sterner challenges, from Altaic and Sino-Tibetan. Like Japanese, Korean is full of Chinese words; like Japanese, the root of the language has remained that of the original inhabitants. It has been a remarkable achievement.

## SUMMARY

This chapter has finally unearthed whole families of language which are not descended from an Afro-Asiatic parent! It has revealed several reminders of

## Chapter 13     Peoples Of The Pacific

the languages of the people who first arrived in eastern Asia over 40000 years ago. In most cases, the survival of these languages has clearly owed a lot to the protection offered by water, although Korean joins Ket as survivors who had no such luxury. Admittedly, Korean had a peninsula to retreat to and Ket lived on in the cold unfriendly wastes of Siberia; nevertheless, they stand as the sole survivors in mainland Asia (other than reconquests by Austronesian) of that first wave of human settlement.

As the eye searches the coasts of Asia and Europe for other possible refuges, we have to dismiss Sri Lanka and the Chinese island of Hainan as being too easily accessible from the mainland. Other islands are too small. Britain and Ireland may have hosted speakers of languages descended from those of Cro Magnon man, but the arrival of Celtic put an end to such speech if it still existed[32]. And the islands of the Arctic were simply uninhabitable during the Ice Age – most still are. But there is one further land which was accessible during the Ice Age and which has since been protected by water. It is a very large tract of land indeed. I speak of America, the final frontier for the human race.

# 14

# A New Beginning In A New World

America is still known as the 'New World'. Only a little over 500 years ago no-one in Europe, Africa or Asia knew of the existence of America. True, it has now been shown beyond reasonable doubt that the Vikings reached the continent and even stayed for a while[1], but this was not widely known even back in the ancient Viking heartlands. Similarly, it seems highly likely that Chinese expeditions also pre-dated Columbus[2]. It may be that Basque whalers knew of the existence of a land in the west, but if they did they kept it a secret; the world at large had no idea that there was anything the other side of the Atlantic except the Pacific and the Indies. Many have argued and will continue to argue that there was indeed some earlier contact between old and new worlds by Phoenicians, Carthaginians or Romans. Numerous unexplained finds have been made in America which are claimed to prove that visits were made in the past and it is quite possible that some are well founded. It is unfortunate that, to some, belief in early contact across the Atlantic has become almost an article of faith, often tied in with an implicit belief in the existence of the lost continent of Atlantis. It is equally unfortunate that others are not even prepared to consider the possibility that such contact could ever have occurred. Thor Heyerdahl, whose theories that Polynesian culture originated in America I completely disagree with, did the world a service in my view by at least demonstrating that ocean travel would have been possible even using the most primitive craft. His journey across the Atlantic in the reed boat 'Ra' showed a sceptical world that such craft could be built and his much more successful but less well remembered exploits in the Indian Ocean demonstrated that these craft could not only be built but also controlled. Not only so, but the previous two chapters have shown, based on linguistic evidence, that humans have been navigating and colonising across the Pacific and Indian Oceans for thousands of years.

But, whatever the theories of some, the hard evidence seems to be that mankind first reached America in the traditional way, by walking, and that he (and she) did so via the Bering Strait from Russia to Alaska.

## COLONISATION

Perhaps it would be useful to think about the journey from Russia to Alaska for a moment. It is not a journey that many make today! The two continents of Asia and America stand about 50 miles apart at their closest. To make the journey today there are basically two options; either make it by boat in the summer – unlikely to be a calm crossing – or wait until the winter ice allows you to walk across. However, during the depth of the last Ice Age, the sea levels were so greatly reduced that it would have been possible to walk right across the Bering Strait on dry land. In fact, experts suggest that a land route was available between about 23000 and 12000BC[3], with a width which reached 150km when the sea was at its lowest. Of course, being the Ice Age, even if there were not enough snowfall for there to have been many glaciers in north-east Asia, or 'Beringia', as the land now beneath the sea has been named, it would still have been unpleasantly cold in winter. But the journey would certainly have been possible. If the Inuit can survive as they do today, and their predecessors have for 4000 years, just a short walk from the North Pole, then certainly mankind could have reached Beringia before 12000BC. And if mankind could have reached Beringia, you can be pretty sure that someone did! The main controversy surrounds just when, and what happened next.

The problem is that, though there was little glaciation in north-east Asia, there was plenty in North America. Even though the earth has been more or less the temperature it is today for 11000 years, it is estimated that

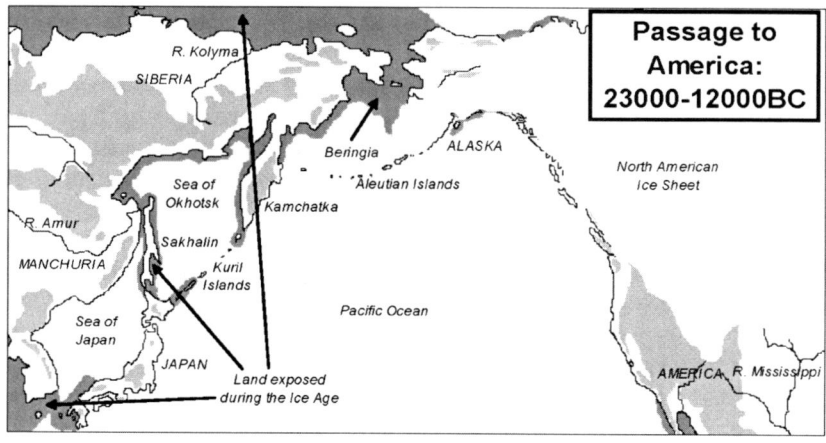

the last mainland Canadian ice sheet only completed its melt in about 2500BC. There was a lot of ice in North America and it stretched, up to 3km in thickness, from Alaska right into the heart of the continent. It barred the way completely from the Arctic coast of Alaska to the Pacific coast. And we are not talking of a few short kilometres distance to travel to cross the ice; it was hundreds of miles in extent. And, according to the experts, it was in position until roughly 8000BC, when it is adjudged that a corridor would have been accessible between the ice sheets on the east and west sides of the Rocky Mountains[4]. Yet there is clear archaeological evidence of settlement in America from at least 12000BC, that is 4000 years <u>before</u> an ice-free passage is thought to have existed. And, in 9500BC, incontrovertible evidence is found right down near the southern tip of South America!

So, are all the assumptions wrong? Clearly there are many possibilities. Perhaps the glaciologists are in error and there really was an earlier passage through from Alaska to the rest of America. Perhaps a very few individuals managed to cross the ice sheet – or, more plausibly, go by boat around it down the coast, via various ice-free islands. And there is another possibility. There have now been several finds in South America which, it is claimed, show evidence for much earlier human habitation. The most famous of these sites are at Pedra Furada in north-east Brazil[5] and Monte Verde in Chile[6], with dates as early as 30000BC, and these have since been augmented by other (admittedly later) sites in Colombia, Venezuela, Peru, Brazil and Argentina[7]. A Central American site, Tlapacoya, is claimed to show evidence of humans from 21000BC[8]. In recent years, there has been increasing support from experts that some of these finds genuinely do prove the earlier presence of humans on the American continent.

A further clue as to the nature of American colonisation comes from genetics. It has been known for many years that there are only four basic human blood types, A, B, AB and O. The proportion of the population in each group varies from one part of the world to another, Europe having the highest incidence of Type A for example, but Native Americans are over 98% Type O[9]! Now Type O is common in the rest of the world but nothing like that common, so what on earth could have led to such an unbalanced population in America? Could it possibly be that the entire population of America, until the arrival of the Europeans, was descended from a mere handful of individuals who, by chance or by 'natural selection', happened to have an unusually high Type O concentration? One might almost go so far as to suggest a single human pair, an American Adam and Eve, were it not for the fact that four separate Mitochondrial DNA types are present. At any rate, it lends weight to the view that most Native Americans are descended from a very few individuals.

# Chapter 14   A New Beginning In A New World

Returning briefly to the archaeological evidence, the opinion of most researchers was, until recently, that humans first arrived in the heart of North America in around 12000BC. This is because there is abundant evidence from that time onwards of what has become known as 'Clovis' culture, betrayed by a particular type of stone spear point. This is also the time that the mammoth population nose-dived, a sure sign that humans were active, either killing and eating mammoths or spreading some virulent disease. However, as I say, belief in the evidence for earlier occupation has been gaining ground. For me, the key point is that undisputed evidence has been uncovered of humans at the southern tip of South America from 9500BC. Now, bearing in mind the time taken to migrate from Africa through southern Asia to Indonesia and Australia, it seems quite inconceivable that the spread of settlement from Alaska to the southern part of South America could have been achieved in anything less than around 10000 years. That would involve a steady 25 miles per generation, compared with 15-20 miles per generation deduced for the spread of early Sino-Tibetan language and culture for instance. In fact I would eat my hat if someone could prove to me that there were no humans in America (except Alaska) before 12000BC; 20000BC seems a much more plausible minimum date, and that's before we even look at the language evidence!

Anyway, enough of speculation; let's take a look at what we actually have in America. The language classification most usually cited nowadays is that proposed by Joseph Greenberg in the 1980's, suggesting that almost all of them fit into a single family known as Amerind; a few, notably Navaho, are left in what is known as the Na Dené family, while Eskimo-Aleut languages, as we have already seen, occupy the far north. The most usual explanation for the Na Dené family is that it represents a second influx of people, one that only reached the northern and western parts of Canada where most Na Dené languages are spoken, except for the case of some West Coast languages and Navaho, which were taken right down into the heart of the continent. However, the Na Dené family never reached further south than the United States. Amerind languages on the other hand stretch from Canada to the tip of South America.

## AMERIND LANGUAGES

The first point to make here is that very few linguists indeed take Greenberg's proposal seriously! They realise of course that ultimately there must have been a common origin for all American languages just as there would ultimately be a common origin for Norwegian and Zulu, but Amerind languages are, in the opinion of the majority, much too varied to be ascribed to a single family. Many are, in my biased opinion, also much too difficult for a human of average brain to speak! However, that is purely the reaction of an English speaker to the ways in which some aspects of language are expressed. When I want to indicate a plural, it is convenient just to add an '*s*'. On learning German, I can cope with substituting '*en*' or '*e*', sometimes '*er*'; even Zulu and the so-called Bantu languages, where I have to stick '*ana*' or '*zi*' or some such alternative onto the front is not impossible. Arabic, with its internal changes to words (*bait* – *house* → *buyut* – *houses*), takes some getting used to, but when I have to check the verb to find out whether a noun is plural or not, the neurons in my brain are simply not wired in that way. I also find it difficult when I have to use a completely different word for '*my mother*' as opposed to '*your mother*' or '*his mother*'!

To be honest, there are few general traits among American languages. Admittedly most are agglutinative. Usually this takes the form of extensive use of suffixes to express 'person' (who did it to whom), 'tense' (past, present, future) and sometimes 'case' (instead of *in, on, from* etc.). Subtleties such as expressing wishes, fears and expectations are also often dealt with by suffixes. However, prefixes are by no means uncommon (also being used in Na Dené languages) and separate words for 'person' are also in frequent use. While most of the languages use postpositions, some use prepositions as we do in English. In short, there is a healthy variety! So let's tackle the problem one step at a time.

## THE LANGUAGES OF NORTH AMERICA

Thanks to the wealth of academic research in the United States and Canada, we now know quite a bit about the various native North American languages, including many which are no longer spoken. It is also fair to say that those indigenous communities which remain have managed to foster a strong spirit of cultural survival, which is good news for language survival also. The principal recognised families are: Algonquian (North-East), Iroquoian (East), Muskogean (South-East), Siouxan (Great Plains), Caddoan (Mississippi), Hokan (South-West), Na Dené (West) and Salish (North-West). In addition, there are several individual languages (Chinook for example) with no generally recognised affiliation.

Now as it happens I believe it is not too hard to make sense of the North American situation, and I can quite see why Greenberg considered them all (except Na Dené) to lie in a single family. If I carry out distance measurements using the full system, selecting representatives from five of these families[10], just over half the results lie between 30000 and 40000 linguistic years, which is certainly close enough to point to genuine relationship. When I turn to the numerals (North American languages all have a complete set of ten), it becomes apparent that the similarity scores are generally significantly above the coincidence level. However, I would like to

# Chapter 14   A New Beginning In A New World

|         | 1       | 2        | 3         | 4         | 5        |
|---------|---------|----------|-----------|-----------|----------|
| Crow    | hawate  | nupe     | dawi      | cope      | tsexo    |
| Pomo    | dan     | xos      | xoxat     | dako      | talko    |
| Quinault| paw     | salli    | chaihla   | mus       | tsilakis |
| Sarcee  | tlikaza | akiya    | tooki     | diitcii   | guutaa   |

|         | 6         | 7         | 8          | 9           | 10        |
|---------|-----------|-----------|------------|-------------|-----------|
| Crow    | akawa     | sapua     | nupupi     | apie        | pireke    |
| Pomo    | xowaloxat | sebaita   | ponamusta  | xutpacem    | pacem     |
| Quinault| sitacha   | tsuups    | tsamus     | tuqwiuh     | panakis   |
| Sarcee  | gustoni   | tsictsidi | tlacdiitci | tlikuyaghaa | gunisnani |

illustrate the sort of thing I mean by this, since I certainly do not want to give the impression that the similarities are strong. It is only by carrying out comparisons over a large number of different language pairs that it is possible to be confident that the average picture obtained is reliable. Take a look at the above table, which gives the numerals from four languages, Crow (Siouxan), Pomo (Hokan), Quinault (Salish) and Sarcee (Na Dené).

The differences between these four are obvious. However, look at the words for *five*. Two begin with *ts* and one with *t*. Pomo and Quinault both have *t-l-k*; in Crow the *k* has become an *x* (pronounced *kh*). A similar series of similarities exists for *seven* and *ten*. Check out the Quinault and Sarcee words for *nine*; they both start with *t*, then either *q* or *k* (similar sounds), a *u* and either *h* or *gh* (similar sounds again). Now admittedly this degree of agreement is hardly impressive, but the point is that it is above the normal coincidence level. It could still simply be coincidence in any individual case, but when we check out several languages in each family, and find that the average is still well above the coincidence score, then probability turns into near certainty. That is what I have done, and the resulting picture would be satisfying vindication of Greenberg's hypothesis were it not for the fact that Na Dené sits quite happily alongside the other families as just another member of the clan! The full results from this comparison are expressed in the next, rather over-sized, family tree.

Please forgive the size; I realise many of the names may be unfamiliar, but I wanted you to get a feel for how it all fits together. As usual, it is the combination of different degrees of change and the geographical locations of each language which gives the best clues as to the origin of the group as a whole, and the crystal-clear picture is that this great expansion of language (and culture) commenced in the western United States. The dates shown on the following map are based on a detailed consideration of the possible change rates at every stage in the family tree. For example Keres, a 'Pueblo Indian' language, has only changed by 12000 linguistic years in total, and a rate of around 0.8 linguistic years per year seems rea-

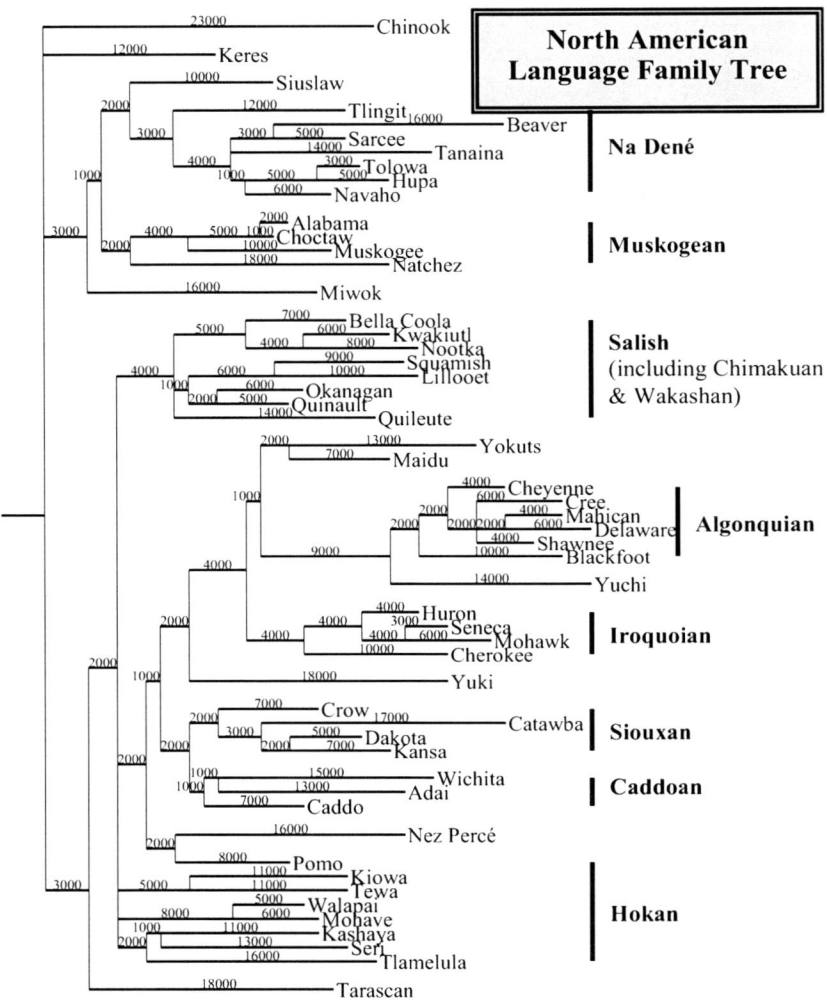

sonable if language has not moved too far. In contrast, the Algonquian languages might reasonably be expected to have changed at up to 3 linguistic years per year during some stages of their long journey eastward.

It is worth picking out one or two more from the crowd. Catawba stands out from the rest of the Siouxan languages; it is spoken 1000 miles to the east of the main bunch and is clearly the result of a long migration across the central United States, which must have commenced in about 5500BC. The journey is reflected in the significant change which has taken place in the language. Tarascan, from central Mexico, seems to be the end

Chapter 14    A New Beginning In A New World

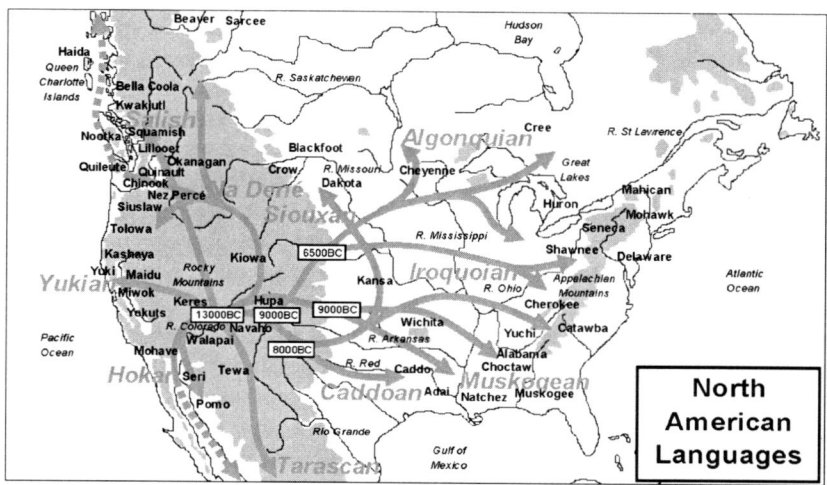

product of an early march south. Tlamelula is one of a cluster of Hokan languages from the far south-eastern end of Mexico (off the map); once again a long migration seems to have taken place for some reason, at a date some time after 8000BC. At the other extreme, Tlingit and Tanaina, both Na Dené languages, are spoken in southern Alaska and they stand as testimony to the spread of Na Dené speakers north through coastal Canada; migration dates in the 8000BC to 6000BC range seem to be indicated.

But can we relate this language spread to any independent evidence of cultural spread? Most definitely! The earliest carbon date obtained for the so-called 'Clovis' culture stands at just after 13000BC and numerous sites give dates from 12000BC onwards. Clovis culture is defined predominantly by a new type of large fluted stone blade or point and it has been found right across the United States. In fact, it seems to have taken no more than a few hundred years to sweep across the continent, trade and imitation seemingly causing a much more rapid spread than that of any ancient language. It is by no means certain just where it all started although the south-west is the location most often proposed[11]. Clovis culture then endured longer in the east, while in the west it had developed by about 10000BC into 'Folsom' culture, identified by its much smaller blades, and this in turn spread steadily eastward. By 8000BC, this had given way to the so-called 'Plano' traditions of the Great Plains[12]. Basically, the drift (or sprint) of cultures seems to have been chiefly from west to east and this is very much reflected in the language movement. The northward spread of Na Dené languages (the Athapaskan branch, represented by Beaver and Sarcee) into Canada is, in my view, to be identified with the northern Plano culture, dating from around 6000BC[13]. But where did the Clovis people come from? And when? Can any light be thrown on the issue from relationship with the languages of Asia?

As it turns out, there are plausible connections with two particular Asian languages, namely Ainu from Sakhalin and northern Japan and Ket from central Siberia, with average distances from six Clovis languages of 41000 and 42000 linguistic years respectively. The relationship with Ket is supported by the recent work of Merrit Ruhlen[14], who found what he considers to be significant similarities in vocabulary between Ket and the Na Dené languages. Personally, I am particularly impressed by the structural resemblance between Ainu and several North American language families. Also, you may remember that Ket and Ainu were found in the last chapter to be just 32000 linguistic years from each other. A plausible explanation would therefore be that the parent tongue was spoken in around 17000BC somewhere in Siberia, since which time Ainu and Ket have changed at a relatively slow 0.85 linguistic years per year while the Clovis languages, being languages on the move, have averaged about 1.4. This certainly ties in with such archaeology as there is, namely the comparisons which have sometimes been drawn between the stone tool culture of Diuktai Cave (and associated sites in the Lena river area of eastern Siberia) and Clovis culture itself[15]. Amazingly, the Diuktai Cave people, who inhabited the Lena river valley throughout the Ice Age, were at the very forefront of world technology in 17000BC. One would therefore expect their culture to have spread widely, including an eastward movement toward Alaska (as well as south to Sakhalin and west to central Siberia). There is absolutely no way that humans could have crossed the great ice sheets of Canada during these times, but they could certainly have made the trip through the islands off the Canadian west coast. In fact, on the Queen Charlotte Islands a language known as Haida is still spoken which doesn't quite fit with the rest of the North American languages (although it is sometimes placed in the Na Dené family). Haida numerals bear unmistakeable similarities to those of both Ainu and Ket (about 28000 linguistic years distant) and the language is almost certainly a remnant from the days when pre-Clovis speakers were making their way south from Alaska[16]. I believe there is also considerable genetic evidence for this wave of human colonisation into North America and that this evidence can be linked to the Mongolia-Manchuria-Siberia region[17]. But were these really the very first humans in America?

As I have hinted, the speed at which Clovis styles spread across the continent is much too rapid for normal population or language spread. Even at an incautious 25 miles per generation it should have taken 2000 years to travel from the Rocky Mountains to the east coast, whereas the archaeological evidence is that adoption of Clovis culture occurred almost simultaneously throughout the United States. This strongly implies the presence of an existing population right across the continent, a view which attracts an increasingly general support today, based on archaeological finds at places such as Meadowcroft Rockshelter – Ohio, Cactus Hill – Virginia, and Topper – South Carolina, all sites which have produced human artefacts below (and therefore earlier than) the Clovis layers[18]. So, while Clovis culture may well have been initiated by a new population recently arrived from Asia, it very much looks as though they found America already occupied when they arrived! It's time to head south in search of further evidence.

## CENTRAL AMERICAN LANGUAGES

Let me first admit that there are still some gaps in this nice neat North American picture. In Florida, a language family known as Timucuan once flourished, and there is no way that I can persuade myself that these languages are part of what might be termed the 'Clovis super-family'. The same is true of a group of languages now spoken in the western United States, including Hopi, Ute and Comanche. They belong to what is known as the Uto-Aztecan family, centred on northern Mexico, and they too are significantly different from any of the Clovis languages. And if American languages exist which are not part of the Clovis group, then the case for a pre-existing human population becomes ever stronger. But before investigating closeness or otherwise to Clovis, let me take you on a quick tour of Central American languages.

Mexico is where the most advanced civilisations were found when Europeans first appeared in the New World. Everyone knows of the Aztecs, the people who were in top spot before the Spaniards intervened. Mexico City is built on the ruins of the Aztec capital Tenochtitlan and there are still significant numbers in the surrounding area who speak Nahuatl, the language of the Aztecs and another member of the Uto-Aztecan family. Further east, the Mayan civilisation was already but a shadow of its former self when the Spanish arrived. It once boasted heavily populated cities right across the Yucatan peninsula of Mexico and Belize, and south into Guatemala and Honduras. The Maya had a written language, and the recent decipherment of their glyphs has vastly improved our knowledge of their civilisation. Mayan languages are still spoken in parts of Guatemala and Mexico – and they are certainly not Uto-Aztecan. Earlier than the Maya, the Olmecs are known as the first of the great civilised peoples of Central America. From about 1200BC, they were constructing settlements, later to be cities, on the Gulf coast of Mexico. They also wrote, and their language was different again. We don't have many available texts, but a widely accepted interpretation has recently been made on the basis of Olmec being of the Mixe-Zoque language family, members of which are still spoken in that part of Mexico[19]. And there is yet another, quite different language family still spoken in central and southern Mexico, namely Otomanguean, Mixtec and Zapotec being modern examples. The final major Central American family is known as Chibchan and it extends from the northernmost part of the South American continent up through Panama and Costa Rica into Nicaragua and Honduras.

Let's start with the Mayan family. The modern family comprises languages which are clearly related to those spoken across the civilised city states of the Mayan world up until about 800AD[20]. With this there is no disagreement. The suggested connection shown on the following map with both the Caribbean language Taino and the Timucuan languages of Florida is much more controversial however[21], and I admit that it is no more than a suggestion based on a comparison of the numerals. If my linguistic distances are correct, Mayan-related language and culture made the 100 mile crossing to Cuba some time around 6000BC, which ties in well with the earliest known archaeological evidence of human occupation in Cuba, dating to about 5000BC (the Casimiroid culture), and originating in the west of the island[22]. In Florida, the archaeological record shows a particularly dramatic change in around 6000BC, with the abrupt end of an earlier so-called 'Palaeoindian' culture, closely related to those of the rest of the south-eastern United States. The millennium between 6000 and 5000BC then seems to bear no evidence of human occupation in Florida at all, and this is followed from about 5000BC by the appearance of a distinctly Caribbean-related culture, presumed to be ancestral to that of the later Timucuan speakers. The logical connection is with the Casimiroid

Chapter 14   A New Beginning In A New World                                    207

people of neighbouring Cuba. In short, the suggestion that both Taino and Timucuan are linked to the Mayan family has real archaeological support.

Moving on; Mayan's immediate neighbour to the west is 'Mixe-Zoque', restricted to a small region on the Gulf coast of Mexico. Today it consists of two very different branches and, looking at the linguistic distance between them and bearing in mind the probability that neither has travelled far, my estimate is that they separated some 12000 years ago, giving an origin in about 10000BC.

Next comes the large Otomanguean family from central Mexico. It includes languages that have changed by between 6500 and 18000 linguistic years since their common ancestor, and this suggests that the original Otomanguean tongue was probably spoken some 9000 years ago, somewhere in Central Mexico. It has been a successful culture, almost certainly the culture of many of the classical civilisations of Mesoamerica, probably including that of Teotihuacan, a city which rivalled ancient Rome for sheer size

To the north, the Uto-Aztecan family covers the whole of northern Mexico and parts of the western United States, and it too dates from the distant past. The six members shown have changed by between 11000 and 16000 linguistic years since they first separated; 10000 years is a reasonable estimate for the time which has elapsed since.

At the other end of Central America, Chibchan tongues are spoken, both in the northernmost part of South America itself and also in Panama, Costa Rica, Nicaragua and Honduras. If I draw up a family tree, I find these languages have changed by between 12000 and 30000 linguistic years since their common ancestor, suggesting that this was spoken as much as 16000 years ago. Two of the languages shown on the map, Sinitacan from Guatamala and Miskito from Nicaragua and Honduras, which are generally considered Chibchan languages, are not even close enough for me to be at all sure they are genuinely part of the same family.

So, we have five distinct language families in Central America and they have all been there a very long time! But are these families related to each other – or to the Clovis languages of the north? The next table shows distances derived from the full vocabulary, grammar and sound system between representatives of the five families as well as the Clovis group. Uto-Aztecan is represented by Hopi and Nahuatl, Otomanguean by Mixtec, Mixe-Zoque by Popoluca, Mayan by Yucatec and Chibchan by Teribe. Navaho, Cree, Cheyenne, Cherokee, Alabama and Seri represent the Clovis super-family.

These measurements are most revealing. None of the five families is at all close to the Clovis languages; and Otomanguean is clearly also very distant from the other four. However, Uto-Aztecan, Mixe-Zoque, Mayan and Chibchan look much more likely to be related. The family tree I am

| Linguistic years | Clovis | U-A | Oto | M-Z | May | Chi |
|---|---|---|---|---|---|---|
| Clovis | 0 | 45000 | 67000 | 48000 | 64000 | 49000 |
| Uto-Aztecan | | 0 | 61000 | 35000 | 58000 | 36000 |
| Otomanguean | | | 0 | 54000 | 44000 | 79000 |
| Mixe-Zoque | | | | 0 | 58000 | 31000 |
| Mayan | | | | | 0 | 30000 |
| Chibchan | | | | | | 0 |

suggesting is based on the distances in the table, supplemented by a comparison of the numerals within each family. In the case of Mayan (Yucatec), I have taken the distance to Chibchan (Teribe) seriously but have treated the much larger measurements to Uto-Aztecan (Hopi and Nahuatl) and Mixe-Zoque (Popoluca) as simply indicating 'significantly more than 40000 linguistic years'.

If this family tree is anywhere near the truth, in particular if I have chosen the root point appropriately (based primarily on a consideration of inter-relationships between Chibchan languages), then the implication is very clear indeed. For some reason, a wave of language (and therefore culture) moved north-west through Central America, originating somewhere in the Panama region. The small change shown to the Chibchan languages

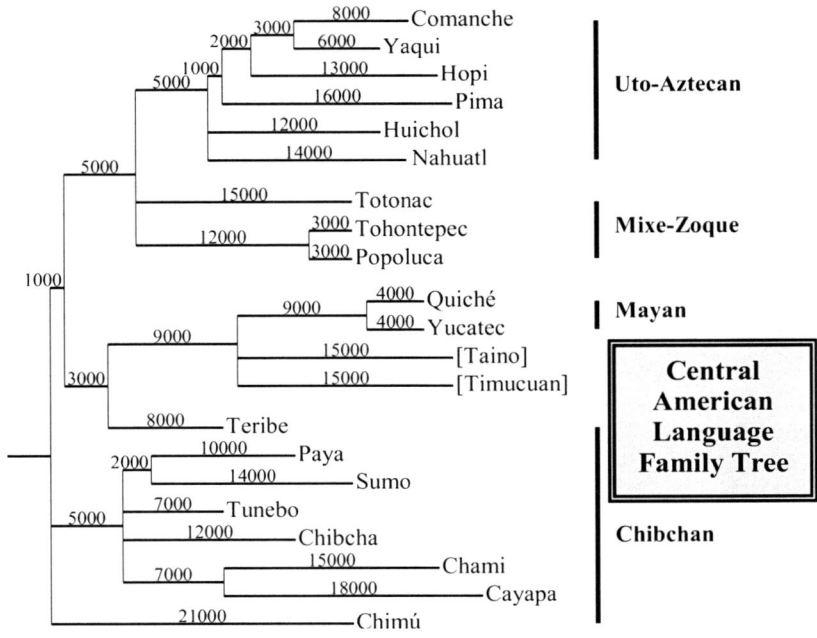

Teribe and Tunebo tells us not only the likely region of origin but it also suggests an approximate date, roughly 14000BC. In about 13000BC, while the language would still have been in Panama or Costa Rica, the ancestor of Mixe-Zoque and Uto-Aztecan separated, taking around 5000 years to reach the US border. Mayan represents a second wave, separating in about 9000BC. I think we can deduce that this culture was at a comparable level to Clovis from the fact that some of the Clovis languages (e.g. Tarascan) penetrated deep into Mexico while several Uto-Aztecan languages took root in the United States.

So, not only was the first Clovis language by no means the first language in America, but the cultural heart of pre-existing American society seems to have lain far to the south, in Panama or even South America itself. A reasonable question would be whether there is any archaeological support for these deductions and I would say the answer is a reasonably confident "yes". Although Clovis culture is often claimed to be the first American culture, it most certainly wasn't. Sites in Venezuela, at the northern end of the South American continent, have produced evidence for a surprisingly advanced stone tool culture usually known as 'El Jobo' which, though possibly slightly inferior to Clovis, predates it by a millennium or so[23]. The spread of El Jobo technology could quite reasonably be linked to the success of Chibchan languages and to the progress of related culture north-west through Central America.

A further reasonable question would be: "what about Otomanguean?" The wave of El Jobo-derived culture would have to have passed right through what would become Otomanguean territory, yet there is absolutely no connection apparent between Otomanguean and the other language families. It seems to have materialised from thin air! This is certainly extremely odd and demands an explanation – but for that you will have to be patient until later in the chapter.

So, it's official. There was life in America before Clovis. But just how much earlier did the very first Americans arrive? It's time to pluck up courage and to enter the linguistic maze which is South America.

## SOUTH AMERICAN LANGUAGES

South American languages have not been studied nearly as extensively as those of most of the rest of the world. The suggested number of families present range from Greenberg's single 'Amerind' family to twenty or more. There are still several hundred Native American languages in daily use in South America but only two have made it anywhere near the world stage. Quechua was the language of the Inca Empire, arguably the largest empire on the planet in its day. As such it was a language of government, and use of it was imposed over a very wide area from Ecuador down to

Chile and Argentina. Today, there are about 6 million Quechua speakers, most in Peru, speaking closely related dialects, all descended from the Inca language. The other truly successful language is Guaraní. In everything but name it is the national language of Paraguay. However, the more usual situation is for a language to be spoken by a few hundred or so, occasionally a few thousand, with the significant danger that future generations will be turning to Spanish, Portuguese, or one of the other major languages.

The following map shows the locations of ten language families from the northern two thirds of the continent. In each case, I have constructed an approximate family tree based purely on the first five numerals (since most South American languages rely on lengthy expressions for anything higher) and this is the basis for the rather tentative start dates shown on the map.

The situation is clearly quite complex; equally clearly, it has developed over a long period of time. Ten distinct families is bad enough, but when you realise that many of the languages shown (for example Timote, Yanomami, Jívaro, Ticuna, Leco) are not included in these ten, then you realise that South America is not an easy place to make sense of – linguistically. However, looking at the suggested dates, as usual based on change rates between about 0.7 and 2.0 linguistic years per year, it becomes thoroughly unsurprising that so many families and individual languages exist. And if language had reached Paraguay by 14000BC (the Waikuruan family), then experience elsewhere in the world suggests that it must have arrived in Panama several thousand years earlier. At 15 miles per genera-

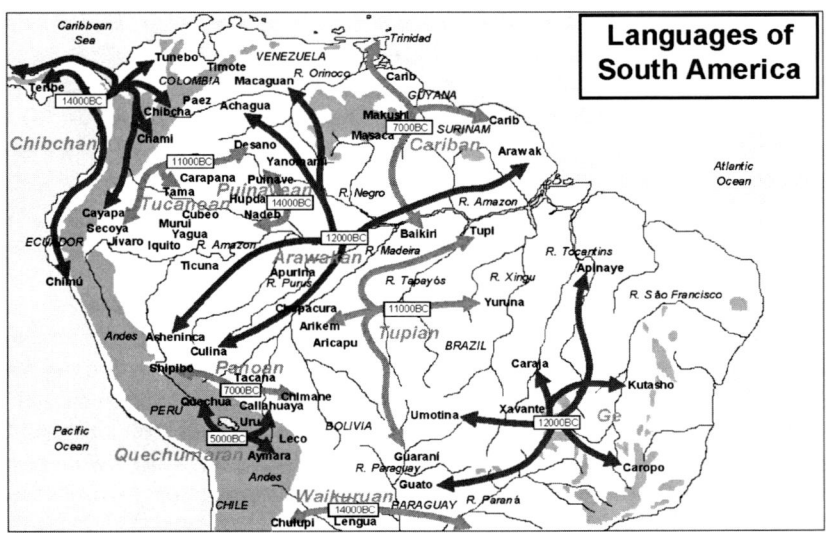

# Chapter 14   A New Beginning In A New World

tion, 17000BC looks like a latest possible date for the first human to have set foot on South American soil.

To look deeper into the inter-relationships between families, I have used the full vocabulary-grammar-sound system on five selected languages[24], as well as comparing the first five numerals of over fifty more. Taking a statistical view of the evidence (i.e. averaging across several languages for each family), I believe the family tree shown is a fairly close approximation to the way nine of the South American language families, plus the majority of the unattached languages, inter-relate. Don't worry about the detail unless you are particularly interested, but notice the fact that Chibchan is one of the nine related families, which means that the

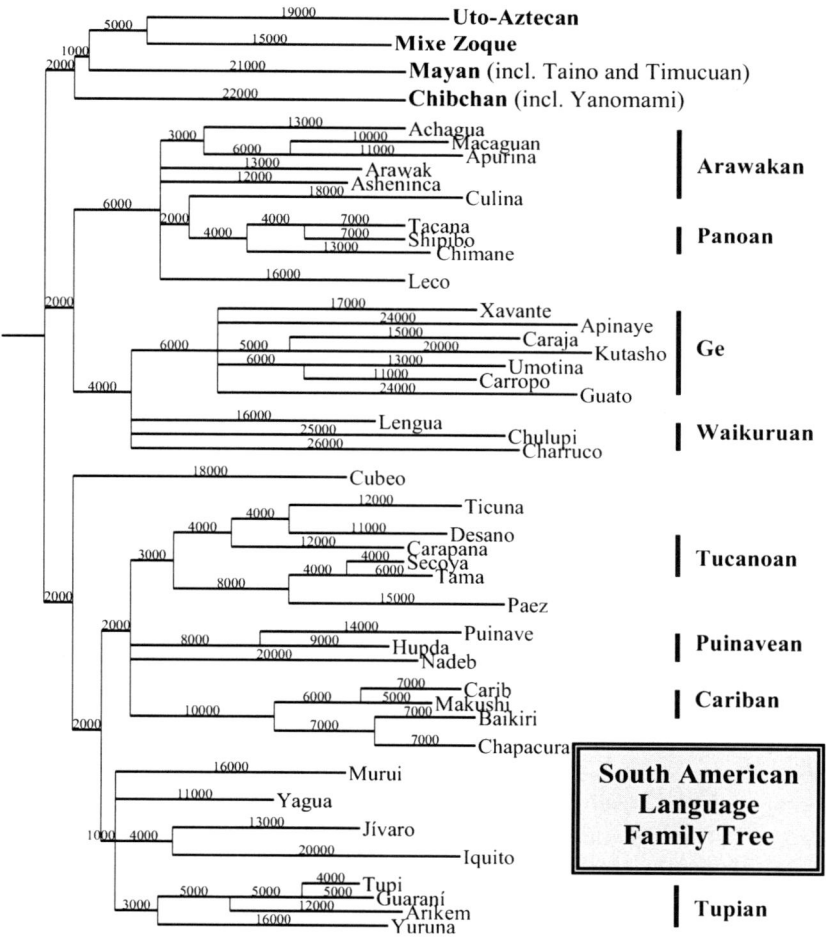

other Central American families (Mayan, Mixe-Zoque and Uto-Aztecan) are also part of the same 'super-family', a grouping which is big enough for me to use Greenberg's term 'Amerind'.

However, this still leaves the Quechumaran languages, which are outside my measurement range from most other families. In the southern third of the continent it also leaves the Chilean language Mapuche (sole surviving representative of the 'Araucanian' family) and the Argentinian language Tehuelche and its relatives (the 'Chon' family). However, using the full vocabulary-grammar-sound system, Quechua (Quechumaran) is clearly related to Teribe (Chibchan), at 26000 linguistic years, and Mapuche (Araucanian) is almost certainly related to Quechua, at 35000 linguistic years. And Tehuelche numerals are 'in range' of Mapuche, at 33000 linguistic years. All of this points to a colonisation route down the Pacific coast of South America, spilling over the southern Andes and into Argentina. The fact that these languages can also be traced back to Chibchan means that all South American language families can be considered as members of a single Amerind super-family, together with most Central American tongues.

As far as date is concerned, I can do no better than my earlier estimate of 17000BC for initial arrival in South America. Since archaeologists are certain that mankind had reached Tierra del Fuego in the far south of the continent by 9500BC, this gives 7500 years for the 4500 mile journey from Panama, which is more or less what would be expected. As well as reflecting the language evidence, the dates shown on the following map also match the accumulating archaeological evidence for the spread of human occupation in South America pretty well. Key early archaeological dates are[25]: Taima-Taima (northern Venezuela), 14000BC; Piedra Museo (Argentina), 13250BC; Los Toldos (Argentina), 12950BC; Monte Verde (Chile), 12850BC[26]; Lapa do Boquete (eastern Brazil), 12000BC; Pachamachay (central Peru), 11850BC; Tibitó (central Colombia), 11750BC; Quebrada Jaguay (coastal Peru), 11075BC; Pedra Pintada (central Brazil), 11075BC.

Admittedly, the very early dates claimed for Monte Verde and those for Pedra Furada in northern Brazil are not supported by these deductions; but then neither are they widely accepted by archaeologists as yet. In general, however, I would contend that the story of South American colonisation is revealed in a highly plausible way by the language evidence. The rates of language spread work out at up to 15 miles per generation, consistent with rates found elsewhere in the world. Furthermore, at 15 miles per generation this demands that arrival in the north-west United States had taken place by about 24000BC (consistent with the archaeological date of 21000BC for Tlapacoya in Mexico) and that humans were probably in Alaska by 27000BC, which closely matches the earliest date for

Chapter 14   A New Beginning In A New World                                                   213

which claims have been made for evidence of human activity in Alaska[27].

As we have seen, archaeologists believe that mankind's first steps out into the Middle East were made at least 65000 years ago. They know that Central Asia was occupied 40000 years ago, and the evidence for human occupation in eastern Siberia stretches back at least 25000 years, possibly well over 30000 years[28]; it is therefore quite possible that the Bering Strait had been reached by 27000BC. Interestingly, this date is also quite compatible with the majority of those proposed based on genetic studies[29].

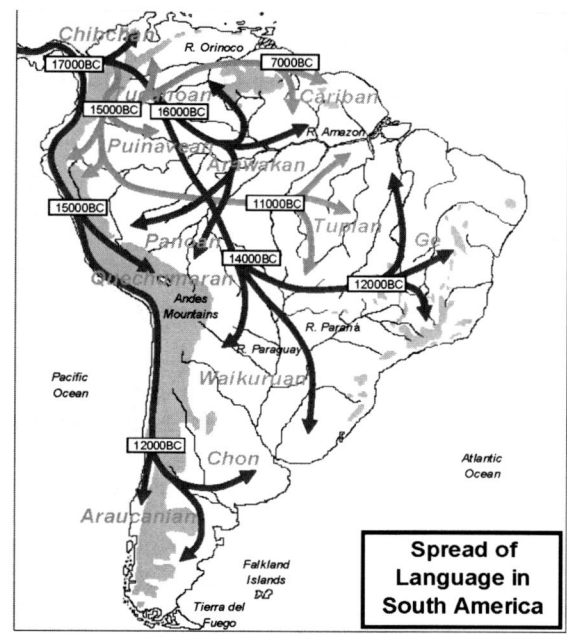

One can easily imagine that one fine summer a tribe or family group was attracted by the possibilities on the other side of the then quite narrow

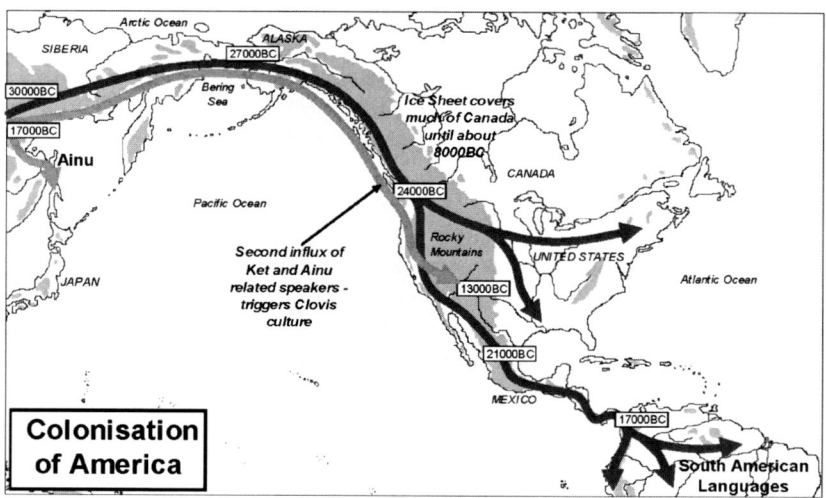

and very shallow Bering Strait, so they crossed and then over-wintered in Alaska. During this period the glaciers of the Rocky Mountains would certainly have been more extensive than today, but they were nowhere near their fullest extent – that would take another 9000 years or so. It seems that a group descended from those who first crossed to Alaska to settle must have made their way, generation after generation, south to warmer lands.

It's logical; it matches the evidence pretty well; but is it the whole story?

## MITOCHONDRIAL HAPLOGROUP B

If the picture I have just painted, of initial colonisation in about 27000BC followed by a second influx which arrived in the United States in about 13000BC is complete, there should be no discernible relationship between American languages and those of the rest of the world other than the faint resemblances found between the Clovis languages and Ket and Ainu. But there most certainly is! Likewise, if the current South and Central American populations are all descended from ancestors who left Asia nearly 30000 years ago, then this should be apparent in their genes; but it certainly isn't!

Mitochondrial Haplogroup B is an enduring mystery. It is one of four very widely distributed haplogroups found in Native American populations (the others being A, C and D), but it is quite different from the other three in two important respects. Firstly its age in America, based on the current level of diversity, is usually put at 12000 to 15000 years[30], compared to well over 20000 years for the others; secondly, there is virtually no Haplogroup B in Siberia, Alaska or Canada, i.e. along the expected colonisation route. However, it is common all down the western side of North, Central and South America, with much lower levels in the eastern United States and east of the Andes in South America; it is also common in eastern Asia and the Pacific. It is an intriguing situation, which clearly had a real, though currently elusive, cause.

Turning to help from languages, an obvious place to look would be the Austronesian family, where Haplogroup B is particularly common. After all, we know that Austronesian speakers got at least two thirds of the way across the Pacific. Furthermore the fact that Polynesians cultivated the sweet potato, indigenous to South America, definitely implies contact[31], as does the finding of prehistoric chicken remains in South America. But, be that as it may, I can detect absolutely no relationship in any of the languages I have studied. Nor, so far as I am aware, have others.

But mainland Asia is quite another story. According to my measurement system, a string of 'Amerind' languages show a marked resemblance

Chapter 14    A New Beginning In A New World    215

(32000 to 37000 linguistic years) to one particular Asian family. The Amerind languages are Nahuatl, Hopi, Teribe and Quechua, representing three different language families, all located on or close to the Pacific coast; the Asian family is Altaic. Can this really be put down to coincidence?

Well actually I have to admit it can. The similarity is pretty much entirely in grammatical form, and there are only so many different ways in which the grammar of a language can be structured. But, just because it could be coincidence, that doesn't mean it is! Consider the following points.

a) I had deduced earlier that the language of northern China during the so-called Yang Shao period, from about 5000BC to 3000BC, was of the Mongolian-Tungusic branch of the Altaic family.
b) In around 3000BC, Yang Shao was replaced by Lung Shan culture, centred on the north-eastern coastal provinces of China.
c) The most likely cause for Lung Shan's rise would appear to be contact with Austro-Asiatic seafarers, the people who also kick-started the impressive Austronesian colonisation of the Pacific. Archaeology supports this in that both Lung Shan culture and that of the succeeding Shang dynasty bear strong similarities, particularly in art, to the cultures of South-East Asia, Indonesia and Polynesia.
d) If Austro-Asiatic seafarers reached the Sino-Tibetan-speaking Lung Shan area, they almost certainly also reached the Altaic-speaking Yang Shao area just to the north, notably the Shandong peninsula, jutting 200 miles out into the Yellow Sea. If so, they would have brought their art and their knowledge of boat-craft but, as in Taiwan, their language may have disappeared. The speech of the resulting composite culture would quite likely still have been Altaic.
e) The 'victory' of Lung Shan over Yang Shao was often a violent one, as seen in the archaeology of numerous settlements. The inhabitants of the Shandong peninsula would have had ample cause to flee the Lung Shan advance by whatever means they had available which, in the end, meant by boat.
f) Boatloads of refugees would have made their way around the coasts of the Yellow Sea, settling wherever they could. Some would have drowned; others would have been caught by adverse winds and driven out to sea; some may even have been swept out past Japan – and if you drop a bottle into the sea off Japan, it is likely to reach Mexico some six months later!
g) A succession of experts has remarked on the similarity of much Central and South American art with that of Shang Dynasty China[32] (and, by extension, with South-East Asia, Indonesia and Polynesia).

Now the possibility that I am implying probably sounds much too far-fetched for you to believe[33]. On the other hand, it is an interesting coincidence that the advanced cultures of Central America, Ecuador and Peru sprang into life seemingly independently at about the same time[34] – and that the time in question was about 3000BC. It also seems inescapable that something must have been responsible for the surprisingly close correspondence between Central and South American cultures, a closeness which is much too clear to stem from the time of initial American colonisation[35]. I could also mention that the cultivated American cotton plant (cotton growing is attested in Ecuador from around 3000BC) is a cross between indigenous and South-East Asian varieties, and that the 'quipu', the Inca system of using knotted strings for record keeping, was also used in China before writing was invented[36]. Remember also that the key strength of Austro-Asiatic culture, very likely inherited by the Altaics of Shandong, was seafaring. They would surely not have set out with the intention of crossing the Pacific – but their seafaring ability may well have enabled them to survive the journey.

But could the arrival of a ragged bunch of foreigners really have influenced so many languages, not to mention the DNA of the population? They would certainly have had a far greater technological capability than the Americans of that time, and a much more advanced appreciation of the possibilities of agriculture[37]. Logically, as in the case of the English colonists of the 17th Century, their numbers would have mushroomed once they had survived the difficult first few years. As seafarers, they would have continued to spread their culture up and down the Pacific coast of America, just as their cultural forebears had around the coasts of eastern Asia. Very likely, as had happened at least once before, in 6000BC, pidgin languages developed, with the newcomers 'corrupting' the languages of the indigenous Americans with their own Altaic grammar. These adapted forms of speech could even have become the dominant languages of mixed communities all along the Pacific coast, communities which would naturally have gone on to dominate far inland as well.

Of course this is all pure conjecture – but something is responsible for Haplogroup B! Somehow, the genes of eastern Asia reached Central and South America, apparently without going through Siberia or Alaska. And although the time depth of Haplogroup B in America (over 12000 years) suggests something rather earlier than 3000BC, this may simply imply that several women were on board ship, representing a Chinese population which was already many thousands of years old. One thing is for sure; the mystery of Haplogroup B has a solution somewhere – and it is hard to dream up any alternative which is less far-fetched than this one!

## OLMEC HEADS

My apologies for the obscure heading; you may be aware that one of the most remarkable legacies of Olmec civilisation, the first city-building Central American civilisation, which dates to the period from 1200 to 400BC, lies in a series of giant carved stone heads, some weighing several tonnes. Considerable engineering research has gone into investigating just how these massive stone blocks could have been moved the several kilometres necessary from the quarry site in a land without large beasts of burden (Native Americans had eaten their last indigenous horse many thousands of years previously!). The Olmecs therefore join the ancient Egyptian pyramid builders and the constructors of Stonehenge as engineers in advance of their time. In fact, there has been plenty of speculation as to whether some Egyptian or European influence may have been responsible for the Olmecs' remarkable abilities. As you have seen, I would rather credit Altaic speakers from northern China!

But there is one further fascinating feature of the Olmecs' head sculpting and that is the fact that some of the facial characteristics look strangely Negroid. Now, generations of experts have explained this away as nothing more than a representation of some elements of the local population but, to the casual observer of these heads, the nagging feeling remains that there is more to it than this. Indeed, one might wonder why there should be Negroid-looking elements in the local population anyway! So can languages help us to solve the mystery?

In the certain knowledge that I am inviting the ridicule of every 'expert' in the field, I believe the answer is "yes". There is one particular family of Central American languages which, to me, stands out as being quite different from all others. It is Otomanguean. I remarked earlier on the strange fact that the wave of language and culture which spread northwest from Panama must have flowed right through what would, from about 7000BC, become Otomanguean territory, yet Otomanguean appeared to be quite unrelated. In fact, as I look around the world's languages, I find nothing remotely like Otomanguean in either grammar or word form in the whole of America, Eurasia or Australasia. It is only when I arrive in West Africa that I find anything with noticeable similarities! African languages are the subject of the next chapter, but here you should know that the Otomanguean language Mixtec measures just 30000 linguistic years from the southern Nigerian languages Efik and Igbo. There are shared grammatical forms such as the use of prefixes on verbs and tone to distinguish between tenses; there are even broad similarities in the types of word used[38].

## Chapter 14  A New Beginning In A New World

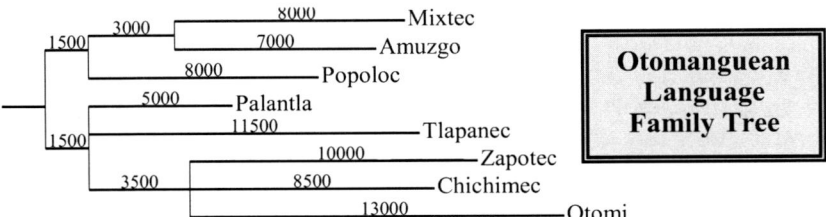

Consider also the geography. The Benguela current brings a strong flow of water north along the Atlantic coast of Africa, which is diverted west by the West African land mass. The current crosses the Atlantic, runs across the north coast of South America and heads straight for the Gulf of Mexico. Admittedly, there is a variable swirl of current off the coast of Nigeria which would mean that, depending on the time of year, a boat set adrift off Nigeria would probably travel south before being picked up by the Benguela current and taken across the Atlantic, but the end result would be the same. One might wonder at just what circumstances could have given rise to such a journey, presumably by at least a small family group. However, in 7000BC sea levels were rising fast. All over the world islands had been created where once continuous land stood – I have already had cause to mention Taiwan, Japan and Sakhalin – and it is certain that some of these newly-created islands were eventually drowned by the ocean. On many occasions and on the fringes of all the world's continents, populations which had first been cut off by rising sea levels would then, after a few more thousand years, have had to abandon their new island homes. For some, without the required sea-going technology, it may have been impossible to cross even a fairly narrow stretch of water without getting swept away on the current. In such cases off the West African coast, the result would be that survivors would have been washed up some weeks later on the shores of a completely different continent!

This is speculative of course; but there is absolutely nothing speculative about the closeness between Otomanguean and the Nigerian languages; and the Olmec heads are real enough. The scenario may have been completely different, but I suggest the result was that a party of West Africans ended up on the Gulf coast of Mexico. Furthermore, those Africans would probably have been at a higher level technologically than the population of Mexico at that time, not high enough to bring metal or agriculture but high enough for them to thrive, multiply and dominate right across central Mexico[39], just as Altaic speakers may have done 4000 years later and Spanish speakers certainly did just 500 years ago. If the Negroid features depicted some 6000 years later on carved stone heads mean anything, then it is certain that African genes continued to make up

Chapter 14    A New Beginning In A New World

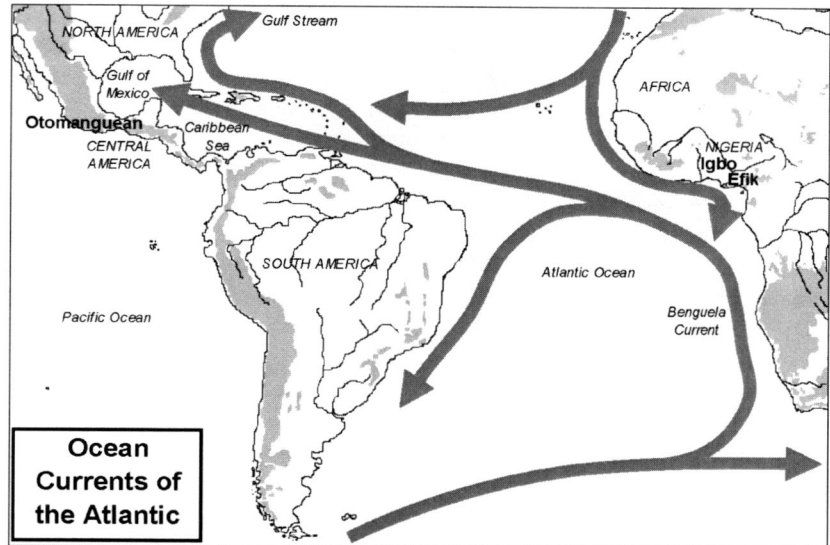

a significant element in the local population. Unfortunately, the influx of slaves from West Africa during much more recent times means that it is practically impossible to use genetics to shed any further light on the matter; there is a 10% African Mitochondrial DNA element in modern Central American populations, but it is clearly not straightforward to deduce the date at which it first arrived in America.

## SUMMARY

This study of Native American language has revealed several quite stunning issues concerning the distant past, some practically certain, some probable and some merely possible. Disputed archaeology suggests that humans have been in America for well over 20000 years; the differences between today's language families effectively prove the case. The much later expansion of Clovis culture across the United States can confidently be linked to a second influx of colonists from Asia. The remarkable similarities between the culture of Shang China and those of Central and South America have led a few researchers to propose early contact between the continents; the grammatical affinity between a string of American languages on and near to the Pacific coast and languages of the Altaic family offers significant support. Negroid features on Olmec heads have invited speculation about an African presence in Central America; a study of the affinities of Otomanguean language makes this highly plausible and suggests a likely date. But none of these deductions could have been made using conventional glottochronology or any other currently used language comparison technique, and I do not believe you will read of them elsewhere; only by having a system which takes sensible account of grammar has it been possible to look so deeply back in time.

But the bottom line is that not only Otomanguean but every other American language stems, in the end, from Africa. Clearly we need to take a serious look at Africa itself now. If Africa really was the mother continent, the continent within which the human race originated, then perhaps evidence for the antiquity of its human inhabitants is still present in its languages. Let's take a look and see.

# 15

# Roots

Anthropologists are now agreed; Africa was the place of origin of the human race. Genetics has established that the variety among African genes is greater than anywhere else on earth, reflecting the greater time available for this diversity to arise. Among the most 'different' (from the majority) are the Pygmy peoples of central Africa and the Bushmen of the Kalahari and, while we have no right to expect any direct correlation between genes and languages, it has to be worth exploring what may lie hidden amongst the modern languages of Africa.

First, a reminder: since the work of Joseph Greenberg in the 1960s, most linguists have been content to divide Africa into just four language families. The Afro-Asiatic family we have already met, accounting for about 40% of the land area of the continent. Of the other three, by far the most widespread is known as Niger-Congo, named after two of Africa's greatest rivers. According to Greenberg, Niger-Congo languages stretch from Senegal in the extreme west, through the whole of West Africa south of the Sahara, right across central Africa to Sudan, Uganda and Kenya, and right across the entire southern part of the continent, with the exception of a relatively small area in Namibia and Botswana. This is therefore a fair sized family, and one might reasonably wonder whether it has any more substance to it than the all-embracing version of 'Amerind' did. Yet it appears that few linguists are seriously challenging the basic correctness of Greenberg's proposal – which is a good sign!

## AN INTRODUCTION TO NIGER-CONGO: THE BANTU LANGUAGES

The Bantu languages, which have been mentioned more than once already, comprise part of the Niger-Congo family and are spoken right across the southern third of Africa. They form an easily recognisable group with a very distinctive grammar. These languages make extensive use of prefixes to verbs and nouns. For example, to form the plural of a noun, the usual procedure is to alter the front end in some way. Thus, *mti* means *tree* in Swahili whereas *miti* means *trees*; *mtu* means *person* whereas *watu* means *people*. In a similar way, the verb is made up of various parts for subject, object, tense/mood, negative (if applicable) and, finally, the actual bit that tells you what is happening; for example *alinitafuta* in Swahili means *he* (*a*) *look-* (*tafuta*) *-ed* (*li*) *for me* (*ni*). To investigate this important group, I have begun by comparing three of the more widely spoken members, namely Zulu (from South Africa), Chichewa (the national language of Malawi) and Swahili (from East Africa). I have then added a further 27 languages from right across the Bantu-speaking belt by using the numer-

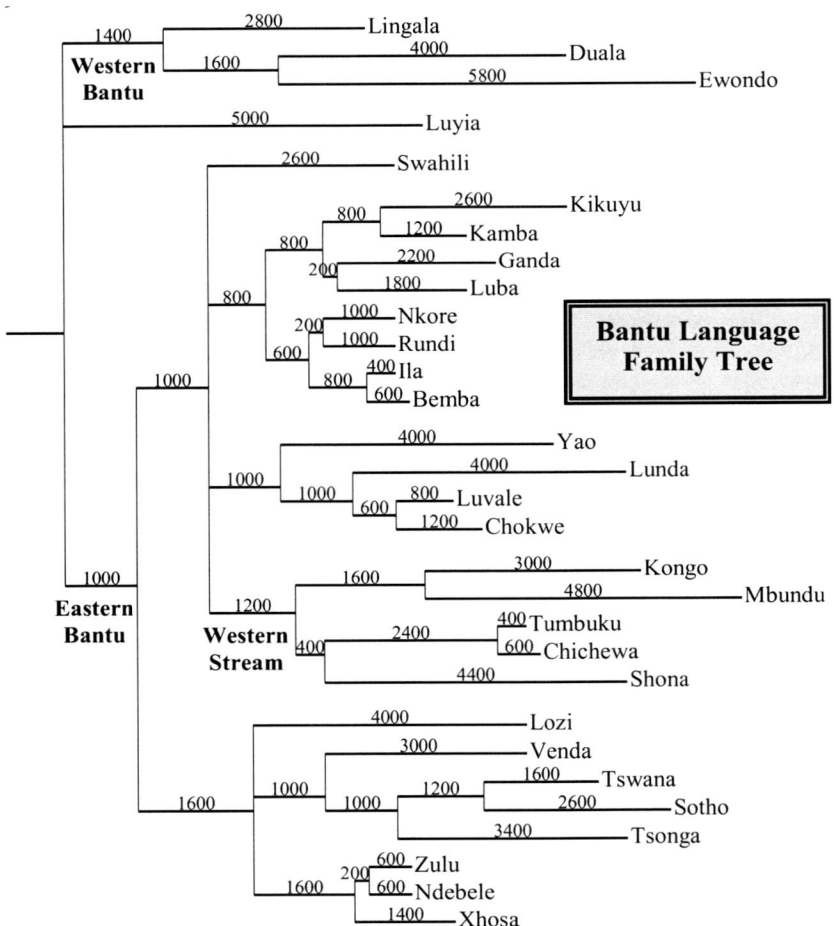

## Chapter 15   Roots

als 1 to 10 (but cheating slightly because of the awkward way in which some of the languages express the numerals from 6 to 9). This gives me the family tree shown, in which the root point, representing the ancestral Bantu language, has been determined by comparing distances to other Niger-Congo languages.

By recent standards the Bantu languages form a very closely related group. And yet they cover a third of the continent of Africa! There can, of course, be only one explanation; they are a very recent phenomenon. The languages have spread out rapidly from somewhere – looking at the lengths of the arms in the family tree and noting the locations of each language geographically, that somewhere must have been in central Africa, probably the eastern Congo region – and at some time in the relatively recent past. Since the languages have been on the move a great deal, and new populations have had to learn them, we would expect a very rapid rate of change. We have seen numerous examples of languages which have changed at over 2 linguistic years per year during periods of expansion and migration and the Bantu expansion has occurred over a very short period and over a vast distance. With total changes ranging between 4200 and 9600 linguistic years, the whole expansion process may have commenced no more than 3000 years ago.

I've given a lot of detail here because I want to illustrate the near one-to-one correspondence between language and culture in this case. For a start, there is a very strong correlation between the Bantu language expan-

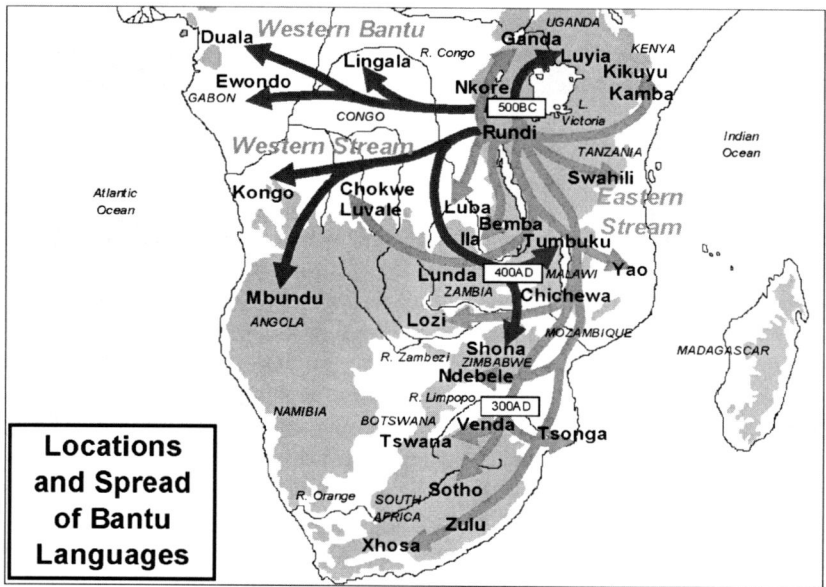

Locations and Spread of Bantu Languages

sion and the sudden appearance of a particular pottery style from the equator right down to South Africa, a pottery with close affinities to that of the Sudan in the 1st Millennium BC. There is also a strong correlation with the spread of iron working and of a pastoralist economy[1]. The pottery can be traced through 'Urewe ware', found to the south-west of Lake Victoria in the last few centuries BC and then extending in all directions to several descendent pottery types. All these closely related pottery types can, in my opinion, be correlated almost precisely with language movements. The northward spread of Urewe ware is represented in the family tree by the Luyia language of Uganda; Lingala, Duala and Ewondo (so-called Western Bantu languages) are the end product of its western movement; 'Kwale ware' can be traced spreading east through southern Kenya and northern Tanzania, as did the ancestor of Kikuyu and Kamba; 'Lelesu ware' spread through central Tanzania – so did Swahili; 'Kalambo ware' penetrated as far as north-west Zambia – languages from Lunda to Chokwe; 'Mulambo and Nkope wares' spread south to Malawi, Mozambique and South Africa – mirrored by languages from Venda to Tsonga; 'Gokomere and Ziwa wares' reached Zimbabwe and South Africa, matching the locations of Ndebele, Zulu and Xhosa. Finally, the so-called 'western stream' of Bantu archaeology ('Chandwe, Kapwirimbwe and Kalundo wares') can be seen arriving in the southern Congo in the 4th Century AD before spreading into Zambia and Zimbabwe, displacing other Bantu cultures in the process. Linguistically, this brings in Tumbuku, Chichewa and Shona, while Kongo and Mbundu spread out into western Congo and northern Angola.

Speakers of the western stream languages had clearly reached a slightly higher level either technologically or socially, and in this context you might note that the early centres of power in sub-equatorial Africa were those of the Shona (constructors of the famous site of Great Zimbabwe) and the Kongo[2], both members of the western stream.

It is quite remarkable that the culture and language of one small area south-west of Lake Victoria should so rapidly have taken over so much of the African continent; but it certainly did. The key development was clearly the use of iron, allowing the production of tools and, more particularly, weapons, which were vastly superior to those in use previously. The origin of this technology was most certainly to the north, probably the Iron Age civilisation of Kush, which ruled Sudan from the 8th Century BC, although the exact circumstances by which a knowledge of iron was transmitted to one particular community near Lake Victoria are totally unknown.

It's a fascinating story – though it hardly helps us to penetrate the distant past! But Bantu is actually just one branch, some would say a subbranch, of the vast Niger-Congo family, a branch which just happened to be in the right place at the right time; what about the wider family?

Chapter 15    Roots                                                     225

## MEET THE REST OF THE FAMILY

I don't wish to get involved in the question as to just what the classification of Niger-Congo branches should be, since there are numerous different opinions amongst linguists; however, what I would like to do is to give an impression of the general scale of this family and, to do this, I will now bring in eight further African languages. Four are from Nigeria: Yoruba, Igbo, Efik and Basa. Twi (otherwise known as Asanti) is from Ghana, Mandinka from Mali, Wolof from Senegal, and Katcha is from Sudan. Controversially, I have also included measured distances to the Otomanguean language Mixtec, from Mexico, for the reasons given in the last chapter. In the following table 'Bantu' represents the average of Swahili, Chichewa and Zulu.

Now, there is no way that distances as high as 96000 linguistic years should be treated as remotely reliable; their inclusion simply serves to warn us of trouble. And the main sources of the trouble appear to be Wolof and Mandinka, which are clearly immensely different from the other languages (and from each other) and I am afraid that, by the standards used for all other parts of the world, neither Wolof nor Mandinka can possibly be allowed to remain within the Niger-Congo family. Nor indeed are they measurably close to any other families except for a surely coincidental distance of 34000 linguistic years between Mandinka and Japanese-Korean! Wolof and Mandinka, representing groups of languages known as 'Atlantic' and 'Mande' respectively, have therefore been excluded from the Niger-Congo family tree shown[3].

Looking at the family tree, which includes a further seventeen languages at distances determined using the numerals 1 to 10, there would seem to be six distinct strands of language represented, some of which subdivided at an early date to form more than one branch[4]. By the way, do not be deceived by languages which appear to be on their own; each represents a sizeable group of related tongues.

| Linguistic years | Wol | Man | Bas | Twi | Yor | Igb | Efi | Kat | BAN | Mix |
|---|---|---|---|---|---|---|---|---|---|---|
| Wolof | 0 | 54000 | 45000 | 53000 | 90000 | 50000 | 46000 | 47000 | 50000 | 86000 |
| Mandinka | | 0 | 44000 | 96000 | 79000 | 57000 | 61000 | 48000 | 58000 | 96000 |
| Basa | | | 0 | 43000 | 35000 | 28000 | 29000 | 36000 | 26000 | 54000 |
| Twi | | | | 0 | 38000 | 34000 | 18000 | 29000 | 39000 | 45000 |
| Yoruba | | | | | 0 | 25000 | 29000 | 50000 | 60000 | 37000 |
| Igbo | | | | | | 0 | 12000 | 40000 | 39000 | 30000 |
| Efic | | | | | | | 0 | 28000 | 42000 | 31000 |
| Katcha | | | | | | | | 0 | 32000 | 38000 |
| BANTU | | | | | | | | | 0 | 55000 |
| Mixtec | | | | | | | | | | 0 |

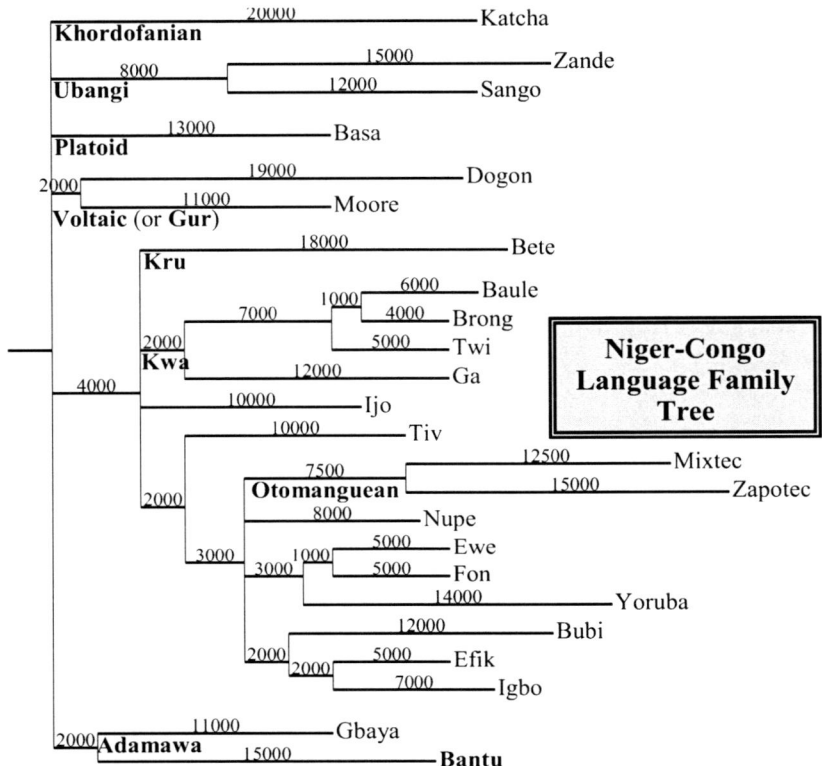

Now, it would be unnecessarily bold to attempt a detailed history based on this family tree alone, but there are certainly some important points which should be made. The only fixed point so far deduced is a date some time in the 1st Millennium BC for the start of the Bantu phenomenon (accepting the pottery dating evidence). Before this date the peoples of central Africa lived, as some still do, as hunters and gatherers. It would not have been an existence which required much movement, in the way that was necessary for the people of northern Asia for instance. Tropical Africa may have its dangers and difficulties, but it is reasonably bountiful regarding food supplies. It is a fair guess that people lived in small groups, in villages or temporary camps, and that they rarely travelled further than was necessary to reap the harvest of the jungle. I am sure it was far from idyllically peaceful in reality, but I cannot see that the conditions would have led to rapid language change. As we have seen several times, a rate of change of 0.7 to 0.8 linguistic years per year seems to be typical where a hunter-gatherer society remains relatively undisturbed. Only where significant disturbance or movement occur does a faster rate apply.

Chapter 15    Roots

However, in the case of Niger-Congo we are fortunate enough to have a further clue. The position of Bubi in the family tree is most interesting. Bubi is only spoken on the small island of Bioko (formerly Fernando Po), now part of Equatorial Guinea, which lies about 30 miles from the African mainland, and the language has changed by 12000 linguistic years since it divided from its nearest continental neighbours, Efik and Igbo[5]. Those same neighbours have changed by 7000 and 9000 linguistic years during the same period. But when did the languages divide? When was Bioko colonised? Personally, I feel pretty confident that the island of Bioko was never colonised by boat. It is much more likely that the island itself actually separated from the mainland <u>after</u> it had been colonised! It didn't move of course, but the 30 mile stretch of water separating the island from the mainland has not always been there. During the Ice Age, and until about 10000BC, Bioko would simply have been an area of high ground near the west coast of Africa. But by 10000BC the waters were rising fast, and not too long afterwards the people of Bioko would have found themselves marooned. About 12000 years have passed, years during which the language of the islanders has changed by 12000 linguistic years, at 1 linguistic year per year; that of the mainlanders has changed by 7000 to 9000 linguistic years, at 0.6 to 0.75 linguistic years per year, more or less the rate found for languages spoken by settled peoples throughout the world. I suggest, therefore, that a rate of 0.7 linguistic years per year is assigned to the least changed Niger-Congo languages (Basa, Moore, Ijo, Gbaya), which leads to a date of around 16000BC for the original Niger-Congo tongue. Incidentally, the experience of Bioko, yet another island formed by melting Ice Age glaciers, lends substance to my suggested history of Otomanguean, possibly once spoken on land now covered by the waters of the Bight of Biafra.

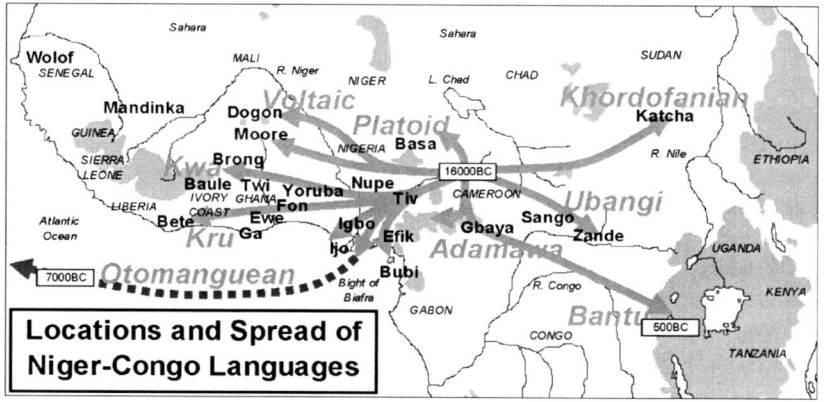

Locations and Spread of Niger-Congo Languages

The point of origin for Niger-Congo pretty much defines itself by the locations of the languages of each branch – I have shown it as being somewhere on the Nigeria-Cameroon border[6]. It is therefore absolutely certain that a highly significant development occurred in that region in around 16000BC, about 4000 years after the time that the Afro-Asiatic family suddenly sprang into life from its base in East Africa. The technological development concerned was almost certainly similar in the two cases and consisted of advances in stone-working and the production of greatly improved spears, arrows and the like, although the archaeology of Nigeria and Cameroon is much less researched than that of Kenya[7]. It is probably significant also that the climate of equatorial Africa had been drying since about 26000BC and, by 16000BC, much of what we know as the forest belt had become grassland. This change would have posed serious challenges to humans, both in ensuring drinking water supply and in the types of animals available to hunt, and it may be that necessity became the 'mother of invention', first in East Africa and then in Nigeria. As to why this particular community expanded so vigorously, rather than others which presumably also had access to similar technology, I believe we have to look once again to the way society was organised. Judging by the chieftain-orientated structure of much of West Africa, I think we can infer that it was probably the adoption of this type of society which, as in the case of the Afro-Asiatic speakers, made success possible.

At this stage I feel you should reward yourself by having a go at pronouncing the *gb* sound in Igbo and Gbaya. It is a very typical sound of central and western Africa, together with its partner *kp*. Basically, you have to try to say the two sounds at the same time; you pretend you are about to utter a *g*, and then change it to a *b* at the last moment. I find it strangely satisfying though I am sure my pronunciation is far from perfect.

## THE ATLANTIC AND MANDE FAMILIES

But what about Wolof and Mandinka? Their average distances to nine genuine Niger-Congo languages are 53000 and 62000 linguistic years respectively – and they are 54000 from each other. I think we just have to face the fact that, if they are connected to the Niger-Congo family, the connection is from much further back in time than the 18000 years during which the rest of the family has been developing. The Atlantic languages in particular are enormously diverse, to the extent that not all linguists would admit that they even form a single family. The following figure gives my interpretation of the evidence for both the Atlantic and Mande families, with suggested start dates and routes of spread, based on family trees derived from the numerals alone. They are therefore indicative only.

## Chapter 15   Roots

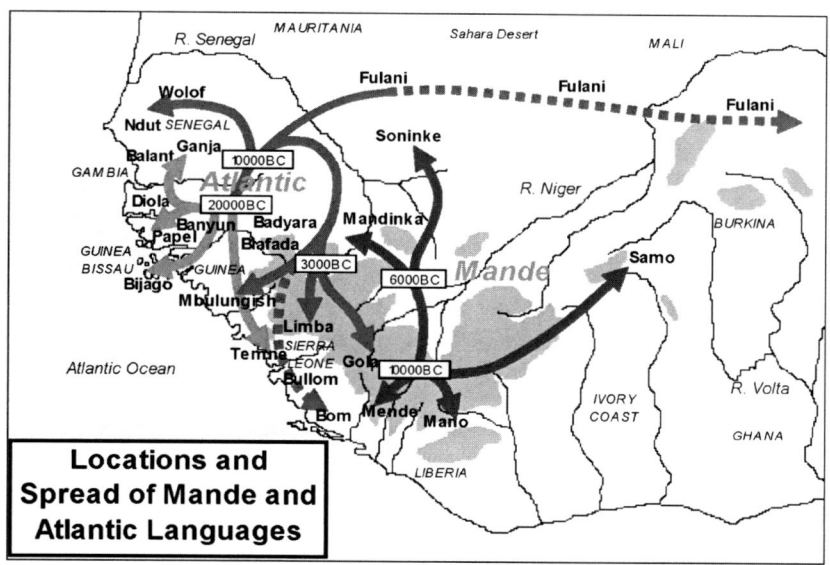

**Locations and Spread of Mande and Atlantic Languages**

We could also ask whether there is any relationship between Niger-Congo, Mande or Atlantic and the Afro-Asiatic family dealt with in Chapter 9. But although there are one or two relatively low measured distances between individual languages, these can readily be explained by secondary contact (Arabic and Swahili; Berber and Twi); there is no clear sign at all of true relationship. In two cases the measurements of grammar, vocabulary and sound are all below the coincidence level, the level of similarity we would expect between alien life forms and humans! The overall average distance from eight Afro-Asiatic languages to nine Niger-Congo languages and to Mandinka and Wolof (assigning a pretty arbitrary 130000 linguistic years for cases at the pure coincidence level) are 58000, 76000 and 66000 linguistic years respectively, way outside my confidence threshold. Taking 0.7 linguistic years per year for these ancient times, any common origin would have to be well before 30000BC.

So what was the world like in 30000BC anyway? Well, for a start, humans had only recently completed the colonisation of Europe and there may still have been pockets of Neanderthal territory in Spain and Portugal. But the first faltering footsteps outside Africa had been taken over 30000 years previously and, by 30000BC, almost all of Asia had been colonised. So, even if we are close to a common ancestor for Niger-Congo, Mande, Atlantic and Afro-Asiatic, this has not brought us even remotely close to the first human language. But Africa has more to tell us yet. There are two more language families which, though they are much less important in terms of numbers of speakers, may yet be highly revealing in terms of human history.

## NILO-SAHARAN LANGUAGES

The Nilo-Saharan family is comparatively small in world terms, with only a few million speakers, but the languages stretch from Songhay, spoken on the fringes of the Sahara in West Africa, to Nubian, spoken in the Nile valley in Egypt and Sudan, to Masai in Kenya and Tanzania. This is a very large tract of territory for relatively few speakers and it means that they are scattered quite thinly on the ground amongst speakers of Afro-Asiatic and Niger-Congo languages.

I should admit here that there is no unanimous agreement on the oneness of this family (although I am fully persuaded of it myself). There is also no agreement on the most appropriate division into branches. Never mind; let's not lose sight of the main point here which is to understand the family as a whole. Personally, I would suggest that the following principal groups of Nilo-Saharan language can be discerned.

| | |
|---|---|
| Saharan: | Songhay and a few others, from Mali, Niger, northern Nigeria and Chad; |
| Maban: | from southern Chad and south-western Sudan; |
| Central Sudanic: | southern Sudan, Central African Republic and northern Congo; |
| Western Nilotic: | southern Sudan and western Uganda; |
| Southern Nilotic: | eastern Uganda and western Kenya; |
| Eastern Nilotic: | Kenya and northern Tanzania; |
| Koman: | a small group of languages in western Ethiopia and eastern Sudan; |
| Northern Sudanic: | languages from 'Fur' in western Sudan to Ethiopia and Eritrea; |
| Nubian: | Nubian itself plus one or two relatives. |

My family tree for Nilo-Saharan is based purely on a comparison of the numerals 1 to 10 for thirty-two languages from all sides of the family. Distances to individual languages have been averaged to obtain those to each branch. Of course, the limitations of the system have to be borne in mind but it at least allows a feel for the relative closeness of the family to be obtained.

I have had to take an educated guess as to the root point – as you can see, I have opted for a point with four strands of language emerging – but it is hard to see any possibility other than that the Nilotic branches are the shortest. And this most certainly means that the geographical location of

# Chapter 15    Roots

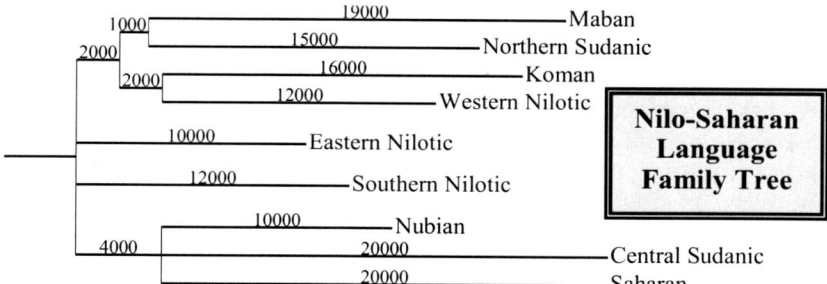

**Nilo-Saharan Language Family Tree**

the first Nilo-Saharan tongue was somewhere around the upper Nile. It is a slightly complicated picture, but I believe the following map matches the data satisfactorily[8].

The date shown for the origin of this family, 12000BC, allows a change rate of about 0.7 linguistic years per year for the least changed, the Eastern Nilotic language Kalenjin, but demands change rates of 2 linguistic years per year and above for the more travelled languages, Songhay, Kanuri and some of the Northern Sudanic and Maban tongues. Admittedly, distance travelled cannot explain all the results; the Central Sudanic languages (Kaba, Kresh, Kaliko) seem to have changed more than their location would imply, whereas Nubian and Dongolawi have changed less. However, it must be remembered that other factors (lifestyle, domination by other groups) also contribute strongly and the detailed prehistory of central Africa is completely unknown. In the particular case of the

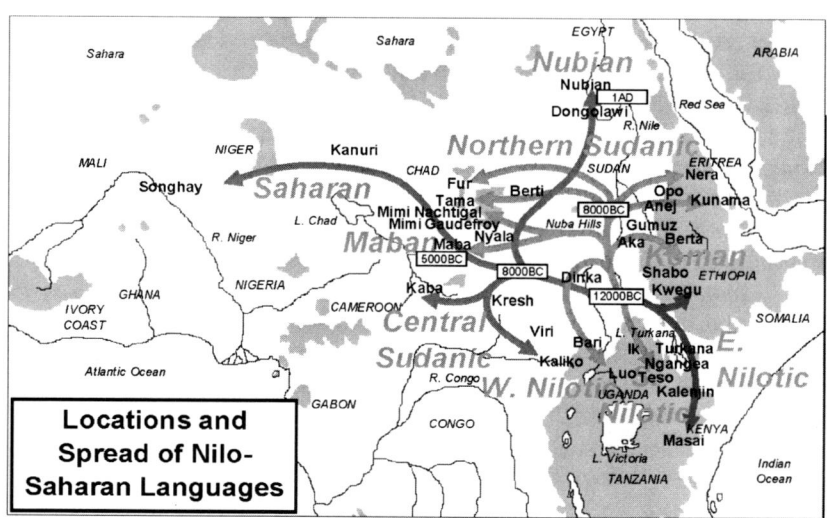

**Locations and Spread of Nilo-Saharan Languages**

Central Sudanic languages, they almost certainly suffered a long period of domination by Afro-Asiatic (Chadic) speech.

But does the overall picture make sense? By 12000BC, we have just seen that Niger-Congo culture was spreading out across the forest belt of Central Africa and it certainly reached north-east to the Nuba Hills of southern Sudan where languages of the Khordofanian branch are still spoken today. In fact, looking at the difference between the remaining Khordofanian languages, the least changed has undergone a sizeable 15000 linguistic years of development since dividing from its brothers and sisters and, even allowing for a mobile lifestyle, I can't help feeling that 11000BC represents a latest likely date for their arrival in the Nuba Hills. So it looks as though the expansion of Nilo-Saharan was later than that of Niger-Congo and that it therefore required the displacement of Niger-Congo language across the grass-covered plains of central Africa, but that Niger-Congo culture endured both in the forests to the south (the Congo basin) and also in the less accessible Nuba Hills. Khordofanian languages have remained an isolated island of Niger-Congo speech since about 8000BC.

But what about Afro-Asiatic? According to Chapter 9, that began in about 20000BC somewhere in Ethiopia. It started well too. We have seen that Afro-Asiatic speech spread rapidly north along the Nile to Egypt and then the Middle East, giving birth to Indo-European, Uralic, Dravidian etc. It also (so I suspect) spread rapidly east along the coasts of Arabia to India, spawning Sino-Tibetan. But it didn't spread rapidly south or west! The relevant map in Chapter 9 suggests that it only shifted a few hundred miles in the course of nine millennia, between 20000BC and 11000BC. Why? Of course, I don't know the real reason, but it seems clear that the capabilities which allowed Afro-Asiatic culture to expand north and east (notably microlithic technology) did not impress their neighbours to the south and west. In fact, from 12000BC, these neighbours seem to have made a better job of things than the Afro-Asiatics. The language evidence is that Nilo-Saharan speech and culture spread out steadily across lands which must previously have hosted Afro-Asiatic tongues, as well as those where Niger-Congo had been spoken. The Cushitic and Omotic branches of Afro-Asiatic were safe (and Indo-European and Sino-Tibetan had already escaped!), but the ancestors of the other branches were pegged back in Kenya and western Ethiopia. It was only from about the $8^{th}$ Millennium BC that the tables were turned. I suggested in Chapter 9 that it was a significant change to a much wetter climate, generating extensive wetlands right across central Africa, that gave the impetus for the spread of the Chadic and South Cushitic branches of Afro-Asiatic, reclaiming territory from Nilo-Saharan. It may have been the same ability to exploit wetlands which, a couple of thousand years earlier, allowed the ancestor of the Semitic and Berber branches to spread down the Nile to central

Sudan. Nilo-Saharan culture was still king of the drier grasslands, however, and this is reflected today in the pastoralist economy which most Nilo-Saharan speakers have adopted. It has also meant that Nilo-Saharan was able to reclaim the former wetlands once the climate shifted back to drier conditions, which has left the Chadic branch of Afro-Asiatic isolated in Chad and northern Nigeria.

It is a complex picture and it is easy to lose sight of the processes which were really at work. Please remember we are rarely talking in terms of a significant migration of population. The recent almost genocidal expulsion of Nilo-Saharan speakers from the Darfur region of western Sudan by Arabic speakers is an unusual and rather modern phenomenon. The process of language spread has usually been achieved by one culture coming to dominate its neighbour, either peacefully or by means of force, and this is possible when the dominating culture has achieved a higher level of technology or social organisation. In such cases, subsequent generations of the dominated culture come to speak the language of their superiors and, eventually, to adopt their culture. In the cases discussed here, it seems to be the technical and economic factors which were of most importance. Niger-Congo culture had a certain level of stone blade technology, enabling a spread east across Sudan. However, this was overtaken by tool developments in the east, which allowed Nilo-Saharan speakers to exploit the grasslands much more efficiently. A few thousand years later, it was Afro-Asiatic speakers who learnt to live off the wetlands most effectively.

Perhaps the most surprising members of the Nilo-Saharan family are Nubian and its close relatives. As you can see, they appear to stem from one of the more southerly strands of language and this is supported by the fact that related languages (Meidob and Hill Nubian – not shown on the map) are spoken far to the south, in the Nuba Hills region. The circumstances which led to Nubian language being able to spread north are quite unknown. The current degree of divergence suggests that arrival on the middle Nile may date from as little as 2000 years ago which, if true, would preclude their being the languages spoken in the historically attested lands of Kush and Nubia during ancient Egyptian times[9].

But can Nilo-Saharan be linked in any way to the other families of Africa? Luo is one of the most important members of the family; it is spoken in Uganda by about three million people, and it is a representative of the Western Nilotic branch. By the full measurement system, it shows a certain closeness to some of the Niger-Congo languages, particularly those of Ghana and Nigeria. The average calculated separation from the modern Niger-Congo languages is 45000 linguistic years, almost close enough to be taken seriously. The equivalent distances to Mande, Atlantic and Afro-Asiatic are 58000, 58000 and 51000 linguistic years respectively. The evidence therefore suggests that Nilo-Saharan may well have sprung from the same original root as Niger-Congo, perhaps between 25000 and 20000BC. Nilo-Saharan languages are highly tonal, making use of variations in tone for grammatical purposes, for example the tense of a verb (whether past, present or future). This is a trait also found in many Niger-Congo languages (and also in Otomanguean) but it is much less common in the Afro-Asiatic, Mande or Atlantic families.

However, while this look at Nilo-Saharan has certainly broadened our appreciation of events in the northern half of Africa, it has not actually taken us any further back in time; and this leaves us with just one remaining language family on the planet, a family which today is in serious trouble and which may well not survive for too many more generations.

## KHOI-SAN LANGUAGES

The world knows these as the 'click' languages. You may have imagined that you require some special adaptation of the throat muscles in order to generate these sounds, but not at all. There are a lot of different types of click, but they are essentially variations on the noises we might make to show disapproval (a sort of 'tut-tut' noise), to encourage a horse (gee-up) or to simulate a cork coming out of a bottle. I admit it needs a little practice to make these sounds as part of normal speech, but it certainly isn't impossible; Khoi-San-speaking children seem to learn the art without trouble!

Khoi-San languages are spoken by Hottentots and Bushmen, the original inhabitants of Namibia and parts of southern Angola, Botswana and the Cape region of South Africa. Nowadays, there are few Khoi-San languages left and each has relatively few speakers. There may be as many as 100000 Nama speakers; most languages only have a thousand or so. However, one extremely interesting point is that there are two languages spoken by two quite different tribes in Tanzania (over a thousand miles from the main Khoi-San speaking group), Sandawe and Hadza, which are thought by most to be members of the family. They are both click languages (not that that is necessarily evidence enough[10]) and they show other similar traits. This suggests that the range of the Khoi-San language family may have been much greater before the Bantu explosion, probably stretching right across the southern half of the continent. In recent centuries, i.e. since some sort of recorded history has existed, the Bushmen have been pushed further and further back into the Kalahari region, from the Cape, from Botswana and from Angola. Hottentots used to dominate an area stretching right across the Kalahari towards fertile Zimbabwe. However, the incursions of Bantu speakers from the north and Afrikaans-speaking settlers from the south have spelt disaster for both groups. There is a famous ancient Egyptian depiction of an expedition to the land of 'Punt', which shows the queen of the land with what is now recognised as

## Chapter 15  Roots

a typical trait of both Hottentot and Bushman women, steatopygia, or the storage of excess fat around the buttocks[11]. Now, no-one knows where Punt was, though most assume it must have been somewhere on the East African coast. Could this be an indication that a people who were ethnically related to modern Hottentots and Bushmen inhabited parts of East Africa three or four thousand years ago?

!Kung is a language spoken by the Bushmen (the '!' is a click sound). It is one of several quite closely related languages in the Kalahari region. According to the measurement system used here, it scores at least 50000 linguistic years from all Niger-Congo, Mande, Atlantic, Afro-Asiatic and Nilo-Saharan languages. In about a third of the cases, the correspondence is no better than the pure coincidence level. If I substitute an arbitrary 130000 linguistic years for these coincidence level cases, then the average comes out at 86000 linguistic years and, to reach that distance, languages changing at 0.7 linguistic years per year would have seen over 60000 years pass since their common origin. Of course, this is far outside the realms where the measurement can be taken seriously. But it means one thing: that common ancestor was spoken a hell of a long time ago! (this time the '!' is mine). It seems that the languages of Africa have been slowly drifting apart, sub-dividing (and being rendered extinct) in just the same way as elsewhere in the world, but for longer and, until recently, with less movement of population and culture. The picture indicated by the languages is absolutely consistent with the belief of anthropologists that Africa was the cradle of human life. The evidence from a comparison of Khoi-San with other language families stretches so far back in time that it is simply off the map!

Checking out the main group of Khoi-San languages, it is quite clear that they are all related, although some linguists would sub-divide them into three separate families. Individual language to language distances may be up to about 30000 linguistic years, so the process of division and spread has been going on in the Kalahari region for quite a while, probably nearly 20000 years. However, the link with the Tanzanian languages, Sandawe and Hadza, is much more tenuous and certainly much more remote in time. The fact that they are click languages is not enough; so are Ndebele, Zulu and Xhosa, all Bantu languages. One has to presume that Ndebele, Zulu and Xhosa have inherited the click sounds from the Khoi-San languages spoken in the region only a few hundred years ago, since Bantu speech arrived in southern Africa only very recently.

To be truthful, Sandawe and Hadza find themselves in the Khoi-San family by default. Linguists are quite sure they are not members of Afro-Asiatic, Niger-Congo or Nilo-Saharan, and physically the speakers most closely resemble the Bushmen, so Khoi-San seems their only natural home, but they are much too distant for real confidence[12]. By the full measurement system here, they average 48000 linguistic years from !Kung, and

66000 from an average of 20 languages from the other African families. However, they at least score a more moderate 23000 from each other. So, assuming that Sandawe and Hadza really are related to the rest of Khoi-San, the common origin was probably at least 25000 to 30000 years ago. Logically, the Khoi-San family might be identified with the Nachikufian culture, which commenced in Zambia in about 30000BC and then spread up into Tanzania, suggesting that Khoi-San language once stretched from coast to coast. Indeed, the Bantu languages clearly replaced something; that is self-evident. And the evidence seems to be that they most probably replaced Khoi-San type languages right across southern Africa. It would be expected, therefore, that Egyptian expeditions to East Africa in the 2$^{nd}$ Millennium BC would have come across Khoi-San speakers; the ancestor of the Bantu languages was then still spoken in the northern Congo basin.

An interesting question is to what extent the Bantu advance involved the replacement of the original population. I have been arguing strongly that language spread is quite different from population spread, because it is the spread of a culture, of an idea or a way of life, and this can be transmitted from group to group with relatively little movement of people. However, my impression is that the Bantu advance did indeed involve a substantial genetic change to the population, even more significant than the genetic impact of the spread of agriculture in Europe or India. The physical differences between most of the Bantu language speakers and Khoi-San speakers are very noticeable[13]. This is much less true towards the southern tip of Africa, where Khoi-San culture was relatively advanced (local Bantu words for cattle and sheep derive from Khoi-San originals)

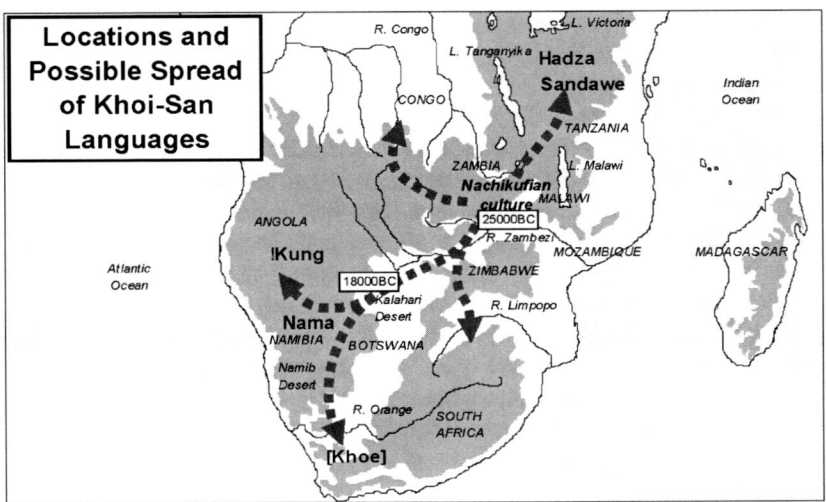

and where Bushman and Hottentot characteristics can be seen in Bantu speakers. It is also not true of those Pygmy groups which now speak a Bantu language; but Pygmies are now few and far between. It must surely have been the case that they – and the Bushmen – once covered a much wider area than their present ranges, but that the territory has now been taken over by the iron-using Bantus and, more recently still, by Indo-Europeans.

Khoi-San languages are no older than any other on the planet – all are the same age. However, the enormous difference between this family and all others leads to an appreciation of the antiquity of human language and the long history of its changing form.

## HUMANKIND

It was always going to be important to study African languages because of the role of Africa as the mother continent. The strong message which I take from African languages is that the process of spread, division and extinction, while it has been basically the same as elsewhere, has been going on for longer. Evidence remains of seven separate language (and therefore cultural) expansions, stemming from different regions of the continent, between Senegal, Ethiopia and Zambia. They commenced between about 20000BC and 10000BC, times when humans were beginning to get to grips with what can really be achieved using thin razor-sharp flakes of stone. Before that, one would not imagine that the pace of change was any quicker, either in culture or in language. But in reality all we can say is that the common ancestor to these seven language groups was spoken many tens of thousands of years ago. The arrows and dates shown on the following map are therefore purely illustrative. And there still remains a massive gap between the most speculative dates for language separation and the origin of our species as a whole, and I think we just have to admit that this gap is simply too wide ever to be bridged by language study alone.

Drifting away from the subject of language for a moment, there seems to be plenty of archaeological evidence that East Africa was the original cradle of our race. It was in Ethiopia that the oldest human skull yet unearthed recently made its appearance[14], dating back 160000 years, and East Africa remained a centre of advanced culture throughout human pre-history. The study of Mitochondrial DNA also revealed a few years ago now that the entire human race is descended from a single unknown African female (so-called 'Mitochondrial Eve') some 150000 years ago – give or take 10000 years or so[15]. This does not of course mean that she was the only woman of her race but it does imply that the total number of Homo Sapiens was at that time only a thousand or so individuals; any more and it would be mathematically highly improbable that no other

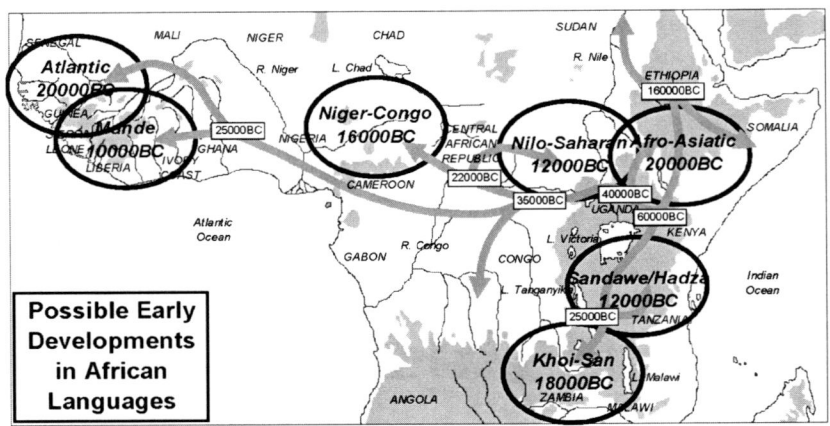

female's line of descent survived[16]. But there were certainly plenty of other human-looking 'people' about. I have mentioned the Neanderthals of Europe several times and have also referred to Homo Erectus, who was then living (in various sub-species forms) in both Africa and southern Asia. However, this particular East African community must have thought of themselves as distinct from all others; they kept themselves to themselves and never interbred with outsiders.

Perhaps 2000 generations passed, some 50000 years, during which time the territory inhabited by these people slowly expanded to cover most of eastern Africa. Outside this area, although the only clear evidence found is that of very small human-like creatures on the Indonesian island of Flores, one would presume that communities of various Homo Erectus types continued to survive. However, as Homo Sapiens mastered more and more different environments, the pace of expansion quickened. They filled the forest belt of central Africa, their stature diminishing with each new generation, reflecting the greater success of smaller individuals in a forest environment. These were the ancestors of the Pygmies and Bushmen. People also started spreading across the drier lands to the north and south. Here, success came to the tall and the swift – as well as of course to the intelligent – and this is reflected in the taller of Africa's modern inhabitants. These people adapted to each new environment they met and, at some time prior to 65000BC, they stood at the northern end of the Red Sea at the gateway to Asia. From there, there was no stopping them; by 50000BC they were in India, by 40000BC they had filled South-East Asia, with other groups entering Europe and Central Asia, and by 35000BC they had also reached Australia and New Guinea. Finally, in around 27000BC, the first band of humans set foot on the continent of North America.

It is a sobering thought though that the human race of 27000BC, our physical and cultural ancestors, were still living in the Old Stone Age using

Chapter 15    Roots                                                                 239

crude stone tools. It is probable that no community anywhere on the planet had yet felt the need for numerals greater than *five*!

But all that was about to change; by 20000BC a spirit of engineering innovation was blowing across the plains, leading to ever greater complexity of tool making, and the innovation centres have been revealed by archaeology to be in East Africa, Western Europe and, most surprisingly, eastern Siberia. We know nothing of the early language of Western Europe, but we know that in both East Africa and Siberia counting to *ten* became normal and culture spread out rapidly from both centres, taking language with it.

Then, in about 17000BC, something remarkable happened; a community living on the eastern coast of Ethiopia or Somalia developed the first skills of boat-craft. They were soon across the Red Sea and it wasn't long before their descendants started spreading east around the coast of Arabia. As existing populations were 'absorbed' into this early Sino-Tibetan-speaking community, the culture positively swept around the shores of the Indian Ocean.

But the final chapter began in about 15000BC when another highly successful band of Africans, having spread their culture north down the Nile valley, spilled out into Palestine. It was this band, probably numbering just a few hundred at the time, who were to transform every continent on the planet. They were the ones who carried the seeds of today's civilisation. At the time, all they had going for them was the latest in Stone Age technology combined with an ability to organise themselves into large and effective communities. Yet this was enough. Their culture spread inexorably outwards from Palestine; by 11000BC it had filled Turkey and the Middle East as far as Iran; from Iran it covered the plains of Central Asia before sweeping both west into Europe (Uralic, Basque, Etruscan) and east into Siberia, Mongolia and northern China (Altaic, Samoyedic, Chukchi-Kamchatkan). It also moved rapidly south-east across India (Austro-Asiatic, Dravidian).

A crucial technological step then took place somewhere on the shores of the Bay of Bengal in about 6000BC with the development of true seafaring, which brought the bearers of this new culture (Austro-Asiatic speaking) right around the coasts of South-East Asia and Indonesia. It was these people whose arrival led to a great technological leap forward in North-West Australia and also to the ocean-going exploits of the Polynesians, both in about 4000BC. They left their mark on the civilisations of China, and may even have enabled Asiatic civilisation to cross the Pacific to Central and South America in around 3000BC.

Perhaps I have strayed rather beyond language in this chapter, but I wanted to give a flavour for the role of language study in the wider world of human history. I hope it has been a thought-provoking experience. Let me close with a question. "What happened in around 6000BC?" This may seem a strange question to ask since I have given little hint until now that anything particular happened, but I want to draw your attention to a strange set of circumstances.

1) In Australia, a language spoken in the eastern hill country of Queensland or New South Wales suddenly started spreading across the greater part of the continent, forming the Pama-Nyungan family.
2) In Florida, human presence suddenly seems to have ceased, followed a thousand years later by re-colonisation by Timucuan speakers from the Caribbean.
3) In the plains of Central Asia, the steady outward spread of Uralic and Altaic language was suddenly reversed, bringing a rapid tide of Mongolian-derived culture (i.e. North Caucasian) back west from the Altai Mountain region.
4) In northern Asia, one particular language of the Ural Mountains (ancestral Finno-Ugric) suddenly started spreading out east and west, apparently replacing other closely related Uralic tongues.
5) In southern Russia, Indo-European speech suddenly started spreading out from the Caucasus region across the steppe lands to the north.
6) In North Africa, the ancestor of Egyptian was suddenly able to move from the Sahara to the Nile valley, despite closely related Afro-Asiatic cultures already being present.

These six are the clearest cases, although I could add issues such as the spilling out of the ancestral Dravidian language across the Indus plain – when the Indus valley should logically have already been host to similarly advanced culture; also the strong spread east of Algonquian, Iroquoian and Siouxan language across the great plains of North America. Individually, each event could plausibly be explained by this or that cultural or economic development which gave advantage to people in a certain place and therefore to whatever language they happened to be speaking. Taken together, however, I feel entitled to at least ask the question as to whether some world-wide phenomenon may have occurred, something which could have led to massive depopulation of whole sectors of the planet. It's not the sort of question that is usually asked when considering human prehistory but I will leave it with you as a final example of an issue which the study of language can raise.

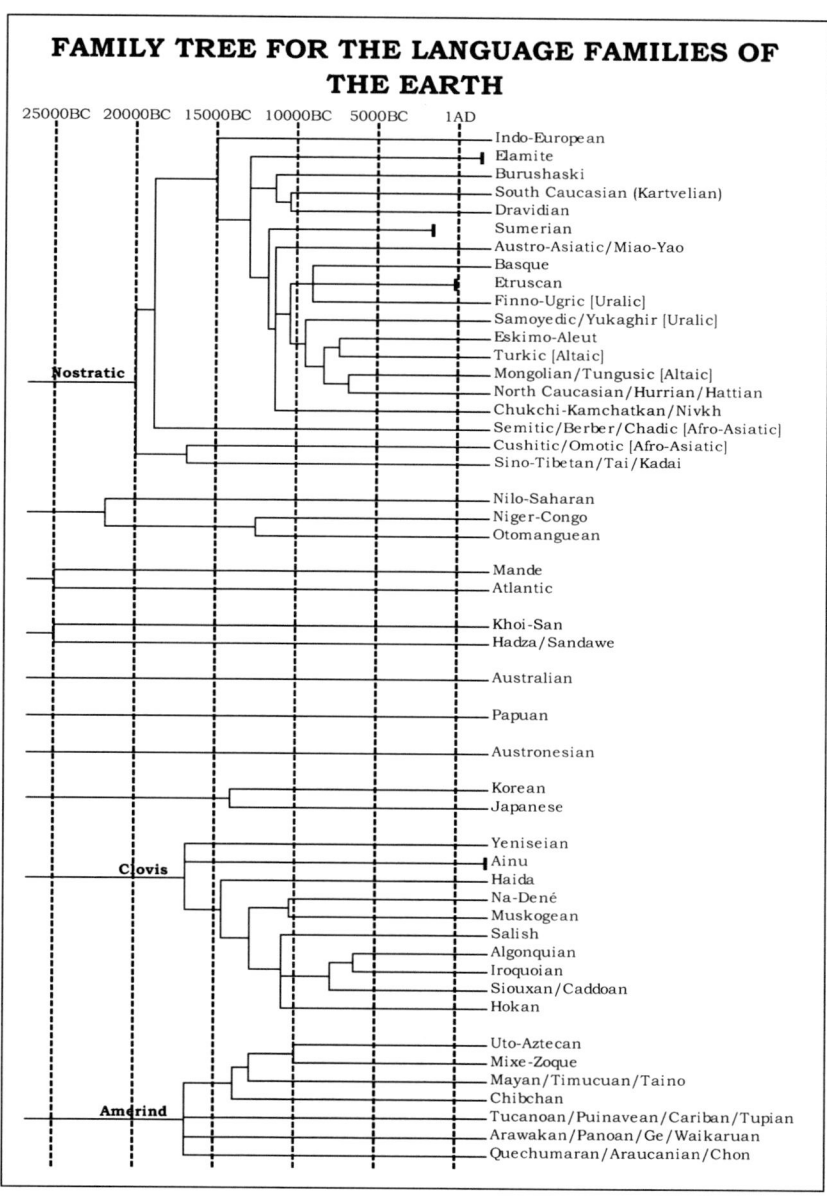

# Notes

## Chapter 1: Introduction

1. It seems that an increasing consensus is developing on this subject and without a doubt it has been the study of Mitochondrial DNA which has been largely responsible. Since Cann, Stoneking and Wilson's article in *Nature* in 1987, the concept of 'Mitochondrial Eve', the mother of us all, has dominated thinking about our species' origin. More recently, study of the Y Chromosome has opened up male line genealogy, and this has led to some disagreement on the date of our common male ancestor, but the broad message is still compatible with that from Mitochondrial DNA.
2. I shall be using the term *Homo Sapiens* to designate fully modern humans, although technically *Homo Sapiens Sapiens* is the correct term. Technically, Neanderthal man is also Homo Sapiens: *Homo Sapiens Neanderthalensis*.
3. In making the comparisons between languages shown in this book, I have made use of a combination of dictionaries, learning aids (many on the web), published texts and specialist papers, too many to list individually. In all, I have characterised some 135 different languages with regard to their vocabulary, grammar and sound, and in many cases it has been necessary to consult several sources in order to find all the information I needed. Where I have received direct specialist assistance, this is acknowledged.
4. Based once again on DNA studies, it is estimated that Neanderthal man diverged from the ancestor of Homo Sapiens something like 300000 years ago. If any more recent interbreeding with our ancestors ever occurred – and the debate over this is ongoing – no clear record has yet appeared in modern human DNA. See Tattersall, 1995, for an excellent introduction to the subject.
5. There is absolutely no agreement on the rapidity with which physical characteristics might be expected to change in a population. The most obviously observed characteristic is skin colour, and it is clear from the continuing pale colour of European colonists in Australia and the dark

colour of African Americans that two or three hundred years is nowhere near enough time to effect real change. At the other end of the scale, the population which first left Africa about 65000 years ago has since diversified into Australians, Chinese, Eskimos and Europeans – and everything in between!

## Chapter 2: The Languages of the Earth

1. I have used the English versions for languages and places where they exist; hence the use of *Persian*, *French* and *Japanese* rather than *Farsi*, *Français* and *Nihongo*.
2. Greenberg, 1963.
3. Greenberg, 1987.
4. The Nostratic super-family is the subject of a vast literature of theories and counter-theories. For example see Dolgopolsky, 1998, or Bomhard and Kerns, 1994, as well as Pedersen, 1962.
5. Ruhlen, 1994.
6. See for example Blažek and Bengtson, 1995.
7. This approach has become known as the 'Comparative Method'. It is undeniably an intellectually rigorous approach but, since it is restricted to the issue of identifying common roots, it includes no actual measure of the degree of separation between two languages.

## Chapter 3: Language Change

1. For example, Caesar describes the tribe known as the 'Belgae' as dwelling on both sides of the channel (having invaded Britain from France/Belgium); see Julius Caesar's *The Conquest of Gaul*.
2. Taken from Jack Lynch's edited version, published in 2002.
3. Taken from The Oxford Shakespeare, published in 1969.
4. Taken from an edition by A Pollard, published in 1924.
5. Taken from an edition by E V Gordon, published in 1937.
6. Lees, 1953; Swadesh, 1972.
7. Gardner, 1988.

## Chapter 4: Measuring the Change

1. The most common usage of the term 'half-life' is to describe radioactive decay, where the half-life is the time for the number of radioactive particles to halve. However a similar 'logarithmic decay' process applies to such effects as the loss of bubbles in a foam or the change in DNA from one generation to another. The common factor is that the processes are all essentially random.

2. In practice, I suggest that this effect would only become significant when dealing with time periods of some thousands of years. For more recent times one would expect that linguists would readily be able to recognise words which are cognate.
3. This suggestion will not prove popular with linguists for two reasons: (a) it introduces an element of subjectivity and (b) it demands little linguistic training beyond an appreciation of sound mutation.
4. Because the effect of different probabilities of change applying to different words is opposite to that of gradual changes in word form, there is a tendency for the two to cancel out in Swadesh and Lees' system. This certainly reduces the errors that there otherwise might have been, but it does not return the real change curve to that of logarithmic decay.
5. Actually this case, the relationship between Vietnamese and Cantonese (or any other of the Chinese languages) is a controversial one. Experts now agree that Vietnamese should be placed in a quite different family from Chinese, but the similarities with the Chinese languages are undeniable. See Chapter 12 for my assessment.
6. Many of the deductions which linguists have made about language ancestry have been based on sound (phonetics), for example the well known division of Indo-European branches into 'Kentum' and 'Satem' languages, depending on the word used for *a hundred*. After 30 years of language study, embracing languages from all parts of the world, I have to say I believe this to be a serious mistake. It seems quite clear that the sounds of a language are often inherited from an earlier language of the region; i.e. even where a people change their language, they do not so easily change the sounds their mouths make. Modern examples would be Welsh and Irish accents of English, the adoption of click sounds by some southern Bantu languages in Africa, and shared phonetics in three quite different Indian language groups (Indic, Dravidian and Munda). The reliance placed on the study of comparative phonetics is, in my opinion, a millstone round the neck of historical linguistics.
7. 'Ln' stands for 'Naperian' or 'Natural' Logarithm, commonly used in mathematics. You can find the function on most calculators.
8. 'e' is a special number to mathematicians (about 2.718), which is used (among other things) to generate Naperian/Natural Logarithms.

## Chapter 5: Divide and Conquer

1. Schmidt, 1872.
2. The most confusing case is presented when comparing two or more languages which still lie on a language gradient. The chief example given in this book is that of Punjabi, Hindi and Bengali, discussed in Chapter 7.

# Chapter 6: The Germanic Tribes

1. The mention of a 'Frisian' tribe in a 1st Century AD Latin text in no way contradicts the view that the separation of today's Germanic languages had not even commenced at that date. Tribal names were conferred on a people or a region. If the language changed, the name by which the people were known would not necessarily change with it, and their name would then attach itself to the new language. A more modern example is the Indic language Nepali, whose name is inherited from the unrelated 'Newari' language it displaced.
2. Pytheas' work *On the Ocean* (Cunliffe, 2001), published around 320BC, is no longer extant. We know of it through references made by other authors, in this case Pliny in his *Natural History*. Pliny quotes Pytheas as stating that a people called 'Guiones' (or Gotones) inhabited an 'estuary of the sea' a day's journey from the amber-producing island of 'Abalus', adjacent to the 'congealed sea'. Their neighbours are recorded as the 'Teutoni'. Most agree that Guiones or Gotones are Goths and Teutoni are certainly Teutons; the congealed sea is usually taken to be ice-covered, which suggests the northern Baltic (largely ice-covered each winter). However, whether Abalus is Bornholm, Öland, Gotland or even Åland is impossible to know for sure. Similarly, the estuary in question could be that of the Oder or the Vistula, both of which flow into large gulfs of the Baltic Sea. Personally, I favour the Gdansk region of northern Poland, where the Vistula flows into the Baltic, as the home of the Goths, and Gotland (meaning land of the Goths), which lies 140 miles to the north, as Abalus. The Teutons would therefore have inhabited the land immediately to the west, i.e. present day north-east Germany. At that stage, western Germany would have been Celtic (the La Tène culture) and the Germanic tribes only moved west when, as Julius Caesar was informed, they invaded Celtic lands towards the end of the 2nd Century BC (Delaney, 1986).
3. It seems to have become accepted as fact (e.g. Dalby, 1998; Bragg, 2003; Biddulph, 1995) that Frisian is the language most closely related to English, and it is certainly true that much commonality (e.g. *goes-goose*; *stoarm-storm*; *rein-rain*; *sliepe-sleep*) exists, apparently closer than other Germanic languages. Nevertheless, this entirely depends on which aspects of language are studied. I could pluck out similar, strong parallels between English and Swedish (*rum-room* cf. Frisian: *keammer*; *liv-life* cf. Frisian: *libben*). The truth is that all Germanic languages have steadily changed from an original and it will inevitably be possible to find examples of strong similarities between any Germanic language pair, and other examples where the similarity is much less strong. Without any means of quantifying the difference between languages,

such observed similarities are of limited use. It should also be noted that the relatively late separation of Dutch and Frisian is further evidence against Frisian being especially close to English. At the time of the Saxon invasion of southern Britain, the ancestor of Dutch, Frisian and German would still have been a single language.
4. Anglo-Saxon artefacts such as those found at the famous warrior burial site at Sutton Hoo are duplicated by numerous similar objects found in Sweden. This certainly suggests a genuine closeness of culture and extensive trade during the early centuries of Anglo-Saxon colonisation in Britain.
5. It is commonly stated as fact that the outlying regions of a language zone are the most conservative. I believe this is entirely down to an erroneous perception of the evidence. Naturally, when a change to the language spoken in the heart of a territory occurs, this leaves the old unchanged version in many of the outlying regions. However, when a change occurs in one of these outlying regions, this still leaves the unchanged version in the other outlying regions, as well as the heartland, and it is therefore less noticeable. I suggest that it is purely because change in individual outlying regions is less noticeable that the language of such regions is often thought of as conservative.

## Chapter 7: The Indo-Europeans

1. Most famously, Sir William Jones, a British judge on service in India, reported in 1786 that Sanskrit bore remarkable similarities to Latin, Greek, Gothic and Celtic.
2. The Urnfield culture is first recognised in Hungary and western Romania in the mid $2^{nd}$ Millennium BC (e.g. Phillips, 1981). By 1000BC it had reached into Germany, France and even northern Spain, as well as northern Italy. There is no real sign of change in Britain however until the $7^{th}$ Century BC, when the first recognisably Celtic artefacts appear, both in Britain (Laing, 1979) and in Ireland (Piggott, 1965). This is also the time when a stratified and somewhat warlike society began to develop (Pryor, 2003). It is at this stage that I suggest Goidelic language may have crossed the English Channel.
3. Hallstatt is the name of a salt mine in Austria, in use for nearly three thousand years. An adjoining village and cemetery have been thoroughly investigated over the years since 1846, revealing an advanced Iron Age civilisation, dating principally from 800BC to around 500BC. The society was highly stratified, and the standard of craftsmanship displayed in the prestige goods found was extremely high. One particularly interesting find was a well-preserved (due to the salt) fragment of tartan cloth, reminiscent of Celtic tartans today.

4. Dates have been taken from Bernard Grun's *Timetables of History*.
5. The Khazars were a Turkic speaking nation who carved out an empire for themselves in modern Ukraine and southern Russia in about 650AD. Within Khazar borders the Slavs were a subordinate people. The empire finally collapsed around 1000AD. (Information taken from *Catastrophe* by David Keys)
6. The Chernyakhovo culture (Mongait, 1961) describes the inhabitants of non-coastal Ukraine during the first five centuries AD. The evidence reveals a prosperous and peaceful society (no fortifications) with strong trade links to the Roman Empire.
7. Every text I see describes Slovene as a 'South Slavonic' language; after all Slovenia was once part of the country known as Yugoslavia (meaning South Slav land). However, the truth is that Slovene cannot be easily understood by speakers of Serbo-Croat or the other South Slavonic languages and it should certainly not be bracketed with them. Those linguists who remark on the similar features between Slovene and Slovak should perhaps ask themselves why, rather than continue to maintain the traditional 'South Slavonic' label.
8. Settlements of the Zarubintsi Urnfield culture lie principally in the northern Ukraine and adjacent Russian territory and date to the period from 200BC to 200AD. They were fortified and served a mixed farming community.
9. See Klima, 2004.
10. Prussian was spoken in what is now north-east Germany and northwest Poland, in territory which had once been Gothic speaking.
11. This split between Slavonic and Baltic seems to have occurred at the time that Iranian speaking tribes swept into the Ukraine (see notes 22 and 23). It therefore seems probable that the invaders drove a wedge between northern (Baltic) and southern (Slavonic) elements of the population.
12. My sources for the numerals are Andrew Dalby's *Dictionary of Languages* and Mark Rosenfelder's website, which quotes the numerals 1 to 10 (where they exist) in over 5000 languages.
13. The Yadava clan are supposed to have migrated south from the Delhi region to Gujarat during the early 1st Millennium BC. Archaeologically, the incidence of a distinctive black and red ware across west and central India may possibly be associated with this cultural movement. An Iron Age horse-riding culture can also be traced spreading south from Gujurat through Maharashtra and Karnataka states (i.e. down the western side of India) during the 1st Millennium BC. The *Mahavamsa*, which tells the history of Sri Lanka, then dates the initial Sinhalese settlement of the island to the year of Buddha's death, 504BC (see Dalby, 1998).

14. The Maurya Dynasty came to power in about 320BC, ruling from Pataliputra (modern Patna) on the Ganges River. Under king Asoka, the empire covered most of Afghanistan as well as Pakistan and the whole of northern India as far south as Karnataka (see Keay, 2000). After Asoka's death in 231BC, the empire fragmented. The language of this empire was Prakrit, ancestral to most of today's Indic languages.
15. In 320AD, the Gupta Dynasty was founded (by Chandragupta), also centred on Pataliputra, and the empire grew to cover the whole of northern India and Bangladesh, but not Afghanistan or southern Pakistan. It lasted until the Huns invaded in 510AD (Keay, 2000).
16. The Persians dominated the Indus Valley from Darius I's conquest in about 520BC until the coming of Alexander the Great in 327BC.
17. The principal dispute is between those who consider the Aryans to be indigenous to India and those who see them as invaders. The Aryans appear in the Rigveda, whose origin is generally dated to the 2$^{nd}$ Millennium BC, but the question is whether they should also be identified with the inhabitants of the Indus Valley civilisation, which came to an end during that millennium.
18. Shalmaneser III of Assyria (859–824BC) controlled much of the Middle East from his homeland in northern Iraq and he is the first to record the presence of 'Madai' (Medes) and 'Parsua' (Persians) in western Iran. Archaeologically, I would suggest that the presence of Iranian speakers is accompanied by the red and cream pottery found at sites such as Sialk in Central Iran, visible from around 1000BC (Curtis, 1989).
19. The Parthian Empire emerged in the 3$^{rd}$ Century BC from territories conquered by Alexander the Great in Central Asia (Turkmenistan). By the mid 1$^{st}$ Century BC, Parthia was a serious threat to the Roman Empire, holding a frontier on the Euphrates River, and with its capital at Ctesiphon on the Tigris. The Parthian Empire finally disintegrated in the early 3$^{rd}$ Century AD following several devastating wars against the Romans (Wells, 1984). It is often claimed that the Kurds should be identified with the 'Kardoukhoi' mentioned by Xenophon in 400BC, and perhaps also with the 'Khirikhi' defeated by Tiglath Pileser 1 of Assyria around 1100BC (according to current majority opinion); however, I am of the view that these peoples are much more likely to have been ancestors of modern Georgians (see Chapter 11).
20. It is generally agreed that horses were first domesticated by early Indo-Europeans in approximately 4000BC, probably in the Ukraine. However, at that stage, they were only suitable as beasts of burden and, shortly afterwards, as drawers of wheeled vehicles. Horse riding was only possible later following the breeding of stronger animals and

is betrayed in the archaeological record by 'bits'. Renfrew, 1987, suggests this may have first occurred in about 2000BC in the Carpathian region of western Ukraine. The earliest claim of which I am aware (based on a bridle cheek piece found in Latvia) is dated to the mid 3rd Millennium BC (Loze, 2004). However, the truth may be that adoption of horse riding was gradual, dependent on the breeding of ever stronger horses.

21. Mongait, 1961, distinguishes three phases of 'pit grave' culture, all of which are likely to represent Indo-European speakers. The first, from the 3rd Millennium BC, is located between the Dnieper and the Volga (eastern Ukraine and southern Russia) and coincides with the first use of the two-wheeled cart. Phase 2, with 'Catacomb' type graves, is a clear development from Phase 1 and is from the first half of the 2nd Millennium BC. However, Phase 3, the 'Timber Grave' (or Andronovo) culture, was quite different; it arrived in the mid 2nd Millennium BC and stretched from the Altai Mountains to the Ukraine. Its centre of development was clearly in the east, i.e. in the Iranian language zone.

22. The Timber Grave culture of the second half of the 2nd Millennium BC gave rise to that of the Cimmerians, who swarmed into Eastern Europe from about 800BC. The next wave was that of the Scythians, and they were followed in the 3rd Century BC by the Sarmatians. Culturally, there was no significant difference between the three groups other than the ongoing technological development of the Iron Age. All were semi-nomadic pastoralists; all were clearly Iranian speakers.

23. Several researchers have drawn strong parallels between Celtic and Scythian or Sarmatian art (e.g. Kendrick, 1927; Piggott, 1965). There was certainly contact between them, as evidenced by Scythian raids deep into Celtic territory in southern Germany and France (Piggott, 1965). It could be argued that raids into Germanic territory (eastern Germany, Czech Republic, Poland) produced a similar effect on Germanic art. Finally, the fact that Iranian speaking tribes smashed into the Slavonic-Baltic heartland is more than sufficient to explain some of the observed similarities between the two branches, similarities which have led several researchers to some very inaccurate conclusions regarding early Slavonic history.

24. The history of the Hittite Empire has been revealed most clearly by the many thousands of inscribed tablets recovered from Bogazköy in Turkey, but also by Egyptian records and, of course, by archaeology. It appears that they took over domination of central Turkey some time early in the 2nd Millennium BC and that the empire survived numerous ups and downs before being destroyed around 1200BC (according

to most commentators – rather later in my view). Descendent kingdoms survived in northern Syria and southern Turkey until the 8th Century BC (e.g. Bryce, 1998).
25. The first Tocharian texts were discovered in the Tarim Basin in western China in the early years of the 20th Century and have been dated to the 6th to 9th Centuries AD. Earlier evidence for Tocharian speech has been deduced from the presence of loan words in Prakrit documents from the 3rd Century AD. Tocharian is thought to have died out under the domination of Turkic speakers in around 1000AD.

## Chapter 8: Indo-European Origins

1. It used to be taken as virtually proven that Indo-European appeared in Pakistan with Aryan invaders in the early 2nd Millennium BC (e.g. Piggott, 1950). The confidence with which this opinion was put forward was based largely on the archaeological investigations carried out by Sir Mortimer Wheeler which, in his opinion, showed evidence for mass slaughter of an earlier population. However, this interpretation of the evidence is widely rejected today, especially in India, and this has led many to suggest that there never was any Aryan invasion, which then leads to the possibility (not supported by this book) that Indo-European languages have a much longer history in India and Pakistan than previously thought. For a recent balanced view, admitting that a serious change in society occurred in the early 2nd Millennium BC with strong connections to Central Asia, see Agrawal (undated).
2. The earliest evidence for agriculture in Europe comes from Nea Nikomedia in Greece, dated to the early 7th Millennium BC. By 6200BC agricultural communities (the Starčevo-Körös-Criş culture) had filled the lower Danube valley (Serbia, southern Hungary, Romania, Bulgaria). There then seems to have been a pause (Baldia, 2003) until about 5600BC, before a culture known as 'Linear Band' after their pottery decoration style spread agriculture across Germany, Holland and Poland, as well as back south into Hungary. In the east, this developed through several pottery styles into 'Corded Ware', the name given to the first agricultural societies of the Baltic states and western Russia, eventually reaching Finland (by the late 4th Millennium BC). In the west, agriculture crossed the sea to Britain in about 4300BC. It appears that a less well documented spread of agriculture also occurred through the Mediterranean lands to Italy (Cardial/Impressed pottery, 6000–5600BC), France (La Hoguette culture, 5500BC) and, eventually, Spain.
3. Gimbutas, 1970; Childe, 1950.

Notes                                                                 251

4. I confess to being amazed at this view. When faced with the historically known changes to Latin (becoming Italian, French, Spanish etc.), it seems impossible to argue that the comparatively slight differences between Slavonic languages have taken many thousands of years to develop. Yet this is what is agued by proponents of the so-called 'Palaeolithic Continuity Theory' (e.g. Alinei, 2003).

5. The script in which the earliest Greek was written is known as 'Linear B'. It was famously deciphered in 1952 by Michael Ventris.

6. A script similar to Linear B (known as Linear A) was used on the island of Crete in the mid 2$^{nd}$ Millennium BC but, though it can be read based on the Linear B interpretation, it cannot be understood. However, it is clearly not Indo-European. The most confident interpretation I know is that put forward by Cyrus Gordon (Gordon, 1975), who considered Linear A to be a Semitic language. This has not been widely accepted however.

7. In the opinion of most, the Mycenaean (i.e. early Greek) civilisation collapsed some time in the 12$^{th}$ Century BC and very little is then known until the 8$^{th}$ Century, when classical Greek civilisation began to emerge.

8. My personal view is that the laryngeal sounds in Hittite were derived directly from the previous language of the region, Hattian (see Chapter 11), as was much of Hittite vocabulary.

9. The period known as Early Bronze II saw a flowering of civilisation in Turkey. However, it was followed by widespread destruction of settlements at the Early Bronze II/III interface, in about 2200BC.

10. There has been a lot of debate about the dating of the Middle Eastern Bronze Age. Personally, I subscribe to the view that the Hittites came to prominence in the late 16$^{th}$ Century BC and that their empire was destroyed in around 1050BC; these dates are about 150 years later than those most commonly cited.

11. The Hittite Empire really had a remarkable history. More than once they lost their heartland to outside invasion and had to fight to recover it. Without natural frontiers, there were potential enemies on all sides, who continually had to be pacified. See Bryce, 1998, for details.

12. Archaeologically, 3000BC marks the appearance of a crude type of pottery in northern Greece known as Dhimini ware, which has clear parallels in the pottery of those who ravaged much of the rest of Greece in about 2200BC.

13. It seems that Albanian society has always tended to be conservative. As the spread of Urnfield cultures progressed through the 2$^{nd}$ Millennium BC, Albania remained an island where barrow burial was still practised. When flange-hilted swords were fashionable in both

Central Europe and the Aegean (late 2$^{nd}$ Millennium BC), Albania remained unaffected.
14. See Duridanov, 1976.
15. Mallory, 1991, agrees with this identification. The Afanasievo culture can be detected from around 3000BC in the southern Urals and then western Siberia, and one notable feature is that the skeletons found have been European-looking rather than Mongoloid. Afanasievo people were replaced in about 1200BC by the so-called 'Karasuk' culture (Mongait, 1961) with Mongoloid skeletal features. This may logically have been the prime reason for the Tocharian-speaking Afanasievo people moving south into the Tarim Basin.
16. The usual identification of the inhabitants of the Tarim Basin as 'Tocharian' stems from the fact that the Greeks met them during their occupation of Central Asia following Alexander the Great's conquest and their name for the people was 'Tokharioi'. The same people then turned up as conquerors of Afghanistan, northern Pakistan and northwest India in the 2$^{nd}$ Century AD (Keay, 2000).
17. Corded Ware cultures (see note 2) predate the arrival of Indo-European. However, my belief is that the north Ukraine area saw a fusion of Corded Ware and Indo-European (specifically Germanic) cultures during the 3$^{rd}$ Millennium BC. It was from this area that the livestock-herding Fatyanovo culture can be discerned spreading east through central Russia as far as the Volga-Oka region during the 2$^{nd}$ Millennium BC (Mongait, 1961). Mallory, 1991, makes the point that Fatyanovo culture, though it used Corded Ware, was intrusive and later than the earlier widespread Corded Ware cultures of northern Europe.
18. The Lusatian (or Lausitz) culture stretched from the western Ukraine through Poland, eastern Germany and the Czech Republic roughly between 1500 and 500BC, paralleling the Urnfield culture to the south. Lusatians were arable farmers but fortified settlements and royal burials speak for a hierarchical society. For Pytheas, see Chapter 6, note 2.
19. The earliest Urnfield sites are in Romania and Hungary (Piggott, 1965), dated to the mid 2$^{nd}$ Millennium BC. I believe it is possible to read in the pottery the fact that the northern zone (Slovakia, Austria – sleek undecorated ware) had become culturally distinct from the southern zone (Hungary, northern Serbia, Croatia – dark-faced ware). Logically, the northerners spoke ancestral Celtic while the southerners spoke early Italic. The culture of Hungary in particular was notably stable, settled and prosperous (Sandars, 1978).
20. The first appearance of burial urns in Italy occurs in the Po valley (northern Italy) at the end of the 'Terremarra' period, just before

1000BC, and is strongly associated with the 'Villanovan' culture (Pallottino, 1955).
21. Of the other Italic languages, Umbrian and Oscan are the best known (from surviving texts) and they are both very closely related to Latin.
22. Piggott, 1965, makes the point that the Tripolye culture is quite distinct from that of the Corded Ware zone to the north. It is therefore most likely to have been Indo-European speaking. However, it clearly owes much to the previous culture of the region, often known as 'Danubian', a derivative of Linear Band Pottery (see note 2). Mongait, 1961, sees a distinct change in Tripolye culture around 2000BC, including a change in burial custom, suggesting conquest, probably from the east. Germanic speakers are the obvious suspects. It may have been at this stage that the ancestral Italic-Celtic speakers were displaced across the Carpathians into western Romania and Hungary. Hood, 1967, also sees clear parallels between the art of the Tripolye people and that of the Dhimini ware people of Greece (see note 12).
23. Prior to 3000BC, the distinction between the different Indo-European languages of the Ukraine region would have been relatively modest. I suggest that the steppe land of the south was home to speakers of ancestral Slavonic, Greek etc.; the Italic-Celtic speakers would have inhabited the more wooded territory to the north, while Germanic-Tocharian speakers lived further north still, in the middle Dnieper region.
24. Common Indo-European vocabulary includes words for tree types (*oak*, *beech*, *willow*), and animals (*wolf, bear, horse, sheep, goat, cow, dog*), but only a general word for *grain* and another for *metal*. It is hardly conclusive, but these words fit in with a location in southern Russia during early pastoralist days (Lehmann, 1973).
25. Barber, 1999.
26. The title is *Archaeology and Language* (Renfrew, 1987).
27. The levels are Anau II and Hissar II; the typical pottery is a plain grey/black ware and the production technique represents a total change in comparison with earlier levels. Dating is made easier by the presence of Akkadian-style tools and weapons from the Early Dynastic Period, which covers the first two thirds of the 3$^{rd}$ Millennium BC.
28. Perhaps the best evidence comes from the settlement of Rana Ghundai in western Pakistan, which was destroyed by fire in about 2000BC and reoccupied at a much more basic level by a people who produced a much cruder pottery type than that used previously. Similar destruction levels are observed at other sites in the region (Piggott, 1950).
29. The empire of Mitanni, based in eastern Turkey, northern Syria and northern Iraq, thrived from about 1500 to 1300BC (according to most

historians); that of the Kassites, based at Babylon in Iraq, lasted from about 1550 to 1150BC. While the dates are open to dispute, the Indo-European nature of their names and the definitively Indic nature of their gods (Mitra, Varuna, Indra) is widely recognised. A Hurrian text on the subject of chariot racing, discovered in the Hittite capital, Hattusas, uses numerals *one*, *three*, *five* and *seven*, as well as the word for *turning*, which are very close to the Sanskrit words (Piggott, 1950).

30. The land which is now Armenia was part of the kingdom of Urartu (Hurrian speaking – see Chapter 11) until the 6th Century BC when the Scythians and Medes combined forces to destroy it. However, Armenians were probably already present. There are references to 'Armens' in the annals of Assyrian kings from the late 2nd Millennium BC and plenty of references to Armenia from Persian Empire times, not to mention archaeological evidence for the arrival of a suspiciously Indo-European looking culture (e.g. warrior burials) in the late 2nd Millennium BC, but there is no absolute certainty that the Armenian language had arrived until the setting up of the first definitely Armenian-speaking kingdom in 190BC.

31. Chapter 7 showed early Slovenian as having spread across the Hungarian plain in about the 6th Century AD. This would have been the language which was superseded by Hungarian.

32. Mitochondrial DNA studies have now been complimented by studies of the Y Chromosome, defining male ancestry. Wells, 2002, reports that some 70% of Europeans are from a population which spread from Central Asia at least 30000 years ago, whereas about 20% stem from a much more recent Middle Eastern population. This last element should logically be associated with the spread of agriculture, matching the 17% from Mitochondrial DNA.

33. There is much discussion as to the most appropriate length to take for a generation. Some take 20 years, which may be about right for a 'first-born' type generation; others take as much as 30 years. 25 years appears to me to be a reasonable compromise.

34. The calculation assumes that the territory is divided into 180 bands, each representing the advance made in a particular generation. As each new band of territory is occupied, the genetic composition of the new inhabitants is assumed to be made up of a certain percentage from the population of the previous band and the remainder from the original inhabitants. Thus, the genes of the advancing agriculturalists are diluted to an ever greater extent at the leading edge of the advance.

35. Metspalu et al, 2004.

36. The prime site is Mehrgarh, situated in western Pakistan, whose earliest levels date to around 7000BC, perhaps a little earlier. Both wheat

and barley were grown and both sheep and goats had already been domesticated.
37. This statement is perhaps not quite true. Wells, 2002, reports a significant Y Chromosome spread from eastern Europe across Central Asia, and into Iran and northern India of relatively recent date. This data is consistent with the spread of a male-dominated society such as Indo-European seems to have been, particularly if the first phase of spread occurred into sparsely populated lands. Dating is problematic but it seems that it could be recent enough to tie in with Indic-Iranian language movement. I should also note that one of the seven sources of European Mitochondrial DNA reported by Sykes, 2001, was the Caucasus, accounting for 6% of the population. While this seems a small percentage, if it was indeed the spread of Indo-European culture which was responsible for the spread of this DNA type over a period of around 5500 years, and if one supposes a steadily diluting wave of progress westwards, then each new generation at the front of the wave would actually have retained only 6–7% from the genes of the pre-existing population. So, while the evidence is much less certain than in the case of the spread of agriculture, it does perhaps exist.
38. The only clear evidence associating Indo-European language with agriculture is the fact that the Uralic languages of central Russia and the Baltic have adopted elements of Indo-European, probably Indo-Iranian, vocabulary related to agriculture.

## Chapter 9: Out of Africa

1. Ancient Hebrew is almost identical to the languages used in inscriptions from Lebanon (Byblos) and Jordan (the Mesha stela). I believe it is quite permissible to speak of 'Canaanite' as the general early 2$^{nd}$ Millennium BC language of Palestine, Lebanon and coastal Syria, one of whose dialects later became Hebrew.
2. In the second half of the 2$^{nd}$ Millennium and the first half of the 1$^{st}$ Millennium BC, Akkadian was the general diplomatic language of the Near and Middle East. Even letters to and from Egypt were written in Akkadian. In effect, it played the same role as Latin in Europe in the Middle Ages and, today, English.
3. Texts from the city of Mari have provided a tremendous wealth of information, covering a period from the mid 3$^{rd}$ Millennium BC until the city's destruction in the 17$^{th}$ Century BC (by most reckonings). The language of the early texts is similar to that of the Ebla archive, unearthed to great excitement in the 1970s, and dating to the mid 3$^{rd}$ Millennium BC. From the contemporary city of Nabada, there has

been a much more modest trickle of finds, but many of the language forms were once again similar to those from Ebla and Mari.
4. The earliest known Akkadian inscription comes from a queen's tomb in the southern Iraqi city of Ur, with a date somewhere around the middle of the 3$^{rd}$ Millennium BC. However, Semitic names occur significantly earlier in Sumerian inscriptions.
5. In fact, two successive cultural changes took place in Palestine during the 4$^{th}$ Millennium BC (see for example Kenyon, 1970). The first, definitely related to Egypt, brought 'Ghassulian' culture to the south. However, Ghassulian culture was then replaced in central Palestine by the culture known as 'Proto-Urban', whose origins are less certain. It was Proto-Urban culture which was directly related to that of the later Bronze Age cities. I suggest that Ghassulian culture may have been South Semitic speaking and that it was superseded by the next cultural wave, which was North Semitic speaking.
6. In fact, there are extremely early signs of agriculture in the Nile valley, tools with tell-tale 'sickle gloss' having been found in southern Egypt and northern Sudan dating to about 10000BC (Grimal, 1992). However, for some reason these early developments seem to have been snuffed out until pastoralism reached the Nile (from the Sahara) in the 6$^{th}$ Millennium BC. Arable farming, using Middle Eastern crop types, spread south from Palestine in the 6$^{th}$ and 5$^{th}$ Millennia BC.
7. It is certainly true that no significant towns have been discovered in northern Egypt or the far south of Palestine before the 4$^{th}$ Millennium BC. In central Palestine, however, the Proto-Urban people inherited territory which had already seen millennia of agricultural and urban development and this clearly gave them a head start.
8. Archaeological evidence shows South Semitic culture spreading south through Arabia, replacing the previous hunter-gatherer society and introducing irrigation and agriculture to the Marib valley of Yemen during the 3$^{rd}$ Millennium BC. Sabean civilisation thrived in Yemen during the 1$^{st}$ Millennium BC, courtesy of the irrigation possible following construction of the Marib dam. The dam unfortunately gave way in the 6th Century AD and has only been rebuilt in the last few years. The first written inscriptions in the Sabean language date from the 6$^{th}$ Century BC.
9. Ethiopian culture from the second half of the 1$^{st}$ Millennium BC shows clear parallels with that of the Sabeans (notably in its architecture and in the use of Sabean writing) and Sabean influence is thought to have been responsible for the first use of iron in Ethiopia. However, it was not until around 350AD that South Semitic civilisation, centred on the city of Axum, achieved regional dominance in Ethiopia (Phillipson, 1977).

Notes 257

10. The origin of the Capsian culture of the Sahara is generally dated to about 8000BC. It was a hunting culture, during times when the Sahara supported buffalo, elephant, rhinoceros as well as deer etc, which then made the transition to pastoralism. The prime direction of spread was certainly from south to north. The earliest pottery appears on the southern edge of the Capsian zone as far east as the Nile from about 7000BC, and the culture can be seen to have made steady progress through to Algeria and Morocco, replacing the earlier Oranian (or Ibero-Maurusian) culture fully by 3000BC. Gómez-Casado et al, 2000, make the point that this movement of culture is not reflected in any noticeable genetic change to the population.

11. The camel is not indigenous to Africa and was introduced about 2000 years ago from Asia. However, there is evidence both from rock art and from the writings of Herodotus that horses and chariots were in use across the Sahara during the 1st Millennium BC, and it may be that this was the period during which Saharan Berber first spread. If Herodotus is correct, then the chariot-driving 'Garamentes' were probably the ancestors of the Tuareg.

12. A relatively early colonisation date is demanded by the difference which has since arisen between the individual Guanche languages. The lack of subsequent interaction between islands suggests that boats could not be controlled, which further suggests that colonisation may even have been achieved by drifting on the Canaries Current flowing south along the North African coast rather than by means of developed boatcraft. As to what prompted groups of people to throw themselves on the mercy of the ocean currents, this remains a total mystery.

13. Wilkinson, 2003, presents a discussion of the evidence.

14. In fact, there were two quite different cultural zones in Egypt during the 5th and 4th Millennia BC (Bard, 1994). The northern zone, identified here as Semitic speaking, had clear affinities to the Sinai and Palestine (Ghassulian then Proto-Urban) and was the more advanced with respect to agriculture. The southern zone had affinities to Saharan society. Archaeologically, it is quite clear that north Egyptian culture, at settlements such as Maadi, was replaced by southern culture at a date some time in the late 4th Millennium BC, and it cannot be denied that this ties in well with what historians had already deduced from inscriptional evidence. Incidentally, a similar culture to that of southern Egypt also seems to have spread south down the Nile, which means that the as yet undeciphered Meroitic language of the kingdom of Kush (now northern Sudan) is, in my opinion, likely to be related to ancient Egyptian.

15. Real evidence in support of this change rate in settled hunter-gatherer society is given in Chapter 15.

16. In fact, such is the degree of difference between those few remaining representatives of South Cushitic that some members may actually have split even earlier than the separation date shown for Dahalo and the Chadic languages (7500BC). This in turn implies that the parent tongue must, at that time, have been spoken close to the current South Cushitic zone. Archaeologically, the Saharan Capsian culture (see note 10) extends well into the Chadic language zone and is also paralleled by the so-called Kenya Capsian, dated to between 11000BC and about 5000BC (Phillipson, 1977), which must surely be associated with South Cushitic language.
17. This wetland fishing culture is quite well known amongst linguists and is most frequently associated with a quite different language family, Nilo-Saharan (see Chapter 15). See, for example, Dalby, 1998.
18. I note that Blench, 2005, one of very few linguists who have also seriously considered the archaeological evidence, has also arrived at almost exactly the same location, although with a more recent date. He simply suggests that the origin of the family was over 10000 years ago.
19. See Phillipson, 1977.
20. Rock art depicting animals, birds and fish has recently been discovered at Qurta in southern Egypt, and is approximately dated to 14000-13000BC. It betrays the presence of a relatively advanced hunting and fishing culture along the banks of the Nile.
21. Kebaran culture, named after Kebara cave in Israel, is known as 'Epipalaeolithic', which means that quite advanced stone tool production was in use compared to the preceding 'Palaeolithic' age. It is generally dated to around 14000BC or slightly earlier and can be found not only in Israel but in Jordan and Syria. In around 11000BC, the culture known as Natufian arose in the same area, and it was Natufians who were the very first to practise agriculture in a serious way. Rye may even have been grown as early as 11000BC.

## Chapter 10: To the Urals and Beyond

1. Advanced microlith-using cultures existed from about 18000BC in both Europe (Solutrean) and Siberia (Diuktai) as well as East Africa.
2. See Chapter 8, note 36.
3. Dalby, 1998.
4. It is interesting that there is no record of any Dravidian speech in Karnataka, where Kannada is now the principal language, during Asoka's reign in the 3rd Century BC, nor indeed during the time of the Chalukya kings of Maharashtra and Karnataka in the 7th Century AD (Keay, 2000). It seems that Dravidian culture was only able to claim

Karnataka under the powerful Pallava and Chola dynasties of Tamil Nadu (between the 6th and 13th Centuries AD).
5. I should acknowledge that not all scholars agree that 'Hariyupiya', the location of a battle described in the Rigveda (Roy, 1989), should be identified with Harappa.
6. Decipherment of the Indus Valley script has kept numerous experts busy for decades. So far as I can determine, no-one has come close to an interpretation which inspires the confidence of more than a few (Robinson, 2002). Majority opinion probably favours the view that the language was Dravidian but this seems to be based more on 'gut feeling' than any real evidence.
7. I believe there is now enough evidence from inscriptions to state that both Iberian and Aquitanian, known from the late 1st Millennium BC, were closely related to Basque, implying that there may have been a string of related pre-Celtic tongues in France and northern Spain.
8. 'Pit-comb' pottery, named for the technique used to texture the pottery surface, actually only appears in the late 4th Millennium BC. The term is a general one for the pottery cultures between the Ural Mountains and the Baltic, through to Scandinavia. Prior to the development of pottery, the Ural-Kama culture located just west of the Urals in the 4th Millennium BC was probably also Finno-Ugric. In the Baltic states, Pit-comb sites can be seen giving way to the intrusive Corded Ware culture, the first farming culture of the region, in approximately 3000BC (Kriiska, 2000).
9. See Beekes and van der Meer, 1991.
10. The best known classical source for Etruscan history is Herodotus. He states that they were 'Lydians', i.e. from western Turkey. This is repeated by Virgil. Other authors (Dionysius, Strabo) suggest they were 'Pelasgians', the term used for the non-Greek-speaking population of Greece, presumed to be the pre-existing non-Indo-European people of the Aegean. The inhabitants of Lemnos were regularly named as Pelasgians. Archaeologically, it is undeniable that Etruscan culture was a blend of existing Italian (Villanovan) culture with an 'orientalising' influence (Pallottino, 1955).
11. In addition to the Epipalaeolithic Kebaran culture of Israel, Syria and Jordan (14000–11000BC), there was an approximately contemporary culture in the Zagros Mountains of Iran (known as Zarzian) and also in southern Turkey (Okuzini cave).
12. Summarising the evidence, Denisova, 2004, suggests that, as the Baltic ice sheet melted, colonisation of the eastern European plain occurred from both west and east, meeting more or less on the Latvia-Lithuania border. The eastern population can be related by its flint artefacts to

the Svidrian culture of the late Palaeolithic period, which eventually stretched from the river Volga to Poland.
13. Although Pryor, 2003, emphasises the cultural continuity from Mesolithic to Neolithic in Britain, it is undeniable that the evidence points to a fairly dramatic change from mobile hunter-gatherer to much more settled farmer during the centuries before and after 4000BC. While many of the customs and practices remained the same, the economy changed radically. Whether the language did or not is pure conjecture.
14. The particular culture named after the settlement at Vinča in Serbia is seen by most (e.g. Phillips, 1981) as an early 5$^{th}$ Millennium development from Starčevo-Körös-Criş (see Chapter 8, note 2). A fairly uniform society (often known as Hungarian Tell culture) appears to have arisen throughout Hungary, Serbia and western Romania and then to have spread south to Bulgaria and Greece (Renfrew, 1973). In Hungary, it endured until the coming of the Indo-Europeans (Urnfield culture) in the mid 2$^{nd}$ Millennium BC.
15. About 210 letter-like signs have been noted on artefacts from Vinča culture sites, notably Tordos and Tarteria, dating to around 4000BC (Rudgley, 1998). Of these, 50 have direct parallels in the 2$^{nd}$ Millennium BC Linear A script from Minoan Crete (Haarmann, 1989). Others have noticed similarities to signs found at Troy on the Turkish coast and the great early 20$^{th}$ Century archaeologist Flinders Petrie also thought he could detect resemblance to the earliest Egyptian signs (preceding hieroglyphs).
16. Babaev, 2002, notes strong similarities in the phonetics of Etruscan and Cretan Linear B (an early form of Greek), which used the same sounds as Linear A.
17. Since writing these words I have noticed one or two attempts at a Nostratic history. They tend to place the point of origin in the Middle East rather than East Africa (e.g. Croft, 2000), but I cannot deny that certain points of commonality exist.

## Chapter 11: Huns, Mongols and Tatars

1. This deduction is based purely on Louis Bazin's interpretation of the only ten Hunnish words ever recorded in writing, advice given by a Buddhist monk to a Hunnish king (Dalby, 1998).
2. The periods of Avar and Khazar rule in the Ukraine were probably responsible for initiating the dispersal of the northern Slavonic tribes.
3. I believe that the earliest Altaic-speaking agricultural society of Siberia was probably the Karasuk culture (from about 1200BC), with a bronze industry similar to that in northern China (Mongait, 1961). However,

it is quite possible that Altaic languages were spoken by agriculturalists in China at a much earlier date.
4. Peiligang is the name given to a millet-growing culture of the Yellow River area of northern China and east to the coast in Shandong province, dating from approximately 6500BC to 5000BC. At what stage millet was first seriously domesticated is not clear.
5. There is evidence of semi-settled life in Chukotkia from about 1000BC (Mongait, 1961), but I would suggest that this is more likely to be attributable to Eskimo-Aleut speakers than to Chukchi-Kamchatkan.
6. Data on Ket was kindly supplied by Marina Kilina of Tomsk University.
7. Ruhlen, 1998.
8. Dumond, 1987.
9. The Arctic Small Tool tradition is the name give to the first human culture to inhabit the north coast of Canada and the islands of the Arctic. It is first recorded in about 2200BC in western Alaska and it then spread eastward, replacing the so-called Northern Archaic tradition (probably comprising Na-Dené speakers) in some locations on the Canadian mainland (Dumond, 1987).
10. The Gutians conquered central Iraq in the late 3rd Millennium BC and ruled for about 100 years. All that is known besides a list of kings is that they came from the east, i.e. from the Zagros Mountains of Iran, and that they were a regular enemy of the Akkadian kings of Iraq as well as the Elamites. Their northern neighbours were the Lullubi, also regular opponents of the Akkadians (Roux, 1966). The early 1st Millennium BC sees the same area inhabited by a people known as 'Khirikhi', whose name alone strongly suggests ancestral Georgian.
11. The first historically attested Georgian kingdom, known as Kartli (or Iberia), arose in the late 4th Century BC and was centred on the eastern part of the modern state. At that time western Georgia was inhabited by the 'Colchians', known to the Greeks, whose language, I suggest, was probably North-West Caucasian (related to modern Abkhaz).
12. If this history of the North Caucasian languages is correct, then the level of culture associated with them can be seen in Level I at Anau in Turkmenistan, with copper and painted pottery from the mid 5th Millennium BC (Piggott, 1950). It is therefore unsurprising that this culture was able to gain ascendancy over Indo-European as it pushed west across the Russian steppe. One has to suppose that the ancestor of Indic and Iranian was pushed north and that it only advanced south and east when domestication of the horse gave Indo-European speakers the upper hand (from about 3500BC).

13. In the texts from Hattusas, Hattian is used exclusively for religious purposes.
14. Hattian language should, in my view, certainly be associated with the Kura-Araxes culture and with 'Khirbet Kerak' ware pottery. This very distinctive pottery type developed in the southern Caucasus region but was then spread rapidly south through eastern Turkey, Syria and northern Palestine in the mid 3$^{rd}$ Millennium BC, always associated with the violent destruction of pre-existing settlements. Most remarkably, single pieces of Khirbet Kerak ware were reverently interred with each royal burial at the eastern Turkish site of Alaca Höyük, burials which are usually dated to around 2000BC.
15. Mitanni has already been mentioned in Chapter 8 in connection with Indo-European (Indic) names, of both people and gods. However, while the origin of the Mitannian ruling class was clearly Indo-European, they equally clearly adopted the language of the population at large, which was Hurrian.
16. The Hurrians can first be seen with the founding of the city of Alalakh on the lower Orontes river, and they appear in Sumerian and Akkadian records throughout the 3$^{rd}$ Millennium BC. They then formed a barrier to Hittite advance in eastern Turkey during the first half of the 2$^{nd}$ Millennium BC, and reached the peak of their power as the kingdom of 'Mitanni' during the 15$^{th}$ and 14$^{th}$ Centuries BC. At that stage, Hurrian language and culture was spread right across northern Syria, northern Iraq and eastern Turkey.
17. Data on Sumerian was kindly supplied by Dr Alasdair Livingstone of the University of Birmingham, UK.
18. The earliest evidence for a sedentary population in the Middle East has been found at Zawi Chemi in the northern Zagros Mountains of Iran, dating from the 10$^{th}$ Millennium BC, including the remains of storage pits such as would typically be used for grain.
19. The earliest Sumerian cities date from the late 6$^{th}$ and early 5$^{th}$ Millennia BC.
20. It was Bishop Caldwell who first drew attention to similarities between Elamite and the Dravidian languages in the 19$^{th}$ Century. It is clear that many linguists now consider the link to be as good as proven.

## Chapter 12: Behind the Great Wall

1. Watson, 1966, and Hay, 1973, for example, both draw attention to striking parallels between Yang Shao pottery and that found at Anau (particularly Level Ib) and other sites in Turkmenistan.

2. That Yang Shao culture is directly ancestral to that of modern China has become a cornerstone of belief amongst many Chinese historians and it is true that aspects of modern Chinese culture, notably cookery, are found in Yang Shao society. However, this definitely does not mean that the language spoken was Sino-Tibetan – any more than the continuity of British culture in the last two millennia BC requires that Celtic languages were already spoken there. Language spread frequently results in a composite culture, containing elements of both old and new.
3. The closeness between inscriptions from Chou times and modern Chinese is sufficient for us to be absolutely sure that the structure of the language was Sino-Tibetan.
4. I am indebted to George Starostin of the Russian State Academy for the Humanities for information on the sounds of ancient Chinese numerals.
5. The current 'politically correct' view is that Lung Shan stemmed directly from Yang Shao (both cultures being ancestral to modern Chinese), although this seems to fly in the face of the discontinuities found at archaeological sites, differences in burial custom and the introduction of a new and wheel-made pottery type. That many aspects of life continued unchanged from one era to the next is clear, but the overall change seems amply large enough to expect a linguistic difference. It is also of note that Lung Shan culture is predominantly a culture of north-east China, excluding the Wei River area where Yang Shao seems to have originated. However, there was strong continuity from Lung Shan through to the Shang dynasty (1500–1050BC). The deduction that Lung Shan was probably Sino-Tibetan speaking is based on the famous 'oracle bones' from Shang dynasty times, bones which were apparently used for divination, many of them being inscribed with characters that were clearly ancestral to the modern Chinese script. Unfortunately, since the characters denote concepts rather than sounds, it is impossible to deduce much about the nature of the Shang language.
6. All experts agree that there was a notable discontinuity between the Shang dynasty and the succeeding Chou, based once more in the Yellow River region. The combination of date (mid 11th Century BC), location (western China) and technology (horses, chariots) gives rise to the suspicion that contact with Indo-Europeans (Tocharian speakers) may have helped the Chou in their rise to power.
7. Agreement with this conclusion would be academic suicide for a professional linguist such is the strength of opinion against it today. The principal argument appears to be that modern Tai languages are clos-

er to modern Chinese than to ancient Chinese, suggesting recent influence rather than true genetic relationship. The counter-argument here would be, of course, that ancient Chinese is not actually a direct ancestor of modern Chinese.
8. Most commentators are content to admit that the geographical origin of Sino-Tibetan language is unknown, although the assumption is often made that it lies in the Yellow River region (e.g. Su et al, 2000). Dalby, 1998, reflects another common view, supporting south-east China.
9. It is clear that belief in the reliability of the evidence for this extremely early cultivation of rice is now widespread (e.g. Xu, 1998) although some researchers continue to question the interpretation of the evidence (Liu, 2000).
10. Rice growing appeared in eastern China with the Hemudu culture, centred around the Shanghai region, which flourished from about 5000BC. In South-East Asia, sites such as Nun Nok Tha in Thailand reveal that rice was probably grown from about 4000BC in the north of the country.
11. The current Tai/Kadai debate was originated by the work of Paul Benedict, who suggested that both Tai and Kadai languages should be bracketed with Austro-Asiatic and Austronesian and not with Sino-Tibetan. He had convinced himself that the very obvious similarities between Tai and Sino-Tibetan were down to secondary contact and, as so often happens in academia, others have followed the strong lead he gave. I am pleased to note a certain retreat from Benedict's position in some recent literature.
12. In case you should doubt that a population can subsist largely on fish, archaeologists have discovered that the people of coastal Peru between about 9000BC and 3000BC lived on a 90% fish diet (Moseley, 2001).
13. The currents in the Indian Ocean change depending on the time of year. However, throughout the summer months, the drift would be eastward right around the coasts of India itself and it seems quite likely that the principal route taken by Sino-Tibetan speech may have been along the coast rather than inland across the Indian subcontinent.
14. Before linguists made the connection between the Munda languages and the rest of Austro-Asiatic, it was recognised that the closest similarities lay with the Uralic languages of northern Europe and Asia, and it is still common to read that this is where the Munda languages originated (e.g. Muscat, 1989).
15. The culture of Afghanistan was comparatively advanced during these times, some suggesting that domestication of sheep and goats may already have taken place.

16. Chinese military domination of Vietnam began in around 200BC and China had practically full control until Vietnamese independence in 939AD. Chinese cultural dominance has continued until much more recent times.
17. Ban Chiang, a site in north-east Thailand, shows continuous occupation from about 3600BC to around 200AD. Bronze appears in approximately 1500BC. The earliest phase, in which rice agriculture was adopted, probably represents Sino-Tibetan culture; later developments may be attributable to Austro-Asiatic settlers.
18. See Fernández-Armesto, 2001.
19. The very large change in Nicobarese may also be partly due to the influence of word taboos, meaning that there has been a continuing pressure to formulate new vocabulary.
20. Besides the claim for the existence of a Munda substratum in northern Pakistan and India, there are two particular languages which may represent departures from the Austro-Asiatic stem dating to before the language's arrival in eastern India. These are Kusunda (now practically extinct), a language of Nepal, and Nahali, spoken on the Narmada river in west central India. Nahali, in particular, shows such a mixture of influences that experts are divided as to its proper family. The numerals are Dravidian but the underlying structure of the language may be closer to Munda.

## Chapter 13: Peoples of the Pacific

1. Yam and Taro have been cultivated in Indonesia and New Guinea for many thousands of years, notably in the highlands of New Guinea (Fernández-Armesto, 2001). Pig domestication also took place at an early date.
2. Sykes, 2001.
3. Rice agriculture only arrived in Taiwan in about 3000BC; however, taro was grown from about 5000BC. Paiwan speakers were therefore already agriculturalists in 4000BC, but those who then emigrated to the Philippines and Indonesia would not have known rice.
4. When the full range of indigenous Taiwanese languages is considered, it is found that Atayal and Paiwan represent the two main branches and I believe that 9000BC is therefore a realistic date for the origin of the family as a whole.
5. Cham was the language of the state of 'Champa', which occupied present-day southern Vietnam from around 200BC until 1471AD, the year in which the Vietnamese invaded from the north.
6. This extremely high measured change rate is probably exaggerated by the different ways in which these languages mutate compared to most

other language families, i.e. greater vowel stability accompanied by increased likelihood of consonant changes.
7. Mahdi, 1997, points out that the Tamil word for *large boat* is the same as the Polynesian-Malagasy word, which suggests that south India was a significant stop-over point.
8. Burney et al, 2003.
9. Sykes, 2001.
10. In fact, evidence of Austronesian influence (specifically Makasar, a language of Celebes) has been found in some northern Australian languages.
11. The three Austronesian languages are Malay, Tagalog and Maori; the Austro-Asiatic languages are Santali, Mon and Vietnamese.
12. Archaeologically, the first Neolithic farming cultures of Taiwan and the adjacent Chinese coast, known as Dapendeng and Fuguodan respectively, can be traced from the $5^{th}$ Millennium BC. Chang, 1989, draws attention to the strong similarities between them and proposes that they could both be Austronesian speaking. I suggest they are more likely to signal the arrival of Austro-Asiatic-speaking seafarers, who colonised the coasts, both on the Asian mainland and on Taiwan. They brought taro cultivation with them rather than rice, the principal staple of most of China. When rice agriculture eventually arrived in Taiwan, in about 3000BC, it came with archaeological cultures (Tanshishan on the mainland, Fengbitou on Taiwan) with parallels to the early stages of Lung Shan (see Chapter 12, note 5).
13. If I am correct in associating these Austro-Asiatics with the development of Dapendeng culture on Taiwan (see note 12), then clearly they came in significant numbers and, from archaeological evidence, they started to arrive in the $5^{th}$ Millennium BC.
14. In Chapter 12, the confusing effects of secondary contact between Tai and Kadai and between Vietnamese and Chinese were noted. It is therefore no surprise to see that the extensive contact which occurred on Taiwan between Austro-Asiatic and Austronesian speakers has also given rise to similar confusion.
15. Cultural similarities have been noted between Lung Shan civilisation (and that of the subsequent Shang dynasty) and South-East Asia (e.g. Hay, 1973).
16. Several researchers have reported Austro-Asiatic substrata in south-east Chinese languages. This suggests a period of Austro-Asiatic colonisation, presumably coinciding with the Fuguodan archaeological culture.
17. As far as I can ascertain, experts put the formation of the Taiwan Strait at 8000–10000BC (e.g. Chang, 1989). My estimate for the date of the ancestral Austronesian tongue of 9000BC is therefore reasonable.

18. The earliest known evidence for human habitation on Taiwan itself dates from around 30000BC.
19. Skeletal remains of anatomically modern humans have been found in Skhul and Qafzeh caves in Israel dated by a range of techniques to between 66000 and 128000 years old. Putting all the evidence together, it seems the real dates are probably in the range 80000 to 100000 years ago. Nonetheless, more recent Mitochondrial DNA evidence (Maca-Meyer et al, 2001) puts the beginnings of the diversification of non-African DNA at 59000–69000 years ago and this is now supported by Y Chromosome studies (Wells, 2002). Perhaps the most likely explanation is found in the fact that Neanderthal remains in nearby caves at Tabun and Kebara are dated both to over 100000 years and also to around 60000–65000 years. It is quite plausible that Homo Sapiens emerged from Africa 100000 years ago but didn't get very far! There may have been little to choose at that date between the survival abilities of Neanderthals and modern humans and the Neanderthals may have managed to reclaim the lost territory, pushing our ancestors back into Africa. It was only about 65000 years ago or so that Homo Sapiens was able to break the Neanderthal stranglehold.
20. It is true that Neanderthals once inhabited Central Asia. However, Wells, 2002, demonstrates from genetic studies that Homo Sapiens had certainly reached Central Asia well before 40000 years ago.
21. Genetically, this first eastward spread is evidenced by a particular Y Chromosome variant (M130) and a Mitochondrial DNA marker (M), whose frequency in today's populations increases from relatively little in India to more in Malaysia and Indonesia to a majority in Australia. Significant incidence of M130 is also found in north-east Asia and North America, but much less in China.
22. Authentic Homo Erectus finds, dating to 1.6 million years ago, have been found on the nearby island of Java, and more recent claims have been made that a 27000 year old specimen from the Solo River region is also a genuine Homo Erectus. Although the Flores evidence is still hotly disputed, some suggest that the dwarf-size Flores people lived between 95000 and 13000 years ago, based on the circumstantial evidence of stone tools and fire hearths, whereas the first evidence for Homo Sapiens on the island is dated to about 11000 years ago, 9000BC (Brown et al, 2004).
23. Archaeological evidence of occupation on the Andaman Islands only dates back about 2000 years. However, the genetic difference between the Andaman Islanders and all other humans suggests a much longer separation, perhaps as much as 30000 years.
24. Foley, 1991.

25. The Australian evidence is most interesting. No-one doubts that Homo Sapiens was in Australia from about 35000 to 40000 years ago; there is plenty of evidence. However, at Nauwalabila rockshelter, a layer bearing manufactured stone artefacts has been dated to between 53000 and 60000 years ago, and this, many believe, signals the first appearance of humans on the continent. Furthermore there are claims that pollen evidence shows that fire was being used to control the environment up to 130000 years ago! Personally I find it hard to believe any date much earlier than 40000 years ago for the first Homo Sapiens in Australia, bearing in mind the genetic evidence that non-African humans only started to diverge 59000 to 69000 years ago (note 19), and it has to be a possibility that the manufacturers of the Nauwalabila tools may not, in fact, have belonged to our species at all. After all, the Neanderthals of Europe and western Asia were at a similar technological level to our ancestors at this time, and the evidence from Flores (note 22) is that Homo Erectus was able to cross the open sea. In fact, claims have been made that Homo Erectus traits can be seen in fairly recent Australian fossils (e.g. Thorne and Macumber, 1972) and even in modern skeletal forms (Vanhollebeke, 2002), reopening the discussion as to whether any interbreeding between Homo Sapiens and other hominids may have occurred. At present, however, the genetic evidence is firmly against this.
26. Reed, 1998, conveniently publishes his vocabulary on a regional basis.
27. The same rockshelter (Nauwalabila) that produced the evidence for hominid presence at least 53000 years ago also produced evidence for a very significant change in technology about 6000 years ago (4000BC) with the introduction of nicely finished stone spear points. This same date, 4000BC, also signalled a significant increase in intensity of occupation at the adjacent Anbangbang rockshelter.
28. The Ainu have a distinctive, almost European, appearance. It has to be supposed that they represent a population descended from the earliest colonisers of north-east Asia but that, over many thousands of years, they have developed their own unique genetic traits.
29. To be strictly truthful, Ainu also has a low measurement to Georgian (29000 linguistic years), but I have discounted this as coincidental similarity in grammar since it is not supported by measurements to other languages which are related to Georgian, i.e. the Dravidian languages, Elamite, Burushaski.
30. The word 'Jomon' actually describes the typical pottery form.
31. The earliest evidence for agriculture in Korea is dated to about 4000BC and the culture with which it is associated shows clear similarities to that of the Amur and Sungari river region of Manchuria, notably its grey comb-marked pottery.

32. The Pictish language, spoken in eastern Scotland until about 1000 years ago has not yet been deciphered, although inscriptions exist. Most commentators suppose it to have been a Celtic language, related to Welsh and the language of southern Scotland, but many also suggest that it may have been pre-Celtic. If this is true, it could have been related to Basque, descended from European agriculturalists who may have settled Britain from about 4300BC; however, it is almost as likely to have been a remnant from Mesolithic times and possibly earlier.

## Chapter 14: A New Beginning in a New World

1. A Viking settlement has been discovered at L'Anse aux Meadows in Newfoundland.
2. Menzies, 2002, gives plenty of evidence for suggesting that Chinese fleets reached parts of the Americas several decades before Columbus.
3. These dates lie around the average of the different estimates made by various experts.
4. Here again, estimates differ wildly.
5. The Pedra Furada evidence concerns stone fragments discovered in deposits in the floor of a rockshelter, deposits which can be dated reasonably accurately using radiocarbon. Sceptics claim that the supposed 'tools' have simply been formed by stones fracturing having fallen from the roof; however, one of the excavators (Fabio Parenti) has produced persuasive evidence (from experiments) that such natural fracturing could not possibly account for the tool-like shapes he found. The earliest such 'tools' date to over 30000 years ago (Renfrew and Bahn, 1996).
6. The site at Monte Verde has also given rise to supposedly man-made artefacts (including some of wood) and I believe it would be fair to say that back to a date of 12850BC, there is widespread acceptance that this does indeed imply that man was present (Meltzer et al, 1997). However, it has been claimed that evidence for hearths has been found dating to 33000 years ago, with associated stone tools, with evidence of wear and, in one case, mastodon blood residue (Gruhn, 2000).
7. Gruhn, 2000.
8. Davies, 1983; Katz, 1972.
9. Sykes, 2001.
10. The languages selected were: Cree and Cheyenne (Algonquian family); Cherokee (Iroquoian family); Alabama (Muskogean family); Seri (Hokan family) and Navaho (Na Déné family).
11. Faught, 1998, suggests Aubrey, Texas as the site with the oldest proven Clovis artefacts, although Haynes, 2002, puts both Paleo Crossing, Ohio, and Big Eddy, Montana, as older still.

12. Archaeological cultures known under the general heading 'Plano' stretch from northern Canada down to the Gulf of Mexico and, while there are significant regional differences, there is plenty of evidence of commonality.
13. There is much disagreement as to whether Na Dené speakers represent a separate population who entered America at a relatively late date. For example Torroni et al, 1992, confidently asserted that genetics supported a separate entry for Na Dené speakers, whereas Silva et al, 2002, equally confidently asserted that their genetic study showed no such evidence. If I had to guess, I would suggest that people continued to arrive from Alaska and that western Canada was populated both from the south and the west as the ice sheet retreated. The dominant culture, however, that of the Northern Plano tradition, arrived from the south with (in my view) the Na Dené languages.
14. Ruhlen, 1998.
15. The earliest confidently dated traces of human occupation in the Lena valley are from about 23000BC although several scholars believe there is evidence for a much earlier arrival (Vasiliev et al, 2002). Even in the earliest deposits, the stone tool evidence is for a relatively advanced culture (i.e. microblades). A single find at one site, Uptar, has drawn comparisons with Clovis styles (McConaughy, 2004).
16. The 40 mile wide Hekate strait which separates the Queen Charlotte Islands from other islands immediately adjacent to mainland Canada would have been largely dry land during the Ice Age, when pre-Clovis speakers were migrating south, but would have been very much as today by the time Na Dené speakers were heading back north (I estimate 6000BC).
17. The genetic wave I refer to is identified by the M130 Y Chromosome marker, associated with Homo Sapiens' initial eastward penetration of southern Asia as far as Australia, but which also appears to have been carried north through eastern Asia to Mongolia (where 50% of the male population carry it), north-east Asia and North America. It is not found in Central or South America however (Wells, 2002).
18. McConaughy, 2004.
19. The interpretation was by Justeson and Kaufman, 1993. However, both Mayan and Mixtec glyphs bear very close similarities to the Olmec script. Also, while Olmec civilisation is generally linked to the famous sites of San Lorenzo and La Venta on the Gulf of Mexico, Olmec-related culture extended right across central Mexico as far as El Salvador and indeed several researchers consider the Pacific coast to be the true centre of the culture based on the relative numbers of finds (Katz, 1972).

Notes 271

20. As far as we can tell from the Mayan glyphs, which are phonetic, a very similar language was used up until about 800AD right across the classical Mayan-speaking world, comprising the southern Yucatan peninsula, with adjacent areas of Guatemala and Honduras. However, the current linguistic difference between the Yucatec (northern) and Quiché (southern) languages – about 8000 linguistic years – suggests that there must have been significant differences outside the literate civilised south.
21. It is most commonly stated that Taino is an 'Arawakan' language, originating in South America.
22. Two quite distinct peoples seem to have colonised the islands of the Caribbean. A culture known as 'Ortoiroid' spread from South America north through Trinidad and the islands of the Lesser Antilles as far as Puerto Rico, while the 'Casimiroid' culture also reached Puerto Rico, but by way of Cuba and Hispaniola. Evidence for both is found in Puerto Rico from around 5000BC, suggesting that the bearers of both cultures probably set off from their respective continental points of origin a thousand or so years earlier. Interestingly, Martínez-Cruzado et al, 2001, have demonstrated that, genetically, the Native American element in the population of Puerto Rico most closely matches that of the eastern United States!
23. El Jobo and associated sites in Venezuela have produced evidence for a stone tool technology which was quite different from that of Clovis culture, making use of thicker, cruder spear tips. Dates tend to range from 14000 to 12500BC. Baker, 2004, discusses the possible interrelationships between the archaeological cultures of early America.
24. The selected languages were: Teribe (Chibchan family); Carapana (Tucanoan family); Asheninca (Arawakan family); Guaraní (Tupian family) and Xavante (Ge family).
25. Gruhn, 2000.
26. This date is that accepted as genuine by most researchers (e.g. Gruhn, 2000; McConaughy, 2004), rather than the still disputed evidence from over 30000 years ago.
27. The first widely acknowledged evidence for human presence in Alaska only dates from a little before 11000BC. Earlier dates relate to animal bones with supposed butchering marks or else to locations for which the dating is suspect.
28. Refer to note 15.
29. Torroni et al, 1994, who studied Mitochondrial DNA, estimate 22000 to 29000 years ago for initial colonisation. Others (e.g. Silva et al, 2002) speak of about 20000 years for each of the four Mitochondrial DNA lineages. The Y Chromosome marker which distinguishes the first wave of American colonisation (M3) can be traced back through

Siberia to Central Asia; the route taken was therefore north of the great Asian mountain mass, through the plain of the Lena river. Although Wells, 2002, estimates an age of only 20000 years for M3's direct ancestor, M242, which would make M3 younger still, he acknowledges a wide margin of uncertainty. The reason for the massive uncertainty levels which continue to be quoted is the disagreement on the rate of genetic mutation which is occurring. Early studies based their estimates principally on rates determined from large differences between primate species, but more recent work has tended to opt for evidence from changes in human DNA over some thousands of years. Both require a lot of assumptions and reference to either palaeontology, archaeology or even linguistics.

30. Torroni et al, 1994.
31. I am not aware that anyone has satisfactorily explained the Polynesians having sweet potatoes. Thor Heyerdahl was among those who suggested that South Americans reached Easter Island, accounting for local legends of there having been two quite different peoples on the island. From there, it is possible that sweet potatoes could have been traded westward over the centuries, reaching as far as New Guinea by the time the Spaniards arrived.
32. Hay, 1973, discusses the affinities of Shang dynasty culture, demonstrating very clearly the continuity from Lung Shan times. However, he remarks that the only comparable art forms are to be found in Pacific and South American cultures. Once again, the non-specialist is struck by the similarity in decorative style used on Shang artefacts and those from Central and South America.
33. Arguments for there having been early trans-Pacific contacts have been made by a few researchers, notably Heine-Geldern, 1954, mainly based on similarities in culture between Asia and South or Central America.
34. Serious adoption of agriculture commenced in around 3000BC both in Mexico and Ecuador, although earlier experiments had taken place over the previous couple of thousand years.
35. Some aspects of culture were almost universal across the whole of both North and South America, notably human sacrifice, and may therefore date back to the dawn of mankind's appearance in America. However, it is harder to explain such details as the jaguar cult, widespread in Olmec Mexico but also paralleled from Colombia to Bolivia (Davies, 1983), and the construction of ceremonial platforms and sunken ball-courts in both regions, commencing in the late $3^{rd}$ or early $2^{nd}$ Millennium BC (Moseley, 2001; Davies, 1983). Davies also draws attention to very similar multi-chambered tombs on the Pacific coasts of both Mexico and Ecuador. Perhaps most striking of all to the non-

specialist is the very similar art forms in the two regions, not only the use of grotesque faces and animal forms, but more particularly the styles of decoration, which spill over into the glyphs used in Central American writing systems.
36. Cook, 2003.
37. In speculating about a possible early crossing of the Pacific, one has to bear in mind the cultural elements which were not transmitted as well as those that might have been. American cultures made no use of the plough, they only began to discover metal much later, and they hardly used wheels. These points suggest that, if such a journey was made, it can have been no later than about 3000BC. If a date had to be selected, then the fact that the Mayan calendar commenced in 3114BC may be relevant. Although American calendars are considerably different from all others, the system of naming days is paralleled in China.
38. The use of tone as a means of distinguishing between tenses is actually very rare outside Africa – arguably a good enough reason on its own to suspect relationship. Unfortunately, despite the forms of words being similar and several instances where common roots are far from impossible, the distance is just too great for conventional linguistics (using the comparative method) to stand any realistic chance of confirming or denying this suggestion.
39. The culture of central Mexico in 7000BC was a descendent of El Jobo. While it is quite impossible to state with any certainty, the culture of West Africa may then have been at a similar level (at least, both would have counted to ten!).

## Chapter 15: Roots

1. Phillipson, 1977.
2. The Shona kingdom reached its height in the late 15th Century, at which time it dominated an area significantly larger than modern Zimbabwe. The Shona successfully defended themselves against Portuguese attack throughout the 16th Century. The opposite side of the continent was ruled by the Kongo people, whose kings were (at least initially) recognised by the Portuguese as their equals.
3. The usual reason cited for including Mande and Atlantic languages within Niger-Congo lies in the fact that they make use of a 'noun class' system. However, since vocabulary similarity is at the coincidence level and other aspects of grammar are also quite different, it would seem that use of a noun class system alone is insufficient justification for their inclusion.
4. The most controversial of those I have shown is Dogon, really a small group of languages spoken in the hills of southern Mali. There is

ongoing discussion among experts as to whether it should be included as a Voltaic language, as I have shown it, or as a member of the Mande family. I have placed it as shown after considering the full range of 26 words used in my measurement system, as well as grammatical points.
5. Bubi is often listed as Western Bantu. However, the measurements made here place it firmly in with the Nigerian languages.
6. Blench, 2005, comes up with a similar location but a much later date (6000BC).
7. It seems that West Africa was very sparsely populated until about 10000BC, at which date microlithic technologies appeared (Blench, 2005) with evidence that wild grain was being harvested.
8. Once again Blench, 2005, agrees with the location. His date, 16000BC, is earlier than mine however.
9. The kingdom of Kush was a neighbour and frequent enemy of ancient Egypt, centred on northern Sudan, where the Nubian branch of Nilo-Saharan is now spoken. Kush was a literate and sophisticated society and, in addition to large numbers of pyramid tombs, the Kushites have left us extensive records in a language we know as Meroitic, but which has not yet been deciphered. My personal view, based on the archaeological similarities between early Egyptian and early Kushite culture, is that Meroitic is most likely to be a relative of Egyptian.
10. The Indian language Manipuri has also developed a click sound, the only case I am aware of outside Africa.
11. The depiction is found in the mortuary temple of Queen Hatshepsut and dates from the mid $2^{nd}$ Millennium BC.
12. George Starostin (undated) has recently published a detailed evaluation of the inter-relationships within the Khoi-San family, including both Sandawe and Hadza, using conventional glottochronology. Although he remarks on certain common roots and traits, he is unable to determine a meaningful measurement of distance between the two Tanzanian languages and the rest of the Khoi-San family.
13. The Hadza, hunter-gatherers from the Lake Eyasi region, and the Sandawe, pastoralists from about 100 miles to the south-east, are both physically quite different from the surrounding South Cushitic, Nilotic and Bantu tribes, and resemble the Bushmen of south-west Africa. This strongly suggests that the disappearance of Khoi-San language has also been accompanied by the disappearance of the people themselves. The scattered Pygmy peoples of the Congo and further south in Angola and Botswana are thought by some to be remnant populations who once spoke a Khoi-San type language, although no evidence of such a language has yet been uncovered among the Pygmies.
14. White et al, 2003.

15. See Sykes, 2001. The estimate for the original Y Chromosome, the father of us all, is rather more recent, although also rather more uncertain. Wells, 2002, suggests between 40000 and 140000 years.
16. The point here is that a surprisingly large number of blood lines die out in any given generation. The mathematics is complicated, but it is possible to simulate the passing on of DNA by assigning a random number of daughters to each female in any generation (number from zero to several – but with varying probabilities). By this technique it is possible to judge that, over 150000 years, all but one of about 500 female blood lines would disappear. Furthermore, if male reproduction is considered then it seems probable that the variability in numbers of descendants would be even greater in many societies (multiple wives for the few), possibly explaining the more recent date deduced for our common biological father (note 15).

# Bibliography

D P Agrawal, *The Indus Civilisation = Aryans equation: Is it really a problem?*, http://www.infinityfoundation.com/mandala/h_es/h_es_agraw_indus.htm, accessed August 2005.

Mario Alinei, "Interdisciplinary and linguistic evidence for Paleolithic continuity of Indo-European, Uralic and Altaic populations in Eurasia, with an excursus on Slavic ethnogenesis", *Conference on Ancient Settlers in Europe*, Kobarid, Slovenia, 2003.

Anon, *The Battle of Maldon*, ed. E V Gordon, Methuen & co, London, 1937.

Cyril Babaev, *Ancient Languages of the East Mediterranean*, http://indeuro.bizland.com/archive/article9.html, accessed June 2002.

Tony Baker, *Clovis First / Pre-Clovis Problem Revisited*, http://www.ele.net/art_folsom/pre-clovis_2004/preclovis2004.htm, 2004, accessed September 2004.

Maximilian Baldia, *The Earliest Bandkeramik (LBK): The Central and North European Neolithic/Copper Age Chronology*, http://www.comp.archaeology.org/Bandkeramik.htm, 2003, accessed March 2004.

Elizabeth Barber, *The Mummies of Ürümchi*, Macmillan, 1999.

Kathryn Bard, "The Egyptian predynastic: a review of the evidence", *Journal of Field Archaeology*, Fall, 1994.

R S P Beekes and L B van der Meer, *De Etrusken Spreken* (The Etruscan Language), Coutinho, Muiderberg, 1991.

Joseph Biddulph, *Notes on Frisian*, Joseph Biddulph Publisher, Pontypridd, Wales, 1995.

Václav Blaûek and D Bengtson, "Lexica Dené-Caucasia", *Central Asiatic Journal*, Vol 39, 1995, pp11–50.

Roger Blench, *Language, Archaeology and the African Past*, http://homepage.ntlworld.com/roger_blench/RBOP.htm, 2005, accessed September 2005.

Alan Bomhard and John Kerns, *The Nostratic Macrofamily: A Study in Distant Linguistic Relationship*, Mouton de Gruyter, Berlin, 1994.

Melvyn Bragg, *The Adventure of English*, Hodder & Stoughton, London, 2003.

Peter Brown, T Sutikna, M J Morwood, R P Soejono, Jatmiko, E Wayhu Saptomo and Rokus Awe Due, "A new small-bodied hominin from the late Pleistocene of Flores, Indonesia", *Nature*, 431, 2004, pp1055–1061.

Trevor Bryce, *The Kingdom of the Hittites*, Oxford University Press, 1998.

David Burney, Guy Robinson and Lida Pigott Burney, "Sporormiella and the late

# Bibliography

Holocene extinctions in Madagascar", *National Academy of Science*, Vol 100, No 19, 2003, pp10800–10805.
Julius Caesar, *The Conquest of Gaul*, translated by S A Handford, Penguin, London, 1951.
Rebecca Cann, Mark Stoneking and Allan Wilson, "Mitochondrial DNA and human evolution", *Nature*, 325, 1987, pp31–36.
Luigi Cavalli-Sforza, *Genes, Peoples and Languages*, Allen Lane, The Penguin Press, 2000.
Kuang-chih Chang, "The Neolithic Taiwan Strait", *Kaogu*, 6, 1989, pp541–550.
Geoffrey Chaucer, *Canterbury Tales: The Nun's Priest's Tale*, ed. A Pollard, Macmillan, London, 1924.
V G Childe, *Prehistoric Migrations in Europe*, Aschehoug, Oslo, 1950.
Michael Cook. *A Brief History of the Human Race*, Granta Books, 2004.
John Croft, *Master Nostratic Synthesis*, http://freepages.genealogy.rootsweb.com/~jamesdow/Tech/croftide.htm, 2000, accessed September 2004.
David Crystal, *The Cambridge Encyclopedia of Language*, Cambridge University Press, 1987.
Barry Cunliffe, *The Extraordinary Voyage of Pytheas the Greek*, Penguin Press, 2001.
John Curtis, *Ancient Persia*, British Museum Publications, 1989.
Andrew Dalby, *Dictionary of Languages*, Bloomsbury, London, 1998.
Nigel Davies, *The Ancient Kingdoms of Mexico*, Penguin Books, 1983.
Frank Delaney, *The Celts*, Hodder & Stoughton, 1986.
Raisa Denisova, *Latvijas senākā apdzīvotība* (The most ancient population of Latvia), Latvijas Vēsture, No 2, 1994.
Aharon Dolgopolsky, *The Nostratic Macrofamily and Linguistic Palaeontology*, McDonald Institute for Archaeological research, Cambridge, UK, 1998.
Don Dumond, *The Eskimos and Aleuts*, Thames & Hudson, London, 1987.
Ivan Duridanov, "Ezikyt na Trakite" (The Language of the Thracians), *Nauka i izkustvo*, Sofia, 1976.
Michael Faught, *Underwater archaeology, Paleoindian origins and histories of settlement*, http://www.flmnh.ufl.edu/natsci/vertpaleo/aucilla11_1/uw.htm, 1998, accessed October, 2004.
Felipe Fernández-Armesto, *Civilisations*, Pan Books, London, 2001.
William Foley, *The Yimas Language of New Guinea*, Stanford University Press, 1991.
John Gardner, *Nichts geht mehr Mr Bond*, translated by Hilde Linnert, Wilhelm Heyn, Munich, 1988.
Marija Gimbutas, *Proto-Indo-European Culture: the Kurgan Culture during the 5th to the 3rd Millennia BC*, in G Cordona, H M Koenigswald and A Senn (editors), *Indo-European and Indo-Europeans*, University of Pennsylvania Press, Philadelphia, 1970.
E Gómez-Casado, P del Moral, J Martínez-Laso, A García-Gómez, L Allende, C Silvera-Redondo, J Longas, M González-Hevilla, M Kandil, J Zamora and A Arnaiz-Villena, "HLA genes in Arabic-speaking Moroccans: close relatedness to Berbers and Iberians", *Tissue Antigens*, Vol 55, Issue 3, 2000.
Cyrus Gordon, *Forgotten Scripts*, Thames & Hudson, 1975.

Joseph Greenberg, "The languages of Africa", *International Journal of American Linguistics, Supplement*, Vol 29, Part 2, 1963.
Joseph Greenberg, *Language in the Americas*, Stanford University Press, 1987.
Nicolas Grimal, *A History of Ancient Egypt*, translated by Ian Shaw, Blackwell, Oxford, 1992.
Ruth Gruhn, "The South American twist: Clovis first doesn't fit the rich prehistory of the southern continent", *Scientific American Discovering Archaeology*, Jan/Feb, 2000, pp51–53.
Bernard Grun, *The Timetables of History*, 3rd Edition, Simon & Schuster, 1991.
Harald Haarmann, "Writing from old Europe to ancient Crete: a case of cultural continuity", *The Journal of Indo-European Studies*, 17/3–4, pp251–275, 1989.
John Hay, *Ancient China*, The Bodley Head, 1973.
G. Haynes, *The Early Settlement of North America*, Cambridge University Press, 2002.
Robert Heine-Geldern, "Das Problem vorkolumbischer Beziehungen zwischen Alter und Neuer Welt und seine Bedeutung für die allegemeine Kulturgeschichte", *Proceedings of the Austrian Academy of Sciences*, No 24, 1954.
Herodotus, *The Histories*, translated Aubrey de Sélincourt, Penguin, London, 1954.
Sinclair Hood, *The Home of the Heroes*, Thames & Hudson, London, 1967.
R W Hutchinson, *Prehistoric Crete*, Penguin Books, Middlesex, 1962.
Tore Jansen, *Speak*, Oxford University Press, 2002.
Samuel Johnson, *A Dictionary of the English Language*, 1755; edited version by Jack Lynch, Levenger Press, 2002.
John Justeson and Terence Kaufman, "A decipherment of the Epi-Olmec hieroglyphic writing", *Science*, 259, 1993, pp1703–1711.
Friedrich Katz, *The Ancient American Civilisations*, Weidenfeld & Nicolson, 1972.
John Keay, *India: a History*, Harper Collins, London, 2000.
T D Kendrick, *The Druids*, Methuen & Co Ltd, 1927.
Kathleen Kenyon, *Archaeology in the Holy Land*, 3rd Edition, Earnest Benn, London, 1970.
David Keys, *Catastrophe*, Arrow, Random House, 2000.
László Klima, "The linguistic affinity of the Volgaic Finno-Ugrians and their ethnogenesis", *Studio Historica Fenno-ugrica 1*, Oulu, Finland, 1996, pp21–33.
Aivar Kriiska, "Corded ware culture sites in north-eastern Estonia", *De temporibus antiquissimis ad honorem Lembit Jaanits*, Muinasaja teadus 8, Talinn, pp 57–79, 2000.
Lloyd Laing, *Celtic Britain*, Routledge and Kegan Paul, 1979.
R B Lees, "The Basis of Glottochronology", *Language*, 29, 1953.
Winfred Lehmann, *Historical Linguistics, an Introduction*, Rinehart & Winston, New York, 1973.
Philip Lieberman, *On the Origins of Language*, Macmillan, New York, 1975.
Zhiyi Liu, "Were 'rice paddies' near Pengtoushan and Jiahu sites", *Agricultural Archaeology*, 2000, pp70–72.
Ilze Loze, *Indo-Europeans in the eastern Baltic in the view of an archaeologist*, http://vip.latnet.lv/hss/loze.htm, undated, accessed November 2004.
Nicole Maca-Meyer, Ana González, José Larruga, Carlos Flores and Vincente

Cabrera, "Major genomic mitochondrial lineages delineate early human expansions", *BMC Genetics*, 2, 13, 2001.
Waruno Mahdi, *Maluku and Melanesia*, http://w3.rx-berlin.mpg.de/~wm//PAP/Mol-n-MN.html, 1997, accessed December 2004.
J P Mallory, *In Search of the Indo-Europeans*, Thames & Hudson, New York, 1991.
J C Martínez-Cruzado, G Toro-Labrador, V Ho-Fung, M A Estevez-Montero, A Lobaina-Manzanet, D A Padovani-Claudio, H Sanchez-Cruz, P Ortiz-Bermudez and A Sanchez-Crespo, "Mitochondrial DNA analysis reveals substantial Native American ancestry in Puerto Rico", *Human Biology*, Vol 3, No 4, 2001, pp491–511.
Mark McConaughy, *Clovis First and pre-Clovis Meadowcroft Rockshelter Discussion*, http://people.delphiforums.com/MCCONAUGHY/Meadowcroft/Clovis%20First.htm, 2004, accessed October 2004.
John McWhorter, *The Power of Babel*, William Heinemann, London, 2002.
D J Meltzer, D K Grayson, G Ardila, A W Barker, D F Dincauze, C V Haynes, F Mena, L Nunez and D J Stanford, "On the Pleistocene antiquity of Monte Verde, southern Chile", *American Antiquity*, 62(4), 1997, pp659–663.
Gavin Menzies, *1421: The Year China discovered the World*, Bantam Press, 2002.
Mait Metspalu, Toomas Kivisild, Ene Metspalu, Jüri Parik, Georgi Hudjashov, Katrin Kaldma, Piia Serk, Monika Karmin, Doron Behar, Thomas Gilbert, Phillip Endicott, Sarabjit Mastana, Surinder Papiha, Karl Skorecki, Antonio Torroni and Richard Villems, "Most of the extant mtDNA boundaries in south and southwest Asia were likely shaped during the initial settlement of Eurasia by anatomically modern humans", *BMC Genetics*, 5(1), 26, 2004.
Alexandr Mongait, *Archaeology in the USSR*, translated by M W Thompson, Penguin Books, 1961.
Michael Moseley, *The Incas and their Ancestors*, revised edition, Thames & Hudson, 2001.
George Muscat, *Santali: a New Approach*, Vinay Press, Bihar, India, 1989.
Massimo Pallottino, *The Etruscans*, translated by J Cremona, Penguin Books, 1955.
Holger Pedersen, *The Discovery of Language*, translated by J W Spargo, Indiana University Press, 1962.
Patricia Phillips, *The Prehistory of Europe*, Penguin Books, 1981.
David Phillipson, *The Later Prehistory of Eastern and Southern Africa*, Heinemann, London, 1977.
Stuart Piggott, *Prehistoric India*, Penguin, London, 1950.
Stuart Piggott, *Ancient Europe*, Edinburgh University Press, 1965.
Francis Pryor, *Britain BC*, Harper Collins, London, 2003.
A W Reed, *Aboriginal Words of Australia*, Reed New Holland, Sydney, 1998.
Colin Renfrew, *Before Civilisation*, Penguin Books, 1973.
Colin Renfrew, *Archaeology and Language*, Jonathan Cape, 1987.
Colin Renfew and Paul Bahn, *Archaeology: Theories, Methods and Practice*, Thames & Hudson, 1996.
Andrew Robinson, *Lost Languages*, Nevraumont Publishing Company, New York, 2002.
Mark Rosenfelder, *Numbers from 1 to 10 in over 5000 languages*, http://www.zompist.com/numbers.shtml, undated.

Georges Roux, *Ancient Iraq*, Pelican Books, 1966.
S B Roy, *The Early Aryans of India*, New Delhi, 1989.
Richard Rudgley, *Lost Civilisations of the Stone Age*, Century Press, London, 1998.
Merritt Ruhlen, *The Origin of Language*, John Wiley & Sons, New York, 1994.
Merritt Ruhlen, "The origin of the Na Dene", *Proceedings of the National Academy of Science (USA)*, Vol 95, 1998, pp13994–13996.
Nancy Sandars, *The Sea Peoples: Warriors of the Ancient Mediterranean*, Thames & Hudson, London, 1978.
Augustus Schleicher, *Die Darwinische Theorie und die Sprachwissenschaft*, Weimar, 1863.
Johannes Schmidt, *Der Verwanddschaftsverhältnisse der Indogermanischen Sprachen*, Weimar, 1872.
William Shakespeare, *Romeo and Juliet*, The Oxford Shakespeare, ed. W J Craig, Oxford University Press, London, 1969.
Wilson Silva, Sandro Bonatto, Adriano Holanda, Andrea Ribeiro-dos-Santos, Beatriz Paixao, Gustavo Goldman, Kiyoko Abe-Sandes, Luis Rodriguez-Delfin, Marcela Barbosa, Maria Luisa Paco-Larson, Maria Luisa Petzel-Ehrler, Valeria Valente, Sidney Santos and Marco Zago, "Mitochondrial genome diversity of Native Americans supports a single early entry of founder populations into America", *American Journal of Human Genetics*, 71(1), 2002, pp187–192.
George Starostin, *A lexicostatistical approach towards reconstructing proto-Khoisan*, http//starling.rinet.ru/Texts/khoilex.pdf, undated, accessed September 2005.
Bing Su, Chunjie Xiao, Ranjan Deka, Mark Seielstad, Daoroong Kangwanpong, Junhua Xiao, Daru Lu, Peter Underhill, Luca Cavalli-Sforza, Ranajit Chakraborty and Li Jin, "Y chromosome haplotypes reveal prehistorical migrations to the Himalayas", *Human Genetics*, 107, 2000, pp582–590.
Maurice Swadesh, *The Origin and Diversification of Language*, Routledge, London, 1972.
Bryan Sykes, *The Seven Daughters of Eve*, Bantam Press, 2001.
Ian Tattersall, *The Last Neanderthal*, Nevraumont, New York, 1995.
Alan Thorne and P G Macumber, "Discoveries of late Pleistocene man at Kow Swamp", *Nature*, 228, 1972, pp316–319.
J R R Tolkien, *The Hobbit*, George Allen & Unwin, London, 1937.
Antonio Torroni, Theodore Schurr, C C Yang, E J Szathmary, R C Williams, M S Schanfield, G A Troup, W C Knowler, D N Lawrence, K M Weiss et al, "Native American mitochondrial DNA analysis indicates that the Amerind and the Nadene populations were founded by two independent migrations", *Genetics*, 130(1), 1992, pp153–162.
Antonio Torroni, James Neel, Ramiro Barrantes, Theodore Schurr and Douglas Wallace, "Mitochondrial DNA clock for the Amerinds and its implications for timing their entry into North America", *Proceedings of the National Academy of Science*, USA, Vol 91, 1994, pp1158–1162.
Jim Vanhollebeke, *Pintubi-1. a Modern Australoid points to the Past*, http://canovanograms.tripod.com/pintubi1/, 2002, accessed January 2005.
Sergey Vasiliev, Yaroslav Kuzmin, Lyubov Orlova and Vyacheslav Dementiev, "Radiocarbon-based chronology of the Palaeolithic in Siberia and its relevance to the peopling of the New World", *Radiocarbon*, Vol 44(2), 2002, pp503–530.

Bibliography

William Watson, *Early Civilisation in China*, Thames & Hudson, 1966.
Colin Wells, *The Roman Empire*, Fontana Press, 1984.
Spencer Wells, *The Journey of Man: a Genetic Odyssey*, Penguin Books, London, 2002.
T D White, B Asfaw, D DeGusta, H Tilbert, G D Richards, G Suwa and F C Howell, "Pleistocene Homo Sapiens from middle Awash, Ethiopia", *Nature*, 423, 2003, pp742–747.
Toby Wilkinson, *Genesis of the Pharaohs*, Thames & Hudson, London, 2003.
Keith Windschuttle and Tim Gillin, "The extinction of the Australian pygmies", *Quadrant*, June 2002.
Yun Feng Xu, "Origin and distribution of rice", *Agricultural Archaeology*, 1998, pp246–254.

# INDEX

## LANGUAGES

| Language | Chapter | Language | Chapter |
|---|---|---|---|
| !Kung | 15 | Asheninca | 14 |
| Abkhaz | 11 | Assamese | 7 |
| Achagua | 14 | Atayal | 13 |
| Achehnese | 13 | Avar | 11 |
| Adai | 14 | Aymara | 14 |
| Afar | 9 | Azeri | 11 |
| Afrikaans | 6 | Badyara | 15 |
| Ahom | 12 | Bai | 12 |
| Ainu | 13 | Baikiri | 14 |
| Aka | 15 | Balant | 15 |
| Akha | 12 | Baluchi | 7 |
| Akkadian | 9 | Banjar | 13 |
| Alabama | 14 | Banyun | 15 |
| Albanian | 8 | Bari | 15 |
| Aleut | 11 | Basa | 15 |
| Amharic | 9 | Bashgali | 7 |
| Amuzgo | 14 | Basque | 10 |
| Andamanese | 13 | Bats | 11 |
| Anej | 15 | Baule | 15 |
| Angami | 12 | Beaver | 14 |
| Anglish | 6 | Beja | 9 |
| Apinaye | 14 | Bella Coola | 14 |
| Apurina | 14 | Bemba | 15 |
| Aquitanian | 10 | Bengali | 7 |
| Arabic | 9 | Berta | 15 |
| Arawak | 14 | Berti | 15 |
| Aricapu | 14 | Bete | 15 |
| Arikem | 14 | Bhojpuri | 7 |
| Armenian | 8 | Biafada | 15 |

283

| | | | |
|---|---|---|---|
| Bijago | 15 | Chokwe | 15 |
| Blackfoot | 14 | Chorasmian | 7 |
| Bodo | 12 | Chukchi | 11 |
| Bom | 15 | Chulupi | 14 |
| Brahui | 10 | Chuvash | 11 |
| Breton | 7 | Circassian | 11 |
| Brong | 15 | Comanche | 14 |
| Bubi | 15 | Coptic | 9 |
| Bugis | 13 | Cornish | 7 |
| Bulang | 12 | Cree | 14 |
| Bulgarian | 7 | Cretan | 10 |
| Bullom | 15 | Crow | 14 |
| Burmese | 12 | Cubeo | 14 |
| Burushaski | 10 | Culina | 14 |
| Buyang | 12 | Czech | 7 |
| Buyi | 12 | Dahalo | 9 |
| Caddo | 14 | Dakota | 14 |
| Callahuaya | 14 | Danish | 6 |
| Canaanite | 9 | Dargwa | 11 |
| Cantonese | 12 | Delaware | 14 |
| Caraja | 14 | Desano | 14 |
| Carapana | 14 | Dinka | 15 |
| Carib | 14 | Diola | 15 |
| Carropo | 14 | Divehi | 7 |
| Catalan | 7 | Dogon | 15 |
| Catawba | 14 | Dogri | 7 |
| Cayapa | 14 | Dong | 12 |
| Cebuano | 13 | Dongolawi | 15 |
| Cham | 13 | Duala | 15 |
| Chami | 14 | Dutch | 6 |
| Chamorro | 13 | East Norse | 6 |
| Chapacura | 14 | Eblaite | 9 |
| Charruco | 14 | Efik | 15 |
| Chechen | 11 | Egyptian | 9 |
| Cherokee | 14 | Elamite | 11 |
| Cheyenne | 14 | English | 3,6 |
| Chibcha | 14 | Eskimo | 11 |
| Chichewa | 15 | Estonian | 10 |
| Chichinec | 14 | Etruscan | 10 |
| Chimane | 14 | Ewe | 15 |
| Chimú | 14 | Ewondo | 15 |
| Chinook | 14 | Faeroese | 6 |
| Choctaw | 14 | Finnish | 10 |

# Index

| | | | |
|---|---|---|---|
| Flemish | 6 | Hupa | 14 |
| Fon | 15 | Hupda | 14 |
| French | 7 | Huron | 14 |
| Frisian | 6 | Hurrian | 11 |
| Fulani | 15 | Iberian | 10 |
| Fur | 15 | Icelandic | 6 |
| Ga | 15 | Igbo | 15 |
| Galician | 7 | Ijo | 15 |
| Ganda | 15 | Ik | 15 |
| Ganja | 15 | Ila | 15 |
| Garo | 12 | Ingush | 11 |
| Gbaya | 15 | Inuit | 11 |
| Gelao | 12 | Iquito | 14 |
| Georgian | 11 | Irish | 7 |
| German | 6 | Italian | 7 |
| Ghalames | 9 | Itelmen | 11 |
| Gola | 15 | Japanese | 13 |
| Gondi | 10 | Javanese | 13 |
| Gothic | 6 | Jingpaw | 12 |
| Greek | 7,8 | Jívaro | 14 |
| Guanche | 9 | Kaba | 15 |
| Guaraní | 14 | Kabile | 9 |
| Guato | 14 | Kalenjin | 15 |
| Guernsiase | 7 | Kaliko | 15 |
| Gujurati | 7 | Kam | 12 |
| Gumuz | 15 | Kamba | 15 |
| Hadza | 15 | Kamilaroi | 13 |
| Haida | 14 | Kannada | 10 |
| Hakka | 12 | Kansa | 14 |
| Hattian | 11 | Kanuri | 15 |
| Hausa | 9 | Kashaya | 14 |
| Hawaian | 13 | Kashmiri | 7 |
| Hebrew | 9 | Katcha | 15 |
| Hill Nubian | 15 | Kawa | 12 |
| Hina | 9 | Kazakh | 11 |
| Hindi | 7 | Keres | 14 |
| Hittite | 7,8 | Ket | 11,14 |
| Hlai | 12 | Khanty | 10 |
| Hmong | 12 | Kharia | 12 |
| Hopi | 14 | Khasi | 12 |
| Huichol | 14 | Khmer | 12 |
| Hungarian | 10 | Khoe | 15 |
| Hunnish | 11 | Khotanese | 7 |

| | | | |
|---|---|---|---|
| Khowar | 7 | Macedonian | 7 |
| Kikuyu | 15 | Magahi | 7 |
| Kiowa | 14 | Mahican | 14 |
| Komi | 10 | Maidu | 14 |
| Kongo | 15 | Maithili | 7 |
| Konkani | 7 | Makasar | 13 |
| Korean | 13 | Makushi | 14 |
| Korku | 12 | Malagasy | 13 |
| Koryak | 11 | Malay | 13 |
| Kresh | 15 | Malayalam | 10 |
| Kunama | 15 | Manchu | 11 |
| Kurdish | 7 | Mandarin | 12 |
| Kurukh | 10 | Mandinka | 15 |
| Kusunda | 12 | Manipuri | 12 |
| Kutasho | 14 | Mano | 15 |
| Kwakiutl | 14 | Mansi | 10 |
| Kwegu | 15 | Maori | 13 |
| Lak | 11 | Mapuche | 14 |
| Lao | 12 | Marathi | 7 |
| Laqua | 12 | Masaca | 14 |
| Latin | 7 | Masai | 15 |
| Latvian | 7 | Mbulungish | 15 |
| Lawa | 12 | Mbundu | 15 |
| Laz | 11 | Mehri | 9 |
| Leco | 14 | Meidob | 15 |
| Lemnian | 10 | Mende | 15 |
| Lengua | 14 | Meroitic | 9n,15n |
| Lezghian | 11 | Migrelian | 11 |
| Lillooet | 14 | Mimi Gaudefroy | 15 |
| Limba | 15 | Mimi Nachtigal | 15 |
| Lingala | 15 | Min | 12 |
| Lisu | 12 | Miskito | 14 |
| Lithuanian | 7 | Miwok | 14 |
| Lozi | 15 | Mixtec | 14 |
| Luba | 15 | Mohave | 14 |
| Lunda | 15 | Mohawk | 14 |
| Luo | 15 | Mon | 12 |
| Luri | 7 | Mongolian | 11 |
| Lushei | 12 | Moore | 15 |
| Luvale | 15 | Mordvin | 10 |
| Luyia | 15 | Mubi | 9 |
| Maba | 15 | Mundari | 12 |
| Macaguan | 14 | Murui | 14 |

# Index

| | | | |
|---|---|---|---|
| Muskogee | 14 | Pima | 14 |
| Nadeb | 14 | Polish | 7 |
| Nahali | 12 | Pomo | 14 |
| Nahuatl | 14 | Popoloc | 14 |
| Nama | 15 | Popoluca | 14 |
| Natchez | 14 | Portuguese | 7 |
| Navaho | 14 | Prakrit | 7 |
| Naxi | 12 | Prasun | 7 |
| Ndebele | 15 | Prussian | 7 |
| Ndut | 15 | Puinave | 14 |
| Nenets | 11 | Punjabi | 7 |
| Nepali | 7 | Quechua | 14 |
| Nera | 15 | Quiché | 14 |
| Newari | 12 | Quileute | 14 |
| Nez Percé | 14 | Quinault | 14 |
| Ngangea | 15 | Rajasthani | 7 |
| Nicobarese | 12 | Romanian | 7 |
| Nivkh | 11 | Romansch | 7 |
| Nkore | 15 | Roshani | 7 |
| Nootka | 14 | Rundi | 15 |
| Norwegian | 7 | Russian | 7 |
| Nubian | 15 | Sabean | 9 |
| Nupe | 15 | Sami | 10 |
| Nyala | 15 | Samo | 15 |
| Okanagan | 14 | Samoan | 13 |
| Ongbe | 12 | Sandawe | 15 |
| Opo | 15 | Sango | 15 |
| Oriya | 7 | Sanskrit | 7 |
| Oromo | 9 | Santali | 12 |
| Oscan | 7 | Sarcee | 14 |
| Ossete | 7 | Sariqoli | 7 |
| Otomi | 14 | Scottish Gaelic | 7 |
| Paez | 14 | Scythian | 7 |
| Paiwan | 13 | Secoya | 14 |
| Palantla | 14 | Semelai | 12 |
| Palaung | 12 | Seneca | 14 |
| Pa-o | 12 | Serbo-Croat | 7 |
| Papel | 15 | Seri | 14 |
| Pashai | 7 | Sgaw | 12 |
| Paya | 14 | Shabo | 15 |
| Persian | 7 | Shan | 12 |
| Phrygian | 8 | Shawnee | 14 |
| Pictish | 13n | Shina | 7 |

| | | | |
|---|---|---|---|
| Shipibo | 14 | Thracian | 7 |
| Shona | 15 | Tibetan | 12 |
| Shughni | 7 | Ticuna | 14 |
| Sinatacan | 14 | Tigrinya | 9 |
| Sindhi | 7 | Timote | 14 |
| Sinhala | 7 | Tiv | 15 |
| Siuslaw | 14 | Tlamelula | 14 |
| Slovak | 7 | Tlapanec | 14 |
| Slovene | 7 | Tlingit | 14 |
| Sogdian | 7 | Toba | 13 |
| Somali | 9 | Tocharian | 7,8 |
| Songhay | 15 | Tohontepec | 14 |
| Soninke | 15 | Tolowa | 14 |
| Sora | 12 | Totonac | 14 |
| Sorbian | 7 | Tripuri | 12 |
| Sotho | 15 | Tsat | 13 |
| Spanish | 7 | Tsez | 11 |
| Squamish | 14 | Tsonga | 15 |
| Sumerian | 11 | Tswana | 15 |
| Sumo | 14 | Tulu | 10 |
| Sundanese | 13 | Tumbuku | 15 |
| Svan | 11 | Tunebo | 14 |
| Swahili | 15 | Tungus | 11 |
| Swedish | 6 | Tupi | 14 |
| Tabasaran | 11 | Turkana | 15 |
| Tacana | 14 | Turkish | 11 |
| Tagalog | 13 | Turkmen | 11 |
| Tahitian | 13 | Twi | 15 |
| Taino | 14 | Udmurt | 10 |
| Tama | 14 | Uighur | 11 |
| Tamasheq | 9 | Ukrainian | 7 |
| Tamil | 10 | Umbrian | 7 |
| Tanaina | 14 | Umotina | 14 |
| Tarascan | 14 | Uru | 14 |
| Tashelhet | 9 | Ute | 14 |
| Tatar | 11 | Uzbek | 11 |
| Tehuelche | 14 | Venda | 15 |
| Telugu | 10 | Vietnamese | 12 |
| Temne | 15 | Viri | 15 |
| Teribe | 14 | Wagiman | 13 |
| Teso | 15 | Wakhi | 7 |
| Tewa | 14 | Walapai | 14 |
| Thai | 12 | Welsh | 7 |

Index                                                                                                                289

| | | | | |
|---|---|---|---|
| West Norse | 6 | Yimas | 13 |
| Wichita | 14 | Yokuts | 14 |
| Wollayta | 9 | Yoruba | 15 |
| Wolof | 15 | Yucatec | 14 |
| Xavante | 14 | Yuchi | 14 |
| Xhosa | 15 | Yukaghir | 11 |
| Yagua | 14 | Yuki | 14 |
| Yangula | 13 | Yuruna | 14 |
| Yanomami | 14 | Zande | 15 |
| Yao | 15 | Zapotec | 14 |
| Yaqui | 14 | Zhuang | 12 |
| Yi | 12 | Zulu | 15 |
| Yiddish | 6 | | |

## LANGUAGE FAMILIES, BRANCHES ETC

| Language | Chapter | Language | Chapter |
|---|---|---|---|
| Adamawa | 15 | Central Sudanic | 15 |
| Afro-Asiatic | 2,9 | Chadic | 9 |
| Algonquian | 14 | Chibchan | 14 |
| Altaic | 2,11 | Chimakuan | 14 |
| Amerind | 2,14 | Chinese | 12 |
| Anatolian | 7,8 | Chon | 14 |
| Araukanian | 14 | Chukchi-Kamchatkan | 11 |
| Arawakan | 14 | Cushitic | 9 |
| Aslian | 12 | Dené-Caucasian | 2 |
| Athapaskan | 14 | Dravidian | 2,10 |
| Atlantic | 15 | Eastern Nilotic | 15 |
| Austric | 2 | Eskimo-Aleut | 2,11 |
| Austro-Asiatic | 2,12 | Eurasiatic | 2 |
| Austronesian | 2,13 | Finno-Ugric | 10 |
| Baltic | 7 | Ge | 14 |
| Bantu | 15 | Germanic | 6,8 |
| Barito | 13 | Goidelic | 7 |
| Berber | 9 | Gur | 15 |
| Bodic | 12 | Hokan | 14 |
| Bodo-Garo | 12 | Ijoid | 15 |
| Brythonic | 7 | Indic | 7,8 |
| Burmese | 12 | Indo-European | 2,6,7,8 |
| Caddoan | 14 | Indo-Pacific | 13 |
| Cariban | 14 | Iranian | 7,8 |
| Caucasian | 2,11 | Iroquoian | 14 |
| Celtic | 7,8 | Italic | 7,8 |

| | | | |
|---|---|---|---|
| Kadai | 2,12 | Pama-Nyungan | 13 |
| Kartvelian | 11 | Panoan | 14 |
| Khoi-San | 2,15 | Papuan | 2,13 |
| Koman | 15 | Platoid | 15 |
| Kordofanian | 15 | Puinavean | 14 |
| Kru | 15 | Quechumaran | 14 |
| Kwa | 15 | Saharan | 15 |
| Lower Sepik | 13 | Salish | 14 |
| Maban | 15 | Samoyedic | 11 |
| Mande | 15 | Sino-Tibetan | 2,12 |
| Mayan | 14 | Siouxan | 14 |
| Miao-Yao | 2,12 | Slavonic | 7,8 |
| Mikir-Meithei | 12 | South Caucasian | 11 |
| Mixe-Zoque | 14 | South Cushitic | 9 |
| Mon-Khmer | 12 | Southern Nilotic | 15 |
| Munda | 12 | Tai | 2,12 |
| Muskogean | 14 | Timucuan | 14 |
| Na-Dené | 2,14 | Tucanoan | 14 |
| Naga | 12 | Tungusic | 11 |
| Niger-Congo | 2,15 | Tupian | 14 |
| Nilo-Saharan | 2,15 | Turkic | 11 |
| Nilotic | 15 | Ubangi | 15 |
| North-Central Caucasian | 11 | Uralic | 2,10,11 |
| North-East Caucasian | 11 | Uto-Aztecan | 14 |
| Northern Sudanic | 15 | Voltaic | 15 |
| North-West Caucasian | 11 | Wa | 12 |
| Nostratic | 2,10,11,12 | Waikuruan | 14 |
| | | Wakashan | 14 |
| Nubian | 15 | Western Nilotic | 15 |
| Omotic | 9 | Yeniseian | 11 |
| Otomanguean | 14,15 | | |
| Palaeosiberian | 2,11 | | |

## ARCHAEOLOGICAL SITES AND CULTURES

| Language | Chapter | Language | Chapter |
|---|---|---|---|
| Afanasievo | 8 | Ban Chiang | 12 |
| Alaca Höyük | 11n | Big Eddy | 14n |
| Anau | 8,11 | Bogazköy | 7 |
| Andronovo | 7,8n | Cactus Hill | 14 |
| Angbangbang | 13n | Capsian | 9 |
| Arctic Small Tool | 11n | Casimiroid | 14 |
| Aubrey | 14n | Chandwe | 15 |

Index

| | | | |
|---|---|---|---|
| Chasseen | 10 | Lapa do Boquete | 14 |
| Chernyakhovo | 7 | Lapita | 13 |
| Clovis | 14 | Lelesu | 15 |
| Corded Ware | 8 | Linear Band | 8n,10 |
| Danubian | 8n | Los Toldos | 14 |
| Dapendeng | 13n | Lung ShanL | |
| Dhimini | 8n | 12,13n,14 | |
| Diuktai | 10n,14 | Lusatian | 8 |
| Dnieper-Donetz | 8 | Maadi | 9n |
| El Jobo | 14 | Meadowcroft | 14 |
| Faiyum A | 9n | Mehrgarh | 8n |
| Fatyanovo | 8n | Mohenjo Daro | 10 |
| Fengbitou | 13n | Monte Verde | 14 |
| Folsom | 14 | Mulambo | 15 |
| Fuguodan | 13n | Nachikufian | 9,15 |
| Ghassulian | 9n | Natufian | 9n |
| Giyan | 11n | Nauwalabila | 13n |
| Gokomere | 15 | Nea Nikomedia | 8n |
| Hallstatt | 7,8 | Nkope | 15 |
| Harappa | 10 | Northern Archaic | 11n |
| Hattusas | 7,8n,11n | Nun Nok Tha | 12n |
| Helwan | 9 | Okuzini | 10n |
| Hemudu | 12n | Oranian | 9 |
| Hissar | 8 | Ortoiroid | 14n |
| Hoabinhiam | 12 | Pachamachay | 14 |
| Hungarian Tell | 10n | Palaeoindian | 14 |
| Ibero-Maurusian | 9n | Paleo Crossing | 14n |
| Jia Lake | 12 | Pedra Pintada | 14 |
| Jomon | 13 | Pedro Furada | 14 |
| Kalambo | 15 | Peiligang | 11,12 |
| Kalundo | 15 | Pengtoushan | 12 |
| Kapwirimbwe | 15 | Piedra Museo | 14 |
| Karasuk | 8n,11n | Pit-Comb | 10 |
| Kebaran | 9,10 | Plano | 14 |
| Khabur | 11n | Proto-Urban | 9 |
| Khinsky | 11 | Qafzeh | 13n |
| Khirbet Kerak | 11n | Quebrada Jaguay | 14 |
| Kurgan | 8 | Rana Ghundai | 8n |
| Kwale | 15 | Rössen | 10 |
| La Hoguette | 8n | San Lorenzo | 14n |
| La Tène | 6n,7,8 | Shang | 12n,14 |
| La Venta | 14n | Sialk | 7n |
| L'Anse aux Meadows | 14n | Skhul | 13n |

| | | | |
|---|---|---|---|
| Solutrean | 10n | Troy | 8,10n |
| Starcevo-Körös-Cris | 8n,10n | Uptar | 14n |
| Svidrian | 10 | Ural-Kama | 10n |
| Taima-Taima | 14 | Urewe | 15 |
| Tanshishan | 13n | Urnfield | 7,8 |
| Tarteria | 10n | Villanovan | 8n,10n |
| Terremarra | 8n | Vinca | 10 |
| Tibitó | 14 | Xinglong Wa | 11 |
| Timber Grave | 7 | Yang Shao | 12,14 |
| Tlapacoya | 14 | Yayoi | 13 |
| Topper | 14 | Zarubintsi | 7 |
| Tordos | 10n | Zarzian | 10n |
| Tripolye | 8 | Ziwa | 15 |

Lightning Source UK Ltd.
Milton Keynes UK
173672UK00001B/14/A